T0189743

Computer Communications and Networks

Series Editor
Anthony Sammes
Swindon, United Kingdom

Titles in this series now included in the Thomson Reuters Book Citation Index

The Computer Communications and Networks series is a range of textbooks, monographs and handbooks. It sets out to provide students, researchers, and non-specialists alike with a sure grounding in current knowledge, together with comprehensible access to the latest developments in computer communications and networking.

Emphasis is placed on clear and explanatory styles that support a tutorial approach, so that even the most complex of topics is presented in a lucid and intelligible manner.

Springer is seeking to publish quality books in areas including, but not limited to:

Computer Networks (general) - Data Communications - Distributed Computing - Parallel and Systolic Computing - Network and Information Security - Network Architecture - Wireless Ad Hoc and Sensor Networks - Mobile Computing - Virtual Private Networks - Advanced Network Protocol Design and Analysis - Protocol Verification and Validation - Network Testing - Network Management - Reliability and Fault Tolerance - Performance Modelling - Quality of Service - Routing and Traffic Engineering - Web Computing - Network Programming - Grid Computing

More information about this series at http://www.springer.com/series/4198

Zaigham Mahmood
Editor

Cloud Computing

Challenges, Limitations and R&D Solutions

 Springer

Editor
Zaigham Mahmood
University of Derby
United Kingdom

North West University
S Africa

ISSN 1617-7975
ISBN 978-3-319-35303-6   ISBN 978-3-319-10530-7 (eBook)
DOI 10.1007/978-3-319-10530-7
Springer Cham Heidelberg New York Dordrecht London

Printed on acid-free paper

Springer is part of Springer Science+Business Media (www.springer.com)

Dedication

This tenth publication is dedicated to my parents Ghazi Ghulam Hussain Bahadur *and* Mukhtar Begum *who spent the prime of their lives in fighting for the freedom and independence of their country. At a very young age, my father joined a paramilitary movement with the mission to engage in peaceful struggle to free the country from foreign occupation. Although the struggle for independence started many decades before, his organization together with similar movements and political parties, decided to stage a much more decisive countrywide peaceful protest on 19 March 1940. The government, fearing the shutdown of the country, had already banned the gatherings but people were out in such huge numbers that the army patrolling the streets received orders to* shoot to kill. *Live bullets were fired; many thousands were killed or injured and many more taken as political prisoners. That day, my father was leading a group of 313 men—totally unarmed. Several dozen of them were martyred or injured; many were captured and tried. There were 13 who were sentenced to* political imprisonment for life—*my father was one of the 13. His organization honored him with the titles of* Ghazi *(survivor in the*

fight between right and wrong) and Bahadur *(valiant). Four days later, an all-party
confederation passed a unanimous resolution
demanding the* formation of an independent
state. *Soon after, a declaration was signed
to transfer power to the leading political
party. Eventually, after another 7 years, the
country achieved independence on 14 August
1947. On this day, all freedom fighters were
released;* my father also returned home ghazi
*and victorious. My mother, a young girl
at the time, was no less courageous in her
struggles: she fully supported her husband's
mission and raised a young girl independently, single handedly, while my father was
away. Now that the mission was achieved,
my father devoted his time to engage in the
study of Oriental languages and theology,
bringing up his family and serving the community.* Achieve excellence … make a difference: *my parents would constantly remind
us. They most certainly were excellent in
what they did and made a huge difference.
They are my heroes and my inspiration
in life.*

Zaigham Mahmood
19 March 2014

Preface

Overview

Cloud Computing is an attractive paradigm that allows consumers to self-provision cloud based software systems, application services, development platforms and virtualized infrastructures. Large enterprises can migrate their applications and data to cloud environments to achieve the benefits of scalability, availability and reduction in capital expenditure; small organisations and start-up ventures can realize benefits by leasing ready-made development environments and computing infrastructure on a pay-as-you-go basis; and general public can enjoy the use of cloud based application such as email systems and storage space, which are often freely available.

The benefits that the cloud paradigm promises are numerous and already proven. However, like any other emerging technology, the limitations, issues and barriers are also many. There are issues of security due to virtualisation and multi-tenant nature of cloud environments; concerns with respect to the loss of governance and control; legal and jurisdiction implications of entrusting private and confidential data to cloud providers; and concerns due to evolving cloud related standards. The lack of knowledge on the part of the cloud consumers is also resulting in vendor lock-ins and inappropriate service level agreements.

Notwithstanding the above, cloud consumers are becoming more knowledgeable and beginning to dictate what they require. Cloud providers are also learning from experience and beginning to provide what consumers actually need. Robust new technologies are appearing and standards organisations, in the process of developing the necessary controls, are keen to enforce the standards for the benefit of all. Other cloud related industries are also appearing to provide specialist services to support cloud providers as well as the cloud consumers. Alongside this, researchers, practitioners and R&D departments within the organisations are coming up with strategies and solutions to resolve the existing issues and remove the barriers. New areas being investigated include: cloud security, interoperability, service level agreements, identity and access management, cloud governance, big data analytics and broker services. New frameworks and methodologies are also being developed for construction, deployment and delivery of cloud services to benefit all.

This book, *Cloud Computing: Challenges, Limitations and R&D Solutions,* aims to present discussions on issues and limitations relating to the cloud computing paradigm and suggest latest research methodologies, emerging developments and R&D solutions to benefit the computing community. In this volume, 39 researchers and practitioners of international repute have presented latest research developments, current trends, state of the art reports, case studies and suggestions for further development of the cloud computing paradigm.

Objectives

The aim of this text is to present the current research and R&D solutions to the limitations, barriers and issues that currently exist in the cloud computing paradigm. The key objectives include:

- Capturing the state-of-the-art research and practice relating to cloud computing issues
- Exploring limitations and barriers with respect to cloud provision and cloud environments
- Analyzing the implications of the new cloud paradigms for the benefit of consumers
- Discussing R&D solutions and strategies with respect to concerns relating to the cloud paradigm
- In general, advancing the understanding of the emerging new methodologies relevant to the cloud paradigm

Organization

There are 14 chapters in *Cloud Computing: Challenges, Limitations and R&D Solutions.* These are organized in three parts, as follows:

- Part I: *Limitations and Challenges of Cloud Environments.* This section has a focus on issues and limitations of the cloud computing paradigm. There are three chapters in this section. The first chapter looks into the security issues of public clouds. The second contribution focuses on architectural choices for DBM Systems for cloud environment and the third chapter discusses the challenges and issues with respect to QoS and SLAs.
- Part II: *Current Developments and R&D Solutions.* This second part comprises six chapters. The first contribution discusses a methodology for cloud security management, while the second chapter suggests a framework for secure data storage and identity management in the cloud. The third contribution presents a simulation tool for energy aware cloud environments and the chapter, that follows, presents an efficient congestion control system for data center networks.

The fifth chapter is devoted to looking into energy aware VM consolidation in the IaaS provision. The last contribution in this section focuses on software defined networking for cloud related applications.

- Part III: *Advances in Cloud Technologies and Future Trends*: There are five chapters in this part. The first chapter discusses future developments with respect to virtualization and cloud security and the second contribution discusses recent trends in QoS data warehouses in relation to the selection of cloud based services. The next chapter focuses on cloud federation approaches. The forth contribution discusses the security aspects of database-as-a-service provision and the final chapter looks into the future to see how the next generation utility computing infrastructures will be designed.

Target Audiences

The current volume is a reference text aimed to support a number of potential audiences, including the following:

- *Enterprise architects, business analysts and software developers* who are keen to adopt the newer approaches to developing and deploying cloud-based services, taking into account the current research.
- *IT infrastructure managers and business leaders* who need to have a clear understanding and knowledge of the limitations and issues that currently exist in the emerging cloud computing paradigm.
- *Students and lecturers* of cloud computing who have an interest in further enhancing the knowledge of the current developments and R&D solutions to the barriers, limitations and issues that currently exist.
- *Researchers* in this field who wish to have the up to date knowledge of the current practice, mechanisms and research developments relevant to the cloud paradigm to further develop the same.

Zaigham Mahmood
University of Derby UK & North West University S Africa

Acknowledgements

The editor acknowledges the help and support of the following colleagues during the review and editing phases of this text:

Rodrigo N. Calheiros, University of Melbourne, Australia
Prof. T. Chandrakumar, Thiagarajar College of Engineering, Tamil Nadu, India
Ganesh Chandra Deka, Ministry of Labour & Employment, Delhi, India
Fortis Florin, Research Institute e-Austria Timisoara, Timisoara, Romania
Kahina Hamadache, SingularLogic S.A., Nea Ionia, Attica, Greece
Dr. Attila Kertesz, University of Szeged and MTA SZTAKI, Hungary
Ping Lin, Avaya Canada Corp, Belleville, Ontario, Canada
Flavio Lombardi, Roma Tre University of Rome, Italy
Abhishek Majumder, Tripura University, Tripura West, India
Prof. Hamid Mcheick, Université du Québec à Chicoutimi, Québec, Canada
Joarder Mohammad Mustafa Kamal, Monash University, Victoria, Australia
Prof Saswati Mukerjee, Anna University, Chennai, India
Kashif Munir, King Fahd University of Petroleum & Minerals, S Arabia
Dr. S Parthasarthi, Thiagarajar College of Engineering, Madurai, India
Dr. Pethuru Raj, IBM Cloud Center of Excellence, Bangalore, India
Dr. Muthu Ramachandran, Leeds Metropolitan University, Leeds, UK
Yasir Saleem, Sunway University, Selangor, Malaysia
Dr. Mahmood Shah, University of Central Lancashire, UK
Sukhpal Singh, Thapar University, Patiala, India
Dr. Fareeha Zafar, GC University, Lahore, Pakistan

I would also like to thank the contributors to this book: 39 authors and co-authors, from academia as well as industry from around the world, who collectively submitted 14 chapters. Without their efforts in developing quality contributions, conforming to the guidelines and meeting often the strict deadlines, this text would not have been possible.

Grateful thanks are also due to the members of my family—Rehana, Zoya, Imran, Hanya and Ozair—for their continued support and encouragement. Best wishes also to Eyaad Imran.

17 July 2014   Zaigham Mahmood
                                    School of Computing and Mathematics,
                                                University of Derby, UK
                            & Business Management and Informatics Unit,
                    North West University, Potchefstroom, South Africa

Other Springer Books by Zaigham Mahmood

Continued Rise of the Cloud: Advances and Trends in Cloud Computing

This reference text presents the latest research and trends in cloud technologies, infrastructure, and architecture. Contributed by expert researchers and practitioners in the field, this book presents discussions on current advances and practical approaches including guidance and case studies on the provision of cloud-based services and frameworks. ISBN: 978-1-4471-6451-7.

Cloud Computing: Methods and Practical Approaches

The benefits associated with cloud computing are enormous; yet the dynamic, virtualized and multi-tenant nature of the cloud environment presents many challenges. To help tackle these, this volume provides illuminating viewpoints and case studies to present current research and best practices on approaches and technologies for the emerging cloud paradigm. ISBN: 978-1-4471-5106-7.

Software Engineering Frameworks for the Cloud Computing Paradigm

This is an authoritative reference that presents the latest research on software development approaches suitable for distributed computing environments. Contributed by researchers and practitioners of international repute, the book offers practical guidance on enterprise-wide software deployment in the cloud environment. Case studies are also presented. ISBN: 978-1-4471-5030-5.

Cloud Computing for Enterprise Architectures

This reference text, aimed at system architects and business managers, examines the cloud paradigm from the perspective of enterprise architectures. It introduces fundamental concepts, discusses principles, and explores frameworks for the adoption of cloud computing. The book explores the inherent challenges and presents future directions for further research. ISBN: 978-1-4471-2235-7.

Contents

Part I   Limitations and Challenges of Cloud Environments

1   **Attacks in Public Clouds: Can They Hinder the Rise of the Cloud?**   3
    Saeed Shafieian, Mohammad Zulkernine and Anwar Haque

2   **Distributed Database Management Systems: Architectural
    Design Choices for the Cloud**   23
    Joarder Mohammad Mustafa Kamal and Manzur Murshed

3   **Quality of Service and Service Level Agreements for Cloud
    Environments: Issues and Challenges**   51
    Inderveer Chana and Sukhpal Singh

Part II   Current Developments and R&D Solution

4   **A Methodology for Cloud Security Risks Management**   75
    Mariam Kiran

5   **SecDSIM: A Framework for Secure Data Storage and
    Identity Management in the Cloud**   105
    Shaga Praveen and G. R. Gangadharan

6   **CloudReports: An Extensible Simulation Tool for
    Energy-Aware Cloud Computing Environments**   127
    Thiago Teixeira Sá, Rodrigo N. Calheiros and Danielo G. Gomes

7   **Cloud Computing: Efficient Congestion Control in Data
    Center Networks**   143
    Chi Harold Liu, Jian Shi and Jun Fan

8   Energy-Aware Virtual Machine Consolidation in IaaS Cloud
    Computing 179
    Md Hasanul Ferdaus and Manzur Murshed

9   Software-Defined Networking (SDN) for Cloud Applications 209
    Lin Lin and Ping Lin

Part III   Advances in Cloud Technologies and Future Trends 235

10 Virtualization and Cloud Security: Benefits, Caveats, and
    Future Developments 237
    Flavio Lombardi and Roberto Di Pietro

11 Quality-of-Service Data Warehouse for the Selection of
    Cloud Services: A Recent Trend 257
    Ahmad Karawash, Hamid Mcheick and Mohamed Dbouk

12 Characterizing Cloud Federation Approaches 277
    Attila Kertesz

13 Security Aspects of Database-as-a-Service (DBaaS)
    in Cloud Computing 297
    Faria Mehak, Rahat Masood, Yumna Ghazi,
    Muhammad Awais Shibli and Sharifullah Khan

14 Beyond the Clouds: How Should Next Generation Utility
    Computing Infrastructures Be Designed? 325
    Marin Bertier, Frédéric Desprez, Gilles Fedak, Adrien Lebre,
    Anne-Cécile Orgerie, Jonathan Pastor, Flavien Quesnel,
    Jonathan Rouzaud-Cornabas and Cédric Tedeschi

Index 347

About the Editor

Professor Zaigham Mahmood is a published author of 11 books, 5 of which are dedicated to Electronic Government and Human Factors; and the other 6 focus on the subject of Cloud Computing including: Cloud Computing: Concepts, Technology & Architecture; Cloud Computing: Methods and Practical Approaches; Software Engineering Frameworks for the Cloud Computing Paradigm; Cloud Computing for Enterprise Architectures; Continued Rise of the Cloud: Advances and Trends in Cloud Computing; and Cloud Computing: Challenges, Limitations and R&D Solutions. Additionally, he is developing two new books to appear in 2015. He has also published more than 100 articles and book chapters and organized numerous conference tracks and workshops.

Professor Mahmood is the Editor-in-Chief of *Journal of E-Government Studies and Best Practices* as well as the Series Editor-in-Chief of the IGI book series on *E-Government and Digital Divide*. He is a Senior Technology Consultant at Debesis Education UK and Associate Lecturer (Research) at the University of Derby UK. He further holds positions as Foreign Professor at NUST and IIU universities in Islamabad Pakistan and Professor Extraordinaire at the North West University Potchefstroom South Africa. Professor Mahmood is also a certified cloud computing instructor and a regular speaker at international conferences devoted to Cloud Computing and E-Government. His specialized areas of research include distributed computing, project management, and e-government.[1,2]

---

[1] School of Computing and Mathematics, University of Derby, Derby, UK
e-mail: z.mahmood@debesis.co.uk

[2] Business Management and Informatics Unit, North West University, Potchefstroom, South Africa

Contributors

Marin Bertier   Inria, Campus universitaire de Beaulieu, Rennes, France

Rodrigo N. Calheiros   Department of Computing and Information Systems, The University of Melbourne, Parkville, VIC, Australia

Inderveer Chana   Computer Science and Engineering Department, Thapar University, Patiala, Punjab, India

Mohamed Dbouk   Ecole Doctorale des Sciences et de Technologie, Lebanese University, Hadath-Beirut, Lebanon

Frédéric Desprez   Inria, Campus universitaire de Beaulieu, Rennes, France

Roberto Di Pietro   SPRINGeR Research Group, Maths and Physics Department, Roma Tre University, Rome, Italy

Jun Fan   School of Software, Beijing Institute of Technology, Beijing, P.R. China

Gilles Fedak   Inria, Campus universitaire de Beaulieu, Rennes, France

Md Hasanul Ferdaus   Faculty of Information Technology, Monash University, Churchill, VIC, Australia

G.R. Gangadharan   Institute for Development and Research in Banking Technology, Hyderabad, India

Yumna Ghazi   School of Electrical Engineering and Computer Science, National University of Sciences and Technology, Islamabad, Pakistan

Danielo G. Gomes   Group of Computer Networks, Software Engineering and Systems (GREat), Universidade Federal do Ceará, Fortaleza—CE, Brazil

Anwar Haque   Bell Canada, Hamilton, ON, Canada

Joarder Mohammad Mustafa Kamal   Gippsland School of Faculty of Information Technology, Monash University, Clayton, VIC, Australia

Ahmad Karawash Department of Computer Science, University of Quebec at Chicoutimi (UQAC), Chicoutimi, Canada

Ecole Doctorale des Sciences et de Technologie, Lebanese University, Hadath-Beirut, Lebanon

Attila Kertesz MTA SZTAKI, Budapest, Hungary

Software Engineering Department, University of Szeged, Szeged, Hungary

Sharifullah Khan School of Electrical Engineering and Computer Science, National University of Sciences and Technology, Islamabad, Pakistan

Adrien Lebre Inria, Campus universitaire de Beaulieu, Rennes, France

Lin Lin Avaya Canada, Belleville, ON, Canada

Ping Lin Avaya Canada, Belleville, ON, Canada

Chi Harold Liu School of Software, Beijing Institute of Technology, Beijing, P.R. China

Flavio Lombardi SPRINGeR Research Group, Maths and Physics Department, Roma Tre University, Rome, Italy

Mariam Kiran Department of Computer Science, University of Sheffield, Bradford, Bradford, UK

Rahat Masood School of Electrical Engineering and Computer Science, National University of Sciences and Technology, Islamabad, Pakistan

Hamid Mcheick Department of Computer Science, University of Quebec at Chicoutimi (UQAC), Chicoutimi, Canada

Faria Mehak School of Electrical Engineering and Computer Science, National University of Sciences and Technology, Islamabad, Pakistan

Manzur Murshed Faculty of Science and Technology, Federation University, Churchill, VIC, Australia

School of Information Technology, Faculty of Science, Federation University Australia, Churchill, VIC, Australia

Anne-Cécile Orgerie Inria, Campus universitaire de Beaulieu, Rennes, France

Jonathan Pastor Inria, Campus universitaire de Beaulieu, Rennes, France

Shaga Praveen Institute for Development and Research in Banking Technology, Hyderabad, India

Flavien Quesnel Inria, Campus universitaire de Beaulieu, Rennes, France

Jonathan Rouzaud-Cornabas Inria, Campus universitaire de Beaulieu, Rennes, France

Saeed Shafieian   School of Computing, Queen's University, Kingston, ON, Canada

Jian Shi   School of Software, Beijing Institute of Technology, Beijing, P.R. China

Muhammad Awais Shibli   School of Electrical Engineering and Computer Science, National University of Sciences and Technology, Islamabad, Pakistan

Sukhpal Singh   Computer Science and Engineering Department, Thapar University, Patiala, Punjab, India

Cédric Tedeschi   Inria, Campus universitaire de Beaulieu, Rennes, France

Thiago Teixeira Sá   Group of Computer Networks, Software Engineering and Systems (GREat), Universidade Federal do Ceará, Fortaleza—CE, Brazil

Mohammad Zulkernine   School of Computing, Queen's University, Kingston, ON, Canada

Part I
Limitations and Challenges of Cloud Environments

Chapter 1
Attacks in Public Clouds: Can They Hinder the Rise of the Cloud?

Saeed Shafieian, Mohammad Zulkernine and Anwar Haque

Abstract Since the advent of Cloud Computing, security has been one of the main barriers to the adoption of the Cloud paradigm, especially by large organizations dealing with customers' sensitive information. The rapid growth of the Cloud has made it a desirable attack target for both external attackers and malicious insiders. Many of the security attacks that occur in non-Cloud environments can occur in the Cloud as well, but some of those may be exacerbated, and some may remain unaffected in the new Cloud paradigm. There are also new threats that have arisen, and Cloud users now face Cloud-specific attacks that did not exist or rarely occurred in traditional environments. In this chapter, we discuss attacks that are exacerbated by exploitation of the multi-tenancy attribute in public Clouds that occur because of the virtualization technology or are due to the pay-as-you-go model in the Cloud. We discuss some of the most common threats and attacks with respect to the Cloud attribute exploitations which are capable of exacerbating attacks by causing more potential consequences, or making detection and prevention mechanisms more challenging. We also assess the attacks to find out how they may affect confidentiality, integrity, and availability of data and services for Cloud users. Being aware of the threats to the Cloud may help organizations and individuals have a more informed switch to the Cloud from their non-Cloud environments. This will also keep up the rise of the Cloud.

Keywords Cloud · Security · Denial of Service · Security attack · Virtualization · Multi-tenancy

S. Shafieian (✉) · M. Zulkernine
School of Computing, Queen's University, Kingston, ON K7L 2N8, Canada
e-mail: saeed@cs.queensu.ca

M. Zulkernine
e-mail: mzulker@cs.queensu.ca

A. Haque
Bell Canada, Hamilton, ON L8P 1P8, Canada
e-mail: anwar.haque@bell.ca

© Springer International Publishing Switzerland 2014   3
Z. Mahmood (ed.), *Cloud Computing,* Computer Communications and Networks,
DOI 10.1007/978-3-319-10530-7_1

1.1   Introduction

Cloud Computing is rapidly becoming the de facto standard for hosting and running medium- to large-scale software applications and services on the Internet [1]. Many companies, individuals and even government sectors are switching to the Cloud environment due to several advantages that this new paradigm offers, including the reduction of operational and training costs, the reduction of upfront capitalizations, rapid scalability, ease of development, unlimited storage, and ubiquitous accessibility. By using the Cloud paradigm, Cloud consumers may be able to concentrate more on the core application functionality instead. Cloud Computing is not a new technology but a combination of existing technologies such as the Web and virtualization. Therefore, any vulnerability in one of these underlying technologies may be exploited as a security attack in the Cloud.

There are, however, disadvantages in utilizing the Cloud infrastructure, most notably issues related to security, privacy, and trust. According to independent surveys [2, 3], the most daunting obstacle in switching to the Cloud from a traditional architecture is security concerns. All of these surveys and studies show the significance of security in the Cloud from the perspective of both providers and consumers. If security issues are well addressed and potential consumers are aware of them, it may help a more confident transition to the new Cloud environment and will consequently help the continued rise of the Cloud.

1.1.1   Cloud Computing

The most commonly referenced definition of the Cloud is the one proposed by the U.S. National Institute of Standards and Technology (NIST) [4]. Based on this definition, the Cloud model is composed of five essential characteristics, three service models, and four deployment models. The five characteristics of the Cloud are on-demand self-service, broad network access, resource pooling, rapid elasticity, and measured service.

The three service models of the Cloud include Software as a Service (SaaS), Platform as a Service (PaaS), and Infrastructure as a Service (IaaS). Each of these service models can be deployed as any of the four deployment models: private, community, hybrid, and public.

Regarding the three service models and the four deployment models, there can be six different combinations of service and deployment models for any Cloud. However, some of these may only exist in theory and not offered by any Cloud Service Provider (CSP), the entity which offers the Cloud services. In this chapter, we only focus on one of these combinations, i.e., the public IaaS Cloud, which is one of the most frequently used combinations and is offered by most prominent CSPs.

In the IaaS model, all the Cloud infrastructure resources are provisioned for the consumer. In this model, the consumer is normally able to deploy and run any operating systems or software applications in the Cloud. Famous examples of IaaS include Amazon EC2, Rackspace Cloud, Google Compute Engine, IBM Smart-Cloud, and Microsoft Azure. In the public deployment model, the Cloud infrastructure is provisioned to be openly used by the general public. Unlike the other deployment models, in the public model the infrastructure only exists on the premises of the Cloud provider.

One of the most important attributes in a public IaaS Cloud is multi-tenancy. Multi-tenancy enables different consumers to have virtual machines (VMs) on the same physical machine. This attribute is not considered as one of the five essential Cloud characteristics mentioned earlier, but it normally exists in public Clouds and is the main justifying factor for the lower costs in the Cloud as compared to non-Cloud environments. All the VMs running on top of the same physical machine are controlled by a hypervisor. A hypervisor, also called a virtual machine monitor (VMM), controls all the guest operating systems running on top of a host operating system.

1.1.2 Cloud Attributes Affecting Security

We identify attributes which may be exploited to exacerbate the attacks in the Cloud compared to non-Cloud environments. By exploiting these attributes, attackers may be able to launch attacks that have more consequences or are harder to detect or prevent in a public Cloud. By "having more consequence," we refer to either affecting more users or causing more asset losses. These attributes are as follows:

- *Ubiquitous Network Access:* Cloud consumers can access and provision all the services and resources provided by the CSP using public networks especially the Internet and via conventional devices.
- *Measured Service:* The CSP measures the provided service to its consumers based on appropriate units. Consumers can monitor and track their resource usage online through the transparent measured service.
- *Multi-tenancy:* In a public IaaS Cloud, different consumers may have their VMs coresident with other consumers' VMs on the same physical server. This allows for lower resource usage costs compared to the single-tenant model in traditional environments or private Clouds.
- *Off-premise Infrastructure:* In a public Cloud, the infrastructure is owned and operated by a third party and is off premises of the consumer's organization. As a result, the consumer loses physical control over their resources, and needs to rely on the CSP's physical security measures.

The ubiquitous network access and measured service are essential Cloud characteristics, and are therefore required to be provided by any CSP regardless of the service or the deployment model. Multi-tenancy does not exist in the private Cloud as there is only one consumer utilizing the Cloud resources. Nevertheless, multi-tenancy is a vital attribute in all public Clouds. Finally, off-premise infrastructure is an intrinsic attribute in any public Cloud which contributes as one of the major concerns for any Cloud consumer. Each of the aforementioned attributes might be exploited in order to exacerbate the attacks. If an attack is exacerbated in the Cloud through exploitation of one of the Cloud attributes, it means that the attribute contributes in increasing attack motivation, attack consequence, or making detection, prevention, and response mechanisms for that specific attack more challenging compared to those in non-Cloud environments.

1.1.3   Chapter Overview

We consider security as the preservation of confidentiality, integrity, and availability. Here, we are concerned mostly with the IaaS security. For the two other service models, most of the countermeasures and mitigation techniques are to be taken by the CSPs. For example, Amazon is responsible for maintaining security from the physical level of the data centers up to the hypervisor level. On the other hand, consumers are kept responsible for all the rest such as operating system (OS) security, application security, etc. [5]. As a result, the Cloud consumers are not free to implement their desired security solutions and need to rely on the provided level of security by the CSP. For the IaaS model, a consumer has the highest degree of control over infrastructure compared to other models. On the other hand, a CSP has the lowest responsibilities for maintaining security in the IaaS. Regarding maintaining confidentiality, integrity, and availability as the three pillars of security, a CSP is generally responsible for only preserving availability in the IaaS and the remaining two attributes should be of the consumer's concern [6].

In this chapter, we discuss and assess attacks in public IaaS Clouds. We are mainly focused on two groups of attacks: attacks that are common between the Cloud and non-Cloud environments but are exacerbated in the Cloud by exploiting multitenancy, and attacks that occur because of the virtualization technology or the utility pricing model used in the Cloud. We provide Cloud scenarios as to how each of the attacks occurs in the Cloud and discuss current solutions for them. We compare the first group of attacks with those in non-Cloud environments based on the proposed Cloud attributes that affect security. Furthermore, we assess how any of these attacks could compromise confidentiality, integrity, or availability in the Cloud.

1.1.4   Chapter Organization

The rest of the chapter is organized as follows: Section 1.2 provides the related work and discusses the motivation for a new survey. Section 1.3 discusses attacks in the public Cloud and provides assessment in terms of the Cloud attributes which may be exploited in order to exacerbate the attacks. Moreover, it shows how attacks compromise confidentiality, integrity, and availability in the Cloud. Finally, Sect. 1.4 concludes the chapter and discusses some open issues.

1.2   Related Literature

There exist a number of surveys in the literature that discuss general Cloud security issues and provide overviews of the challenges [7–25]. In this section, we discuss the works that propose classifications with respect to the attacks in the Cloud.

Gruschka et al. [26] suggest a classification of the attacks in the Cloud based on the notion of attack surfaces. They identify three major participants in a Cloud environment: users, services, and the Cloud provider. They suggest six combinations of possible interactions between any two of these entities proposing that an attack in the Cloud exploits one or a combination of these surfaces.

Srinivasan et al. [27] also propose a classification of the security challenges in the Cloud. They categorize the security challenges as being either based on architectural and technological aspects, or process and regulatory-related aspects. They suggest different subcategories within each of those two categories. In another work, Chow et al. [28] identify the security concerns in the Cloud as traditional security, availability and third-party security. They suggest different subcategories within each of the mentioned categories.

Grobauer et al. [29] categorize vulnerabilities in the Cloud as core technology or Cloud-specific vulnerabilities. They suggest that Cloud Computing is built on three core technologies i.e., Web applications and services, virtualization, and cryptography. A vulnerability is Cloud-specific if it is inherent in a core Cloud technology, is caused mainly due to one of the NIST's essential Cloud characteristics, is because of inefficiency of the conventional security controls in the Cloud, or is common in prominent Cloud offerings.

You et al. [9] propose a classification of Cloud security issues into three different categories: data security, virtualization-related security, and application-related security. They describe each category in terms of security issues and threats related to each category.

Sen [30] proposes a classification of security issues in the Cloud consisting of traditional security concerns, availability issues, and third-party data control-related issues. The author claims that the traditional security concerns will be aggravated by moving to the Cloud. By pointing out real availability incidents for well-known CSPs such as Amazon and Google, the author identifies availability issues as one of the biggest concerns for critical applications hosted in the Cloud. Legal, contractual, and auditability issues are also identified as concerns raised by third-party data control.

Molnar et al. [31] classify threats that arise from moving from self-hosting to Cloud-hosting into two sets: threats that may be caused by having leased resources instead of owned ones, and threats which may be caused by having shared instead of dedicated resources. For the first group, they identify threats to infrastructure assembly, contractual threats, and legal and jurisdictional threats. The second group consists of threats from other tenants, legal and jurisdictional threats, threats to availability and service costs, and restricted audit, detection, and response capabilities. They also discuss countermeasures to each group of threats.

1.3   Attacks in the Cloud

In this chapter, we investigate attacks in the Cloud from the perspective of consumers and clients who do not operate the Cloud infrastructure themselves. We are interested in the IaaS service model because in the other service models there is little freedom for a consumer in terms of countermeasures they can put in place to mitigate the security vulnerabilities. We consider public deployment model of the Cloud since it is the most-widely used model. Public model has not been customized for specific high-security demand entities like financial institutions or government sectors. As a result, it may be the most vulnerable model to the attacks.

Many of the attacks that can occur in a Cloud environment are preexisting attacks that have occurred in non-Cloud environments before. Due to the nature of the Cloud, which is a combination of existing technologies such as the Web and virtualization, any security vulnerability that can occur in the presence of these technologies has the potential of occurring in the Cloud as well. However, there are attacks that may only occur in the Cloud environment because of the specific Cloud paradigm and architecture. In this section, we provide an overview of some of the attacks that are common between the Cloud and non-Cloud environments but may be exacerbated in the Cloud through exploiting multi-tenancy. Furthermore, we discuss and assess attacks that occur due to the virtualization technology used in the Cloud. In this chapter, we do not discuss well-known Web-based attacks such as cross site scripting (XSS), cross site request forgery (CSRF), SQL injection (SQLI), and phishing. These attacks can all occur in the Cloud because of the similar underlying technologies used as non-Cloud systems. However, these have been well studied, and we refer the interested reader to the related references on these attacks [e.g., 32].

1.3.1   Common Attacks

There are attacks that are common between the Cloud and non-Cloud environments. These attacks, however, may be exacerbated in the public Cloud via exploitation of the inherent multi-tenancy attribute in the public Clouds. Here, we discuss three attacks that may be aggravated in the Cloud because of the coresident consumers sharing the same physical hardware.

1.3.1.1   Distributed Denial of Service Attacks

Distributed Denial of Service (DDoS) attacks are one of the dominant attacks in the Cloud [2]. In a DDoS attack, the adversary exploits a number of compromised machines called bots to compose a botnet in order to consume critical resources at the victim's machine(s). The goal of the attacker is to force a computer or network to become incapable of providing normal services by blocking access to or degrading services. DDoS attacks can target different layers of a computer system stack including network device level, operating system level, and application level [33]. Using internet protocol (IP) spoofing techniques, the attacker may be able to send attack packets from spoofed IP addresses. This might make the fraudulent traffic difficult to filter and the source of attack undistinguishable.

The Cloud is a combination of preexisting technologies such as Web and networks, so DDoS attacks can be targeted to Cloud machines. However, there are differences between a DDoS attack on the Cloud and non-Cloud environments. In the context of the Cloud, the attack can also be launched from within the Cloud by exploiting a number of VMs as internal bots in order to flood malicious requests towards the victim's VM(s) [7]. This may make detecting such an attack very difficult, if intrusion detection and prevention systems operate only at the perimeter of the Cloud. In this case, they may be unable to detect DDoS attacks launched from within the Cloud. This can increase the chance of having successful DDoS attacks on the Cloud. Another difference between the Cloud and non-Cloud environments which exacerbates DDoS attacks in the Cloud is that unlike non-Cloud environments, a DDoS attack in the Cloud can have impact on multiple consumers as several consumers may be using the compromised physical machine.

The conventional countermeasures to mitigate DDoS attacks include Intrusion Detections Systems (IDSs) and Intrusion Prevention Systems (IPSs). These systems can be both software-based and hardware-based and deploy various techniques such as resource multiplication, traffic pattern detection, and traffic anomaly detection to prevent and detect DDoS attacks [34–36]. Yu et al. [37] propose using idle resources to form multiple parallel IPSs in the Cloud in order to help the attacked machine to defeat a DDoS attack. This may save the victim from having its resources blocked or degraded, but it may incur a considerable amount of charges for many idle resources that might have been used.

1.3.1.2 Keystroke Timing Attacks

Keystroke timing attacks occur when the attacker tries to steal the victim's confidential information, especially login passwords, via eavesdropping on their keystrokes. Song et al. [38] show that the timing information of keystrokes may leak information about the keys' sequence types. They show that by applying advanced statistical techniques on timing information collected from the network, an attacker can learn substantial information about the characters the victim has typed in a secure shell (SSH) session.

In a Cloud environment, the attacker's goal is to measure the time between keystrokes while the victim is typing a password. If the inter-stroke times are measured with sufficient resolution, they can be used to perform password recovery. Having coresidency, the attack can be launched in real time via measuring cache-based loads while the victim is typing sensitive information. However, a successful attack requires the two VMs to share the same CPU core at the time of the attack which decreases the chance of having a successful attack [39]. We are not aware of any countermeasures for keystroke timing attacks other than avoiding coresidency in the Cloud. A mitigation technique used in Amazon EC2 is to frequently change the processor cores among VMs such that the chance of a successful attack decreases.

1.3.1.3   Side-Channel Attacks

Due to the multi-tenancy attribute in the public Clouds which enables multiple VMs to run on the same physical machine, a consumer's VM could be running on the same server as their adversary. This may allow the adversary to infiltrate the isolation between the VMs and compromise the consumer's confidentiality. A side-channel attack consists of two main steps: placement and extraction. In the placement phase, the attacker tries to place his/her malicious VM on the same physical machine as that of the target consumer. Ristenpart et al. [39] show that by using careful empirical mappings on Amazon EC2 public IaaS Cloud, they can increase the chance of placing the malicious VM on the right physical machine. In fact, they suggest that two VM instances in EC2 are likely to be coresident if they have matching Xen Dom0 IP addresses, small packet round-trip times, or numerically close EC2 internal IP addresses. After the intruder manages to place a VM coresident with the target, the next step involves extracting the confidential information via a cross-VM attack. One of the ways to do this is through side-channels, i.e., cross-VM information leakage due to the sharing of the physical resources, for instance a CPU's data cache. By using a technique called Cloud cartography, the EC2 service can be mapped in order to make an educated guess as to where the potential target VMs are located. This can be achieved by using network probing tools. The cache-based side-channel attacks have been shown to be able to extract Rivest Shamir Adleman (RSA) and advanced encryption standard (AES) secret keys [17, 18]. In a recent work, Zhang et al. [42] were also able to extract the ElGamal decryption key from a victim VM managed by the modern Xen hypervisor.

Zhang et al. [43] propose a technique called HomeAlone to allow a tenant to verify their exclusive residency of the physical machine on which their VMs are running. This happens when a tenant has purchased isolated resources from a CSP, but they still need to verify physical isolation of their VMs. The proposed technique employs an L2 memory cache side-channel not as an attack but as a defensive detection tool. The technique helps the tenant ascertain whether there is a rival VM coresident with their VMs on the same physical machine. To achieve this, all the friendly VMs silence their activity in a selected cache region for a specific period of time. The tenant then measures the cache usage during this period and checks to see if there is any unexpected activity. Any activity during this period would indicate the presence of a rival VM.

One of the proposed solutions to mitigate side-channel attacks includes obscuring the internal structure of the services as well as the VM placement policy. These should be done by CSPs in order to complicate the placement procedure for an attacker. The other approach is to minimize the information that can be leaked once

Table 1.1 Consequences of Cloud attribute exploitations

Attack	Ubiquitous network	Measured service	Multi-tenancy	Off-premise infrastructure
DDoS	+	+	+	+
Keystroke timing	0	0	+	0
Side-channel	0	0	+	0

+: exacerbated, 0: not affected

the attack occurs [39]. Godfrey et al. [44] propose a server-side approach to mitigate cache-based side-channel attacks. They modify the Xen hypervisor so that a cache flush occurs only when a context switch changes to a VM that has the ability to establish a side-channel with the first. However, none of these countermeasures stops an adversary, launching side-channel attacks, and the best solution would be for the consumer to utilize physical machine resources exclusively. Although more costs would be incurred by the underutilization of the resources, the consumer makes sure no such attacks can occur.

1.3.1.4   Discussion

DDoS, keystroke timing and side-channel attacks may all be exacerbated in the Cloud compared to non-Cloud environments. Table 1.1 shows the consequences of Cloud attribute exploitations by attacks. As shown in Table 1.1, all these attacks may be exacerbated in the Cloud through exploitation of the multi-tenancy attribute. A DDoS attack may be exacerbated via exploitation of other attributes too. In a Cloud environment, not only do there exist DDoS attacks initiated outside of the Cloud but also there can be DDoS attacks launched from inside the Cloud by exploiting VMs to form an internal botnet. Here, exploitation of ubiquitous network access and multi-tenancy attributes may exacerbate the DDoS attack, making it more difficult for firewalls and intrusion detection systems to detect, as attacks are coming from an internal as well as an external source. Moreover, as the consumer is charged according to measured services, this attribute can also incur more charges to the victim due to the unwanted inbound and outbound traffic and resource usage. Having off-premise infrastructure may also delay an immediate response to the attack. There is another opportunity for an attacker to perform DDoS attacks in the Cloud: usually with public CSPs, one can register for an IaaS service by just entering credit card information or even benefit from trial periods without entering any valid data. Due to this type of loose registration, attackers can exploit VMs while hiding their identities [45]. In this way, an adversary can launch attacks against victims that reside both inside and outside the Cloud, by exploiting the Cloud resources. For those DDoS attacks launched from inside the Cloud against victims that are inside as well, firewalls and intrusion detection and prevention systems might not be able to block the attacks.

In our assessment of the attacks in the Cloud, we also consider keystroke timing attacks as having more consequence in a Cloud rather than a non-Cloud environment due to multi-tenancy attribute exploitation. The keystroke timing attacks require coresidency with the victim's VM. This can happen when there are multi-tenant consumers in an IaaS Cloud. Multi-tenancy attribute of the Cloud may be exploited to exacerbate the keystroke timing attack by increasing the chance of having a successful attack. However, this attack may be very difficult to succeed in practice if the CSP migrates VMs between different cores of a physical machine processor as implemented in Amazon EC2. If the attacker VM and the victim's VMs are using one of the cores on a four-core processor, the chance of having a successful keystroke timing attack would be less than 25 % [39].

Side-channel attacks can also occur in Cloud as well as non-Cloud environments. However, even in a non-Cloud environment which uses virtualization technology such as Virtual Private Server (VPS) hosting, the attacker has no way of placing their malicious VM on a target server. Therefore, the placement step which is the first required step in performing a successful side-channel attack cannot be performed, leaving little chance of success for the attacker. Nonetheless, in a public Cloud scenario, an adversary may be able to place their malicious VMs coresident with the victim's VMs by exploiting the multi-tenancy attribute, and launching a successful side-channel attack as described earlier. As a result, multi-tenancy exploitation may exacerbate side-channel attacks by bringing more motivation to the attacker, compared to traditional environments.

1.3.2   Cloud-Specific Attacks

Cloud-specific attacks are those attacks that occur via exploiting vulnerabilities in the virtualization or utility pricing. These attacks may also occur in any non-Cloud environment which uses virtualization technology. Nevertheless, multi-tenancy and pay-as-you-go features offered by the public Clouds, make the Cloud an ideal attack target for adversaries targeting to exploit such vulnerabilities. In this section, we discuss this class of attacks in the Cloud.

1.3.2.1   VM Denial of Service Attacks

A Virtual Machine Denial of Service (VM DoS) attack occurs when the adversary who is the owner of a VM in the Cloud exploits a vulnerability in the hypervisor in order to consume all or most of the available resources of the physical machine the VM is running on [11]. This will lead to other tenants being deprived of the required resources and encountering malfunctions with their services.

The VM DoS attack can occur in any environment that uses the virtualization technology and offers coresidency to the consumers. Most current hypervisors are capable of detecting excessive resource consumption by the VMs running on top of them. After detecting a malicious VM, one of the techniques to prevent denial of service for other VMs residing on the same physical server is to restart the malicious VM. This costs less than restarting the entire physical machine.

1.3.2.2   Hypervisor Attacks

A Cloud administrator who has privileged access to the hypervisor is able to penetrate into guest VMs through the hypervisor even without having any direct privileges on the target VMs. For example, if Xen is used as the hypervisor, the XenAccess library allows a privileged VM to view the contents of another VM's memory at runtime. This technique is called virtual machine introspection [46]. In another type of hypervisor attack, a malicious administrator installs a malicious hypervisor into a Cloud server to eavesdrop on a consumer's activities and steal their sensitive information. Moreover, considering the root-level access of system administrators, it may be difficult for a guest OS to detect the fraudulent activity using conventional detection mechanisms [47].

Santos et al. [48] propose a Trusted Cloud Computing Platform (TCCP) for ensuring the confidentiality and integrity of computations that are outsourced to IaaS services. They suggest that the approach enables a closed box execution environment preventing a user with full privileges on the host VM to gain access to the guest VMs.

Another type of attack targets vulnerabilities in a hypervisor scheduler. Zou et al. [49] show that an attacker can exploit a VM so that it uses more processor time than its fair share and escapes the periodic sampling performed by the hypervisor. In this attack, the adversary makes the processor idle just before the scheduler tick occurs and resumes the run after the tick finishes. This enables the attacker VM to consume most of the processor cycles without incurring any charges and deprives the cotenant VMs from consuming their required cycles. They have implemented sample hypervisor scheduling attacks on Amazon EC2 to demonstrate the practicality of these types of attacks. The proposed solutions to this attack include using a high-precision clock or a random scheduler to prevent scheduler escaping.

1.3.2.3   Cloud Malware Injection Attacks

In a Cloud malware injection attack, the adversary tries to inject a malicious VM into the Cloud with different purposes including eavesdropping, functionality altering, or blockings [10]. The attacker needs to create their own malicious VM instance into an IaaS Cloud. In order for this attack to be successful, the malicious instance should be designed in such a way that the Cloud treats it as a valid instance.

In Amazon EC2 public IaaS Cloud, a consumer can simply create an image of their VM, called Amazon Machine Image (AMI). Once the image is created, it can be easily made public by editing AMI permissions and changing the visibility from private to public. As a result, if a malicious image is created in this way, it will be visible to all other EC2 consumers, and they can launch VM instances based on this image. All the VMs created based on the malicious image may be vulnerable to attacks such as stealing of sensitive data.

One of the countermeasures to be taken by CSPs in order to resolve these types of attacks is not to allow an image to go public unless it has been fully scanned to ensure that it is free from any potential malware. However, new malware may not be detected by malware detection tools, thus, consumers should always undertake the risk of using public images, and do not solely rely on the service provider's security measures.

1.3.2.4   VM Image Attacks

Typically, in a Cloud environment such as Amazon EC2, VM images are shared among Cloud consumers. These include both CSP-provided and user-provided images. CSP-provided images help consumers instantiate their required VMs rapidly by providing them with the standard OSs and applications. On the other hand, a user is able to make an image of their VM and make it publicly available to all other users of the Cloud. VM images can be easily saved, copied, encrypted, moved, and restored.

There are three types of risks associated with VM images: publisher's risk, retriever's risk, and Cloud administrator's risk [50]. The publisher risks disclosing their sensitive information, such as saved passwords, browsing history, cookies, etc., by sharing a VM image for the public. On the other hand, there is a high risk for the consumer who runs vulnerable or malicious images. When a malicious VM is run by a victim consumer, the attacker is in fact bypassing security measures such as intrusion detection and prevention systems and firewalls around the Cloud network. The Cloud administrator also risks distributing the images with malicious content over the Cloud network. The infected machines appear shortly, infect other machines, and disappear before they can be detected. As a result, the infections would persist indefinitely and the system may never reach a steady state [51].

Inadequate data deletion can be the root for another type of VM image attack [52]. Cloud consumers normally delete their VMs after they are finished using them in order not to incur the cost of having idle VMs. Nevertheless, if the data is not properly deleted, there is the risk of being recovered by a malicious CSP insider or even by another Cloud consumer who has been allocated the same disk area on that specific server. This can occur due to the fact that in many OSs when data is deleted, its space is marked as free by the system, but the contents will remain on the disk. In a recent work, Balduzzi et al. [53] show that 98 % of Windows images and 58 % of Linux images in Amazon EC2 contain software with critical vulnerabilities based on analyzing a total of 5303 Amazon machine images.

These types of attacks are similar to malware injection attacks when a malicious VM becomes publicly available in the Cloud. However, when a consumer publishes an image publicly, they need to make sure that any sensitive data has been thoroughly erased in such a way that it will not be recoverable by subsequent users of the image or even CSP administrators.

1.3.2.5   VM Relocation Attacks

VM mobility is one of the advantageous features of using VMs, as opposed to physical machines, and is essential for load balancing and system maintenance. However, it imposes security risks for the owner as VMs can be stolen by malicious insiders even without the owner's awareness. In an offline attack, the adversary can simply copy the entire victim's VM to a remote machine or even a portable storage device [51]. Moreover, there exist attacks that can occur in a live VM migration scenario. A live VM migration is normally done by copying memory pages of a VM from the source hypervisor to the destination hypervisor over the network. The attacks have been empirically demonstrated on Xen and VMware, the two most deployed hypervisors [54]. One of these attacks includes initiating unauthorized migration of a victim VM to the attacker's physical machine. The adversary can then gain full control over the victim's VM or launch attacks that exploit coresidency such as side-channel. Another type of attack is to initiate an unauthorized migration of a large number of VMs to a victim machine in order to cause denial of service for the victim. Mutual authentication of the source and the destination hypervisors is a suggested solution in order to achieve a secure migration and prevent potential attacks.

1.3.2.6   Resource-Freeing Attacks

Resource-freeing attacks (RFAs) are a new type of attack in the Cloud that exploit the coresidency and resource sharing among VMs in order to modify the workload of a victim VM to release resources for an attacker VM [55]. Any hypervisor such as Xen tries to provide performance isolation by allocating required resources to each VM. However, if two VMs require heavy use of the shared memory or the processor at the same time, the performances of both VMs degrade, since the hypervisor is not able to allocate the required resources to both VMs. The competition to acquire resources may lead to a malicious consumer crashing the rival VM in order to free resources for their own use.

A hypervisor scheduler may provide a fair-share allocation of the processor by distributing idle processor time to running VMs (work-conserving), or by putting a limit on the maximum amount allowed for each VM (non-work-conserving). The former increases performance, but reduces isolation, whereas the latter increases the isolation with the cost of decreasing the performance. A resource-freeing attack can occur only when a work-conserving scheduler is used. The first step to launch an RFA attack is to increase the resource usage of the victim so that it reaches a bottleneck. This step is performed by using a helper process that can be run either on the same or another machine. Then, the next step would involve shifting the victim's resource usage to the bottleneck resource. This would free up other resources to be used by the attacker.

An RFA has been shown to be able to increase the performance of a VM by up to 60% on a local test bed, and up to 13% when launched on Amazon EC2 [56]. The low rate on Amazon EC2 is in part due to the fact that non-work-conserving scheduler is used by Xen to schedule processor timing in EC2. One of the ways to prevent RFAs is to use dedicated instances. This costly approach is supported by Amazon EC2 and allows a consumer to request dedicated resources for their VMs on a physical machine. The other approach to prevent an RFA is to use schedulers that do not distribute idle resources, such as non-work-conserving schedulers. However, as previously mentioned, this places a boundary on the maximum resource share to be used by each VM, and may reduce the performance.

1.3.2.7   Fraudulent Resource Consumption Attacks

One of the few unique attacks in the Cloud is Fraudulent Resource Consumption (FRC) [56]. In this Cloud-specific attack, the adversary aims to exploit the utility pricing model of the Cloud by launching an attack similar to a DDoS attack. The utility pricing in the Cloud is similar to the pricing model of utilities such as electricity and gas for which a consumer pays only for the amount they have used.

By fraudulently using the consumer's Cloud resources, the adversary's intension is to divest the victim of their long-term economic benefits. There are two major differences between FRC and DDoS attacks. First, FRC attacks aim to make Cloud resources economically unsustainable for the victim, whereas a DDoS attack aims to degrade or block Cloud services. Second, FRC attacks tend to be more subtle and are carried out over a longer period of time compared to DDoS attacks. In order to fraudulently consume resources, the attacker exploits a botnet to send malicious requests to the Cloud to gradually increase the cost of resource usage for the victim consumer. The idea of FRC attacks is originated from the notion of Economic Denial of Sustainability (EDoS) [57] where an attacker targets the long-term sustainability of the victim.

Detecting an FRC attack could be very difficult because the way an attacker requests Web resources is like that of any legitimate client, and the only differentiating attribute is their intention. An FRC attack occurs just above the normal activity threshold and below the DDoS attack threshold. Therefore, it may be unlikely to be detected by traditional intrusion detection systems. FRC attacks are new and unique to the Cloud because they exploit the utility pricing model of the Cloud, which is not applicable to non-Cloud environments.

In a normal traffic activity to a website, the frequency of visiting a Web page is proportional to the popularity of that page. For example, the Home page is usually the most visited page in normal traffic and the About Us page may be visited less frequently. Now if for a given website, the incoming page requests from a client hit the About Us page much more than the home page, most probably the traffic is being automatically generated from a botnet and therefore should be detected as

Table 1.2 Security attributes affected by the attacks

Style3Attack	Confidentiality	Integrity	Availability
DDoS	N	N	Y
Keystroke timing	Y	N	N
Side-Channel	Y	N	N
VM DoS	N	N	Y
Hypervisor	Y	Y	Y
Malware injection	Y	Y	Y
VM image	Y	Y	Y
VM relocation	Y	N	N
RFA	N	N	Y
FRC	N	N	N

Y compromises, *N* does not compromise

fraudulent. Another approach to mitigate EDoS attacks is to try to verify benign and malicious requests by creating a white list and a blacklist of IP addresses based on the first packet received from a requesting source [58]. As a result, if the first request is from a benign user, all the subsequent requests from the user will be passed to the Cloud server, but if the first packet is detected to be from a malicious user, all the subsequent requests will be denied for that user. The downside of this technique is that it may not be possible to distinguish between malicious and benign users by only examining the first packet received from them.

1.3.2.8 Discussion

Cloud-specific attacks are those attacks that can occur in the Cloud due to the specific Cloud paradigm and technologies. Most of these attacks exploit vulnerabilities in the virtualization. These attacks are able to make Cloud services unavailable or significantly degraded for the tenants. Attackers can also penetrate into other VMs coresident with them in order to steal private information, alter data, etc. Moreover, a malicious VM can escape the fair processor sharing and not incur any charges for the processor cycles that have been used. The other type of attack is to inject a malicious VM in the Cloud. There are also threats associated with sharing VM images and relocating VMs in public Clouds. Fraudulent resource consumption or economic denial of sustainability attacks target the long-term sustainability of the Cloud resources for consumers. These types of attacks are unique to the Cloud and may be among the most difficult attacks to detect.

1.3.3 Security Attributes in the Cloud

The three fundamental attributes of security, i.e., confidentiality, integrity, and availability, can be affected by the attacks in the Cloud. Nonetheless, not every attack compromises every attribute of the triad. Table 1.2 shows how these three attributes of security are affected by different attacks in the Cloud. As Table 1.2 shows, some of the attacks affect all, whereas some others only affect one or two of the attributes. The only exception is the FRC attack. This attack does not compromise any of the three security attributes; however, fraudulent resource consumption is considered an attack which exploits utility pricing model of the Cloud.

Once a DDoS attack occurs, data may not be available to the authorized users, thus violating the availability attribute. Nonetheless, confidentiality and integrity may not be compromised by a DDoS attack. A successful keystroke timing attack may lead to the leakage of sensitive data thus compromising the confidentiality attribute. This attack normally cannot put the other security attributes at risk. Side-channel attacks are able to compromise the victim's confidentiality by extracting confidential information through side-channels.

A VM DoS attack may deprive a victim tenant of the shared resources. As a result, it compromises the availability attribute. If a hypervisor attack is successful, based on the level of privileges the attacker may acquire, any of the three security attributes can be at risk. This is also true for a malware injection attack. By eavesdropping, functionality changing, and blocking services for other VMs, the confidentiality, integrity, and availability of the victims can be compromised. A consumer who publishes their VM to the public, risks compromising the confidentiality of their private data in case of not being thoroughly deleted. Moreover, a consumer who runs a shared VM may put all the three security attributes at risk by inviting potential malware into their VM instance. If a VM is stolen during the process of its relocation, the confidentiality of the victim may be compromised since the adversary gains access to the victim's entire data located on the VM. Finally, an RFA compromises the availability of the victim VM via shifting its resource usage towards a bottlenecked resource.

There are also risks associated with image backups in the Cloud. Image backups should always be stored encrypted, but if an unencrypted backup is accessed by an adversary, the confidentiality of the owner may be at risk. Furthermore, if the attacker alters the contents of the backup, the integrity may also be compromised once the backup image is restored.

1.4   Conclusions and Open Issues

Security concerns are among the biggest barriers that may hinder the rising adoption of the Cloud. In this chapter, we described the attacks that can occur in the public Clouds. We discussed and compared the attacks that are common between the Cloud and traditional systems, but are exacerbated in the Cloud due to exploitation of multi-tenancy. These included distributed denial of service, keystroke timing, and side-channel attacks. Furthermore, we discussed attacks that are specific to the Cloud paradigm. These attacks exploit vulnerabilities in hypervisors and are able to carry out malicious actions such as blocking the Cloud resources for consumers, eavesdropping on consumers' activities, and escaping fair share scheduling. EDoS or fraudulent resource consumption is another type of Cloud-specific attack that exploits the utility pricing model of the Cloud. We also discussed how each of the three security attributes may be compromised by each attack. We believe that when consumer applications run in the Cloud, they generally face more potential attacks, and the evolving nature of the Cloud may also suggest newer threats in future.

This study may help organizations and individuals who are considering the Cloud as the future infrastructure for hosting and running their business applications. These consumers can decide more wisely by identifying the potential attacks on their specific assets and by comparing the consequence of those attacks between the two environments before they move to the Cloud.

In this chapter, we did not investigate attacks in the SaaS and PaaS models of the Cloud. For those two service models, most of the countermeasures are to be taken by CSPs. We discussed attacks in the public IaaS Cloud as it is the most popular Cloud model.

The Cloud should be monitored for new attacks. As the Cloud is yet a new and evolving environment, new Cloud-specific attacks may always be discovered by carefully investigating the underlying interactions between different components in the architecture. There are attacks in the Cloud that require new solutions and countermeasures, or improvements to the current countermeasures. This is especially true for EDoS attacks which are the Cloud-specific variant of DDoS attacks. These attacks are capable of making the Cloud services unsustainable for the victim consumer. Consequently, designing appropriate detection and prevention mechanisms may help the potential victims to become more resilient against these attacks. This is particularly due to the fact that most solutions and countermeasures have only been experimented in controlled lab environments, or have been only proposed without undergoing any experimental validation as a proof of concept.

References

1. Amazon Web Services (AWS) (n.d.) Case studies. https://aws.amazon.com/solutions/case-studies. Accessed 2 Sept 2014
2. Cloud Security Alliance (Feb 2013) The notorious nine—cloud computing top threats in 2013. https://downloads.cloudsecurityalliance.org/initiatives/top_threats/The_Notorious_Nine_Cloud_Computing_Top_Threats_in_2013.pdf. Accessed 2 Sept 2014
3. Internet Data Corporation (IDC) (15 Dec 2009) New IDC IT cloud services survey: top benefits and challenges. http://blogs.idc.com/ie/?p=730. Accessed 2 Sept 2014
4. Mell P, Grance T (Sept 2011) The NIST definition of cloud computing. National Institute of Standards and Technology (NIST), Gaithersburg. http://csrc.nist.gov/publications/nistpubs/800-145/SP800-145.pdf. Accessed 2 Sept 2014
5. Grosse EH, Howie J, Ransome J, Reavis J, Schmidt S (2010) Cloud computing roundtable. IEEE Secur Priv 8(6):17–23
6. Hwang K, Kulkareni S, Hu Y (2009) Cloud security with virtualized defense and reputation-based trust management. In: Yang B, Zhu W, Dai Y, Yang LT, Ma J (eds) Proceedings of the 8th IEEE international symposium on dependable, autonomic and secure computing (DASC '09), Chengdu, 12–14 Dec 2009. IEEE Computer Society, Los Alamitos, pp 717–722

7. Ma X (2012) Security concerns in cloud computing. Proceedings of the 2012 fourth international conference on computational and information sciences (ICCIS 2012), Chongqing, 17–19 Aug 2012, pp 1069–1072

8. Subashini S Kavitha V (2011) A survey on security issues in service delivery models of cloud computing. J Netw Comput Appl 34(1):1–11. (Elsevier, January 2011)

9. You P, Peng Y, Liu W, Xue S (2012) Security issues and solutions in cloud computing. Proceedings of the 32nd international conference on distributed computing systems workshops (ICDCSW), Macau, 18–21 June 2012, pp 573–577

10. Jensen M, Schwenk J, Gruschka N, Iacono LL (2009) On technical security issues in cloud computing. Proceedings of the 2009 IEEE international conference on cloud computing (CLOUD '09), Bangalore, 21–25 Sept 2009, pp 109–116

11. Dawoud W, Takouna I, Meinel C (2010) Infrastructure as a service security: challenges and solutions. Proceedings of the 7th international conference on informatics and systems (INFOS), Giza, 28–30 March 2010, pp 1–8

12. Ren K, Wang C, Wang Q (2012) Security challenges for the public cloud. IEEE Internet Comput 16(1):69–73

13. Sabahi F (2011) Cloud computing security threats and responses. Proceedings of the IEEE 3rd international conference on communication software and networks (ICCSN), Xi'an, 27–29 May 2011, pp 245–249

14. Zhou M, Zhang R, Xie W, Qian W, Zhou A (2010) Security and privacy in cloud computing: a survey. Proceedings of the 6th international conference on semantics knowledge and grid (SKG), Ningbo, 1–3 Nov, pp 105–112

15. Zissis D, Lekkas D (2012) Addressing cloud computing security issues. Future Gener Comp Sy 28(3):583–592

16. Shue CA, Lagesse B (2011) Embracing the cloud for better cyber security. Proceedings of the 8th IEEE international workshop on middleware and system support for pervasive computing, Seattle, 21–25 March, pp 245–250

17. Chaves S, Westphall C, Westphall C, Geronimo G (2011) Customer security concerns in cloud computing. Proceedings of the tenth international conference on networks (ICN 2011), St. Maarten, 23–28 Jan, pp 7–11

18. Takabi H, Joshi JB, Ahn GJ (2010) Security and privacy challenges in cloud computing environments. IEEE Secur Priv 8(6)24–31

19. Behl A (2011) Emerging security challenges in cloud computing: an insight to cloud security challenges and their mitigation. Proceedings of the 2011 world congress on information and communication technologies (WICT), Mumbai, 11–14 Dec, pp 217–222

20. Behl A, Behl K (2012) Security paradigms for cloud computing. Proceedings of the fourth international conference on computational intelligence, communication systems and networks (CICSyN), Phuket, 24–26 July, pp 200–205

21. Pearson S, Benameur A (2010) Privacy, security and trust issues arising from cloud computing. Proceedings of the 2nd IEEE international conference on cloud computing technology and science (CloudCom), Indianapolis, 30 Nov–3 Dec, pp 693–702

22. Tripathi A, Mishra A (2011) Cloud computing security considerations. Proceedings of the IEEE International conference on signal processing, communications and computing (ICSPCC), Xi'an, 14–16 Sept, pp 1–5

23. Sengupta S, Kaulgud V, Sharma VS (2011) Cloud computing security—trends and research directions. Proceedings of the IEEE world congress on services (SERVICES), Washington DC, 4–9 July, pp 524–531

24. Tianfield H (2012) Security issues in cloud computing. Proceedings of the IEEE international conference on systems, man, and cybernetics (SMC), Seoul, 14–17 Oct, pp 1082–1089

25. Bouayad A, Blilat A, Mejhed NEH, Ghazi ME (2012) Cloud computing: security challenges. Proceedings of the colloquium on information science and technology (CIST), Fez, 22–24 Oct, pp 26–31

26. Gruschka N Jensen M (2010) Attack surfaces: a taxonomy for attacks on cloud services. Proceedings of the 3rd IEEE international conference on cloud computing (CLOUD'10), Heidelberg, 5–10 July, pp 276–279

27. Srinivasan MK, Sarukesi K, Rodrigues P, Manoj MS, Revathy P (2012) State-of-the-art cloud computing security taxonomies: a classification of security challenges in the present cloud computing environment. Proceedings of the international conference on advances in computing, communications and informatics (ICACCI '12), Chennai, 3–5 Aug, pp 470–476
28. Chow R, Golle P, Jakobsson M, Shi E, Staddon J, Masuoka R, Molina J (2009) Controlling data in the cloud: outsourcing computation without outsourcing control. Proceedings of the 2009 ACM workshop on cloud computing security (CCSW'09), Chicago, 13 Nov, pp 85–90
29. Grobauer B, Walloschek T, Stocker E (2011) Understanding cloud computing vulnerabilities. IEEE Secur Priv 9(2):50–57.
30. Sen J (2013) Security and privacy issues in cloud computing. arXiv:1303.4814 [cs.CR]
31. Molnar D, Schechter S (2010) Self hosting vs. cloud hosting: accounting for the security impact of hosting in the cloud. Proceedings of the ninth workshop on the economics of information security (WEIS 2010), Harvard University, 7–8 June
32. Shahriar H (Nov 2011) Mitigation of web-based program security vulnerability exploitations. PhD thesis, Queen's University, Canada
33. Douligeris C, Mitrokotsa A (2004) DDoS attacks and defense mechanisms: classification and state-of-the-art. Comput Netw 44(5):643–666
34. Roschke S, Cheng F, Meinel C (2009) Intrusion detection in the cloud. In: Yang B, Zhu W, Dai Y, Yang LT, Ma J (eds) Proceedings of the 8th IEEE international symposium on dependable, autonomic and secure computing (DASC '09), Chengdu, 12–14 Dec 2009. IEEE Computer Society, Los Alamitos, pp 729–734
35. Mirkovic J, Reiher P (2004) A taxonomy of DDoS attack and DDoS defense mechanisms. Comp Comm R 34(2):39–53.
36. Bakshi A, Yogesh B (2010) Securing cloud from DDOS attacks using intrusion detection system in virtual machine. Proceedings of the second international conference on communication software and networks (ICCSN'10), Singapore, 26–28 Feb, pp 260–264
37. Yu S, Tian Y, Guo S, Wu DO (2014) Can we beat DDOS attacks in clouds? IEEE T Parall Distr 25(9):2245–2254
38. Song DX, Wagner D, Tian X, (2001) Timing analysis of keystrokes and timing attacks on SSH. Proceedings of the 10th USENIX security symposium, Washington DC, 13–17 Aug
39. Ristenpart T, Tromer E, Shacham H, Savage S (2009) Hey, you, get off of my cloud: exploring information leakage in third-party compute clouds. Proceedings of the 16th ACM conference on computer and communications security (CCS'09), Chicago, 9–13 Nov, pp 199–212
40. Osvik DA, Shamir A, Tromer E (2006) Cache attacks and countermeasures: the case of AES. In: Pointcheval D (ed) Proceedings of the RSA conference cryptographers track (CT-RSA 2006), 13–17 Feb. Lecture notes in computer science, vol 3860. Springer, Berlin, pp 1–20
41. Percival C (2005) Cache missing for fun and profit. Proceedings of BSDCan 2005, Ottawa, 13–14 May
42. Zhang Y, Juels A, Reiter MK, Ristenpart T (2012) Cross-VM side channels and their use to extract private keys. Proceedings of the 2012 ACM conference on computer and communications security (CCS'12), Raleigh, 16–18 Oct, pp 305–316
43. Zhang Y, Juels A, Oprea A, Reiter MK, (2011) HomeAlone: co-residency detection in the cloud via side-channel analysis. Proceedings of the 2011 IEEE symposium on security and privacy (SP), Oakland, 22–25 May, pp 313–328
44. Godfrey M, Zulkernine M (2013) A server-side solution to cache-based side-channel attacks in the cloud. Proceedings of the IEEE 6th international conference on cloud computing, Santa Clara, 28 June–3 July, pp 163–170
45. Cloud Security Alliance (2010) Top threats to cloud computing V1.0. Cloud Security Alliance, Singapore
46. XenAccess (n.d.) XenAccess library. https://code.google.com/p/xenaccess. Accessed 2 Sept 2014
47. Duncan A, Creese S, Goldsmith M (2012) Insider attacks in cloud computing. Proceedings of the IEEE 11th international conference on trust, security and privacy in computing and communications (TrustCom), Liverpool, 25–27 June, pp 857–862
48. Santos N, Gummadi KP, Rodrigues R (2009) Towards trusted cloud computing. Proceedings of HotCloud'09, San Diego, 15 June, article no 3

49. Zhou F, Goel M, Desnoyers P, Sundaram R (2011) Scheduler vulnerabilities and coordinated attacks in cloud computing. Proceeding of the 10th IEEE international symposium on network computing and applications (NCA), Cambridge, 25–27 Aug, pp 123–130

50. Wei J, Zhang X, Ammons G, Bala V, NingRaleigh P (2009) Managing security of virtual machine images in a cloud environment. Proceeding of the 2009 ACM workshop on cloud computing security (CCSW'09), Chicago, 13 Nov, pp 91–96

51. Garfinkel T Rosenblum M (2005) When virtual is harder than real: security challenges in virtual machine based computing environments. Proceeding of the 10th workshop on hot topics in operating systems (HotOS'5), Santa Fe, June

52. Pearson S (2012) Privacy, security and trust in cloud computing. In: Pearson S, Yee G (eds) Privacy and security for cloud computing. Springer, London, pp 3–42

53. Balduzzi M, Zaddach J, Balzarotti D, Kirda E, Loureiro S (2012) A security analysis of amazon's elastic compute cloud service. Proceedings of the 27th annual ACM symposium on applied computing (SAC '12), Riva del Garda, 26–30 March, pp 1427–1434

54. Oberheide J, Cooke E, Jahanian F (2008) Empirical exploitation of live virtual machine migration. Proceedings of the Black Hat DC Briefings, Washington DC, 18–21 Feb

55. Varadarajan V, Kooburat T, Farley B, Ristenpart T, Swift MM (2012) Resource-freeing attacks: improve your cloud performance (at your neighbor's expense). Proceeding of the 2012 ACM conference on computer and communications security (CCS'12), Raleigh, 16–18 Oct, pp 281–292

56. Idziorek J, Tannian M, Jacobson D (2011) Detecting fraudulent use of cloud resources. Proceedings of the 3rd ACM workshop on cloud computing security workshop (CCSW'11), Chicago, 17–21 Oct, pp 61–72

57. Hoff C (2008) Cloud computing security: from DDoS (distributed denial of service) to EDoS (economic denial of sustainability). http://www.rationalsurvivability.com/blog/?p=66. Accessed 2 Sept 2014

58. Sqalli MH, Al-Haidari F, Salah K (2011) EDoS-Shield—a two-steps mitigation technique against edos attacks in cloud computing. Proceedings of the fourth IEEE international conference on utility and cloud computing (UCC), Victoria, 5–8 Dec, pp 49–56

Chapter 2
Distributed Database Management Systems: Architectural Design Choices for the Cloud

Joarder Mohammad Mustafa Kamal and Manzur Murshed

Abstract Cloud computing has changed the way we used to exploit software and systems. The two decades' practice of architecting solutions and services over the Internet has just revolved within the past few years. End users are now relying more on paying for what they use instead of purchasing a full-phase license. System owners are also in rapid hunt for business profits by deploying their services in the Cloud and thus maximising global outreach and minimising overall management costs. However, deploying and scaling Cloud applications regionally and globally are highly challenging. In this context, distributed data management systems in the Cloud promise rapid elasticity and horizontal scalability so that Cloud applications can sustain enormous growth in data volume, velocity, and value. Besides, distributed data replication and rapid partitioning are the two fundamental hammers to nail down these challenges. While replication ensures database read scalability and geo-reachability, data partitioning favours database write scalability and system-level load balance. System architects and administrators often face difficulties in managing a multi-tenant distributed database system in Cloud scale as the underlying workload characteristics change frequently. In this chapter, the inherent challenges of such phenomena are discussed in detail alongside their historical backgrounds. Finally, potential way outs to overcome such architectural barriers are presented under the light of recent research and development in this area.

Keywords Cloud computing · Distributed database · ACID · CAP · Replication · Partitioning · BASE · Consistency · Trade-offs

J. M. M. Kamal (✉)
Gippsland School of Faculty of Information Technology, Monash University, Clayton, VIC, Australia
e-mail: Joarder.Kamal@monash.edu

M. Murshed
Faculty of Science and Technology, Federation University, Churchill, VIC, Australia
e-mail: Manzur.Murshed@federation.edu.au

© Springer International Publishing Switzerland 2014
Z. Mahmood (ed.), *Cloud Computing,* Computer Communications and Networks,
DOI 10.1007/978-3-319-10530-7_2

2.1 Introduction

In recent years, with the widespread use of Cloud computing based platform and virtual infrastructure services, each and every user-facing Web application is thrusting to achieve both 'high availability' and 'high scalability' at the same time. Data replication techniques are long being used as a key way forward to achieve fault-tolerance (i.e., high availability) and improving performance (i.e., maintaining system throughput and response time for an increasing number of users) in both distributed systems and database implementations [29]. The primary challenges for replication strategies include: (1) replica control mechanisms—'where' and 'when' to update replicated copies, (2) replication architecture—'where' replication logic should be implemented and finally (3) 'how' to ensure both the 'consistency' and the 'reliability' requirements for the target application. These challenges fundamentally depend on the typical workload patterns that the target application will be going to handle as well as the particular business goals it will try to meet.

Even in the absence of failure, some degree of replication is needed to guarantee both 'high availability' and 'high scalability' simultaneously. And, to achieve the highest level of these two properties, data should be replicated over wide area networks. Thus, the replicated system inherently imposes design trade-offs between consistency, availability, responsiveness and scalability. And, this is true for deployments either within a single data centre over local area network (LAN) or in multiple data centres over wide area network (WAN).

A high-level Cloud system block diagram is portrayed in Fig. 2.1, where a typical layout of a multi-tier Cloud application has been shown in a layered approach.

According to Fig. 2.1, end-users' requests originate from the typical client-side applications such as browsers and desktop/mobile apps through HTTP (which is a request/reply based protocol) interactions. Database name server (DNS), Web and content delivery network (CDN) servers are the typical first-tier Cloud services (typically stateless) to accept and handle these client requests. If it is a read-only request, then clients can be served immediately using cached data, otherwise update (i.e., insert, update, delete) requests need to be forwarded to the second-tier services.

Application servers, on the other hand, process these forwarded requests based on the coded logic and process the operation using in-memory data objects (if available) or fetch the required data from the underlying database-tier. Model view controller (MVC) pattern-based logic implementation can be considered as an example. In an MVC application, user requests (typically URLs) are mapped into 'controller' actions which then fetch data from appropriate 'model' representation and finally set variables and eventually render the 'view'. If in-memory representation of the model data is not available then the model component needs to initiate a transactional operation (like using ActiveRecord or DataMapper patterns) in the inner-tier database services. Otherwise, in-memory update can take place and updated information can be later pushed into the database.

Note that, application servers are typically 'stateful' and may need to store state values (e.g., login information) as session objects into another highly scalable key-value store. While in the inner-tier, database can be partitioned (i.e., Shards)

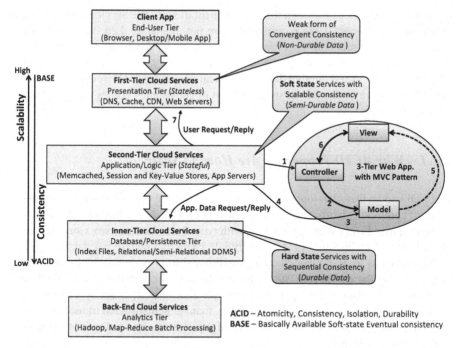

Fig. 2.1 Different service tiers of a typical 3-tier Web application and their interactions within the Cloud computing model. *DNS* database name server, *CDN* content delivery network, *DDMS* distributed database management systems

as well as replicated based on application functionality and requirements. Based on the replica control and placement policies, data can be fetched (if read-only) or updated accordingly and ultimately reply back to the model component in the MVC implementation at the upper-tier.

Our curiosity is to investigate how this end-to-end request–reply procedure access and utilise these durable and consistent data objects into different tiers of a typical Cloud system. And, gradually this will also clarify the system–design trade-offs for different components in a large-scale distributed systems. Read-only user requests for static information (and some form of dynamic information) can be directly served by first-tier Cloud servers based on the data staleness bound. As durability is not guaranteed in this stateless tier, stored information can be lost due to failures. Again, high availability (by means of rapid responsiveness) and high scalability are needed to handle client requests with a typically converging consistency requirement, which also depend on cache expiration and freshness policies.

For read requests which cannot be served due to expiry now can be fetched from the in-memory data objects that reside in the application tier. Update and scan requests typically routed to the second-tier services and mapped according-ly as explained earlier. In this tier, application logics are typically executed using the in-memory data representations which offer scalable consistency with semi-durability. Based on the implementation mechanism of this second-tier services, consistency guarantees reside in the development of soft-state services with reconstructible data pieces. If the required data are not available, then the application logic initiates transactional operations into the inner-tier databases. And they usually offer strong consistency (via atomicity, consistency, isolation and durability (ACID) properties) and durable data (via replication services). However, scalability is hard to achieve in this tier as stronger form of consistency comes with the price of responsiveness.

2.1.1 Why ACID Properties Are Hard to Scale

It is well known that scale-out and utilisation are far more cost-effective using thousands of commodity hardware than through high-end server machines [3]. However, deploying user facing Web applications with typical transactional workload in such shared nothing architecture [41] is not trivial. Again, the underlying database system itself needs to be replicated and/or partitioned to provide required read/write scalability for the end users. The problem resides in the fact that if a transaction needs to access data which span over multiple machines, it is pretty complex to guarantee ACID properties. At the same time, managing distributed transaction and executing them in parallel into a number of replicas to ensure atomic success or abort is also challenging.

Atomicity property (in ACID) requires a distributed commit protocol such as '2-phase commit' (2PC) to run across multiple machines involved in a particular transaction. In the meanwhile, the isolation property insists that the transactions should acquire all of its necessary locks for the total duration of the run of a 2PC. Thus, each transaction (whether it is a simple or complex one) requires a considerable amount of time to complete a 2PC round while performing several round trips in a typical failure-free case. While in case of failure of 2PC coordinator, the total system blocks and a near-success transaction can be aborted due to a single suddenly failed replica.

Again, having data replication schemes in action, to achieve strong system-wise consistency (e.g., possibly via synchronous update) requires to make trade-off with the system response-time (as well as transactional throughput). Finally, in a shared-nothing system with failing hardware ensuring durable transactional operation in the face of strong consistency is far away from reality and practice. As mentioned earlier, real system designers have to make diverse set of trade-offs to ensure different levels of consistency, availability and latency requirements in face of scalable ACID semantics.

2.1.2 CAP Confusion

Current Cloud solutions support a very restricted level of consistency guarantees for systems which require high assurance and security. The issue develops from the misunderstanding of the design space and principle like consistency, availability and partition (CAP) devised by Eric Brewer [10], and later proved by Gilbert and Nancy [16]. According to the CAP principle, the system designer must choose between consistency and availability in the face of network partition. And, this trade-off comes from the fact that to ensure 'high availability' in case of failure (i.e., crash-recovery, partition, Byzantine, etc.) data should be replicated across physical machines.

In recent years, due to the need for higher system throughput in the face of increased workload and high scalability, distributed database systems (DDBS) have drawn the utmost attention in the computing industry. However, building DDBSs are difficult and complex. Thus, understanding of the design space alongside with the application requirement is always helpful for the system designers. Indeed, the CAP theorem has been widely in use to understand the trade-offs between the important system properties—the CAP tolerance.

Unfortunately, today's development trend indicates that many system designers have misapplied CAP to build somewhat restrictive models of DDBSs. The narrower set of definitions presented in the proof of CAP theorem [16] may be one of the reasons. In their proof, Gilbert and Nancy considered 'atomic/linear consistency' which is more difficult to achieve in a DDBS while being at fault and partition tolerant. However, Brewer actually considered a more relaxed definition of the 'Consistency' property referring to the case considered in the first-tier of a typical Cloud application as shown in Fig. 2.1.

In reality, the probability of partition in today's highly reliable data centre is rare although short-lived partitions are common in WANs. So, according to CAP theorem, DDBSs should provide both 'availability' and 'consistency', while there are no 'partitions'. Still, due to extreme workload or sudden failure, it might be the case that the responsiveness of inner-tier services is lagging behind comparing to the requirements for the first-tier and second-tiers services. In such a situation, it would be better to value quick responses to the end users using cached data to be remaining act as available. The goal is to have a scalable Cloud system that remains available and responsive to the users even at the cost of tolerable inconsistency, which can be deliberately engineered in the application logic to hide the effects.

In his recent article [11], Eric Brewer has revisited the CAP trade-offs and mentioned the unavoidable relationship between latency, availability and partition. He argued that a partition is just time bounded on communication. It means that failing to achieve consistency in a time-bound frame, i.e. facing P, leads to a choice between C and A. Thus, to achieve strong ACID consistency in cases either there is a partition or not, a system should both compensate responsiveness (by means of latency) and availability. On the other hand, a system can achieve rapid responsiveness and high availability within the same conditions while tolerating acceptable inconsistency.

To this end, it is fair enough to suggest that design decisions should be made based on specific business requirements and application goals. If an application strives for consistent and durable data, all time scalability will be limited, and high availability will not be visible (due to low responsiveness). Otherwise, if the target is to achieve scalability and high availability, the application should be able to live with acceptable level of inconsistency.

In Sect. 2.2, important components and concepts of distributed databases, i.e., transactional properties, are discussed. Strategies to update replicated data and different replication architectures, partitioning schemes and architectures along with classifications based on update processing overhead and in context of multi-tier Web application have been elaborated in Sect. 2.3. In Sect. 2.4, the evolution of modern distributed database systems has been explored in parallel with the architectural design choices and innovative management of replicated and partitioned databases in details. Finally, Sect. 2.5 concludes with the remarks on the important characteristics (i.e., data replication and partitioning) of modern distributed database systems which have been shaped the Cloud paradigm over the past years and thus provided the opportunity to build Internet-scale applications and services with high availability and scalability guarantees.

2.2 Background of Distributed Database Concepts

In the following sub-subsections, the building blocks of a modern distributed database management system is discussed, which will eventually help the reader to understand the ACID properties and their implications in great extent.

2.2.1 Transaction and ACID Properties

A transaction T_i is a sequence of read operation $r_i(x)$ and write operation $w_i(x)$ on data items within a database. Since, a database system usually provides ACID properties within the lifetime of a transaction, these properties can be defined as shown below:

- *Atomicity*—guarantees that a transaction executes entirely and commits, or aborts and does not leave any effects in the database.
- *Consistency*—assuming the database is in a consistent state before a transaction starts, it guarantees that the database will again be in a consistent state when the transaction ends.
- *Isolation*—guarantees that concurrent transactions will be isolated from each other to maintain the consistency.
- *Durability*—guarantees that committed transactions are not lost even in the case of failures or partitions.

In contrast to a stand-alone database system, a replicated database is a distributed database in which multiple copies of same data items are stored at multiple sites. And, replicated database systems should be acted as a '1-copy equivalence' of a non-replicated system providing ACID guarantees. Thus, within a replicated environment the ACID properties can be redefined as below:

- *1-copy atomicity*—guarantees that a transaction should have the same decision of either all (commit) or nothing (abort) at every replicas which it performs the operation. Thus, some form of 'agreement protocol' is necessary to run among the replicas which should force this guarantee.
- *1-copy consistency*—guarantees that a consistent database state should be maintained across all replicas in such a way that the restrictions imposed by the 'integrity constraints' (e.g., primary/foreign key) while executing a transaction, are not violated after it ends.
- *1-copy isolation*—guarantees that concurrent executions of a set of transactions across multiple replicas to be equivalent to a serial execution (i.e., order) of this set (as if the set of transactions are running serially in a non-replicated system). Also defined as the '1-copy-serialisability' (1SR) property.
- *1-copy durability*—guarantees that when a replica fails then later recovers, it does not only require to redo the transactions that had been committed locally but also make itself up-to-date with the changes that committed globally during the downtime.

2.2.2   *Distributed Transactions and Atomic Commit*

When a transaction attempts to update data on two or more replicas, 1-copy-atomicity property needs to be ensured which also influences consistency and durability properties of the data item. To guarantee this, 2PC protocol [17] is typically used. As shown in Fig. 2.2, initially 2PC is originated from the local replica and the scheme includes all the other remote replicas that hold a copy of the data items that are accessed by the executing transaction.

At phase-1, the local replica sends a 'prepare-to-commit' message to all participants. Upon receiving this message, the remote replica, if it is willing to commit replies with a 'prepared' message, otherwise sends back an 'abort' message. The remote replicas also write a copy of the result in its persistent log which can be used to perform the 'commit' in case of failure recovery. While the coordinating local replica receive 'prepared' messages from all of the participants (means all remote replicas have persistently written the result into log), only then it enters into phase-2.

Fig. 2.2 The 2-phase commit protocol

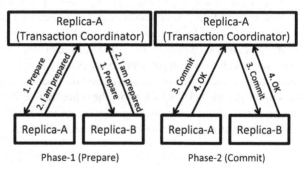

The second round message from the coordinator tells the replicas to actually 'commit' the transaction. 2PC aims to handle every possible failure and recovery scenarios (like in case of the coordinator fails); thus, transactions are often 'blocked' for an unbounded amount of time. '3-phase commit' [40] protocol was proposed lately which is non-blocking. However, it requires more costly implementation in real system as well as only assumes fail-stop-failure model. Thus, in face of network partition, the protocol simply fails to progress. A more elaborate description of distributed transaction processing can be found in [8].

Note that, both 2PC and 3PC protocols are within the solution family of Consensus [50] problems. More recently, Paxos [27, 51], which is another family of protocols (more resilient to failures) to solve the consensus problems, has received much attention in both academia and industry.

2.2.3   Distributed Concurrency Control

Concurrency control mechanism [8] in a database system maintains an impression that concurrent transactions are executing in isolation. There are two families of concurrency control protocols that exist: 'pessimistic' and 'optimistic'. Pessimistic approach is typically implemented using 'locking'. A 'shared lock' is acquired by a transaction to get read-access in the database record (typically the whole 'row' in a database 'table') and an 'exclusive lock' is acquired to have write-access. If a lock cannot be granted by the concurrency control manager, then the involving transaction is blocked in waiting until conflicting locks are released. A shared lock can be granted if there are at most other shared locks currently held on to a record.

On the other hand, an exclusive-lock can only be granted if there are no other locks currently on hold. Thus, read operations are permitted to execute concurrently while write operations must go through serially. Also note that read-only operations may also 'block' during a period of exclusive-lock holds by another transaction. Alternatively, a write operation may also 'block' during a period of shared-lock holds by another transaction. In order to ensure strict serialisability, all acquired locks are typically released only after the transaction commit or abort. This total mechanism can be implemented through either using '2-phase locking (2PL)' or 'strong strict 2-phase locking (SS2PL)' protocol. In phase-1, all required locks are requested and acquired step-by-step from the beginning of a transaction towards its execution. In phase-2, all locks are released in one step based upon commit/abort decision.

As shown in Fig. 2.3, deadlocks can be created by due concurrent transactions racing to acquire locks. In such situations, the concurrency control manager should be able to detect such deadlocks. 2PL/SS2PL can still be used to guarantee 1-copy serialisability; however, it pays the costly penalty in system throughput and latency, i.e., responsiveness. One of the conflicting transactions has to be aborted in all replicas to release its locks, which allow the other transaction to proceed and complete its operations. Sometimes, locking may create unwanted delays through blocking, while the transactional operations could be serialisable.

Fig. 2.3 Deadlocks with pessimistic concurrency control using 2PL

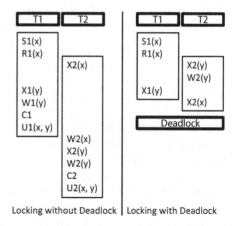

Locking without Deadlock | Locking with Deadlock

Alternatively, simple 'atomic commitment protocol' could be used where all the transactional executions are done within an atomic operation in the participating replicas. Optimistic approach on the other hand, allows concurrent transactions to proceed in parallel. A transaction can create its local copy and perform all the necessary update operations in it. At the end of transaction, a validation phase takes place and checks whether the read-sets of the considered transaction overlaps with the write-set of any transaction that has already successfully validated. If true, it has to be aborted, otherwise it can be committed successfully via writing its changes persistently back to the database.

In DDBS with replication mechanism enabled, a distributed lock manager is required which will try to detect and resolve distributed deadlocks among conflicting replicas in a pessimistic approach. Atomic commit protocols like 2PC/3PC could still be used along with 2PL/SS2PL. One such approach is to achieve global serialisation order instead of distributed locking by using 2PC atomic commit globally while locally applying 2PL/SS2PL. However, achieving global serialisation order is costly and pays the price with restricted system performance. On the other hand, an optimistic approach would try to perform distributed or centralised conflict detection and resolution procedure to rescue. Whichever the case is, the bottom line is implementing distributed concurrency control through locking always creates 'race condition' locally which may lead to deadlocks or alternatively require costly conflict and serialisation order management schemes globally.

Cursor stability (CS) is another kind of concurrency control mechanism which uses short 'read' locks. A read lock on a data item x is acquired and released directly after the read operation is executed. In situations when a data item is accessed by a read-only operation simultaneously and a write operation is blocked for an unbounded amount of time CS can be used in rescue. Short 'read' locks gradually upgraded to exclusive write locks to prioritise the blocked write operations to complete. However, inconsistencies may occur due to 'lost update' from another transaction in progress.

2.2.4 Multi-Version Concurrency Control and Snapshot Isolation

In multi-version concurrency control (MCC or MVCC) approach, a database system always performs update operation by creating a new version of the old data item instead of overwriting it. MVCC typically utilises timestamps or transaction IDs in increasing order to implement and identify new data version copies. The benefit of using MVCC is reads will be never blocked by write operations. Read-only access in the database will always retrieve a committed version of the data item. Obviously, the cost incurs in the storing of multiple versions of the same data items. Database that supports MVCC implementation typically adopts snapshot isolation (SI) [8] which performs better with low overhead working with such multiple data versions. However, SI is less restrictive in nature than serialisability thus may allow non-serialisable operations leading to anomalies. In practice, commercial systems also provide lower level of isolation as it is always hard to scale with increasing number of concurrent transactions with serialisability.

SI assumes whenever a transaction writes a data item x, it creates a new version of x; and when the transaction commits, the version is installed. Formally, if transaction T_i and T_j both write data item x, then T_i commits before T_j and if no other transaction commits in between T_i and T_j and writes x, then T_i's version is directly ordered before T_j's version of x. SI adopts two important properties:

- *Snapshot reads*—provides each transaction a snapshot of the database as of the time it starts, i.e., last installed version. It guarantees high transaction concurrency for read-only operations and reads never interfere with writes.
- *Snapshot writes*—writes that occur after the transaction are not visible. It disallows two concurrent transactions (neither commits before the other starts) to update the same data item. It avoids well-known anomalies that can occur in the use of lower-level isolation guarantee.

2.2.5 Isolation Anomalies

Based on the above discussion on different concurrency control mechanism and isolation levels, it would be better to introduce few isolation anomalies which are typically used to appear in the system [21, 8]:

- *Dirty read*—reading an uncommitted version of a data item. For example, a transaction T_j reads an uncommitted version a data tuple x which has been updated by another transaction T_i. However, if T_i later aborts due to any reason, this will also force T_j to abort as well. This is called 'cascading aborts effect'.
- *Lost update*—overwriting updates by concurrent transactions. For example, T_j writes (i.e., overwrites) x based upon its own read without considering the new version of x created by T_i. T_i's update will be lost.
- *Non-repeatable read*—reading two different versions of a data item during a transaction execution period.

- *Read skew*—if MVCC is allowed, then it might be possible that by reading different versions of multiple data items which are casually dependent on any applied constraint, is violated.
- *Write skew*—similar to read skew, constraints between casually dependent data items may be violated due to two concurrent writes.

2.3   Replication and Partitioning Mechanisms

2.3.1   *Replica Control Strategies*

Replica control strategies can be categorised based on two primary dimensions: *where* updates will be taken place and *when* these updates will be propagated to remote replicas. Considering these criteria, the classification based on [14] is shown in Table 2.1. Considering the 'when' dimension, there can be two classes of replica control mechanisms. One is the '*eager*' *replication* that is a proactive approach, where tentative conflicts between concurrent transactions are detected before they commit while synchronously propagate updates among replicas. Thus, data consistency can be preserved while in the cost of high communication overhead which increases the latency. It is also called the *active replication*. The second is the *lazy replication* which is a reactive approach which allows concurrent transactions to execute in parallel and make changes in their individual local copies. Therefore, inconsistency between replicas may arise as update propagations are delayed by performing asynchronously after the local transaction commits. It is also called as *passive replication*.

Again, based on the 'where' dimension, both 'eager' and 'lazy' replication scheme can be further divided into two categories. One is the *primary copy update* which restricts data items to be updated in a centralised fashion. All transactions have to perform its operations in the primary copy first which then can be propagated either synchronously or asynchronously to other replicas. This scheme is benefited from a simplified concurrency control approach and reduces the number of concurrent updates in different replicas. However, the single *primary copy* itself may be a single point of failure and potentially create bottleneck in the system. On

Table 2.1 Typical classification of replica control strategies [18]

Propagation vs. ownership	Eager	Lazy	Remark
Primary copy	1 transaction 1 owner	N transactions 1 owner	Single owner (can be potential bottleneck)
Update anywhere	1 transaction N owners	N transactions N owners	Multiple owner (harder to achieve consistency)
	Synchronous update (converging consistency)	*Asynchronous update* (diverging consistency)	

the other hand, the second category of *update anywhere* approach allows transactional operations to be executed at any replicas in a distributed fashion. Coordination between different replicas is required which may lead to high communication cost while using *eager update* propagation. While using *lazy propagation* potentially leads to potential inconsistencies which require expansive conflict detection and reconciliation procedure to resolve.

A trade-off is typically considered where high performance can be achieved by sacrificing consistency via using 'lazy' replication schemes. Alternatively, one can get consistency in the price of performance and scalability via using 'eager' replication scheme. Further classification of replica control mechanisms can be deduced in this regard. One of the popular replication technique is to implement read-one-write-all (ROWA) solution where read operations acquire local locks while write operations need distributed locks among replicas.

The correctness of the scheme can be satisfied with '1SR'. 2PC and SS2PL are also required to ensure atomic transactional commits. An improved version of this approach is read-one-write-all-available (ROWAA) which improves the concurrency control performance in the face of failure. Quorum-based replication solutions are also an alternative choice which typically reduces the replication overhead through only allowing a subset of replicas to be updated in each transaction. However, quorum systems also do not scale well in situations where update rates are high. An excellent analytical comparison can be found at [21] regarding this analogy.

In [18], Jim Gray was the first to explore the inherent dangers of replication in these schemes when scalability matters. Gray pointed out that as the number of replicas increase, it also exponentially increases the number of conflicting operations, response time and deadlock probabilities.

For 'eager' schemes, the probability of deadlocks increased by the power of three of the number of replicas in the system. Again, disconnected and failed nodes also cannot use this approach. In the 'lazy' scheme, the reconciliation rates (in *update anywhere*) and the number of deadlocks (in *primary copy*) sharply rise with the increase of the number of replicas.

Alternatively, Gray [18] proposed the *convergence property* instead of strict serialisability provided by the ACID semantics. It considers that if there are no updates within a sufficient amount of time, then all participating replicas will gradually converge to a consistent state after exchanging ongoing update results. He coined the examples of Lotus Notes, Microsoft Access and Oracle 7 which were typically proving such kind of convergence property at that time.

Commercial implementation of replica control schemes also followed the 'lazy' approaches and offered different options for appropriate reconciliation procedure for a long time. Research efforts were also engaged in solving and optimising the inconsistencies that arise from 'lazy' approaches like weak consistency models, epidemic strategies, restrictive node placement, using 'lazy' primary approach and different kinds of hybrid solutions. However, maintaining consistency over the impacts of inconsistency is much simpler to implement, but hard to optimise for scalability.

To meet this challenge, Postgres-R [22] was developed which provides replication through an 'eager' approach using *group communication* primitives, thus totally avoids the cost of distributed locking and deadlocks. The Postgres-R approach uses a 'shadow copy' of the local data item to perform updates, check integrity constraints, identify read-write conflicts and fire triggers. The changes that are made into a shadow copy propagate to the remote replicas at commit time, thus vastly decreases the message/synchronisation overhead in the system. Read operations are always performed locally as following a ROWA/ROWAA approach.

Thus, there are no overheads for read operations in the system. Update (i.e., write) operations of a transaction are bundled together into a write-set message and multicast in total order to all replicas (including itself) to determine the serialisation orders of the running transactions. Each replica uses this order to acquire all locks required by that transaction in a single atomic step. The total order is used to serialise the read/write conflicts at all replicas at the same time. Thus, by acquiring locks in the order in which the transactions arrive, all replicas are performing the conflicting operations in the same order. As a plus point, there will be no chance for deadlocks. In case of read/write conflicts, reads are typically aborted as a straightforward solution while different optimisations can also be possible. After completion/abortion of the write operations in the local replica, the decision is propagated to the remote replicas.

Performance results from [22] indicate that Postgres-R can scale well with increasing workloads and at the same time boost system throughput by reducing communication overheads and by eliminating the possibility of deadlocks. A more detail of this work can be found at [23]. However, replica control, i.e., coordination is still a challenging task in practical systems and two essential properties always need to ensure: (1) Agreement—every non-faulty replicas receive every intended request and (2) order—every non-faulty replica processes the request it receives in the same order. Interested readers can find an elaborate discussion in [51] on how we can maintain these properties, thus understand how state machine replication works using consensus protocol like Paxos [27] and what determinism in database replication really means.

2.3.2   Replication Architectures

One of the most crucial choices is 'where' to implement the replication logic. It might be implemented tightly with the database in its kernel. Alternative approach might be using a middleware to separate the replication logic from the concurrency control logic implemented in the database. Based on these choices, replication logic can be implemented in the following ways (see Fig. 2.4):

- *Kernel-based*—replication logic is implemented in the database kernel and therefore has the full access to database internals. The benefit is that clients can directly communicate with the database. On the other hand, any change in the database internals (e.g., concurrency control module) will directly impact the functionalities of replica control module. Again, refactoring database source code is cumbersome and the implementation is always vendor specific. Also called as 'white-box replication'.

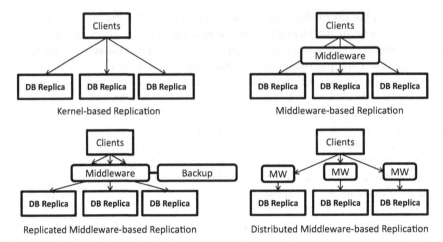

Fig. 2.4 Different replication architectures

- *Centralised middleware-based*—replication logic can be separately implemented into a middleware layer. It provides much flexibility and independence to integrate with any database. However, the functionalities of concurrency control module have to be re-implemented. It is also called as 'black-box replication'. A modified version of this scheme can be called 'gray-box replication' where the database itself should expose the required concurrency control functionalities through specific interface for the middleware to utilise in replica control scheme.
- *Replicated centralised middleware-based*—to avoid single point of failure and bottlenecks, backup middleware can be introduced. However, failover mechanisms are hard to implement to support hot-swap for running transactions and coordinating with the application layer modules.
- *Distributed middleware-based*—every database replica is coupled with a middleware instance and act as a single unit of replication. In case of failover, the total unit can be swapped. Again, the approach is more suitable in WANs reducing the overhead of clients to communicate with the centralised middleware each time it wants to initiate transactional operations.

2.3.3 Partitioning Architecture

It is obvious that replicating data to an extent will increase the read capacity of the system. However, after a certain replication factor, it might be difficult to maintain consistency even if 'eager' replication and synchronous update processing are used. On the other hand, write capacity can be scaled through partial replication where only subsets of nodes are holding a particular portion of the database. Thus,

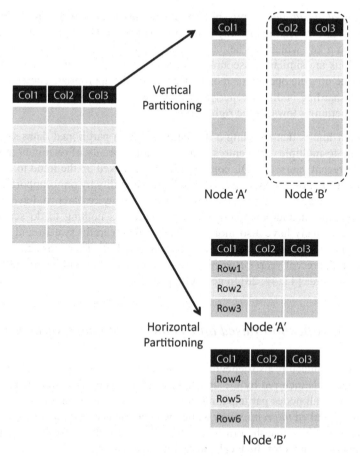

Fig. 2.5 Database partitioning techniques—vertically and horizontally

write operations can be localised and the overheads of concurrent update processing can be reduced. Sharding is a technique to split data into multiple partitions (i.e., Shards). There are two basic ways of partitioning data as shown in Fig. 2.5:

* *Vertical partitioning*—by splitting the table attributes (i.e., columns) and thus creating tables with small number of attributes. It only offers limited scalability in spite of the ease of deployment. The main idea is to map different functional areas of an application into different partitions. Both the datasets and workload scalability are driven by different functional aspects of an application. Thus, it is necessary to pick up the right tables and column(s) to create the correct partition, because the 'join' operations in a relational database will now need to be performed within the application code. Hence, the underlying database will no longer support relational schema, and apparently the application scalability is restricts to its hosting node's resource capacity.

- *Horizontal partitioning*—by splitting the tuples (i.e., rows) across different tables. It allows scaling into any number of partitions. The tuples are partitioned based on a key which can be hash based, range based or directory based. Join operations are similarly discouraged to avoid cross-partition queries. The performance of write operations mostly depends on the appropriate choice of shard key. If sharding is done properly, then the application controller can route the write operations towards the right server.

The bottom line is that sharding a database results in partitioned datasets spread over single-to-multiple data centres, thus forcing the beauty of relational model to reduce. In recent years, NoSQL communities have picked up the trend to abandon relational properties and SQL in favour of high-scalability by only supporting key-value type accesses in their data stores. However, many researchers have already pointed out that abandoning SQL and its feature has nothing to do scalability. Alternatively, many have also indicated ways where careful system and application design can lead to the desired level of scalability [39]. There has been a debate going on in the recent years between these two communities and interested readers may head towards [42, 44, 28] to get a glimpse of it.

2.3.4 Classification Based on Update Processing Overheads

Replication architecture also depends on 'how' data is actually replicated. Depending on the overheads incurred by the update processing operations, data items can be replicated into all nodes participating in the system or into a subset of nodes. The former one is called *full replication* while the later one is called *partial replication*. It is to be noted here that the primary overhead in replication resides in the update processing operations for the local and remote submissions.

There are two basic choices: *symmetric update processing* and *asymmetric update processing*. The former choice requires a substantial amount of resources (i.e., CPU, I/O in the remote replicas); it may also initiate divergence consistency for non-deterministic database operations (like updating a value with current time). Alternatively, in the asymmetric update processing, the operations are first performed locally and only the changes (along with corresponding primary identifiers and after-image values) are bundled together in the write sets, then forwarded to the remote replicas in a single message. This approach of processing still holds even if the system is using 'eager'/'active' replication scheme.

Depending on the update processing approaches, we can consider the trade-offs between using the *full replication* and *partial replication* schemes. Full replication technique requires an exact snapshot of the local database into every other remote replicas, which may face high-system overheads in the face of increased update workloads. Both symmetric and asymmetric update processing introduce a level of overhead as data needs to be updated into every replicas. However, by using partial replication scheme, one can reduce this overhead and localise the update processing based on their origination.

Surprisingly, partial replication also comes with its own challenges. There are several variants of the partial replication, e.g., (1) *pure partial replication*—where each node has only copies of a subset of the data items, but no node contains a full copy of the total database and (2) *hybrid partial replication*—where a set of nodes contain a full set of the data items, while another set of nodes are partial replicas containing only a fraction of the data sets.

Now, depending on the transaction, it might want to access data items on different replicas in a pure partial replication scheme. It is non-trivial to know which operation will access which data items in the partial replicas. Thus, flexibility is somehow reduced by typical SQL transactions which often need to perform 'join' operations between two tables. However, if the database schema can be partitioned accordingly and workload pattern is not changing frequently, then the benefits of localising of update processing can be revealed.

Considering the case of hybrid partial replication, update operations need to be applied fully in the replicas which contain the full set of database. With the increase in the number of transactions, these nodes might create hotspots and bottlenecks. The beauty of the hybrid approach is that while read operations can be centralised to provide more consistent snapshots of data items, the write operations can be distributed among partial replicas to reduce writing overheads. The bottom line is that it has been always challenging to know the transactional properties (like which data items need to access) and apply partial replication accordingly. However, if the application requirements are understood properly and workload patterns are more or less static, then partial replication can exploit the scalability goals.

2.3.5 Classification Based on Multi-Tier Web Architecture

Recalling the example drawn in Fig. 2.1, real-life Web applications are typically deployed in multi-tier Cloud platforms. Each tier is responsible to perform specific functionalities and coordination between these tiers and is necessary to provide the expected services to the end users. Hence, replicating a single tier always restricts scalability and availability limits. Again, apart from being read-only or update operations, workloads can be compute intensive (require more resource and scalability at the application/logic tier) or data intensive (require more ability in the inner database tier).

Again, considering failure conditions, replication logic should work in such ways that the interdependencies between multiple tiers should not lead to multiple workload execution both in the database and application servers [24]. For example, despite failure, 'exactly-one' update transaction should be taken place in the corresponding database tier and its entire replica for a single transactional request forwarded from the application tier. Based on this analogy, there can be two architectural patterns for replicating multi-tier platforms [20] as listed below:

- *Vertical replication pattern*—this pairs one application and one database server to create a unit of replication. Such units can be then replicated vertically to increase the scalability of the system. The benefit of this approach is that replication logic is transparent to both application and database servers; thus, they can work seamlessly. However, challenges reside in the fact that particular application functionalities and corresponding data need to be partitioned appropriately across the whole system to get the target scalability. Much engineering cost and effort are needed for such kind of implementation; thus, in reality, these systems can be still seen very few in numbers.

- *Horizontal replication pattern*—here, each tier implements replication independently and requires some 'replication awareness' mechanism to run in between to make necessary coordination. In contrast to the vertical replication pattern, the beauty here is that one can scale flexibly based on the necessity across individual tier. However, without any awareness support to know whether the cooperating tier is replicated or not, it is not able to provide the utmost performance the system could achieve. In reality, this type of systems can be seen almost everywhere in the computing industry; however, they are still in lack of appropriate replication awareness mechanism which is still left as an open challenge.

To support these two categories, other architectural patterns also need to be considered like replica discovery and replication proxy, session maintenance, multi-tier coordination, etc. Several examples of real implementations based on these patterns can be found at [20, 33, 34, 35]. However, replication control via multi-tier coordination is still an open research problem both in academia and industry.

2.4 Distributed Database Systems in the Cloud

2.4.1 BASE and Eventual Consistency

The BASE (Basically Available, Soft state, Eventually consistent) acronym [36] captures the CAP reasoning. It devises that if a system can be partitioned functionally (by grouping data by functions and spreading functionality groups across multiple databases, i.e., shards), then one can break down sequence of operations individually and pipeline them for asynchronous update on each replicas while responding to the end user without waiting for their completion. Managing database transactions in a way that avoids locking, highly pipelined, and mostly depends on caching raise all kinds of consistency worries into surface.

While ACID can be seen as a more pessimistic approach, BASE, in contrast, envisions for a more optimistic approach. Availability in BASE systems is ensured through accepting partial partitions. Let us consider a 'user' table in a database which is sharded across three different physical machines by utilising user's 'last_name' as a shard key which partitions the total datasets into the following shards A-H, I-P and Q-Z. Now, if one of the shards is suddenly unavailable due to failure or partition, then only 33.33 % users will be affected and the rest of the system is still operational. But, ensuring consistency in such kind of system is not trivial and not readily available like ACID systems. Thus, the consideration of relaxed consistency guarantees arises. One can consider achieving consistency individually across functional groups by decoupling the dependencies between them. As proposed in [36], a persistent pipelined system can tackle the situations where relative ordering and casual relationship is necessary to maintain or one consider de-normalised database schema design.

The 'E' in BASE which stands for 'eventual consistency' [45, 46] guarantees that in the face of inconsistency the underlying system should work in the background to catch up. The assumption is that in many cases it is hard to distinguish these inconsistent states from the end-user perspective which is usually bounded by different staleness criteria (i.e., time-bounded, value-bounded or update-based staleness). Later, Eric Brewer [11] had also argued against locking and actually favoured the use of cached data but only for 'soft' state service developments, while DDBSs should continue to provide strong consistency and durability guarantees. However, this implication of inconsistency requires a higher level of reconfigurability and self-repair capability of a system that tends to expansive engineering effort.

In [45], Werner Vogels from Amazon described several variations of eventual consistency which can also be combined together to provide a stronger notion while ensuring client-side consistency as follows:

- *Casual consistency*—guarantees that if there is any casual dependencies between two processes, then a committed update by one process will be seen by another process and can be superseded by another update.
- *Read-your-writes consistency*—guarantees that after an update of a data item, consecutive reads always get that updated value.
- *Session consistency*—guarantees that as long as the session exist, read-your-write consistency can be provided.
- *Monotonic read consistency*—guarantees if a process reads a particular value of an object, then any subsequent reads will not see any previously committed value.
- *Monotonic write consistency*—guarantees to serialise writes by the same process.

At the server-side consistency, Vogels [45] argues that one should look at the flow of update propagation. One can consider a quorum-based replicated DDBS [35] with N nodes where W nodes replicas are responsible to accept a write and R replicas are contacted while performing a read. Then, if $W+R>N$, then read and write sets are always overlapped, and the system provides stronger form of consistency. Again, if $W<(N+1)/2$, then there is a definite possibility of conflicting writes as the write sets do not overlap. On the other hand, if the read and writes do not overlap as $W+R<=N$, then a weaker form of eventual consistency is provided by the system where stale data can be read. In case of network partitions, quorum systems can still handle read and write requests separately as long as these sets can communicate with a group of clients independently. And, later reconciliation procedures can run to manage conflicting updates within replicas.

In [9], Ken Birman has effectively shown ideas that it is possible to develop scalable and consistent soft-state services for the first tier of the Cloud system if one is ready to give up durability guarantee. He argues that the 'C' from the CAP theorem actually relates to both 'C' and 'D' in ACID semantics. Therefore, by sacrificing durability, one can scale through first to inner-tier Cloud services while at the same time can guarantee strong consistency.

In reality, systems that utilises group communication semantics (e.g., membership management, message ordering, failure coordination, recovery, etc.) can achieve consistent replication schemes to support both high availability and high scalability. Google's Spanner [14] is one of the most prominent examples of this kind. Although these systems can exploit the requirements for first-to-inner service tiers, the consistency guarantee usually comes with a high engineering cost and lacks generalised patterns/solutions.

Lastly, based on the current usage of Cloud systems, inconsistencies can somewhat be tolerated for improving read/write performances under increasing workloads and handling partition cases. However, the level of scalability that Cloud systems can achieve is a long cherished dream for system which prefers high assurance (i.e., both availability and consistency), reliability and security.

2.4.2 Revisiting Architectural Design Space

To overcome the confusion that arises from the CAP theorem, it is necessary to revisit the design space in the light of distributed replication and data partitioning techniques. This insight will also enable to clarify the relationship between the related challenges with ACID and BASE as discussed above. In [1], Daniel Abadi was the first to pinpoint the exact confusion that arises from CAP and clarifies the relationship between consistency and latency. He proposed a new acronym PACELC which he believed to be the actual representation of reality.

PACELC in a single formulation: if there is a partition (P), how does the system trade-off exist between availability and consistency (A and C); else (E) when the system is running as normal in the absence of partitions, how does the system trade-off exist between latency (L) and consistency (C)?

The PACELC formulation is shown in Fig. 2.6 under several considerations like based on replication factor, consistency level, system responsiveness and partition-tolerance level. We will explain this phenomenon with respect to PACELC classification for distributed system design. As Abadi explained in [2], there can be four possible system types as follows:

- *A-L systems*—always give up consistency in favour of availability in case of partition otherwise prefer latency during normal operating periods. Example– Apache Cassandra [4], Amazon's DynamoDB [3] and Riak [38] (in their default settings).
- *A-C systems*—provide consistent reads/writes in the typical failure-free scenarios; however, in failure cases, consistency sacrifices (for limited period until

Fig. 2.6 Design space for
large-scale distributed system
development. *BASE* basi-
cally available, soft state,
eventually consistent; *ACID*
atomicity, consistency, isolation and durability

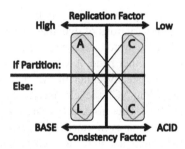

the failure recovers) would remain available. Example: MongoDB [31] and
CouchDB [5].

- *C-L systems*—provide baseline consistency (as defined by the system, e.g., timeline consistency) for latency during normal operations, while in case of partitions
  it prioritises consistency over availability (or, being slow responsiveness which
  imposes high latency). Example: Yahoo! PNUTS [13].
- *C-C systems*—disallow to give up consistency either in the case of partition or
  not and thus incur availability (i.e., responsiveness), and latency costs as the
  trade-off. Example: BigTable [12]/HBase [6] and H-Store [19]/VoltDB [46].

This is to be noted here that, completely giving up availability is not possible at all;
otherwise it will be a useless system. Availability actually spans over two dimensions: (1) resilient to failures, and (2) responsiveness in both failure and failure-free
cases. Interested readers are also encouraged to read Dan Weinreb's blog entry [49]
which further clarifies how availability and latency relate to each other. Similarly,
completely inconsistent systems are also useless; thus, the level of consistency varies in between its weaker and stronger forms. Let us now discuss these system
design choices in more detail under the light of the above mentioned considerations.

2.4.2.1 Consistency Factor

Stronger consistency models which are tightly coupled with a DBMS always ease
the life of the application developer. Depending on the application requirement, giving up ACID properties in favour of BASE is also inadequate in many situations.
However, stronger consistency levels can also be viable to achieve by decoupling
logic from the underlying DBMS and implementing along with the replica control
scheme.

Quorum-based systems are one of the possible choices in this regard where one
can control the level of consistency by restricting read/write quorum requirements.
Alternatively, consistency can be ensured in a much fine-granularity [37]. Ensuring
entity-level or object-level consistency within a single database can also provide a
notion of ACID semantics. Furthermore, entity groups can be considered as a unit
of consistency and even multiple groups might act as a unit.

A-L systems which can be viewed as the BASE equivalent tend to provide different variations of eventual consistency all the time. Similar adaption is also true while the system design space gradually shifts towards C-L systems in failure cases. On the other hand, A-C and C-C systems by default tend to achieve stronger form of consistency either in the case of failure or not. However, as indicated earlier providing ACID level consistency (i.e., serialisability) is challenging and costly in DDBSs. Therefore, providing soft level of consistency guarantees like snapshot isolation or even timeline consistency (as provided in Yahoo's PNUTS [13]) seems to be more adaptable in such scenarios.

2.4.2.2 Responsiveness Factor

Responsiveness is the perceived 'delay' between when an end-user or internal system component takes an action such as clicking on a link or forwarding a request, and when the user/component perceives a response. It wraps up two other technical pieces, namely: (1) latency—initial delay to start receiving replies for a corresponding request, and (2) throughput—total time taken for all the contents of a reply to be received completely. These factors are imposed by the service level objective (SLO) goals while considering the design spaces.

One can consider the '8 second rule' [30] which still fits well to measure the responsiveness of modern Cloud applications. It states that 'if a computer system responds to a user action within 100 ms, it's perceived as 'instantaneous'; within 1 s, the user will still perceive a cause-and-effect connection between their action and the response, but will perceive the system as 'sluggish'; and after about 8 s, the user's attention drifts away from the task while waiting for a response'.

Based upon this observation, A-L systems should be chosen where strict and rapid responsiveness is the requirement. Both the A-C and C-L systems will be better on ensuring flexible responsiveness requirements in the face of failure and failure-free cases, respectively. C-C systems pay the costs to keep the system up-to-date and consistent, therefore, slow responsive will be incurred while they are overloaded.

2.4.2.3 Partition-Tolerance Factor

Partitions are not always created from network/communication outage. Sometimes, it might be the case that the system is overloaded and may not be able to respond within the timeout period. Improper network configurations in the intermediate nodes can also cause similar results. Again, the possibility of partition highly depends on whether the system is deployed in a WAN across multiple data centres or LAN within a single data centre. An interesting discussion of practical database errors which can lead to partitioned networks in DDBS can be found in [43].

Primarily based on the deployment strategies, one can consider choosing A-L or C-L system to deploy across multiple data centre distributed over WAN due to their latency awareness during normal operation periods. On the other hand, A-C and C-C systems will be more preferred in deploying within single data centre over the LAN.

2.4.2.4 Replication Factor

The scalability of today's Cloud systems and DDBS primarily depends on how they are replicated to provide high read/write throughput, although increasing the number of replicas blindly will not make the success. It may create potential bottlenecks and unresponsiveness in the system. As discussed in [2], three types of replication strategies are popularly seen in today's deployment, viz.: (1) Data updates sent to all replicas at the same time (synchronous), (2) data updates sent to an agreed-upon location first (synchronous/asynchronous/hybrid), and (3) data updates sent to an arbitrary location first (synchronous/asynchronous).

Considering the above analogies, option-1 provides stronger consistency level in the costs of increased latency and communication overhead. Thus, it might primarily be suitable for C-C systems. Option-2 with synchronous-update propagation also ensures consistency but only limited to while deployed in LAN/single data centre. With asynchronous propagation, option-2 provides several options for distributing read and write operations. If a primary/master node is responsible for providing read replies and accepting writes, then inconsistencies can be avoided. However, it may be the source of potential bottleneck in case of failures. On the other hand, if reads are served from any node, while the primary node is only responsible for accepting writes, then read results probably reflect inconsistencies.

A combination of synchronous and asynchronous is also possible considering a quorum-based replication strategy. If $R+W>N$, then the system will provide consistent results while gradually divergent in the condition where $R+W<=N$. Both A-L and C-L systems are well suited for the approaches mentioned above under option-2 as they are flexible and dynamic with latency-consistency trade-offs. Option-3, which is similar to option-2 apart from preferring any node to accept reads and writes, can also be used either in a synchronous or asynchronous fashion. While synchronous setting can incur increased latency, potential inconsistencies will arise using asynchronous setting. A-C and some of the C-L systems might be suitable to fit in this category.

To this end, it seems worthwhile to revisit the design choices as it broadens our mind to think beyond what the CAP theorem actually meant. It also helps to visualise how we can fit the multi-tier Cloud application within the architectural model. Although a more analytical approach to explain these trade-offs will be definitely profound. Modern software-as-a-service (SaaS) applications deployed over very large-scale distributed systems strive for the following *performance goals*: (1) Availability or uptime—what percentage of time the system is up and properly accessible, (2) responsiveness—measure of latency and throughput, and (3) scalability—as the number of users, i.e., workloads increase how to maintain the target responsiveness without increasing cost/user.

2.4.3   Data Partitioning and Replication Management

Typical distributed database systems (e.g., HBase [6], Cloud SQL, MongoDB [31] and MySQL Cluster [32]) which usually provide automatic partitioning and load-balancing features only support pre-configured partitioning rules. The system splits and merges the partitions based on the number of nodes (e.g., MySQL Cluster [32]), predefined data volume size (e.g., in HBase [6]), predefined key (e.g., MongoDB [31]) or even based on partitioned schema (Cloud SQL). All of these approaches are unable to adopt to dynamic workload patterns and current resource utilisation profile of the system. Again, sudden increase in workload volume, occurrences of data spikes and hotspots can also influence the change in normal workload characteristics.

However, dynamic partitioning decision making is not possible and often requires human intervention. Hence, these systems normally suffer from sudden workload spikes in any particular partition, hot-spotted partition or database table, partitioning storm and load-balancing problems. These are the potential reasons of restricted system behaviour, unresponsiveness, failures and bottlenecks. In a WAN setting, this leads to replication nightmare and inconsistency problems on top of added latency.

As Cloud systems are growing bigger and bigger day by day with the explosion of big data, automated management of these large-scale distributed systems are often desirable to maintain high scalability and elasticity. Automatic replication/partitioning management schemes are believed to stand as the solution towards these worries and opportunities. These systems can exploit the self-managerial properties (i.e., healing, optimisation, and provisioning) of a typical Cloud platform and ensure more reliability to achieve the target SLO.

Automatic management of partitioning and replication are also necessary in cases where the database is spanned in multiple data centres over WAN in a geographically distributed fashion. It can be also recognised as a classical match for the case of partial replication where individual partitions of the distributed database management systems can be distributed over WAN. The primary challenge here is to maintain rapid consistency among the replicas with an acceptable latency requirement. The trade-offs between replication and partitioning considering partitioning size as an impacting factor can be also explored in this context.

The particular emphasis is on how to find an optimal partition size for load distribution (arise from hot-spotted partitions due to workload pattern) in geo-distributed data centres. Determining an optimal partition size is essential for effective replication and data transfer between physical machines over WAN. In overall, the choice of availability, consistency, and latency play an important role in developing a scheme over WAN where network partitions occur very often and usually are not avoidable.

To understand the significance, one can be motivated by the scenarios of massively multi-player online role playing games (MMOG) and virtual worlds. Scalability in such environment is really challenging and not trivial in contrast to other

Cloud applications. Game and virtual world users are geographically distributed and can personalise the game environment as well as make interactions with other online users. Two kinds of partitioning strategies are generally seen: one is to decompose the game or virtual world based on the application design and functionality, while another possibility is to partition the system, based on the current workload pattern.

Distributing the workloads evenly among the physical servers is really tedious for both of the cases as they may spread in a WAN over several geographical locations. Again, users residing in one system partition are naturally forbidden to access or interact with other users in different partitions. Even if they wish to do so, costly replication process needs to be taken out. Games and virtual worlds like World of Warcraft, Farmville, SimCity, and Second Life are a few of the examples which have such evolving architectures and geographically distributed workload patterns over the WAN; thus, face these challenges. Jim Waldo has mentioned these challenges from a real-world point in [48] while others like the authors in [52, 25, 26] have also discussed related challenges and the significance of reliable scalability issues in MMOG.

Recent development of the Google's Big Data platform Spanner [14] also focused on a geographically distributed consistent data service platform which spans over multiple data centres in the WAN. The argument of whether existing NoSQL solutions are adequate to handle such scalability challenges effectively is still an active topic of discussion among the community [15], and it is believed that the above mentioned approach can direct an appropriate pathway towards the right vision.

2.5   Conclusion

Cloud computing backed up by modern scalable distributed databases provides significant opportunities for the start-up and established businesses as well as presents potential challenges for the system administrators. The development of distributed databases has been continuing over the past four decades, and is still emerging to adopt the Cloud paradigm. However, system designers and administrators should be well aware of the past trials and potential pitfalls. The design space should be well adopted and possible user cases need to be well studied beforehand. This is required to fit target application scenarios into the architectural design space. Although, recent developments have shown notable promises over the past years, most of the approaches are static in nature and not adaptable with dynamic workload behaviours. SaaS applications deployed within Cloud platforms also span over multiple geographical regions and thus require special attentions to adopt with distributed workload characteristics.

Designing a scalable Cloud system requires a high level understanding of the life-cycle management of a modern multi-tier Web application and characterisation of system workloads. These interpretations lead us straight to the exploration of available architectural design choices and off-the-shelf distributed databases to support underlying high scalability and availability requirements. However, the misunderstanding of CAP theorem over the past decade, and consequent developments of hundreds of NoSQL systems providing relaxed consistency guarantees did not hold us back. In reality, all these efforts have helped the system architects to understand the actual design space for Cloud applications and thus have provided the necessary momentum to modernise the development of distributed database systems in a whole. Again, the core building blocks of a distributed database system have also helped in shaping the general ideas behind effective data replication and partitioning strategies. Eventually these apprehensions have influenced the development of high available, high scalable and partition tolerance Internet-scale Cloud applications. Nowadays, without having a clear picture of the architectural design choices in front, it is tedious to design a scalable Cloud platform. The PACELC acronym clearly identifies this challenge and helped us grasp the relationship between ACID and BASE properties. Still, automatic management of data replication and partitioning in line with workload characteristics and issues arise from multi-tenant environments that are potential challenges to deal with. With the rapid advancement in database and system research and development, it can be hoped that innovative solutions will be soon in place to rescue us from back-breaking labours of system administrations and disaster response situations.

In this chapter, a trail of modern distributed database systems has been drawn alongside the challenges which require urgent attention from the research community. The relationship between how to adopt the past to overcome the challenges at present has been also discussed in a great extent. Different data replication and partitioning techniques have been discussed in details which are essential to achieve massive scalability and elasticity for the Cloud applications. Finally, several approaches have been shown as potential way out to achieve Cloud scale modernisation of distributed database management systems in a dynamic environment for the years to come.

References

1. Abadi DJ (April 2010) Problems with CAP, and Yahoo's little known NoSQL system. http://dbmsmusings.blogspot.com.au/2010/04/problems-with-cap-and-yahoos-little.html. Accessed 31 Jan 2014
2. Abadi DJ (2012) Consistency tradeoffs in modern distributed database system design: CAP is only part of the story. Comput IEEE 45(2):37–42
3. Amazon DynamoDB—NoSQL Cloud Database Service (2014) http://aws.amazon.com/dynamodb. Accessed 31 Jan 2014
4. Apache Cassandra Project. http://cassandra.apache.org. Accessed 31 Jan 2014
5. Apache CouchDB. http://couchdb.apache.org. Accessed 31 Jan 2014
6. Apache HBase—Apache HBase Home. http://hbase.apache.org. Accessed 31 Jan 2014
7. Armbrust M, Fox A, Griffith R, Joseph AD, Katz RH, Konwinski A, Lee G, Paterson DA, Rabkin A, Stoica I, Zaharia M (2009) Above the clouds: a Berkeley view of cloud computing. Technical Report UCB/EECS-2009-28, EECS Department, University of California, Berkeley
8. Bernstein PA, Newcomer E (2009) Principles of transaction processing, 2nd edn. Morgan Kaufmann, San Francisco

9. Birman K, Freedman D, Huang Q, Dowell P (2012) Overcoming CAP with consistent soft-state replication. Comput IEEE 45(2):50–58

10. Brewer EA (2000) Towards robust distributed systems (abstract). In: Proceedings of the nineteenth annual ACM symposium on principles of distributed computing (New York, NY, USA, 2000), PODC'00, ACM, p. 7

11. Brewer E (2012) CAP twelve years later: how the "rules" have changed. Comput IEEE 45(2):23–29

12. Chang F, Dean J, Ghemawat S, Hsieh WC, Wallach DA, Burrows M, Chandra T, Fikes A, Gruber RE (2008) BigTable: a distributed storage system for structured data. ACM Trans Comput Syst 26(2), 4(1–4):26

13. Cooper BF, Ramakrishnan R, Srivastava U, Silberstein A, Bohannon P, Jacobsen H.-A, Puz N, Weaver D, Yerneni R (2008) PNUTS: Yahoo!'s hosted data serving platform. Proc VLDB Endow 1(2):1277–1288

14. Corbett JC, Dean J, Epstein M, Fikes A, Frost C, Furman JJ, Ghemawat S, Gubarev A, Heiser C, Hochschild P, Hsieh W, Kanthak S, Kogan E, Li H, Lloyd A, Melnik S, Mwaura D, Nagle D, Quinlan S, Rao R, Rolig L, Saito Y, Szymaniak M, Taylor C, Wang R, Woodford D (2012) Spanner: google's globally distributed database. In: Proceedings of the 10th USENIX conference on operating systems design and implementation (Berkeley, CA, USA) OSDI'12, USENIX Association, pp 251–264

15. Floratou A, Teletia N, Dewitt DJ, Patel JM, Zhang D (2012) Can the elephants handle the NoSQL onslaught? Proc VLDB Endow 5(12):1712–1723

16. Gilbert S, Lynch N (June 2002) Brewer's conjecture and the feasibility of consistent, available, partition-tolerant web services. SIGACT News 33(2):51–59

17. Gray J (1978) Notes on database operating systems. In: Gray J (ed) Operating systems, an advanced course. Springer-Verlag, London, pp 393–481

18. Gray J, Helland P, O'Neil P, Shasha D (1996) The dangers of replication and a solution. SIGMOD Rec 25(2):173–182

19. H-Store: Next Generation OLTP Database Research (2014) http://hstore.cs.brown.edu. Accessed 31 Jan 2014

20. Jimenez-Peris R, Patino Martinez M, Kemme B, Perez-Sorrosal F, Serrano D (2009) A system of architectural patterns for scalable, consistent and highly available multi-tier service-oriented infrastructures. Architecting dependable systems VI. Springer-Verlag, Berlin, pp 1–23.

21. Kemme B (2000) Database replication for clusters of workstations. PhD thesis, Swiss Federal Institute of Technology, Zurich

22. Kemme B, Alonso G (2000) Don't be lazy, be consistent: Postgres-R, a new way to implement database replication. In: Proceedings of the 26th international conference on very large data bases (San Francisco, CA, USA), VLDB '00, Morgan Kaufmann Publishers Inc., pp 134–143

23. Kemme B, Alonso G (2000) A new approach to developing and implementing eager database replication protocols. ACM Trans Database Syst 25(3):333–379

24. Kemme B, Jimenez-Peris R, Pantino Martinez M, Salas J (2000) Exactly once interaction in a multi-tier architecture. In: VLDB workshop on design, implementation, and deployment of database replication

25. Kohana M, Okamoto S, Kamada M, Yonekura T (2010) Dynamic data allocation scheme for multi-server web-based MORPG system. In: Proceedings of the 2010 IEEE 24th international conference on advanced information networking and applications workshops (Washington, DC, USA), WAINA '10, IEEE Computer Society pp 449–454

26. Kohana M, Okamoto S, Kamada M, Yonekura T (2012) Dynamic reallocation rules on multiserver web-based MORPG system. Int J Grid Utility Comput 3(2/3):136–144

27. Lamport L (1998) The part-time parliament. ACM Trans Comput Syst 16(2):133–169

28. Lerner RM (2010) At the forge: NoSQL? I'd prefer some SQL. Linux J. 2010:192. (http://www.linuxjournal.com/article/10720. Accessed 31 Jan 2014)

29. Lindsay BG, Selinger PG, Galtieri CA, Gray JN, Lorie R A, Price TG, Putzulo F, Traiger IL, Wade BW (July 1979) Notes on distributed databases. Research Report, IBM Research Laboratory (San Jose, California, USA) 247–284

30. Miller RB (1968) Response time in man-computer conversational transactions. In: Proceedings of the December 9–11, 1968, fall joint computer conference, part I (New York, NY, USA), AFIPS '68 (Fall, part I), ACM pp 267–277
31. MongoDB http://www.mongodb.org. Accessed 31 Jan 2014
32. MySQL MySQL Cluster CGE. http://www.mysql.com/products/cluster. Accessed 31 Jan 2014
33. Perez-Sorrosal F, Patino Martinez M, Jimenez-Peris R, Kemme B (2007) Consistent and scalable cache replication for multi-tier J2EE applications. In: Proceedings of the ACM/IFIP/USENIX 2007 international conference on Middleware (New York, NY, USA), Middleware '07, Springer-Verlag New York, Inc., pp 328–347
34. Perez-Sorrosal F, Patino Martinez M, Jimenez-Pereis R, Kemme B (2007) Consistent and scalable cache replication for multi-tier J2EE applications. In: Proceedings of the 8th ACM/IFIP/USENIX international conference on Middleware (Berlin, Heidelberg), Middleware 2007 Springer-Verlag pp 328–347
35. Perez-Sorrosal F, Patino Martinez M, Jimenez-Peris R, Kemme B (2011) Elastic SI-Cache: consistent and scalable caching in multi-tier architectures. VLDB J 20(6):841–865
36. Prichett D (May 2008) BASE: an ACID alternative. Queue ACM 6(3):48–55
37. Ramakrishnan R (2012) CAP and Cloud data management. Computer IEEE 45(2): 43–49
38. Riak | Basho Technologies (2014) http://basho.com/riak. Accessed 31 Jan 2014
39. Schram A, Anderson KM (2012) MySQL to NoSQL: data modeling challenges in supporting scalability. In: Proceedings of the 3rd annual conference on systems, programming, and applications: software for humanity (New York, NY, USA), SPLASH '12, ACM, pp 191–202
40. Skeen D, Stonebraker M (1983) A formal model of crash recovery in a distributed system. Software engineering. IEEE Trans SE 9(3): 219–228
41. Stonebraker M (1986) The case for shared nothing. IEEE Database Eng Bull 9(1):4–9
42. Stonebraker M (4 Nov 2009) The "NoSQL" discussion has nothing to do with SQL. http://cacm.acm.org/blogs/blog-cacm/50678-the-nosql-discussion-has-nothing-to-do-with-sql/fulltext. Accessed 31 Jan 2014
43. Stonebraker M (5 April 2010) Errors in database systems, eventual consistency, and the cap theorem. Blog, Communications of the ACM
44. Stonebraker M (2010) SQL databases v. NoSQL databases. Commun ACM 53(4):10–11
45. Vogels W (Oct 2008) Eventually consistent. Queue ACM 6(6):14–19
46. Vogels W (2009) Eventually consistent. Communications of the ACM 52(1):40–44
47. VoltDB http://voltdb.com. Accessed 31 Jan 2014
48. Waldo J (2008) Scaling in games and virtual worlds. Commun ACM 51(8):38–44
49. Weinreb D Improving the PACELC taxonomy. http://danweinreb.org/blog/improving-the-pacelc-taxonomy. Accessed 27 Feb 2013
50. Wikipedia. Consensus (computer science). http://en.wikipedia.org/wiki/Consensus_(computer_science). Accessed 31 Jan 2014
51. Wikipedia. Paxos (computer science). http://en.wikipedia.org/wiki/Paxos_(computer_science). Accessed 31 Jan 2014
52. Zhang K, Kemme B, Denault A (2008) Persistence in massively multiplayer online games. In: Proceedings of the 7th ACM SIGCOMM workshop on network and system support for games (New York, NY, USA), NetGames' 08, ACM, pp 53–58

Chapter 3
Quality of Service and Service Level Agreements for Cloud Environments: Issues and Challenges

Inderveer Chana and Sukhpal Singh

Abstract The increasing use of Cloud computing makes the development of high-quality Cloud-based applications a vital research area. Cloud computing, which provides inexpensive computing resources on the pay-as-you-go basis, is promptly gaining momentum as a substitute for traditional information technology (IT)-based organizations. As more and more users migrate their applications to Cloud environments, service level agreements (SLAs) between clients and Cloud providers become a key element to consider. Due to the dynamic nature of the Cloud, endless supervision of quality of service (QoS) attributes is necessary to honor the SLAs. Thus, Cloud computing faces the challenge of QoS, especially in relation to how a service provider can ensure appropriate QoS for its Cloud services. QoS is an inherent element, part of service-oriented architecture (SOA), to direct nonfunctional quality attributes of a service, such as the response time, price, or the supported security rules. Consequently, there is a requirement to grow architectures in order to respond correctly to the QoS requirements. The architecture should be able to change dynamically the amount of resources made available to the applications it hosts. Optimal resource utilization should be attained by providing (and maintaining at run time) each hosted application with the number of resources which is adequate to guarantee that the application SLA will not be violated. This chapter reflects the essential perceptions behind the QoS provision in the Cloud, identifies current and innovative quality attributes based on customers' desires associated with SLA and identifies metrics to measure the deviation of QoS from predictables, with possible resolution in the outline of architecture for spontaneous supervision of QoS without violation of SLA. The existing intent of Cloud SLAs is inspected with a focus on QoS and customer requirements. Further, foremost research problems and scientific challenges in Cloud SLAs have been considered with possible reasons. Autonomic management architecture for dynamic provisioning of resources

S. Singh (✉) · I. Chana
Computer Science and Engineering Department, Thapar University,
Patiala, Punjab 147004, India
e-mail: ssgill@thapar.edu

I. Chana
e-mail: inderveer@thapar.edu

© Springer International Publishing Switzerland 2014
Z. Mahmood (ed.), *Cloud Computing,* Computer Communications and Networks,
DOI 10.1007/978-3-319-10530-7_3

based on users QoS requirements to maximize efficiency and automatic fulfillment of SLA has also been proposed.

Keywords Cloud computing · Service level agreement (SLA) · Service-oriented architecture · SOA · Quality of service · QoS · Autonomic Cloud computing · SLA challenges

3.1   Introduction

Cloud computing is a computing model for permitting omnipresent, suitable and on-demand service access to a common group of configurable computing resources (e.g., networks, servers, storage, and applications) that can be quickly provided and released with minimum management struggle [21]. Public Cloud platforms are usually superior at providing IT services over the open Internet than the on-premise enterprise IT resources. Therefore, the public Cloud can well serve as a workforce that is expected to work at the local region because processing, storage, and enterprise applications to a middle tier between the company and the Cloud consumer can be done easily [31]. The services provided by a Cloud are shown in Fig. 3.1. As a Cloud offers three types of services such as infrastructure as a service (IaaS), or platform as a service (PaaS), or software as a service (SaaS), it requires quality of service (QoS) to efficiently monitor and measure the delivered services and thus needs to follow service level agreements (SLAs) [1, 11]. The complex nature of the Cloud environment requires a cultured means of handling of SLAs as the demands of the service users vary considerably. The QoS attributes that are frequently part of an SLA (response time, throughput, etc.) vary repeatedly and to implement the contract, these parameters need to be carefully controlled [1, 5].

An SLA is part of a service contract where a service is defined based on the agreement between a provider and a customer [19]. In other words, the term SLA denotes the contracted service and its performance. An SLA is a document that specifies the description of the service level parameter, service level objective, agreed service,

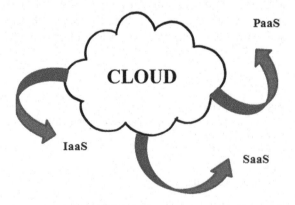

Fig. 3.1 Cloud computing services. *IaaS* infrastructure as a service, *PaaS* platform as a service, *SaaS* software as a service

warranties, and action in case of violation. An SLA is a conveyed bargain that has been documented between two parties which are customer and service provider [2]. The SLA is very significant to define the availability, reliability, and scalability of services. In the literature, the following definitions of SLA are prevalent:

- "SLA is an officially exchanged document that describes (or tries to express) in measurable (and maybe qualitative) terms the service being presented to a customer. Any metrics involved in a SLA should be capable of being controlled on a systematic basis and the SLA should record by whom" [4].
- "A contract is an officially binding bargain between two or more parties. Contracts are subject to particular authorized explanations" [9].

Although, Cloud consumers do not have full supervisory control over the fundamental computing resources, they do require ensuring attributes such as quality, accessibility, trustworthiness, and performance of these resources when users have transferred their fundamental business functions onto their honored Cloud. In other words, it is vital for users to acquire assurances from suppliers on service provisions [18]. Usually, these are delivered through SLAs discussed between the providers and customers [30]. The very first problem is the description of SLA terms in such a way that has a suitable level of granularity, namely the compromises between accuracy and complexity, so that they can ensure most of the user hopes and is comparatively simple to be prejudiced, certified, calculated, and imposed by the resource provisioning mechanism on the Cloud [3, 25]. In addition, different Cloud service models (IaaS, PaaS, and SaaS) will need to express different SLA meta disclaimers [13]. This also increases a number of implementation issues for the Cloud providers. Moreover, innovative SLA mechanisms require to continuously integrate consumer response and customization features into the SLA assessment framework [8].

As the Cloud service models develop and become omnipresent, there is an increase in the probability of clarifying the way the services are provisioned and managed. It, therefore, permits the providers to address the different requirements of their customers. In this perspective, SLAs appear as a significant characteristic which subsequently serve as the establishment for the predictable quality level of the services made available to customers by the providers [38]. Nonetheless, the collection of the recommended SLAs by providers (with marginal overlaps), has directed to manifold different definitions of Cloud SLAs [6]. Moreover, confusions exist on what is (if there is) the difference between SLAs and agreement, what is the marginal quality, what are the terms involved in each one of these documents, and if and how are these associated.

SLAs are a corporate way to officially specify the particular circumstances (both functional and non-functional) under which services are or should be provided. Customers and providers can use top-level SLAs to monitor whether their actual service delivery conforms to the contracted SLA terms [34]. In the case of SLA violations, top-level SLAs permit for penalties or compensations to be paid [16]. In a service-oriented world, services presented are generally self-possessed of or built on a complete set of other services [24]. These services may reside in the domain of the provider itself, or be hosted by external providers. Such services contain business services, software services, and infrastructure services. The quality of a presented service depends comprehensively on the quality of the services it uses [39]. Service quality also depends on the components used and the structure of the basic IT system appreciating the service. Presently, service providers cannot design their service landscapes using the SLAs of dependent services [4, 28]. They have no means by which to control, why a certain SLA violation might have happened, or how to express an associated penalty. SLA guarantee terms are not unambiguously associated to quantifiable metrics, nor are their relation to lower-level services well defined. As a consequence, service providers cannot define the mandatory supervision required in confirming top-level SLAs. This missing relationship between top-level SLAs and (lower-level) metrics is a main obstacle to effective service planning and expectation or improvement processes in service stacks [15, 36].

Further, Cloud computing allows for organizations to move applications and data to remote servers. Due to virtual computing, Cloud computing can deliver better approach to consumption of available resources. Hosted solutions and on-demand server resources are two cases where the use of external vendors may provide for a lower overall price of computing. As the data is moved to remote resources, the control or governance of the data becomes difficult [29].

In this chapter, we first present the concept of SLA in the context of Cloud computing. The remainder of this chapter is then organized as follows: Sect. 3.2 describes interweaving of QoS and SLA with respect to the Cloud; Sect. 3.3 presents the SLA challenges and benefits with respect to Cloud environments; Sect. 3.4 introduces the Cloud SLA (CSLA) architecture; and Sect. 3.5 presents the discussion of work done. Section 3.6 describes our conclusions and future research directions.

3.2   QoS and SLA: Intertwined in the Cloud

This section presents the background of QoS and SLA, SLA Management, SLA of Cloud provider, SLA levels, Metrics in SLA, and SLA deviation in the area of Cloud computing.

3.2.1   QoS and SLA

QoS is increasingly significant when composing services because a degrading QoS in one of the services can dangerously disturb the QoS of the complete composition. Cloud service providers want to confirm that sufficient amount of resources are provisioned to ensure that QoS requirements of Cloud service consumers such as deadline, response time, and budget constraints are met [36]. Consequently, Cloud service providers want to confirm that these violations are avoided or reduced by dynamically provisioning the exact amount of resources in a timely fashion. The success of next-generation Cloud computing infrastructures will depend on how capably these infrastructures will discover and dynamically tolerate computing platforms, which meet randomly varying resource and service requirements of Cloud costumer applications [29]. Logically, based on QoS requirements such as scalability, high availability, trust, and security, these applications will be characterized, identified in the so called SLAs. The current Cloud technology is not completely personalized to honor probable SLAs, though industrial and the academic, both the research groups are presenting increasing interest on problems of QoS assurance within the context of Cloud computing. Broadly, an SLA needs a precise assessment of the characteristics of the required resources [19]. Application services introduced in Clouds (e.g., Web applications, Web services) are frequently characterized by great load inconsistency; therefore, the amount of resources required to honor their SLAs may vary particularly over time [8]. An important challenge for Cloud providers is to automate the management of virtual servers while keeping into account both high-level QoS requirements of hosted applications and resource supervision expenses. Cloud market mechanisms are consistently static and cannot react on dynamic variation of consumer desires [26]. To respond to these issues, there is a requirement of an adaptive methodology for autonomically springing SLA patterns based on consumer requirements. The present research in Cloud SLA limits the capability of matching conformation metrics to acceptable benchmarks [1]. These metrics comprise statistical measures such as standard deviation that want to be computed from the expected and actual outcomes of services delivered to customer. Semantic Web technologies can be used to improve the descriptions and therefore increase the quality of these matches.

3.2.2 Cloud and SLA

Resource reservation is one of the main characteristics in parallel and distributed environment like the Cloud. While preserving the services in the Cloud, we require initiating SLAs through settlement. The settlement between consumers and Cloud service providers fundamentally comprise of parameters like price, time, and other QoS parameters. There are presently numerous methods which resolve the issue of expense and time slot settlement mechanism without taking into account the significant characteristics of QoS [23]. Knowingly handling and assigning resources among numerous consumers in a commercial manner is significant for service providers [41]. Thus, SLA shows a chief role in resource provisioning. In practice, the term SLA is occasionally used to mention the limited delivery time (of the service) or performance.

The Cloud is a parallel and distributed system containing a huge collection of interrelated and virtualized resources that are dynamically self-provisioned and offered as one or more merged computing resources based on SLAs [19]. During negotiation/agreement, there are parameters considered like price, time, and other QoS. Since there is an opposing relationship between price and time-slot feasibilities (e.g., a customer desires to pay a higher price to use a service at a more expected time slot—attaining a higher time-slot utility), expense and time slot have to be exchanged suddenly [25].

Another parameter taken into account is about expanding the QoS through supervising the Cloud services by the use of SLA-based Cloud architecture [13, 36]. Cloud supervising environment comprises of measuring the properties of the network to guarantee that the system functions with required parameters. The management station inquires the state of the network in order to respond to alarm circumstances that may develop in the network system parameter, which is defined as a conjunctive predicate on the local properties of different network elements. In such cases, after identifying local variations, each network element has to successively originate alarms in order to ensure that global parameters are not violated. Even though data may be hosted remotely, it is still an organization's accountability to offer for its security. The problem for the organization is to ponder on what mechanisms it has to provide for the safety of data which it may no longer directly control.

3.2.3   SLA Management

SLA management is the element that retains track of SLAs of consumers with Cloud providers and their satisfaction history. Based on SLA terms, the security mechanism preserves the real usage of resources by needs so that the absolute price can be calculated and charged from the consumers [8]. In addition, the preserved past-usage statistics can be utilized by the service request assessor and admission governor mechanism to expand resource distribution assessments.

An SLA is a document that describes the relationship between two parties: the provider and the consumer. This is obviously a very significant item of documentation for both parties. If used appropriately it should: recognize and describe the consumer's requirements, make all the difficult concerns simpler, decrease areas of clash, inspire dialog in the event of disagreements, and eliminate impossible viewpoints [3, 34]. It should resolve an extensive collection of disputes clearly and unambiguously. Amongst these, the following are some of the most frequent services to provide performance, tracking and reporting problem management, legitimate agreement and resolution of disagreements, consumer responsibilities and accountabilities, reservation and trustworthy information termination. Typical SLA substances [3, 4, 15, 16, 19, 24, 25] to be considered are:

1. *Description of services*: This is the most serious section of the contract as it designates the services and the way in which those services are to be provided. Standard services are frequently separated from adapted services but this disagreement is not of serious concern. The information on the services must be correct and comprised through requirements of what is being delivered.
2. *Performance supervision*: An important part of a SLA deals with supervising and evaluating service level performance. Fundamentally, every service must be capable of being measured and the outcomes inspected and informed. The standards, objectives, and metrics to utilize must be quantified in the contract. The two parties must examine the service performance level consistently.

3. *Problem administration*: The determination of problem administration is to reduce the violent influence of occurrences and difficulties. This regularly specifies that there must be a suitable process to control and solve unexpected occurrences and that there must also be preemptive action to reduce happening of unexpected happenings.

4. *Consumer responsibilities and accountabilities*: It is significant for the consumer to understand that it also has accountabilities to sustain the service delivery process. The SLA describes the association, which of course is a two-way unit. Typically, the consumer must organize for entrance, accommodations, and resources for the provider's workforces who require working on-site.

5. *Licenses and cures*: This section of the SLA stereotypically covers the following vital issues: service quality protections, third party claims, and cures for loopholes.

6. *Reservation*: Reservation is mainly a serious feature of any SLA. The consumer must deliver well-ordered physical and logical entrance to its principles and information. Correspondingly, the contractor must respect and obey with the consumer's reservation rules and techniques.

7. *Catastrophe recovery and commercial strength*: It can be of dangerous status. This factor should be conveyed within the SLA. The topic is catastrophe recovery frequently incorporated within the reservation section; though, it is also regularly involved within the problem administration area. At the highest level, both these areas typically state that there must be acceptable provision for catastrophe recovery and commercial strength forecasting to protect the continuity of the services being distributed.

8. *Service termination*: The SLA agreement naturally covers the following fundamental areas: services are finished at completion of preliminary term, finish for suitability, finish for reason, and expenditures on closure.

3.2.4 SLA of a Cloud Provider

Quality attributes play a significant role in SOA environments [23]. An SLA formally describes the level of service. Organizations seek to develop SLAs for numerous causes. From a simple viewpoint, an SLA is developed between two parties to spell out who are responsible for what, what each party will do, and occasionally more clearly what each party will not do [38]. Also an SLA describes the interaction between a service provider and a service consumer. An SLA contains several elements of details [6, 18, 30], viz.:

1. The set of services the provider will offer.
2. A comprehensive, full definition of each service.
3. The responsibilities of the provider and the consumer.
4. A set of metrics to define whether the provider is providing the service as guaranteed.
5. The inspecting mechanism to supervise the service.

6. The courses of action available to the consumer and provider if the terms of the SLA are not fulfilled.
7. How will the SLA vary with respect to time?

A typical SLA of a Cloud provider has the following components [8, 12–14, 17, 20, 28, 29, 32, 35, 36]:

1. *Service assurance*: It specifies the metrics which a provider struggles to meet over a service agreement time period. Failure to attain those metrics will outcome in service recognition to the consumer. Availability (e.g., 99.9%), response time (e.g., less than 50 ms), catastrophe recovery, and fault perseverance time (e.g., within one hour of discovery) are examples of service assurances. Some service assurances can be on a per action basis, such as zeroing out a VM disk when it is deprovisioned.
2. *Service Assurance Time Period*: It describes the duration over which a service guarantee should be happened. The time period can be a billing month or time occurred since the previous advantage was filed. The time period can also be insignificant, e.g., one hour. The smaller the time period, the more difficult is the service assurance.
3. *Service assurance granularity*: It defines the resource scale on which a provider specifies a service guarantee. For example, the granularity can be as per service, per data center, per instance, or per transaction basis. Related to time period, the service assurance can be inflexible if the granularity of service assurance is fine-grained. Service assurance granularity can also be designed as a cumulative of the deliberated resources, such as contacts. For example, aggregate uptime of all running instances must be greater than 99.95%. Though, such an assurance denotes that some instances in the collective SLA computation can hypothetically have a lesser percentage uptime than 99.95% while still meeting the collective SLA. As significant, collective SLA computation leaves provider the room to better accomplish its presented services.
4. *Service guarantee*: Omissions are the instances that are excluded from service guarantee metric calculations. These omissions typically include misuse of the system by a customer, or any downtime associated with the scheduled maintenance.
5. *Service recognition*: It is the amount credited to the consumer or applied towards upcoming expenditures if the service assurance is not met. The amount can be a comprehensive or restricted recognition of the consumer compensation for the miscalculated service.
6. *Service Violation Measurement and Reporting*: It describes how and who measures and reports the violation of service assurance, respectively.

3.2.5 SLA Levels

Cloud SLAs may provide safety at different stages through infrastructure operating systems (OSs) and applications [8, 38]. Some of the significant attention levels that could be included in a Cloud SLA are described in Table 3.1.

Table 3.1 Cloud SLA levels

SLA levels	Description
Facilities level SLA	Here, the Cloud provider will normally deliver an SLA including the data center services necessary to maintain the customer-owned infrastructure. These comprise items such as electric power, on-site generators, cooling, etc
Platform level SLA	The next level of safety in a Cloud usually covers physical servers, virtualization platforms and hardware related to network retained by the provider and used by the Cloud consumer. Usually, the physical server and virtualization software are hidden by a platform SLA
OS level SLA	OS is the subsequent possible area of coverage for a Cloud SLA. Providers proposing an OS level SLA normally deliver some amount of managed services to a client. This extra service permits the provider to guarantee that the OS is suitably sustained so that it is dependably accessible and normally has some warnings
Application level SLA	This category of SLA delivers safety against application level catastrophes up to and comprising the custom application executing on the infrastructure provided by SLA. Under this model, the Cloud provider is ensuring the availability and performance of their Cloud customer software, which is a hard guarantee to encounter
Availability level SLA	The Cloud network (network among Cloud servers) may be covered by a distinct availability level SLA

3.2.6   Metrics in SLA

Realization of Cloud computing requires that both consumers and suppliers can be confident that contracted SLA are supporting their corresponding business accomplishments to their best degree [19]. Current SLAs usually fail in providing such confidence, exclusively when Cloud providers outsource resources to other Cloud providers. These Cloud providers typically provision very modest metrics, or metrics that hinder an efficient misuse of their Cloud resources [2]. We have identified some of the service-level metrics for specifying fine-grain guarantees of QoS. These metrics sanction resource providers to assign dynamically their resources among the executing Cloud services depending on their request. This is accomplished by including the consumer's service usage in the metric description, but avoiding false SLA violations when the consumer's application does not use all its assigned resources [13, 20, 25].

Through metrics, the defects can be easily identified. Assigning a severity type to defects helps prioritize the development of Cloud services [17, 25]. Table 3.2 demonstrates each type of defect associated with it, as well as SLA that describes the time within which Cloud provider promises to fix the defect measured by metrics.

Normally, a Cloud provider approves the QoS with its consumers through a SLA, which is a two-sided agreement between the consumer and the supplier that states not only the circumstances of a Cloud service, but also describes the contracted QoS between them using a set of metrics. Cloud service providers certainly offer service-level metrics (service accomplishment deadline) to their consumers

Table 3.2 Defect types and SLAs

Defect type	Metric description	SLA
Type 1	Business critical features absent or do not function; program may crash	Fix within 4–24 h
Type 2	Business critical features function most of the time. No work around exists	Fix within 1 week
Type 3	Noncritical features absent or do not function; work around exists	Fix within 2 weeks
Type 4	Inconsequential function may not work as expected, typos in documents, etc	Fix for next software release

for specifying the QoS. The Cloud providers must offer service level metrics that can be used to deliver fine-grain QoS assurances. First, the QoS contract can be obviously expressed using general metrics (e.g., number of processors, frequency of processors, etc.), meanwhile underdone resources are the functioned good. Second, having fine-grain metrics, which assures a given resource distribution during a time period, is particularly significant for service providers that outsource resources to Cloud providers, as we have specified before.

3.2.7 SLA Deviation

Customers desire that composed data should be put into expressive perspective. This situation produces the restriction for a procedure which gathers data from different sources and implements appropriate algorithms for controlling expressive consequences. Such metrics comprise statistical measures such as average or standard deviation that want to be computed from the expected and actual outcomes of services delivered to customer [16]. With the rise of the number of Virtual Machines (VMs), the standard deviation of the customer load falls. Due to this unpredictability, the standard deviations of resource utilization and performance are difficult to measure.

At the application's SLA Level, along with the benchmarks, QoS metrics to estimate the performance and SLA deviation are also required [12, 17, 25, 35]. This is appreciated through a distributed supervising framework that is able to combine supervising information coming from several sources and at different stages. For this trend, the assessment method of the platform is capable to evaluate on the cause of the application's performance deviation, i.e., whether it establishes a breach of the application usage terms and if so, whether the application SLA specifies activities to be executed, whether it is an adequate deviation that can be accurately controlled or a real breach of the SLAs. In the previous situation, more evaluation is required in order to accomplish on the particular nature of the SLA breach to recognize the real object or objects that failed to deliver the granted QoS level [36]. An SLA is typically a two-way written contract which outlines the service and principles the providers deliver to their consumers whether these are scholars, supervisor in universities, and/or other central management teams. It also describes what the providers require from their consumers/service customers in order to provide the service specified. It needs assurance and support from both parties to provision and follow the contract in order for the SLA to work efficiently [6]. In SLA, both the parties (Cloud provider and Cloud consumer) should have specified the possible deviations to achieve appropriate quality attributes. If taking availability as a quality attribute and if it should be 95 %, then it means that the system should be available for 22.8 h per day with maximum deviation of 1.2 h per day (5 %). In the case of system performance, if the desired deadline is 9 ms with deviation (10 %) of 1 ms, then maximum response time should be 10 ms for a particular task without violation of agreement. The Cloud provider's SLA will give an indication of how much actual availability of service the provider views as adequate, and to what amount it is agreeable to require its own financial resources to compensate for unexpected outages. Usually, no Cloud provider considers compensation because 85 % resource providers do not actually provide penalty enforcement for SLA violation presently [10]. There should be penalty delay cost or consumers' compensation if the Cloud provider misses the deadline. Moreover, it provides a risk transfer for IaaS providers, when the terms are violated by the Cloud provider. Penalty delay cost is equivalent to how much the service provider has to give concession to users for SLA violation. It is dependent on the penalty rate and penalty delay time period. The effect of inaccuracy could be reduced by two approaches: first, considering the penalty compensation clause in SLAs with IaaS provider and impose SLA violation; second, adding some slack time during scheduling for avoiding risk [27].

3.2.8 Existing SLA Architectures in the Cloud

Not much has been written in the area of Cloud SLA. We have surveyed only three related architectures in this context. Casalicchio et al. [7] presented an architectural model for the autonomic service provisioning system that investigated the problem from the outlook of an application service provider that uses a Cloud infrastructure to attain scalable provisioning of its Cloud services in the respect of QoS restrictions for autonomic resource management of Cloud-based systems. This architecture describes the functional desires of an autonomic service provisioning system and recognized features and services presented by many IaaS providers that might be used to implement such desires [7].

Happe et al. [33] have proposed a reference architecture for multi-level SLA management that provisions the inclusive supervision of possibly difficult service stacks and discussed how SLAs are used for handling the nonfunctional features of the complete Cloud service life cycle. The presented architecture is based on capabilities extended from an SLA framework constructed around a particular reference application. Emeakaroha et al. [14] have presented DeSVi—an architecture for observing and identifying SLA destructions in Cloud computing infrastructures. This architecture is accountable for the provision of resources and for mapping of tasks, accountable for the implementation of consumer applications, and visualizes the execution of the applications and converts low-level metrics into high-level SLAs.

It is used to recognize the intervals for applications with stable resource consumption only.

However, all these architectures do not take into account the dependency of SLA on QoS requirements? Therefore a new architecture is required that considers SLA deviation status, heterogeneous Cloud workloads and their resource consumption dynamically, assigns priority to Cloud workloads and different states of Cloud workloads and also assures the relation between QoS and SLA.

3.3   SLA Challenges and Benefits in Cloud

This section describes the SLA key challenges along with the reasons of their occurrences as well as benefits and potential barriers/issues of SLA in Cloud computing [11, 18, 21, 31].

3.3.1   SLA Challenges

1. SLAs are hard to express in the Cloud in part because areas of the infrastructure (in specific the network) are outside of the scope of either consumer or provider. This hints to the challenge of offering a predetermined contract for something which is only comparatively in the provider's control [36]. Additionally, as the infrastructure is shared (multi-tenanted) SLA's are more challenging to deliver since they rest on capacity which must be shared [22].
2. The consumer accessing services in the Cloud also face a challenge. New Cloud SaaS providers, who are growing their business and attracting more consumers to their multi-tenanted data center, are unlikely to offer serviceably defined SLA for their services as compared to a data-center provider who can bargain where it supervises all fundamentals of the supplied infrastructure [1]. As their business is increasing and an SLA is a massive threat (since it is a multi-tenanted break of one SLA and is possibly a break of lots), the expenditure might look insignificant and unfortunate to the consumer but is great for a SaaS provider). Additionally with each new consumer, the difficulties on the data center, and therefore danger, increase [12].

Every new consumer brings the advantage of growing stress testing of the SaaS platform and improving growth of abilities within the SaaS provider. While the SLA may remain to be neglected, the risk of dissatisfaction of the data center may well reduce as the SaaS transmits [35]. The objective of an SLA is accordingly not just to deliver a predetermined contract but rather to set out the level of service on which the cooperation between customer and supplier is constructed. In this way, an SLA is about the predictable quality demanded of the supplier and with the above model the expected quality may well improve with more consumers—not reduction as is frequently predicted for a Cloud [17]. SLA's for Cloud providers may well be insignificant and neglected, but the universal risk of using Clouds is not as simple as is often competed. Whereas it is probable that Cloud providers' compromise rundown SLA's, it does not mean that the QoS is, or will stay, underprivileged.

The integration of QoS aware aspects in each Cloud component in order to control and inform the system about its current behavior is required. Further, the optimization of energy consumption in the Cloud computing environment according to user-specified budget constraint is necessary. Thus, maximizing energy efficiency, cost effectiveness, and utilization for applications while ensuring performance and other QoS guarantees, requires controlling important and extremely challenging tradeoffs. These challenges and issues occur due to the following important factors related to the Cloud:

- SLA deviation occurs due to shared nature of the Cloud, and it leads to SLA violations.
- Service quality fluctuations occur due to fluctuations in QoS requirements of different Cloud users.
- Problems in invoices occur due to the various modes of payments along with their own constraints.
- Risk of SLA violations due to urgent execution of Cloud workloads (while assigning priorities to the most urgent workloads), whether the Cloud providers provide the compensation to the user in case of SLA violations or not.
- Difficulty in maintaining the security, due to the multi-tenanted data center, access to the database and type of encryption and decryption.
- Efficient storage is required as memory is wasted due to multiple copies of same data by different or same Cloud users.
- VM migration demands high bandwidth which further leads to complexity.
- Lack of standard QoS-oriented SLA architecture in the Cloud due to heterogeneous nature of Cloud workloads.

The required architecture will focus on developing a resource provisioning and scheduling technique that will automatically manage QoS requirement of Cloud users and would be based on energy efficient usage of the Cloud infrastructure. So, what the customer should deliberate in considering the SLA, in terms of service quality [22, 36, 37], are:

- How does the Cloud SaaS provider determine its progress? The progress of a SaaS service means larger demand on the supplier's data center. Therefore, greater risk that the SLA's will be broken for their multi-tenanted data center.
- How vulnerable is the Cloud SaaS provider in permitting analysis of its services by fresh consumers?
- How well the Cloud SaaS provider engages in planned motivation for service quality alignment with your requirements for service quality?

To address these challenges, SLA can respond to the following issues and questions [2, 3, 6, 8, 9, 13, 16, 19, 25, 38]:

- What are the resources delivered to the consumer? How resources will support the consumer? Are there any limitations to the number of resources?

- How the invoices are created? What are the payment methods? How the services are affected if the customer postpones in compensating invoices? This should comprise refinement period and how the consumer can acquire the services back after the payment when the services are blocked?
- What happens if the SLA is not met? How data is controlled when the service agreement finishes, the sort of data compensated to the company?
- What happens if the service contract is withdrawn? How data is handled and returned to the company?
- How does the service use event logs and who actually has access to the data on the backend?
- Who will check the security of Cloud providers?
- Which of the SaaS employees has root and database access, and will anything prevent them from getting access to your corporate data? What controls are in place?
- Is the held data separated between clients or is it all stored on one huge database out there? How is this data separated? How will the legal question of e-discovery be addressed should it arise as a business concern?
- In terms of service availability, can you get your vendor to sign a service level agreement?
- What security arrangements do you have in place with Cloud service providers that you rely on to deliver your service? What are you doing to build "trust in depth" in the Cloud?

Many significant issues in Cloud computing occur at the boundary between the provider's infrastructure and the Cloud environment [4, 15, 24, 34], e.g.:

- How do you move resources from one side to the other? Is the Cloud application dependent on storage that exists on your side of the boundary?
- What influence will that have on the bandwidth desires? And, how do you perfectly move VMs between the Cloud and your data center as demand raises and failures occur?

These are all legal and motivating problems. But an even larger question forthcoming like a dark Cloud on the perspective is that of the right and authorized grade [8]; i.e., is the matter in the Cloud on the same legitimate footing as the matter in the data center? For example:

- How will the switch occur to a public Cloud when the private Cloud infrastructure gets mixed out? Or would you be using the public Cloud for just executing your services?
- How much confident can be placed on the encryption patterns?
- How safe is the data from natural disasters?
- Is it probable for all of the data to be fully encoded?
- What algorithms are used? Who holds, maintains, and issues the keys?
- And so on.

Thus, it can be construed that SLAs are elements of a quality methodology to help the support teams in classifying and agreeing on what 'good quality' looks like and deliver a framework for quantifying and supervising the realization of service quality [9, 17].

3.3.2 Prospective Benefits

QoS and appropriate SLA collectively offer huge benefits to Cloud computing paradigm. A few of such benefits are listed below:

- Enables strong understanding of the service and accountabilities of all parties
- Helps you to achieve your service consumers viewpoints
- Encourages clearness, responsibility, and reliability
- Notifies team performance, capabilities, and staffing judgments
- Provisions supportive and collective functioning
- Emphases teams on uninterrupted enhancement

3.3.3 Potential Barriers/Issues of SLAs

Following are some of the potential barriers that hinder the implementation of QoS through SLAs:

- Adequate resources not being available at the desired time.
- Lack of assurance from management to implement the solutions within granted schedule.
- Unavailability of desired staff and momentum, in case of urgency.
- SLA's excessive optimization may become difficult and even may lead to rejection.
- The development of SLAs should be team's strength, and if recommendations made within the team are not appreciated, then it may be difficult to preserve staff commitment in the process.

These barriers can be overcome by deliberating the SLAs as follows: Adjust the work roles and responsibilities to reproduce the necessities of the new structure. Note that stronger work roles and responsibilities can help on specific basis but not in terms of the general service nor will this methodology enable endless improvement, added value, and simplicity of service delivery [3, 18]. Observations and prospects of central services will unavoidably adjust as consumers will search for reasonable service delivery and proof of price/profit/worth of services they use [20].

3.4 The Proposed Cloud SLA Architecture

This section proposes Cloud SLA (CSLA) architecture that can ensure better SLAs for both Cloud provider and consumers, as shown in Fig. 3.2. The objective of the proposed CSLA architecture is to reduce the standard deviation of resource

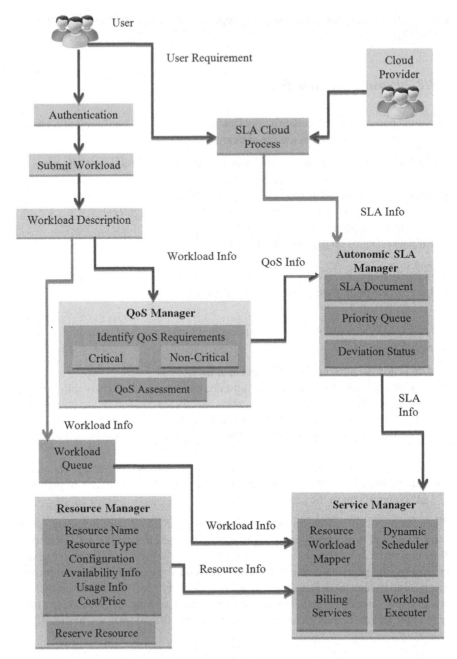

Fig. 3.2 Cloud SLA (CSLA) architecture. *SLA* service level agreement, *QoS* quality of service

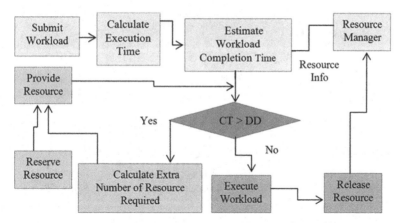

Fig. 3.3 Autonomic service level agreement (SLA) manager in Cloud SLA (CSLA) architecture. *CT* completion time, *DD* desired deadline

utilization and performance to attain a well-proportioned load scattering in the Cloud environments, where the load is characterized as the VM utilization. Furthermore, we define the standard deviation of resource utilization and performance so as, to prevent any hurdle in evaluating the degree of inconsistency. Consequently, the CSLA architecture also targets to reduce the degree of inconsistency. The consideration of standard deviation would aid to avoid the unstable workload of customers during the VMs distribution. The main components of the proposed architecture are as follows:

1. *Authentication*: The user should have valid username and password.
2. *Submit workload*: After authentication, the user will submit their Cloud workload that will be executed in this CSLA architecture.
3. Workload description: All the workload should have their key QoS requirements, based on that the workload is executed with some user defined constraints.
4. *Workload queue*: All the submitted Cloud workloads will be put into a workload queue for execution.
5. *QoS manager*: Based on the key QoS requirements of a particular workload, the QoS manager puts the workload into critical and non-critical queues through QoS assessment.
6. *Autonomic SLA manager*: Based on SLA information, SLA document will be prepared and accordingly urgent Cloud workloads would be placed in priority queue for earlier execution. Deviation status is used to measure the deviation of QoS from predictable with their possible resolution. If the deviation is more than the allowed, then it will allocate the reserve resources to the particular job or workload. Flowchart of autonomic SLA manager in CSLA architecture is shown in Fig. 3.3.
7. *Resource manager*: It contains the information about the available resources and reserved resource along with resource description (resource name, resource type, configuration, availability information, usage information, and price of resource).

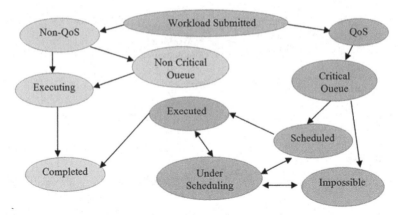

Fig. 3.4 States in Cloud SLA (CSLA) architecture. *SLA* service level agreement, *QoS* quality of service

8. *Service manager*: Based on SLA information, workload information and resource information, the service manger map the workloads to the appropriate resource by taking care of both SLA and QoS. Dynamic scheduler will schedule the workload for execution and billing for that execution will be generated. After payment, the workload executer will execute the workloads.

As shown in Fig. 3.3, the SLA Manager will calculate the execution time of workload and find the approximate workload turnaround time or completion time (CT). If the CT is lesser than the desired deadline (DD), then it will execute immediately with the available resources and release the resource back to resource manager for another execution, otherwise calculate extra number of resources required and provide from the reserved stock for current execution after recreating the SLA document with new user constraints. There are 11 states through which a submitted workload can move as shown in Fig. 3.4.

The first state for every workload is 'workload submission'. Based on key QoS requirements of workload, the next state will be decided either as non-QoS or QoS (quality oriented workloads). After non-QoS state, if there is no other workload pending, then it will execute directly other workload that is waiting into non-critical queue. After successful execution of workload, the workload is completed. On the other hand, all the QoS-oriented workloads are put into critical queue and sorted based on their priority decided by QoS manager and then scheduled for execution. If there is no obstacle (urgency, more resource requirement, etc.), then execute directly with available resources, otherwise put it into under-scheduling state to fulfill the user requirements. If all the conditions meet the given budget, resource, and time constraints, then it will execute, otherwise it will not be executed. CSLA architecture is the key mechanism that ensures that Cloud providers can serve large amount of requests without violating SLA terms. It dynamically manages the resources by using efficient resource scheduling techniques. For instance, when a workload requires low amount of resources, it will assign resources with lower capability, so that new requests can be served.

3.5   Discussion

As designated in the suggested architecture, we observe a very sincere requirement of CSLA architecture to administrate SLAs in the perspective of the Cloud
environment. The proposed CSLA architecture recommends a very flexible design
for handling SLAs between Cloud providers and Cloud users. We perceive this as
one of the strong facets of CSLA architecture where, realistic to the prototype of
SOA, each functionality is delivered as a Cloud service that could not essentially
come from the similar Cloud provider. One vital remark we make in the framework
of Clouds is the absence of standardization. This is especially essential when we
try to relate through manifold Clouds. Even though it is possible to provide service
for diverse Cloud interfaces through a middleware, there is no general collection
of metrics that can be supervised through Cloud providers. There are challenges
to organize the Clouds and we highlight the importance of such determinations in
the light of observing abilities. As a part of these standardization determinations,
we also recommend four types of straightforward metrics for measurements to be
recognized. Clouds would not be capable of scaling indefinitely when a resource
restriction is faced. A service provider may choose to assign the Cloud workloads
or applications or tasks to another provider to avoid important SLA violation penalties. Such a situation generates research prospects in SLA supervision. We proceed
to analyze SLA characteristics like accounting, monitoring of QoS restrictions, and
condition damage in related situations as upcoming research.

3.6   Conclusions and Future Research Directions

This chapter discussed significant factors that could be considered when developing
Cloud SLAs. Four types of metrics have been recognized for specifying fine-grain
guarantees of QoS. The defects in the Cloud service can be easily identified and
SLA deviation can be measured through these metrics. This work mainly focuses
on enhancing the QoS provided by CSLA architecture. The concept and challenges
of SLA-based provisioning and QoS for applications and workloads implementation in the Cloud environment have been presented. We have also proposed and
presented a CSLA architecture that enables adaptive and dynamic provisioning
of the resources based on workload-defined policies for satisfying their own SLA
performance requirements, avoiding the price of any SLA violation and govern-
ing the budgetary cost of the distributed computing resources. Future research in
this area can be recognized in many ways. One such opportunity is based on QoS
requirements, which is considered as a vital characteristic of Cloud computing. The
work presented here can be extended along several lines. From the research method
viewpoint, our investigative method should evolve into theory building and a sup-
position testing as more experimental data about Cloud computing adoption becomes available. From the research output perception, the work regarding different
service and deployment models, the comparative importance of SLA components as

associated to industry-specific features, and new characteristics and perceptions in the innovativeness modeling of the Cloud computing subcontracting judgment can be initiated. Some more QoS parameters can be analyzed and incorporated to find the critical success factors of the CSLA architecture and offer a model that will further help in accomplishing SLA in the Cloud environment using an automated tool.

References

1. Ayadi I, Simoni N, Diaz G (2013) QoS-aware component for Cloud computing. In: ICAS 2013, the ninth international conference on autonomic and autonomous systems (pp 14–20)
2. Bonvin N, Papaioannou TG, Aberer K (2011) Autonomic sla-driven provisioning for Cloud applications. In: Cluster, Cloud and Grid computing (CCGrid), 2011 11th IEEE/ACM international symposium on IEEE, pp 434–443
3. Breskovic I, Maurer M, Emeakaroha VC, Brandic I, Dustdar S (Dec 2011) Cost-efficient utilization of public sla templates in autonomic Cloud markets. In: Utility and Cloud computing (UCC), 2011 fourth IEEE international conference on IEEE, pp 229–236
4. Buyya R, Garg SK, Calheiros RN (2011) SLA-oriented resource provisioning for Cloud computing: challenges, architecture, and solutions. In: Cloud and Service computing (CSC), 2011 international conference on IEEE, pp 1–10
5. Buyya R, Calheiros RN, Li X (2012) Autonomic Cloud computing: open challenges and architectural elements. In: Emerging applications of information technology (EAIT), 2012 third international conference on IEEE, pp 3–10
6. Cardellini V, Casalicchio E, Lo Presti F, Silvestri L (2011) Sla-aware resource management for application service providers in the Cloud. In: Network Cloud computing and applications (NCCA), 2011 first international symposium on IEEE, pp 20–27
7. Casalicchio E, Silvestri L (2011) Architectures for autonomic service management in Cloud-based systems. In: Computers and communications (ISCC), 2011 IEEE symposium on IEEE, pp 161–166
8. Casalicchio E, Silvestri L (2013) Mechanisms for SLA provisioning in Cloud-based service providers. Computer Networks. 57(3):795–810
9. Chazalet A, Dang Tran F, Deslaugiers M, Exertier F, Legrand J (2010) Self-scaling the Cloud to meet service level agreements. In: Cloud computing 2010, the first international conference on Cloud computing, GRIDs, and virtualization, pp 116–121
10. CIO   http://www.cio.com.au. Accessed 26 Nov 2013
11. Dillon T, Wu C, Chang E (2010) Cloud computing: issues and challenges. In: Advanced information networking and applications (AINA), 2010 24th IEEE international conference on IEEE, pp 27–33
12. Duong TNB, Li X, Goh RSM, Tang X, Cai W (2012) QoS-aware revenue-cost optimization for latency-sensitive services in IaaS Clouds. In: Distributed simulation and real time applications (DS-RT), 2012 IEEE/ACM 16th international symposium on IEEE, pp 11–18
13. Emeakaroha VC, Brandic I, Maurer M, Dustdar S (2010) Low level metrics to high level SLAs-LoM2HiS framework: bridging the gap between monitored metrics and SLA parameters in Cloud environments. In: High performance computing and simulation (HPCS), 2010 international conference on IEEE, pp 48–54
14. Emeakaroha VC, Calheiros RN, Netto MA, Brandic I, De Rose CA (2010) DeSVi: an architecture for detecting SLA violations in Cloud computing infrastructures. In: Proceedings of the 2nd international ICST conference on Cloud computing (CloudComp'10)
15. Emeakaroha VC, Netto MA, Calheiros RN, Brandic I, Buyya R, De Rose, CA (2012) Towards autonomic detection of sla violations in Cloud infrastructures. Future Gener Comp Syst 28(7):1017–1029

16. Garg SK, Gopalaiyengar SK, Buyya R (2011) SLA-based resource provisioning for hetero-geneous workloads in a virtualized Cloud datacenter. In: Algorithms and architectures for parallel processing. Springer, Berlin, pp 371–384
17. Goiri Í, Julià F, Fitó JO, Macías M, Guitart J (2010) Resource-level QoS metric for CPU-based guarantees in Cloud providers. In: Economics of Grids, Clouds, Systems, and Services, Springer, Berlin, pp 34–47
18. Huebscher MC, McCann JA (2008) A survey of autonomic computing—degrees, models, and applications. ACM Comput Surveys (CSUR) 40(3):1–31
19. Kertesz A, Kecskemeti G, Brandic I (2011) Autonomic sla-aware service virtualization for distributed systems. In: Parallel, distributed and network-based processing (PDP), 2011 19th euromicro international conference on IEEE, pp 503–510
20. Kounev S, Nou R, Torres J (2007). Autonomic qos-aware resource management in grid com-puting using online performance models. In: Proceedings of the 2nd international conference on performance evaluation methodologies and tools. ICST (Institute for Computer Sciences, Social-Informatics and Telecommunications Engineering), pp 1–10
21. Kumar S, Goudar RH (2012) Cloud computing—research issues, challenges, architecture, platforms and applications: a survey. Int J Future Comput Commun 1(4):356–360
22. Li J, Chinneck J, Woodside M., Litoiu M, Iszlai, G (2009) Performance model driven QoS guarantees and optimization in Clouds. In: Software engineering challenges of Cloud com-puting, 2009. CLOUD'09. ICSE workshop on IEEE, pp 15–22
23. Liu X, Zhu L (2009) Design of SOA based web service systems using QFD for satisfaction of quality of service requirements. In: Web services, 2009. ICWS 2009. IEEE international conference on IEEE, pp 567–574
24. Lodi G, Panzieri F, Rossi D, Turrini E (2007) SLA-driven clustering of QoS-aware applica-tion servers. IEEE Trans Software Eng 33(3):186–197
25. Maurer M, Brandic I, Sakellariou R (2011) Enacting SLAs in Clouds using rules. In: Euro-Par 2011 parallel processing, Springer, Berlin, pp 455–466
26. Nathuji R, Kansal A, Ghaffarkhah A (2010) Q-Clouds: managing performance interference effects for qos-aware Clouds. In: Proceedings of the 5th European conference on computer systems, ACM, pp 237–250
27. Ostermann S, Iosup A, Yigitbasi MN, Prodan R, Fahringer T, Epema D (2009) An early per-formance analysis of Cloud computing services for scientific computing. In: Proceedings of the 1st international conference on Cloud computing (CloudCom 2009), Beijing, pp 1–22
28. Rezaee A, Rahmani AM, Parsa S, Adabi, S (2008) A multi-agent architecture for qos support in grid environment. J Comput Sci 4(3):225–231
29. Rosenberg F, Celikovic P, Michlmayr A, Leitner P, Dustdar S (2009) An end-to-end approach for qos-aware service composition. In: Enterprise distributed object computing conference, 2009. EDOC'09. IEEE international, IEEE, pp 151–160
30. Salehie M, Tahvildari L. (2005) Autonomic computing: emerging trends and open problems. ACM SIGSOFT Software Eng Notes 30(4):1–7 (ACM)
31. Singh S, Chana I (2012) Cloud based development issues: a methodical analysis. Int J Cloud Comput Services Sci (IJ-CLOSER) 2(1):73–84
32. Singh S, Chana I (2013) Advance billing and metering architecture for infrastructure as a service. Int J Cloud Comput Services Sci (IJ-CLOSER) 2(2):123–133
33. Theilmann W, Happe J, Kotsokalis C, Edmonds A, Kearney K, Lambea J (2010) A reference architecture for multi-level sla management. J Internet Eng 4(1):289–298
34. Van HN, Tran, FD, Menaud JM (2009) SLA-aware virtual resource management for Cloud infrastructures. In: Computer and information technology, 2009. CIT'09. Ninth IEEE inter-national conference on Vol. 1, IEEE, pp 357–362
35. Xiao J, Boutaba R (2005) QoS-aware service composition and adaptation in autonomic com-munication. IEEE J Selected Areas Commun 23(12):2344–2360
36. Xu M, Cui L, Wang H, Bi Y (2009) A multiple QoS constrained scheduling strategy of mul-tiple workflows for Cloud computing. In: Parallel and distributed processing with applica-tions, 2009 IEEE international symposium on IEEE, pp 629–634

37. Yang F, Su S, Li Z (2008) Hybrid QoS-aware semantic web service composition strategies. Sci China Series F: Inform Sci, 51(11):1822–1840
38. Yoo S, Kim S (2013) SLA-aware adaptive provisioning method for hybrid workload application on Cloud computing platform. In: Proceedings of the international multi conference of engineers and computer scientists (Vol 1).
39. Zhang P, Yan Z (2011) A QoS-aware system for mobile Cloud computing. In: Cloud computing and intelligence systems (CCIS), 2011 IEEE international conference on IEEE, pp 518–522
40. Zhang Q, Cheng L, Boutaba R (2010) Cloud computing: state-of-the-art and research challenges. J Internet Services Appl 1(1):7–18
41. Zheng Z, Zhang Y, Lyu MR (2010) CloudRank: a QoS-driven component ranking framework for Cloud computing. In: Reliable distributed systems, 2010 29th IEEE symposium on IEEE, pp 184–193

Part II
Current Developments and R&D Solution

Chapter 4
A Methodology for Cloud Security Risks Management

Mariam Kiran

Abstract Cloud computing is an extremely attractive model for both the users and the providers of Cloud-based infrastructure, who have their own business angle for using and providing these services. However, as with many business ventures, as the use of Cloud environments grow, the risks and the threats associated with a successful use of the model also increase. Although, the Cloud paradigm is an evolution of grid systems, Clouds have particular threats specific to virtualized and multi-tenant environments, which need to be managed with proper methodologies to ensure that the entire ecosystem is secure. Security consists of three main aspects—availability, integrity and confidentiality—and each of these needs to be considered to make sure that the complete ecosystem is secure. This chapter presents a comprehensive discussion of the concerns associated with the Cloud security depicting the best practices currently used in the industry. This chapter presents an in-depth analysis of these issues with an innovative holistic approach on how to manage and assess security risks for different kinds of Cloud ecosystems which allows documentation as well as design tools which can be in place to monitor security at both deployment and operation phases. The proposed risk methodology approach allows better management and mitigation of security threats when they occur during the service lifecycle of any kind of Cloud ecosystem and Cloud services provision.

Keywords Cloud computing · Risk modelling · Security · Threats · Service lifecycle

4.1 Introduction

Cloud computing is a market, which was worth US$ 42 billion in 2012, but is technologically still being developed [1]. Being attractive to the IT industry, where the leasing model can allow powerful software tools to be developed on top of the infrastructures, which are not always available, the Cloud brings a number of advantages which include remote accessibilities to resources, elasticity, scalability based on

M. Kiran (✉)
Department of Computer Science, University of Sheffield, Bradford, Richmond Road,
Bradford BD7 4DP, UK
e-mail: m.kiran@bradford.ac.uk

© Springer International Publishing Switzerland 2014
Z. Mahmood (ed.), *Cloud Computing,* Computer Communications and Networks,
DOI 10.1007/978-3-319-10530-7_4

user demands, pay-per-use models to save energy and costs, to name but a few [2]. However, Clouds still have a long way to go to build the trust of the average Cloud users on issues of risks, data securities, the kind of services being processed and the governance characteristics in general [3].

Forrester Research [4] describes the market potential of Cloud computing through the hype curve, divided into 12 segments, based upon level of sharing and business value (see Fig. 4.1). Figure 4.2 shows that Cloud computing is a field, which covers a wide range of abilities being offered, estimated worth around $ 18 billion.

Security is a priority concern for many Cloud computing customers where it can affect the reputation of the providers in terms of confidentiality, resilience and integrity of the company. Kiran et al. [6] have described some of these examples such as data leakage that has been investigated with access control measures like discretionary access control [7] or mandatory access control [8] to control access to an object. Both of these approaches can be used to control access to virtual machines (VMs) via the hypervisor or VM monitor. However, traditional access control models focus on the assumption that the data controller and data owner is in the same trust domain, an assumption which does not hold for Cloud computing. Another example is network access control software like Symantec data-loss prevention [9], which cannot control data leakage within an organisation, as only the end points or network points are scanned for violation of enterprise security policy. Hypervisor attacks are the most serious security threats to the Cloud environment [10] where if infected, such attacks can be used to gain control over a VM (Bluepill) [11]. Even the smart meters cannot monitor false data injections; cyber-attacks having serious implications on the infrastructures [12].

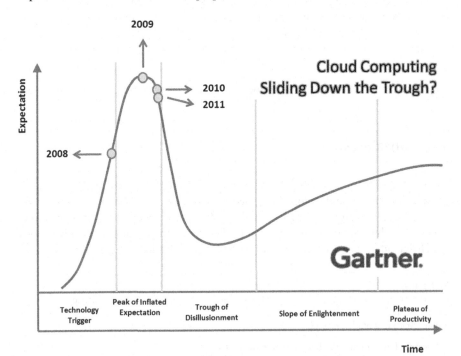

Fig. 4.1 Hype cycle for Cloud computing 2011 [5]

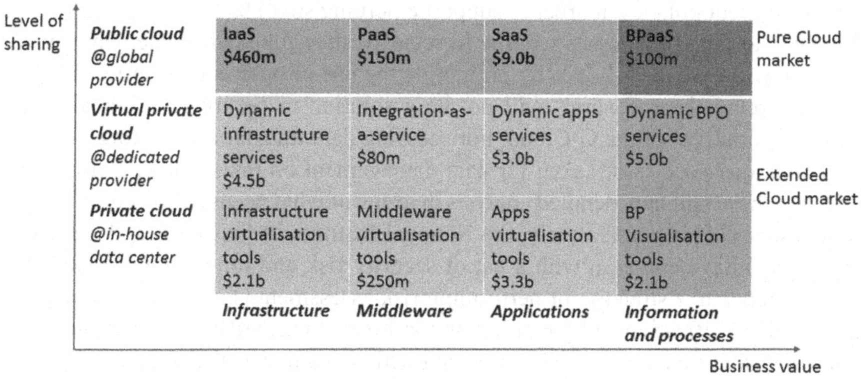

Level of sharing					
Public cloud *@global provider*	IaaS $460m	PaaS $150m	SaaS $9.0b	BPaaS $100m	Pure Cloud market
Virtual private cloud *@dedicated provider*	Dynamic infrastructure services $4.5b	Integration-as-a-service $80m	Dynamic apps services $3.0b	Dynamic BPO services $5.0b	Extended Cloud market
Private cloud *@in-house data center*	Infrastructure virtualisation tools $2.1b	Middleware virtualisation tools $250m	Apps virtualisation tools $3.3b	BP Visualisation tools $2.1b	
	Infrastructure	*Middleware*	*Applications*	*Information and processes*	

Business value

Fig. 4.2 Cloud computing business value [5]. *IaaS* infrastructure as a service, *PaaS* platform as a service, *SaaS* software as a service, *BPaaS* business process as a service, *BPO* business process outsourcing

This chapter discusses the research challenges in security and the best practices employed by the industry with the various policies and measures adopted. Based on these approaches, a uniform risk methodology is presented discussing a step-by-step procedure for handling security risks on Cloud ecosystems. This involves the policies, documentations, governance checks as well as designs tools, which can be implemented based on local infrastructures to implement security checks at the deployment and operations phases of the service lifecycle. The chapter has been organised to present a comprehensive detail on security concerns and findings in the Cloud. Section 4.2 starts with the security concerns and some general characteristics found in industry with a distribution of money spent on the different sectors to improve its issues. Sections 4.3 and 4.4 present different Cloud ecosystems and the service lifecycle as a background on which the methodology applies relevant to security risk assessment. Section 4.5 presents the actual risk assessment methodology introducing the documentation methods, which include reviewer documentation, provider policies, legal implications and risk assessment data sheets that can be filled in advance as a risk report for monitoring security concerns of the Cloud ecosystems. Based on this analysis, the next section identifies six Cloud threat categories which encompass all kinds of threats on Clouds. This identification is extended in Sects. 4.7–4.9, where the risk methodology for the Cloud is presented with accompanying algorithm and simulation results. Section 4.10 discusses the issues with Cloud security testing and the potential future within this domain. This chapter concludes with a case study applying the methodology to a video scalability problem using Clouds and concludes with further future work to be carried out in this domain.

4.2 Security Concerns in Clouds

The UK government is investing in the G-Cloud programme initiative in order to improve the economic sustainability by delivering information and communication technologies (ICT) systems that are flexible, on-demand and in compliance with the government policies in order to support emerging small business suppliers [13]. However, to target the issues relating to security, they released a statement saying that they will ease these issues by promoting the use of open source software [14]. Open sourcing the software's will not be a solution to securing the already being used initiatives of the G-Cloud. For securing data transfer and hosting, various considerations need to be taken for data management on multi-tenancy in Clouds [15]. But these still lack detailed analysis in terms of what needs to be done to target these issues [16]. Comparatively, the National Institute of Standards and Technology (NIST) have come up with a list of security risk and mitigation mechanisms with reference to a strategy for performing risk assessment [17]. Whistle et al. [18] discuss the certification and accreditation for threats in accordance with the government laws analysed per stage accompanied with a detailed analysis.

Security can make or break deals, either convincing organisations to use the Cloud or deferring on security concerns. Best performances in a survey conducted by Ried et al. [4] show the following characteristics on security issues and how they are influenced by various factors, grouping them into three areas:

- *Policies and control*: security control objectives prioritised as functions of requirements for risk, audits and compliance(69 %), policies for protection (85 %), acceptable use (81 %) and regular monitoring, analysis and reporting (70 %) on information assets, baseline security requirements for all applications, databases and network infrastructures (74 %)
- *Organisation*: responsible team with ownership for security (67 %), formal end-user awareness and training programs (70 %), non-disclosure agreements in place and reviewed at intervals (74 %), defined steps for employee termination (67 %)
- *Knowledge and performance management*: audit plans agreed in advisory boards (70 %), compliance with SLAs demonstrated at various intervals (69 %), formal risk ass at regular intervals (52 %)

Risk models in security can be used to define and document some of the security concerns. Pullman [19] conducts an in-depth threat analysis for concerns making sure every part is covered. Microsoft has described a similar threat modelling technique to keep security concerns intact. Figure 4.3 shows a preliminary investigation in threat analysis for data loss in the Cloud and how it can be worked through to assets and mitigation strategies.

Figure 4.3 shows a threat analysis tree of the threat of data loss. The process involves working out each possibility which may have lead to this threat. It then links up with which assets need to be protected for this. As a result of this analysis, various mitigation actions can be identified such as security audits, hardware wipe policy whenever data moved, encrypting data and keeping the protected keys safe. Therefore the risks categories help identify each risk separately and the different models to analyse them separately.

4.2.1 General Security Characteristics

Security is a major concern for organisations and for businesses who are interested in Cloud investments [20–22]. The Aberdeen group [22] conducted a survey of

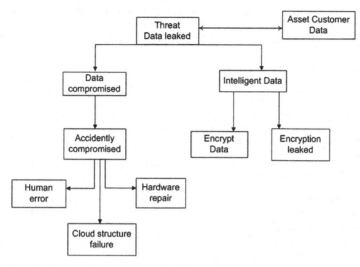

Fig. 4.3 Security threat analysis carried out by Microsoft [19]

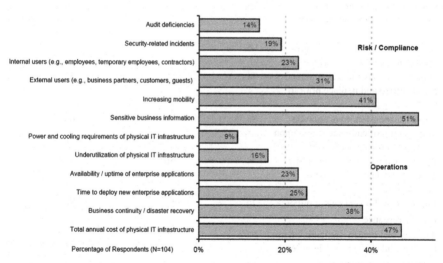

Fig. 4.4 Leading pressures driving the current investments in security for Cloud initiatives. (Adapted from [22])

security practices relating to risks and the leading pressure for areas of investments in the Cloud initiatives. Their findings are presented in Fig. 4.4.

Table 4.1 summarises their findings in terms of the best practices adopted across the different dimensions of security mechanisms on Cloud infrastructures.

Table 4.1 Best practices across various domains [22]. Numbers represent percentage of respondents with $N = 104$

Best practices across following domains	Best in class (%)	Industry average (%)	Laggards (%)
Data security			
Policies and controls to ensure data security (e.g. access controls, data loss prevention, encryption)	85	60	55
Encryption of sensitive data in storage (e.g. file servers, databases, end-user endpoints)	50	46	45
Encryption of sensitive data during transmission (e.g. over public networks, electronic messaging)	70	62	65
Effective key management to support encryption of data in storage and in transmission	56	53	45
An audit function is involved if the integrity of enterprise data has potentially been compromised (e.g. data loss or exposure, unauthorised access)	59	56	55
Identity and access management			
Consistent minimum standards for user authentication and access controls	96	81	70
Minimum authentication requirements for secure remote access	96	86	75
All requirements for access to data are identified and in place prior to access being granted	74	69	50
Timely suspension/revocation/deprovisioning of end-user access upon termination or change in role	85	71	65
Periodic validation that end users have appropriate access rights (attestation)	74	56	55
Enforcement for separate of duties	74	56	50
Data governance			
All data (and objects containing data) have been identified and classified	54	46	32
All data has a designated owner/ steward	58	38	37
Policies and processes are in place for data labelling and data handling	54	51	42
Production data is not replicated or used in non-production environments	64	56	37
Data backup and recovery mechanisms, tested at regular and planned intervals	74	72	63

Table 4.1 (continued)

Best practices across following domains	Best in class (%)	Industry average (%)	Laggards (%)
Policies for secure disposal and complete removal of data from all storage media	70	57	47
Security mechanisms to prevent data leakage	58	56	39
Network access, mobility and application security			
Network infrastructure is designed and configured to restrict connections between trusted and un-trusted segments	81	73	70
Policies ad controls to protect wireless network environments	78	76	65
Policies and controls to limit access to sensitive data from mobile devices (e.g. laptops, smart-phones, tablets)	74	49	40
Policies and controls with respect to code for mobile devices	52	37	35
All functions and application programming interfaces (APIs) that will be used in conjunction with software development are analysed for security risk	52	38	30
Monitoring, auditing, forensics and incident response			
Security-related logs, information and events are retained and regularly reviewed	69	68	58
Monitoring and tracking of security-related incidents and events (e.g. types, volumes, time and cost to remediate)	78	70	56
Communications channels and escalation procedures for security-related incidents and events	59	52	50
Forensic procedures (e.g. chain of custody) for collection, retention and presentation of evidence in support of potential legal action	52	48	35
Segmentation and access controls to prevent compromise and misuses of log data	65	59	55
Access to diagnostic and configuration ports is restricted to authorised individuals and applications	77	68	55

4.3 Cloud Ecosystems

To make them more attractive for users, Cloud providers attempt to hide a lot of the processes in the background to promote the easy usability for users. Having automated security policies and access control measures are examples of these, but there are still a lack of standards to be followed during these activities. These have been on the active research agenda of bodies like NIST [23] and Gartner [5].

NIST describes the Cloud as a convenient model using efficient computing resources stressing on four deployment models [24]:

- Private Cloud: operated for an organisation by either itself or a third party
- Public Cloud: for general public use and is owned by an organisation selling Cloud services
- Community Cloud: an infrastructure that is shared by several organisations, also called federation of Clouds
- Hybrid Cloud: a composition of two, more Clouds or multi-Clouds (community, private, public)

Each of these models or Cloud ecosystems brings different issues in terms of data hosting, security, risks and business models. This chapter discusses Cloud ecosystems in relation to the roles of the actors—namely service provider, infrastructure provider and brokers—involved in the ecosystem, which do not have a direct mapping from the NIST documentations. This is done to ease discussion in the later sections.

Figure 4.5 describes the different Cloud ecosystems and shows the roles of the actors who play in them. A private Cloud involves only a service and an infrastructure provider who communicate directly to each other and possibly in the same geographical location. A Cloud-bursting environment is when one infrastructure provider is close to running out of resources and thus bursts to another. Figure 4.5c describes a federation of infrastructure providers working together as a team to complete the

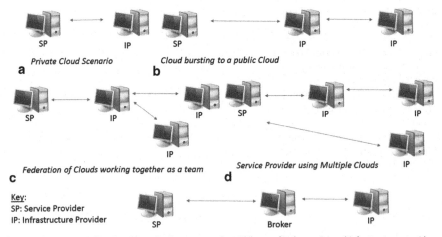

Fig. 4.5 a–e Various Cloud scenarios or ecosystems

service execution. Figure 4.5d shows a similar situation, but this time the infrastructures are working independently of each other and only guided by the service provider. Lastly, Fig. 4.5e describes a situation which involves a broker to mediate between the two parties. The broker can take responsibilities to monitor, test and make sure the service is completed and delivered at the right time to the service provider.

In addition to the Cloud ecosystems, Clouds can be recognised by the form of functionality they offer. These are as follows:

- Software as a service (SaaS): Uses the Web to deliver third-party applications to Clients. Example: Gmail
- Platform as a service (PaaS): Provides framework to build applications on top as well. This provides the client highly scalable infrastructure and hardware for computing. Examples: GoogleAppEngine [25], Heroku [26]
- Infrastructure as a service (IaaS): Third party allows you to install a virtual server on their IT infrastructure

This chapter focuses on Cloud security in terms of the different ecosystems and the security threats that need to be monitored. Functionality models of Clouds form part of these ecosystems, depicting how the services will be offered. Based on the functionality and ecosystems, various threats can be highlighted which would otherwise not need to be monitored in a different scenario. Section 4.7 provides a case study for a video scalability application to demonstrate this use of identifying threats for the particular scenarios.

4.4 Cloud Service Lifecycle

Before we discuss the different kind of threats across the ecosystems, we have to recognise the different phases in which the services can exist. This also highlights that only particular threats will be active during, either the service engineering phase, onboarding or operation phase. The services lifecycle is represented in Fig. 4.6, where the first phase of service engineering is when the service is constructed, the second phase is when the service is actually deployed on to the Cloud and the third phase is when the service is in operation and executing on the Cloud.

4.5 Risk Assessment of Security threats on Clouds

Security can essentially be broken into three main aspects, which, if guaranteed, becomes fully optimal (Fig. 4.7). These are:

Service construction or Engineering	Service onboarding	Service operation

Fig. 4.6 Service lifecycle covering construction, deployment and operation of the service on the Cloud

Fig. 4.7 Security triangle   Availability

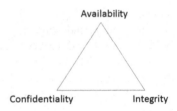

Confidentiality   Integrity

- *Availability*: The data is available when needed.
- *Integrity*: The data is not modified without being detected.
- *Confidentiality*: The data remains undisclosed to unauthorised parties.

Comparing to grid infrastructures, due to their nature, Clouds have additional threats that need to be considered for security reasons. For instance, data access in Clouds is a huge threat because geographically the data can be hosted anywhere as a service. This would not be a threat on Grid infrastructure which are usually business owned and located internally. Therefore there is a need to consider the geographical location and the access rights to the Cloud for safety of the data. Another example is when migrating the VMs securely across the different infrastructures on the Cloud. Depending on the situation, the data manager on the Cloud should consider if the VM's new location still complies with the legal agreements made between the end user and the Cloud for where the data is allowed to be hosted. Various authentication models can be introduced to make it more secure as a mechanism to overcome this threat.

There is a need to identify the different kinds of security issues in Cloud computing. For example, Fig. 4.8 describes how data being hosted in isolation, can be compromised.

Figure 4.8 describes a tree structure which can be used to perform a fault-tree analysis style to find, where human errors, faults and the business being affected helps to determine how to mitigate similar situations if this happens in real life.

4.5.1 Documenting a Security Risk Assessment

Different Cloud ecosystems and the services executing on them, are prone to different number of threats, particularly the public or hybrid Cloud scenarios. In public Clouds, the data is hosted externally on a Cloud, being used by multiple users of the public. Hybrid Clouds can include different Clouds joining to form a federation or multiple Clouds working together to fulfil a service. Threats, such as unauthorised data access, are a problem on public Clouds rather than a private Cloud, where everything is maintained internally. Not having formal procedures in place is a major problem because of these different natures. When using multiple Clouds a few common rules should be maintained to allow uniform protocols that are followed by all Cloud providers in case certain security threats are realised. Cloud networks can be set up with various sensors to gather the informa-

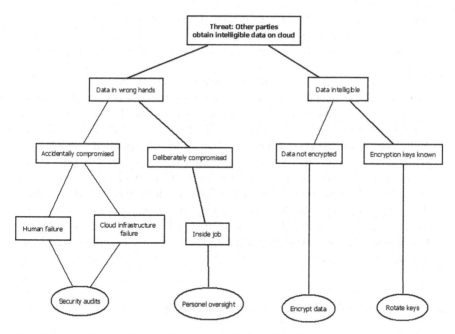

Fig. 4.8 Tree analysis for threat of data leakage. (Adapted from [1])

tion, on how the service is performing on the Cloud within the applications. The introduction of formal methods can make Clouds secure by applying them to the Cloud industry as a whole [6]:

- *Reviewing various documentations*: These include using sniffers to filter output logs produced by the monitoring software installed on the infrastructures. These can include system logs (for details of service start-up, downtimes, file and account access and changes to file privileges), firewall logs (authorisation attempts from various locations and identify the users, if possible), antivirus logs (for detecting malicious code accessing the system), and intrusion detection system logs (detecting the changes to the hypervisor code), and legal implications of security threats have to be set to measure the impact of certain threats.
- *Provider interaction policies*: Policies have to be set for the providers, which include action management policies for necessary legal steps to be taken, if threats happen and how to mitigate them. These should include an incident response plan, which may include communication protocols (how information will be displaced to within the team or outside such as the attacking internet protocol (IP) addresses to block those organisations) [6], software vendors providing the software, (if the actual software being installed is corrupted), internal team management procedures, vulnerability assessment with certain auditing procedures and using these for future incident planning. An important issue is revealing the performance information to Cloud customers. Should the end users be told of threats occurring at the time their services were hosted on the Cloud and when?

In cases of multiple locations hosting data, this can be an attractive requirement from the users to ensure their data is secure.

- *Legal implications on the security aspects*: Data protection and security can be specified in a legal contract, being drawn with the end users and the providers. This may include analysing all privacy concerns specific to the Cloud usage. This may start with analysing the data flow in the Cloud use cases and understanding the legal issues with the multiple vendor situations and how these should be handled. Information security-related standard (ISO/IEC 27001:2005) has recognised protection of personal data including protection against alteration, unauthorised modifications and against unauthorised access as a standard [3]. Further recommendations concerning information security are mainly based on control and industry best practices relevant to Cloud providers (security framework). However, this needs to be defined, clarifying questions concerning intellectual properties and ownership rights in information and services placed *in the Cloud*. This also involves clarifying ownership rights among all potential stakeholders and includes them within the service level agreements (SLAs) drawn.

4.5.2 Security Risk Assessment Data Sheet

An example of a data sheet used to perform a security risk assessment has been described below: This can be filled out by the providers or the end user as part of the SLA, when they try to ask for certain security measures to be taken.

1. Details:

Service name: _____

Department: Service provider/infrastructure provider

Date of this assessment: _____

Risk reference no: _____

2. Hazards overview:

- Example unencrypted data
- Example lost keys

3. Control measures:

(Option to complete this section for any risk which is rated as four or more, or for which the likelihood is three).

For each hazard name responsible person and action

Note: The choice of controls should be implemented according to the following hierarchy:

1. Eliminate the hazard
2. Substitute
3. Reduce

4. Isolate (enclose the hazard)
5. Regulate (e.g. numbers at risk, engineering controls or safe system of work)
6. Protection
7. Discipline

Copies: (a) The original of this form is to be retained by the originating department and a copy is to be supplied to the safety department. (b) Relevant information on risks and preventive/protective measures are required by law to be provided to employees so that they can ensure their own health and safety and not put others at risk.

4. Evaluation of risk:

Hazard details		Services at risk		Fre-quency/ (duration)	Controls in place	Residual risk evaluation	Risk rating
Hazard	Nature of hazard/ adverse effects (how is the hazard likely to put services at risk?)	Insert code and (num-ber of people)	Insert code letter and (dura-tion)	Insert code numbers	Severity of harm score 1–3	Likeli-hood of occur-rence score 1–3	Multiply sever-ity × like-lihood
Unen-crypted data	Third party acquires data	A, B, D (5)	D/(4)	1, 3, 5	3	3	9
Lost keys	Third party has data	A, B, D (10)	D/(4)	2, 4, 5	2	3	6

Key: services at risk:
(a) Operator (skilled), (b) operator (inexperienced), (c) end users, (d) office staff

Key controls:
(1) Data encryption algorithms, (2) refreshing keys, (3) segregating data, (4) assessment of personnel, (5) monitoring login logs

Severity of harm:
(1) Slight, e.g. minor data leaks, less important data, (2) serious, e.g. personal data compromised, (3) major, e.g. business lost, reputation jeopardised

Likelihood of occurrence:
(1) Low (harm will seldom occur), (2) medium (harm will often occur), (3) high (certain or near certain)

Table 4.2 Security threats and their categories (*C* confidentiality, *I* integrity, *A* availability) [6]

Threat category	Description (specific to Clouds)	Factor	Example
External attacks	These include all the threats in scenarios involving use of public infrastructures	C, I, A	Carrying out of denial of service (DoS) attack
Theft	Cloud computing supports multi-tenant architecture with multiple users using same resources. This can lead to the theft of data by an adversary	C, I, A	Gaining unauthorised access to systems or networks
System malfunction	Some software used extensively on Clouds has bugs	A, I	Malfunction of software
Service interruption	Unavailability of service/data due to DoS attacks	C, I, A	Natural disaster
Human error	No control on how users use the system	C	User error
System specific	System specific threats and abuse	C, I, A	Usage control

4.6 Identifying Cloud Threat Categories

Khan et al. [6, 24] describe how the various security threats can be bunched together in six specific categories, represented by Table 4.2. The main differences from grids to Clouds have added a few unique threats, such as data leakage (an unauthorised transmission of data from within an organisation to outside or the unauthorised access to the system, which compromises the confidentiality of the data), usage control (access control to cover conditions independent of environmental factors), hypervisor level attacks (enable an adversary to exploit vulnerability at the virtualisation layer that is running underneath the VMs). Most threats have a domino effect on the other components, where one affects multiple components. For instance, if the hypervisor gets corrupted, all the corresponding VMs, their locations and data can be compromised. Inappropriate use of any technical or data available on the Cloud affects the trust customers place on the Cloud, having implications on the business objectives of the Cloud providers.

4.7 Need for Risk Management

Risk management addresses the possibility that future events may cause adverse effects and is defined as "the process whereby organisations methodically address the risks attaching to their activities with the goal of achieving sustained benefit within each activity and across the portfolio of all activities" [2]. Figure 4.13 describes the stages in a risk management cycle. The most important concepts in risk management are as follows:

- An *asset*: to which has a value and hence for which the party requires protection.
- An *unwanted incident*: an event that harms or reduces the value of an asset.

Fig. 4.9 Risk management process

- A *threat* is a potential cause of an unwanted incident whereas vulnerability is a weakness that opens for, or may be exploited by, a threat to cause harm or reduce the value of an asset.
- *Risk* is the likelihood of an unwanted incident and its consequence for a specific asset, and *risk level* is the level or value of a risk derived from its likelihood and consequence. For example, a server is an asset; a threat may be a computer virus and the vulnerability a virus protection not up to date, which leads to an unwanted incident.

A risk management process consists of a risk identification stage, where it is identified, assessed for likelihood and impact, managed through planning and resolved with a plan on what to do if it occurs. Risk monitoring phase allows it to be continually monitored in case it becomes active in the future (Fig. 4.9).

4.7.1   Cloud Threats Identified

The security risk methodology uses the threat modelling as an approach for identifying the threats and vulnerabilities of the system. Two sources of information were used to collect the threats, unique to Clouds. The sources of information are as follows:

For collection purposes:

- The information security forum [1, 3] for providing data on attacks on IT systems and the frequency of attacks
- The public data on attacks on the Cloud platforms such as Amazon EC2 and Google Apps Engine [8, 9]

For evaluation purposes:

- Defense Advanced Research Projects Agency (DARPA) intrusion detection evaluation data sets [3]

Based on the data collected, a risk catalogue can be created to document the threats, the affected assets and their vulnerabilities. An entry into the risk catalogue can be stated and shown in the example in Table 4.3.

The data from the threat analysis tool [28] helps to identify the form the threats in the form of ids, assets, and the values for priority and likelihood. The ecosystems relate to Cloud scenarios being private, bursting, federation and multi-Clouds. The lifecycle stage shows which phase of the service lifecycle, during execution, is the threat active—during deployment or operation. A risk methodology is then generated

Table 4.3 Example of
the threat entry in the risk
inventory

Threat id	27
Name of threat	Theft of business information
Cloud ecosystem at which active	All (private, bursting, federation, multi, brokerage)
Service lifecycle stage	Operation
Asset affected	Customer data
Priority assigned	4
Likelihood assigned	2

which will use this risk catalogue as a reference database when making decisions on
the security risks in the Cloud.

4.8 Risk Methodology Stages

This section describes the various stages involved when performing a risk assessment
for Cloud computing environments. The methodology follows a 5-stage procedure
from a high level analysis of the system to the asset identification, threat assessment
and then the final evaluation of risk from the matrix to calculate as the assessment of
the risks that need to be managed in order of high probability and impacts.

Stage 1: High-Level Analysis of the System An initial high-level analysis of the
Cloud ecosystem or scenarios, to help identify the actions and assets involved. This
will help isolate the assets involved and how they change over time to identify the
vulnerabilities of the Cloud environment.

Generally security needs to be assessed before deployment of the service to
check for security concerns of other provider or if the SLAs demand certain security
aspects. During the operation, as security concerns are monitored while the service
is executing, certain live data have to be assessed continuously.

Stage 2: Identifying the Assets Involved There are various assets involved either at
the deployment or operation stage such as the SLA or customer data. These can be
monitored in relation to the specific threats in the environment.

Stage 3: Identify the Threats in Each Cloud Deployment Scenario This is where
a threat analysis tool can be used to perform a detailed analysis of each threat.
Figures 4.10 and 4.11 describe the threat distribution across the six threat categories
identified earlier [28].

The threat analysis, accompanied by an expert opinion, sets the threat and vulnerability ratings for each threat from a scale of 1–5 (very low, low, medium, high
and very high). The tool also allows mapping the threat with respect to business
impact produced as an information risk profile. These results have been shown in
Table 4.4.

Stage 4: High-Level Analysis of Each Threat Each of the threats can be further analysed in terms of who/what causes them and the incidents leading up to them, which

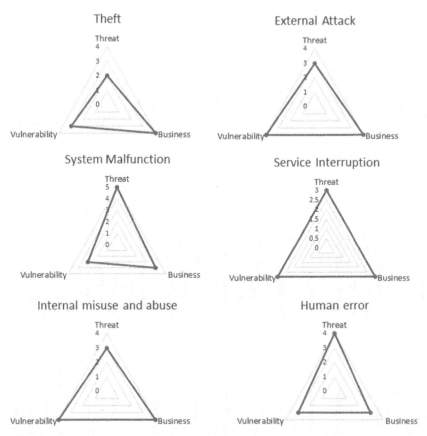

Fig. 4.10 Business impact, threat and vulnerability rating for the six threat caetgories. (Adapted from [28])

Fig. 4.11 Overall threat rating in terms of business impact. (Adapted from [28])

Table 4.4 Threats identified in the various use cases and their details. (Adapted from [24])

Threat category	Threats (threat id) {threat classification: availability (A) confidentiality (C) integrity (I)}	Stage of service lifecycle (deployment/ operation)	Assets involved	Cloud ecosystems	Priority (1—low, 5—high)	Likelihood (1—low, 5—high)
External attacks	Carrying out of denial of service (DoS) attack (T1) {A}	Operation	Customer data, infrastructure of the provider	All	4	3
	Hacking (T2) {I, C}	Operation	Customer data or service	All	3	1
	Undertaking malicious probes or scans (T3) {I, C}	Operation	Hypervisor code	All	4	2
	Cracking password (T4) {A, I, C}	Operation	Customer data or service	All	3	1
	Cracking keys (T5) {A, I,C}	Operation	Customer data or service	All	3	1
	Spoofing user identities (T8) (A, C) {A, C}	Operation	Customer data or service, all services	All	3	1
	Modifying network traffic (T9) {I}	Operation	Software, connections, service (runtime)	All	2	2
	Eavesdropping (T10) {I, C}	Operation	Software, connections, service (runtime)	All	2	1
	Distributing computer viruses (T11) {I}	Operation	Software, connections, service	All	3	1
	Introducing Trojan horses (T12) {I}	Operation	Software, connections, service	All	3	1
	Introducing malicious code (T13) {C}	Deployment and operation	Software, connections, service	All	3	3
	Distributing Spam (T15) {A}	Deployment and operation	Mailing lists	All	1	4

Table 4.4 (continued)

Threat category	Threats (threat id) {threat classification: availability (A) confidentiality (C) integrity (I)}	Stage of service lifecycle (deployment/operation)	Assets involved	Cloud ecosystems	Priority (1—low, 5—high)	Likelihood (1—low, 5—high)
Theft	Gaining unauthorised access to systems or networks (T16) {A, I, C}	Operation	Customer data or service	All	5	4
	Theft of business information (T27) {A, C}	Operation	Customer data	All	4	2
	Theft of computer equipment (T29) {A, C}	Operation	Customer data	All	1	2
System malfunction	Malfunction of software (T34) {I}	Operation	Toolkit, all services	All	1	4
	Malfunction of computer network equipment (T35) {I}	Operation	Toolkit, all services	All	1	5
Service interruption	Natural disaster (T40) {I}	Deployment/Operation	Customer data	All	1	3
	System overload (T41) {A, C}	Operation	Customer data,	All	4	3
Human error	User error (T42) {C}	Deployment/operation	Data	All	5	3
System specific threats and abuse	Data Leakage (T50) {I, C}	Operation	Data	All	5	3
	Usage control (T51)	Operation		All		
	Hypervisor level attacks(T52) {A}	Operation	Data	All	3	2
	Data ownership (T53) {I}	Deployment	Data	All	4	2
	Data exit rights (T54) {I, C}	Deployment	Data, SLA	All	5	3
	Isolation of tenant application (T55) {I, C}	Deployment and Operation	Data	All	5	2
	Data encryptions (T56) {A, I, C}	Operation	Data	All	5	3
	Data segregation (T57) {A, I}	Operation	Data, programs	All	4	2
	Tracking and reporting service effectiveness (T58) {A, I}	Operation	Data, Hosted VMs	All	5	3
	Compliance with laws and regulations (T59) {A, I}	Deployment and operation	Data	All	3	2
	Use of validated products meeting standards (T60) {A, I}	Operation	Data	All	3	3
	Guest virtual machines (T61) {A, I}	Operation	Data	All	1	3

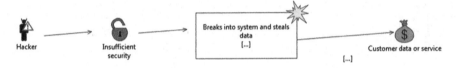

Fig. 4.12 Analysing the threat *hacking*, drawn using the CORAS (A Framework for Risk Analysis of Security Critical Systems) risk modeling tool [27]

Table 4.5 Risk evaluation matrix. (Adapted from [24])

		Consequence				
		Insignificant	Minor	Moderate	Major	Catastrophic
Likeli-hood	*Rare*	T40	T10	T2, T4, T5, T8, T11, T12		
	Unlikely	T29	T9		T3, T27	
	Possible	T41		T13	T1, T50	T51, T52
	Likely	T15,T34				T16
	Certain	T35				

Table 4.6 Range of threats for confidentiality, availability and integrity. (Adapted from [24])

		Likelihood rating				
		Very Low	Low	Medium	High	Very High
Business impact rating	Very High					
	High			Confidentiality		
	Medium			Availability		
	Low			Integrity		
	Very Low					

can then be prioritised depending on this information. This also helps to measure the impact of the security risk on the service and the providers. Figure 4.12 depicts an example of the hacking threat and its related asset and vulnerabilities.

Stage 5: Risk Evaluation Depending on the priority of the assets and likelihoods of the threats occurring, the threat items can be plotted into an evaluation matrix to document their occurrences. Table 4.5 depicts this in relation to the threats identified in Table 4.4.

The likelihood and impact rating is set using the data collected and the threat analysis. The impact values also denote the affect the threat will have on the business such as loss of confidentiality or availability eventually leading to loss of money. The loss in trust has the highest impact (Table 4.6).

Once the inventory has been created for security risks, the level of risk can be calculated by the following algorithms. These are different both for deployment and operation phases.

4.9 Algorithms for Security Risk Assessment

The algorithms used to measure security risks can be unique depending on the deployment and operation phases. These are described below:

4.9.1 Algorithm: Deployment Phase

Security_risk_at_deployment (Cloud_ecosystem)

1. Calculate number of threats recorded, at deployment stage and the involved ecosystem.
2. For each threat, calculate:
   a. probability of likelihood given the asset is affected $(p(B|A))$ = likelihood / 5.0
   b. probability of asset priority $(p(A))$ = priority / 5.0
   c. probability of likelihood regardless of asset $(p(B)) = p(B \mid A)$ $* p(A) + p(A')$
   d. probability of threat occurring $(p(A \mid B)) = ((p(B \mid A) * p(A))) / p(B)$
3. Security risk = sum all probabilities of threats occurring/threats found

The maximum value of the asset priority and the likelihood of it being affected are set in the range 1–5. Based on the list of threats that need to be monitored, these can be assessed based on each asset and the likelihood that each asset actually fails as a result of the threat. Bayes rule can be used to calculate the underlying probability:

Let A = "Something is wrong with asset with its priority"

Let B = Asset has failed as a result

In steps 2c and 2d, the aim is to calculate $P(A \mid B)$, the probability that the asset has indicated a risky event as a result of the threat.

$$P(A \mid B) = P(B \mid A) * P(A) / P(B)$$

$P(B \mid A)$, indicates that likelihood that the asset has been affected when something is wrong but not related to the kind of threat. $P(A)$ gives the asset affected with its priority. $P(B)$ is then defined by calculating the total probability:

$$P(B) = P(B \mid A) \times P(A) + P(B \mid A') \times P(A')$$

Note: A and A' are mutually exclusive where (A') means any kind of fault in the system without this asset being involved.

$$P(A') = 1 - P(A)$$

Assuming $P(B \mid A') = 1$, because this means that $P(B)$ (probability that the asset has failed) given the asset is not present $P(A')$. Thus this determines that if the asset is not present, the system has failed already.

Therefore:

$$P(B) = P(B \mid A)P(A) + 1 \times P(A')$$

Once calculated, using substitution to find $P(A|B)$ probability that the asset has failed due to this threat is given by:

$$P(A \mid B) = P(B \mid A) \times P(A) / P(B)$$

The algorithm above shows how the security risk probability is calculated at deployment stage. Considering the recorded risks in the risk inventory (Table 4.4) for each particular use case and using the values of priority and likelihood as described in the algorithm, the probability of that particular threat can be calculated. The security risk values are depicted in Fig. 4.13 which show the probabilities returned for each of the use cases, private, bursting, federation and multi-Cloud during deployment and operation (Fig. 4.14).

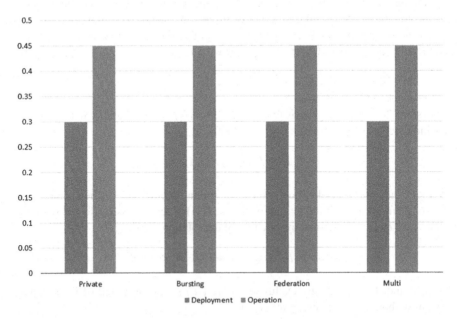

Fig. 4.13 Security risk probability as calculated from the risk catalogue from value 0–1 and the different use cases. (categories are private (private at deployment and operation), bursting (bursting at deployment and operation), federation (federation at deployment and operation), multi (multi-Cloud at deployment and operation))

Fig. 4.14 State changes for each asset from good, attacked or compromised. *Pl1* probability likelihood 1 can be calculated using the risk inventory, *Pl2* probability 2 is calculated at operation depending on the monitored logs, *PlT* the relative probability threshold is measured using the relative probability between Pl1 and Pl2

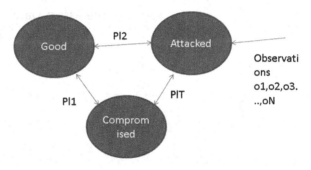

4.9.2 Algorithm: Operation Phase

Security_risk_at_operation (Cloud_ecosystem)

1. Make a list of threats to be monitored at operation stage for the *particular ecosystem.*
2. Make a list of the affected threats to be monitored.
3. For each asset make observations Oi for every 10 min.
4. Return the sample to the risk assessor, which records the probability of the event occurring.
5. Calculate total_event_rate = events_found/total monitored time.
6. Relative risk (RR) = total_event_rate/risk (risk from catalogue).
7. If RR = 1 do nothing, RR < 1 accept risk, if RR > 1 apply mitigation strategy.

A collection of monitoring logs can be parsed to calculate the event rate for the risk assessor to calculate the relative risk. Figure 4.15 shows the states of a particular asset changing with time, 1 h 40 min (collecting 10 min samples). The probability collected is returned to the risk assessor, which calculates the relative risk as shown in the algorithm at operation stage.

Various monitoring logs will be assessing its state during operation. Initially the asset starts with state "good", but because it is to be monitored, it moves into the "attacked" state where the various logs are counting the number of events occurring. This is the event rate returned to the risk assessor.

During this time, if the risk assessor receives an event rate, which is too high, this causes the relative risk to go above 1, the asset moves into a "compromised" state.

When the risk assessor witnesses the assets in a *compromised* state, if then fires relative mitigation strategies to allow the asset to be repaired and go back to a "good" state. Then once in the "good" state, it will then again move to an "attacked" state so that it can be continuously monitored for attacks and return event rates to the risk assessor.

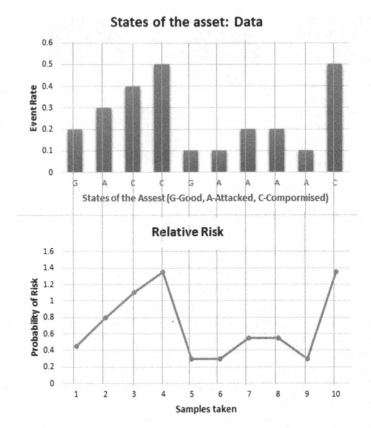

Fig. 4.15 Example of rates counted for asset data. The asset data being monitored for 10 samples and the corresponding state changes (good, attacked, compromised) with event rate (*top graph*) is shown in relation to the relative risk (*bottom graph*)

4.10   Testing Security

A kind of testing, particularly "penetration testing", seeks to get past security proto-cols. Security as a whole involves static design issues, as well as run-time verifica-tion of security. In this sense, security is a measure of reliability, to test if the data is secure assessing in terms of vulnerability, availability and integrity.

Non-functional requirements specify how a system should perform, in terms of its efficiency and reliability in the SLAs. Some of these aspects can also be defined as specific variables, such as response time, scalability, reliability, avail-ability, security or maintainability. Various kinds of testing included here are per-formance testing, security testing or dependability testing for satisfying customer needs.

4.11 Application: Case Study for Video Scalability in Cloud Environment

Khan et al. [29] describe an implementation of threat methodology to assess the video scalability when being distributed as an IaaS on the Cloud. Scalable video is a means of distributing media content to many users using Clouds, as this allows heterogeneous networks to be connected to devices. This is a highly distributed environment with an IaaS focus, but centralized with many users connecting to it.

Security measures have to be taken to make sure copyright laws are intact, pay-per-view models for business value and economic return and it caters to the different levels of bandwidth used by the users. Usually, past models have distributed encrypted video files when broadcasted, such as satellite television, investing in set-top box to subscribe to encrypted channels. Shared encryption keys are used with each subscriber, which changed periodically.

Figure 4.16 describes the unique service lifecycle, which would exist in this particular scenario. To prevent past users accessing the data, when unsubscribed, there will be a continuous pre-deployment stage, where new keys will be generated, deployed and used periodically.

When identifying the threats, some of these do not apply to video broadcasting, from the general Cloud scenarios such as the following [29]:

- *Isolation of tenant application*: Affects integrity, confidentiality and does not apply to video broadcasting.
- *Data encryptions*: Applies to all three availability, confidentiality and integrity and is already covered in the key authentication process during the pre-deployment process.
- *Data segregation*: Affects the availability and integrity also does not affect broadcasting issues.
- Tracking and reporting service effectiveness can be given by customer review and end-user experience affecting the credibility of the server.
- Compliance with laws and regulations of copyright issues and contract breach. Affects the confidentiality and integrity of the business during the pre-deployment stage.

Based on Table 4.4, the threats which apply in this scenario are identified in Table 4.7, with corresponding risk evaluation in Table 4.8 and priority concerns for business in scalable video in Table 4.9.

Fig. 4.16 Service lifecycle for scalable video. (Adapted from [29])

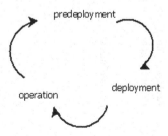

Table 4.7 Threats referring to Table 4.4 which apply to scalable video on the Cloud

Threat category	Threats (video threat id) {Threat classification: availability (A) confidentiality (C) integrity (I)}	Stage of Cloud (Pre/deployment/ operation)	Assets involved	Priority (1—low, 5—high)	Likelihood (1—low, 5—high)
External attacks	(T1.) Carrying out of denial of service (DoS) attack {A}	Operation	Broadcasting server	5	4
	(T2.) hacking {I, C}	Operation	Customer data, comprising service, company reputation	3	1
	(T3.) Undertaking malicious probes or scans {I, C}	Operation	Hypervisor code, virtual machine, video server	4	4
	(T4.) Cracking password {A, I, C}	Operation	Customer data or service	3	1
	(T5) Cracking keys {A, I, C}	Pre-deployment, operation	Customer data or service	2	1
	(T8.) Spoofing user identities {A, C}	Pre-deployment, operation	Customer data or service data, all services	3	1
	(T9.) Modifying network traffic {I}	Operation	Software, connections, service, video streaming (runtime)	2	2
	(T10) Eavesdropping {I, C}	Operation	Software, connections, service (run-time), video streaming	4	3
	(T11) Distributing computer viruses {I}	Operation	Software, connections, service, broadcast is usually patched with security modes	2	1
	(T12) Introducing Trojan horses {I}	Operation	Software, connections, service	3	1
	(T13) Introducing malicious code {C}	Deployment and operation	Software, connections, service, not through video easy to, broadcast is controlled	2	1
	(T15) Distributing spam {A}	Deployment, operation	Mailing lists, server lists	2	1

Table 4.7 (continued)

Threat category	Threats (video threat id) {Threat classification: availability (A) confidentiality (C) integrity (I)}	Stage of Cloud (Pre/deployment/operation)	Assets involved	Priority (1—low, 5—high)	Likelihood (1—low, 5—high)
Theft	(T16) Gaining unauthorised access to systems or networks {A, I,C}	Operation	Customer data or service, extract data from the video	4	3
	(T27) Theft of business information {A, C}	Operation	Customer data	4	2
	(T29) Theft of computer equipment {A, C}	Pre-deployment, Operation	Customer data	1	2
System malfunction	(T34) Malfunction of software {I}	Pre-deployment, operation	Toolkit, all services video server, end user, because of the key generation	1	4
	(T35) Malfunction of computer network equipment {I}	Pre-deployment, deployment, operation	Toolkit, all services, video server, malfunction during the key generation will affect the broadcasting of the video and the server	1	3
Service interruption	(T40) Natural disaster {I}	Pre-deployment, deployment, operation	Customer data, video server	4	1
	(T41) System overload {A, C}	Operation	Customer data, video server	1	2
Human error	(T42) User error {C}	Pre-deployment, deployment, operation	Data	3	3
System specific threats and abuse	(T50) Data leakage {I, C}	Operation	Data, video data	4	2
	(T53) Data ownership {I}	Pre-deployment, deployment	Data relates to video rights	4	2
	(T54) Data exit rights {I, C}	Pre-deployment, deployment	Data, SLA relating to copyrights	4	3

Table 4.8 Risk evaluation Matrix for scalable video

		Consequence				
		Insignificant	Minor	Moderate	Major	Catastrophic
Likelihood	Rare		T5, T11, T14, T15	T2, T4, T12, T8	T40	
	Unlikely	T29, T41	T9		T27, T50, T53,	
	Possible	T35		T42	T3, T10, T16, T54	
	Likely	T34				T1
	Certain					

Table 4.9 Range of threats for confidentiality, availability and integrity for scalable video

		Likelihood rating				
impact		Very Low	Low	Medium	High	Very High
	Very High					
Business rating	High	Availability				
	Medium	Confidentiality				
	Low	Integrity				
	Very Low					

Based on the above analysis, availability is the highest concern, so we can implement changes that target these threats like implementing fast authentication key mechanisms and secure access to data throughput.

The above threat analysis can help determine the important threats to watch for, concentrating staff efforts and costs to make sure they do not occur. This helps manage the critical parts of the systems and also manage the costs.

4.12   Conclusions

Cloud computing refers to *on-demand access to a shared pool of computing resources*, providing reduced costs, reduced management responsibilities and increase in business agility. For these reasons, it is a popular paradigm to be used by end users from different professions. Security is, however, a major player in this equation as it can make or break deals for Cloud users and infrastructure providers alike.

The way forward is to come up with standards on how security can be assessed to minimize the risks in the systems as well as manage the costs as efficiently as possible. This chapter discussed a security risk methodology approach to assess the items which can jeopardise the security of the Cloud ecosystems and the actors involved in the Cloud. By performing a detailed documentation assessment and assigning a likelihood and priority to each of these threats, the items can be listed in order of priority to see which particular measure need to be taken first to reduce that kind of security risk. This allows work to be categorized in terms of the most important first when assessing complex ecosystems such as Cloud environments which have too many components that can go wrong during the service deployment or operation phases.

There is a further need for proper documentation and legal agreements to be drawn up to restore the trust of consumers in Clouds and effectively making business more aware of a detail approach to take when securing their systems.

Acknowledgments This work has been partially supported by the EU within the seventh framework programme under contract ICT-257115—Optimized Infrastructure Services (OPTIMIS).

References

1. Wills G (2009) Technical review of using Cloud for research, University of Southampton, Final Report 2009
2. Foster I, Zhao Y, Raicu I, Lu S (2008) Cloud computing and grid computing 360-degree compared. In GCE '08: Grid Computing Environments Workshop, pp 1–10. IEEE, Nov 2008
3. Catteddu D, Hogben G (2009) Cloud computing: benefits, risks and recommendations for information security, Technical Report, European Network and Information Security Agency (ENISA) 2009
4. Ried S, Kisker H, Matzke P (2010) The evolution of Cloud computing markets. Forrester Research 2010
5. Stamford C (10 Aug 2011) Press Releases, Gartner's 2011 Hype Cycle special report evaluates the maturity of 1,900 Technologies, 2011
6. Kiran M, Khan AU, Jiang M, Djemame K, Oriol M, Corrales M (2012) Managing security threats in Clouds, Digital Research 2012
7. Buyya R, Yeo CS, Venugopal S, Broberg J, Brandic I (2008) Cloud computing and emerging IT platforms: vision, hype, and reality for delivering computing as the 5th utility. Future Gener Comput Syst 25:599–616
8. Information Security Forum (ISF), Information risk analysis methodology (IRAM). https://www.securityforum.org/iram#iramtva. Accessed April 2014
9. Symantec Ltd., Symantec Data Loss prevention. http://www.symantec.com/en/uk/business/solutions/solutiondetail.jsp?solid=sol_info_risk_comp&solfid=sol_data_loss_prevention&om_sem_cid=biz_sem_emea_uk_Google_DLP. Accessed Nov 2010
10. Carpenter M, Liston T, Skoudis E (2007) Hiding virtualization from attackers and malware. IEEE Secur Priv 5(3):62–65
11. Naraine R (2011) Blue pill prototype creates 100 % undetectable malware. http://www.eweek.com/c/a/Windows/Blue-Pill-Prototype-Creates-100-Undetectable-Malware,   2011. Accessed Dec 2013
12. Grid Security (2012) Industry insiders: insufficient security controls for smart meters, Published Online: 10 April 2012. http://www.homelandsecuritynewswire.com/dr20120410-industry-insiders-insufficient-security-controls-for-smart-meters, 2012. Accessed Dec 2013
13. HMGovernment (2010) HMGovernment G-Cloud, Crown copyright, 2010. http://gcloud.civilservice.gov.uk/. Accessed Dec 2013
14. Huddle Inc. Government storage. http://www.huddle.com/campaign/government-storage/. Accessed Oct 2012
15 UK Government (2012) G-Cloud brochures. http://www.fcoservices.gov.uk/eng/files/Government_Cloud_Solutions_Brochure.pdf. Accessed Oct 2012
16. Millman R (2012) SCC launches secure multi-tenancy Cloud on G-Cloud. Published Online: April 30, 2012. http://www.cloudpro.co.uk/cloud-essentials/3493/scc-launches-secure-multi-tenancy-cloud-g-cloud, 2012. Accessed Dec 2013

17. Scarfone K, Souppaya M, Cody A, Orebaugh A (2008) Information security testing and assessment, National Institute of Standards and Technology (NIST), Special Publication 800-115. http://csrc.nist.gov/publications/nistpubs/800-115/SP800-115.pdf. Accessed Sept 2008

18. Whiteside F, Badger L, Iorga M, Shilong Chu JM (2012) Challenging security requirements for US government Cloud computing adoption (draft), Special publication 500-296, NIST, May, 2012

19. Pallman D (2010) Azure Blog, Threat modelling the Cloud, August 2010. http://davidpallmann.blogspot.com/2010/08/threat-modeling-cloud.html#fbid=8qxQ6O6UvEq. Accessed Dec 2010

20. Brink DE (2010) Security and the software development lifecycle: secure at the source. Aberdeen Group December 2010, research brief, 2010

21. Jansen W, Grance T (2011) Draft NIST special publication guidelines on security and privacy in public Cloud computing, Computer Security, Jan 2011

22. Brink D (2011) Security and cloud best practices July 2011, Aberdeen Group, 2011

23. Mell P, Grance T (2009) The NIST definition of Cloud computing, National Institute of Standards and Technology, Oct 2009

24. Khan AU, Kiran M, Oriol M, Jiang M, Djemame K (2012) Security risks and their management in Cloud computing. CloudCom, pp 121–128, 2012

25. Google Inc (2013) GoogleAppEngine platform as a service, Google developers. https://developers.google.com/appengine/. Accessed Dec 2013

26. Heroku Inc (2013) Heroku platform. https://www.heroku.com/. Accessed Dec 2013

27. den Braber F, Braendeland F, Dahl HEI, Engan I, Hogganvik I, Lund MS, Solhaug B, Stolen K, Vraalsen F (2006) The CORAS Model-based method for security risk analysis, SINTEF, Oslo, September, 2006. http://www.uio.no/studier/emner/matnat/ifi/INF5150/h06/undervisningsmateriale/060930.CORAS-handbook-v1.0.pdf. Accessed Dec 2013

28. Khan AU (2013) Data confidentiality and risk management in Cloud Computing, PhD thesis, Department of Computer Science, University of York, 2013

29. Khan AU, Kiran M, Oriol M (2013) Threat methodology for securing scalable video in the Cloud, 8th international conference for internet technology and secured transactions (ICITST-2013), Dec 9–12, 2013, London, UK

Chapter 5
SecDSIM: A Framework for Secure Data Storage and Identity Management in the Cloud

Shaga Praveen and G. R. Gangadharan

Abstract Cloud storage is a model of networked online storage where data are stored in virtualized pools of storage devices. Cloud storage requires users to host their data on the servers of cloud service providers. This raises issues of confidentiality, integrity, and availability of the data stored in the cloud environment. In this chapter, we propose a framework for secure data storage and identity management (SecDSIM) that can store data securely in the servers of cloud service providers using multi-user searchable encryption technique. The framework supports the process of verifying proof of storage correctness of the data by retrieving data identifiers any time around the cloud. The framework also supports dynamic updates for the encrypted data and indexes stored in the servers of cloud service providers.

Keywords Multi-user searchable symmetric encryption · Grade-based access control · Cloud data storage · Identity management · Aided keyword search · Precise keyword search

5.1 Introduction

Cloud computing is a way of delivering IT-enabled capabilities to users in the form of "services" with elasticity and scalability, where users can make use of resources, platform, or software without having to possess and manage the underlying complexity of the technology. Cloud computing becomes popular because of its characteristics including scalability, elasticity, and cost effectiveness. However, from the perspective of a cloud consumer, security of the data in the cloud is one of the main obstacles for adopting cloud computing services [1–5].

Cloud storage is a specific sub-offering within infrastructure as a service (IaaS) of Cloud computing and promises high data availability and reduced infrastructure

G. R. Gangadharan (✉) · S. Praveen
Institute for Development and Research in Banking Technology,
Castle Hills, Road No.1, Masab Tank, Hyderabad 500057, India
e-mail: e-mail: geeyaar@gmail.com

S. Praveen
shagapraveen@gmail.com

© Springer International Publishing Switzerland 2014
Z. Mahmood (ed.), *Cloud Computing,* Computer Communications and Networks,
DOI 10.1007/978-3-319-10530-7_5

costs by storing data of users with remote third-party providers [6]. In recent years, cryptography has become a critical tool in theoretical analysis of security model and architecture for cloud storage and emerged as an important technique in designing secure identity management for cloud storage systems [6–8].

Our goal in this chapter is to propose a multi-user searchable symmetric encryption scheme that provides an efficient isolation and a secure storage mechanism for users' data and to provide an identity management using grade-based access control when users share their data with other trusted users.

5.2 Cryptographic Cloud Storage and Identity Management Schemes

Users are required to store their data on the servers of cloud service providers (CSPs), which discard the control over their data. A CSP physically stores users' data in one location that could lead to several data security and privacy issues such as unauthorized access by internal employees of CSP and by outsiders. As a result, CSPs could not provide confidentiality, integrity, and availability of data. In such cases, a CSP must provide an efficient isolation and secure storage mechanism for users' data.

Mostly, data are accessed through a search operation performed on a cloud storage server. Generally data are stored in encrypted form in a cloud storage server. Traditionally, we download the whole encrypted data on the local machine, decrypt all its contents, and then perform the search on the plain text. Note that this searching scheme is inefficient and impractical.

We now present some of the common cryptography-based cloud storage schemes.

5.2.1 Broadcast Encryption

Broadcast Encryption (BE), introduced by Fiat and Naor [9], distributes encrypted data along with a decryption key to a group of users with whom the broadcaster wishes to share the data via a secure channel. While encrypting the data, the broadcaster can choose a set of users to allow decrypting the data. However, in the real world, there could be a large number of owners who may want to store their data in the cloud as well as a large number of users who may want to access the stored data. Later, several other BE schemes [10–14], are proposed. However, these schemes require public parameters for every user and the public parameters need to be updated every time a user wants to join or leave the system.

5.2.2 Identity-Based Encryption

Identity-based encryption (IBE), introduced by Shamir [15], encrypts the data using a public key encryption scheme in which the public key can be an arbitrary string (called as identity). Boneh et al. [16] presented a secure IBE scheme in which the sender uses the identity of the receiver as the public key to encrypt the data. Canetti et al. [17] proposed the construction of IBE that was provably secure outside the random oracle model. Later Boneh and Boyen [18] gave two schemes with improved efficiency and prove security in the selective-ID model without random oracles. IBE schemes lack management and secure communication models.

5.2.3   Attribute-Based Encryption

In an attribute-based encryption (ABE) scheme, proposed by Sahai and Waters [19], ciphertexts are labeled with sets of attributes and private keys are associated with access structures. Nail et al. [20] proposed a threshold attribute-based encryption which can prevent the collusion attacks. Based on access policy, ABE schemes are classified into two types: Key policy attribute-based encryption (KP-ABE) and cipher text policy attribute-based encryption (CP-ABE). In the KP-ABE scheme, proposed by Goyal et al. [21], the access policy is derived from the user's private key and a set of attributes are used to decrypt the data. In CP-ABE scheme, introduced by Bethencourt et al. [22], the user keys are associated with sets of attributes and the ciphertexts are associated with the access policies.

Several other variations of the CP-ABE-based and KP-ABE-based schemes have been proposed in [23–25]. However these schemes have disadvantages in practice such as the ability to achieve revocation of users' key.

5.2.4   Searchable Encryption

The problem of searching on outsourced encrypted database was solved by Goldrich and Ostrovsky [26] over oblivious random access memory (RAM). However, this approach is unrealistic because it suffers from poly-logarithmic computation and communication overheads. Song et al. [27] proposed the first construction of searchable symmetric encryption scheme in which each word in the document is encrypted independently under a special two-layered encryption scheme called Song, Wagner, and Perrig (SWP). As an extended version to [27], Boneh et al. [28] presented a public-key based searchable encryption scheme. Goh [29] described a secure index (SI) to build a symmetric searchable encryption scheme. However, SWP and SI schemes are slow in retrieving documents.

Curtmola et al. [30] proposed a searchable symmetric encryption that includes a constant computational complexity to perform the search operation on the ciphertext. However, it does not support efficient updates to the database. Later, Kamara et al. [31] proposed cryptography-based public cloud storage scenarios where the service provider is not completely trusted by the user. Here, when a user wants to store data in the cloud storage, the data processor indexes data and encrypts using advanced encryption standard (AES). Then, the data processor encrypts the index using a searchable encryption scheme and the unique key using an

ABE scheme. Further, Kamara et al. [32] used searchable symmetric encryption, search authenticator, and proof of storage to achieve confidentiality, integrity, and verifiability in the cloud. However, these papers compromise on confidentiality by revealing the files that contain a common keyword to a cloud provider while retrieving the encrypted data. Moreover, [31] and [32] are inefficient in handling dynamic updates on indexes. To address the problem of dynamic updates, Kamara et al. [33] presented a dynamic searchable symmetric encryption scheme which provides an efficient dynamic updates to the encrypted data that are stored on third party servers.

Searchable encryption techniques leak information about the search patterns (i.e., the number of keywords of the document collection or metadata that it contains). Furthermore, most of the searchable encryption schemes are inefficient in updating the ciphertext [27–36].

5.2.5 Role-Based Encryption

Zhu et al. [37] proposed a new hierarchical role-based access control model to encrypt the data. Zhou et al. [38, 39] proposed a hybrid scheme called role-based encryption (RBE) that combines access control with cryptography and key distribution to address security requirements for data storage in the cloud. However, these schemes lack the ability of user revocation.

5.2.6 Identity Management

Cryptographic cloud storage techniques provide identity management using several access control mechanisms such as attribute based, identity based, and role based. Torres et al. [40] presented a survey on various identity management techniques or methods for future network. Celesti et al. [41] proposed a reference architecture based on identity management and service provider (IdM/SP) model to address the identity management problem in InterCloud context where identity is managed by the third party. Several access control models that are used for identity and access privilege management are presented in [42].

5.3 Searching on Encrypted Data

Searchable encryption is a technique that provides functionalities to search encrypted data without requiring the decryption key [43]. In this chapter, we follow a keyword-based access scheme, where all the keywords related to the encrypted data are stored in an index. There are two approaches to implement a keyword-based access scheme:

- The first approach is to store an index of the data locally, and for each search operation, query the index and use the results to retrieve the appropriate encrypted data from the cloud storage server.
- The second approach avoids using local storage for indexes; instead, the index is stored in the cloud storage server in an encrypted form. Then, for each search, the index is retrieved and queried locally before the encrypted data are fetched.

Consider the following multi-user scenario. Imagine that Alice wishes to store her medical records on a personal health record (PHR) server, such that the data are available to her anywhere and anytime. She also wants to share some of her medical records to a "physician" for treatment. Bob is a physician who uses the PHR server to treat the patients. If Alice's records are in plaintext, then Bob can simply check the designation of each medical record of her and proceed for treatment. However, Alice wishes to use an encryption scheme to maintain the confidentiality of her medical records. In this setting, if Bob wants to access Alice's medical records designated with "physician", either Alice has to reveal her decryption key to Bob, or Alice has to decrypt her medical records by herself and send only the medical records which are designated with "physician" to Bob. The first solution compromises the confidentiality of all medical records, and the second solution is not efficient.

The above scenario requires a cryptographic technique that is used to store the data securely in cloud storage servers with efficient multi-user retrieval support.

Searchable encryption is a technique that provides functionalities to search encrypted data without requiring the decryption key. Each message of data is associated with a set of keywords. Searchable encryption transforms both the message and the associated keywords into an encrypted form, in such a way that the encrypted keywords can be queried later using a trapdoor. This allows a client to retrieve or decrypt only the messages of the data that contain a particular keyword without decrypting the data.

Let $D=(M_1, M_2,..., M_n)$ be data consisting of n messages $M_1, M_2,..., M_n$. Each message M_i $(i=1,...,n)$ is associated with a metadata item $W_i=\{ W_{i,1}, W_{i,2},...\}$ which is actually a set of keywords chosen from a finite set W. Searchable encryption stores the data D on a server such that:

- A message M_i is retrieved from the server, only in case a particular keyword occurs in its associated metadata W_i, while leaking as little information as possible.
- The confidentiality of the data is preserved as much as possible.

The searchable symmetric encryption is used to retrieve encrypted data from a third party storage server, when the metadata associated with the message contains a particular keyword. Searchable symmetric encryption allows only to the user who stores the data on third party server can search the encrypted data. Initially each message M_i is encrypted, using a standard symmetric key encryption scheme, and stored on a third party server. To store the metadata items on the third party server that can be queried later, searchable symmetric encryption schemes with the following algorithms are used:

- *Keygen$_s$(p):* Given the security parameter p, outputs a master secret key *msk*.
- *Enc$_s$(W, msk):* Given the metadata W, and the master secret key *msk*, outputs a searchable ciphertext S_W.
- *Trapdoor$_s$(W, msk):* Given the keyword W, and the master secret key *msk*, outputs a trapdoor *Tw*.
- *Search(Tw, S$_W$):* Given the trapdoor *Tw*, and the searchable ciphertext S_W, outputs 1 if $W \in W$.

The Keygen, Enc, and Trapdoor algorithms are invoked by the client, and the search algorithm is invoked by the server. If search = 1, the server sends back the encrypted message whose associated metadata is W.

5.4 Grade-Based Access Control

The goal of identity and access control management is to ensure that accesses to data stored in cloud storage servers are given only to authorized users. Access control mechanisms are used to mitigate the risks of unauthorized access to the data, resources, and systems. Figure 5.1 shows a general access control model which includes principal, auction, guard, and protected system. Principal can be a user, a program, etc.; auction can be a query; guard can be a security manager or a server; and a protected system can be repository or a file, etc. Guard verifies the identity of the entity (usually the principal) called authentication. Then the guard checks the access control policies that consist of rules that describe what is allowed and what not to access the protection system.

We introduce grade-based access control (GAC), a new mechanism to provide identity and access control management based on the grades of users. Access to a resource is determined based on the level of the relationship, typically the grades

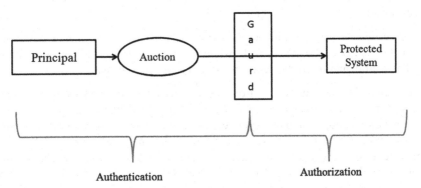

Fig. 5.1 General access control model

Fig. 5.2 Grade-based access control

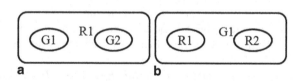

Fig. 5.3 Grades versus roles

of the user in an organization. In other words, the permissions are associated with grades, and users assigned to appropriate grades.

Figure 5.2 shows the basic structure of GAC model. Consider that Alice and Bob are two employees of an organization A holding assistant manager as their roles. Assume that an organization A has implemented the role-based access control mechanism for identity management. Assume that Alice has joined in the organization prior to Bob. Therefore, Alice holds grade II position and Bob holds grade I (assuming grade II is superior to grade I).

Consider that there is a payment approval application that can be accessed by the employees of the organization A who hold their role as senior manager having a minimum of grade II level. In this scenario, if the organization A had not implemented role-based access control mechanism, then Alice could access payment approval application. However, in our case, the organization A has implemented role based access control mechanism for identity management.

In this case, if the organization A wants to give access permission to Alice for payment approval application, then there are two solutions:

- The organization A has to create another account to Alice which holds a role as senior manager and provide access permission.
- The organization A has to promote Alice to senior manager.

None of the above two solutions are practically implementable as organizations may have many employees like Alice. From the above scenario, it is clear that the role-based access control having its own disadvantage, i.e., classifying and providing access permissions to people based on roles makes it more difficult to define granular access controls for each person.

Grades of a user can be of two types as shown in Fig. 5.3. For a role, say R1, there may be different grades, say G1 and G2 as shown in Fig. 5.3a. For different roles, say R1 and R2, there may be same grade, say G1 as shown in Fig. 5.3b. This makes GAC mechanism more flexible than role-based access control.

GAC can provide the functionalities provided by the role based access control. GAC is not replaceable for role-based access control. If we use GAC with role-based access control as a hybrid access control model, it may serve as a better granular and flexible access control mechanism.

5.5   Multi-User Searchable Symmetric Encryption

We extend the concept of multi-user searchable symmetric encryption (mSSE) defined in [30] and apply to our framework for data storage and identity management in the cloud. Table 5.1 specifies the notations used in the rest of the chapter.

We illustrate the modified mSSE scheme as follows.

$$mSSE = \left(GDid, Enc, GAC, Trpdr, Search, Dec\right).$$

Our mSSE is composed of the following six algorithms:

Did ⟵ *GDid(Uid, Date, N):* It takes *Uid,* date (in DDMMMYYYY format), and a 5-digit unique random number as input and generates a unique *Did* for newly created/generated data by the user (see Fig. 5.4). Here we used 5-digit random number because even if a user continuously creates new data or file per second, he can create a maximum of 86400 files per day.

(EnData, EnKws) ⟵ *Enc(w, D):* It takes keywords and data as input and generates *EnData* and *EnKws.*

AData ⟵ *GAC (Uid, pswd, grade):* It takes *Uid, pswd,* and *grade* as input to verify the authorization based on GAC and provides access to the data.

T ⟵ *Trpdr(Uskw):* Trapdoor is an encrypted search keyword provided by the user to access the data.

Table 5.1 Notations

Notation	Description
mSSE	Multi-user searchable symmetric encryption
GDid	Generating data identifier
Did	Data identifier
Uid	User identity
N	5 digit unique random number
EnData	Encrypted data
EnKws	Encrypted keywords
W	Keywords collection
D	User generated data
Pswd	Password
GAC	Grade based access control
AData	Access permission to the data.
Uskw	User search keyword
T	Encrypted user search keyword (Trapdoor)
Enc	Encryption
Dec	Decryption
Ver	Number of times the data accessed
CSP	Cloud service provider

1	1	M	C	M	B	3	1	0	0	0	3	J	A	N	2	0	1	3	7	4	9	1	2
USER ID									DATE OF DATA CREATED										5 DIGIT RANDOM NUMBER				

Fig. 5.4 Data identifier (Did) format

Did ⟵ *Search(T) and EnData* ⟵ *Search(Did):* It takes initially *Trpdr* as input and searches it on "local index" based on aided keyword search which contains *EnKWs*, *Did* and *Ver*. It generates output as a set of *Did*s. Then it takes *Did* as input and searches it on the "cloud index" based on precise keyword search and generates *EnData* as output.

Data ⟵ *Dec(EnData):* It takes *EnData* and decrypts.

5.6   SecDSIM Framework

In this section, we discuss our proposed framework, SecDSIM. It is a secure cryptographic cloud storage based on mSSE which provides identity management using GAC. SecDSIM is composed of the following four components (see Fig. 5.5):

- *User:* User can be an employee of an organization or a trusted employee of a partner company.
- *Dedicated local server (DLS):* DLS resides in the own premises of an organization which manages outgoing data and incoming data. DLS encrypts the data and generates the *Did* for each data received at the first time (as shown in Fig. 5.5) and decrypts the encrypted data received from the CSP.
- *Data Verifier Server (DVS):* DVS checks the *proof of storage-correctness* of the data around the clock by checking the version value of the data.
- *Credential Generator (CG):* CG creates credentials for users.

The following are the steps involved in SecDSIM:

Step 1: *Credential generation*
  Initially CG creates user credentials.

Step 2: *Data creation by user*
  A user creates data and keywords and sends to DLS by using his credentials to encrypt the data.

Step 3: *Preparing encrypted data and passing to CSP communication server*
  DLS verifies user credentials. If the user credentials are valid, then DLS encrypts data and keyword using master key and generates *Did*. The method of generating *Did* is given in algorithm 1. Also, DLS sets a version value *ver* to *EnData* and the associated *Did* (initially this version value is set to zero, i.e., *ver*=0) and sends *EnData*, *Did*, and *ver* to the communication server of CSP. *EnKw*, *Did*, and *ver* are stored in the local index along with some metadata (e.g., data last accessed) for further use.

Fig. 5.5 SecDSIM framework

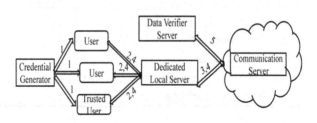

Step 4: *Accessing the data by the user*

Whenever a user wants to access data, the user sends keywords to DLS as a request.

DLS verifies his credentials for accessing the data. If his credentials are valid, then DLS fetches the *Enkw* from the local index (referred as *aided keyword search,* AKS), where a user performs a keyword search.

If the *EnKw* is found in local index, then the corresponding grade in the local index is verified by the user-provided grade for authorization is based on GAC (access privileges are implemented using GAC).

If the user grade satisfies the accessible grade, then the corresponding *Did* from the local index is retrieved and sent to the user.

The user selects the *Did* from the retrieved *Did* list for the user keyword, then DLS sends *Did* as a request to the communication server of CSP for accessing the encrypted data.

The communication server of CSP fetches *Did* from the cloud index what we refer to as *precise keyword search (PKS)*, where communication server performs exact keyword search operation on the cloud index.

If *Did* is found in the cloud index, then the communication server of CSP sends the corresponding *EnData* to DLS and updates the *ver* value of the retrieved *EnData* in the cloud index.

After receiving the *EnData* from the communication server of CSP, DLS decrypts the data and sends it back to the user. DLS updates the *ver* value of the received data in local index. The method of search operation is given in algorithm 2.

Step 5: *Process of verifying proof of storage correctness*

Whenever data verifier wants to check the correctness of the data, DVS sends *Did* to the communication server of CSP to get *ver*. Then DVS compares the *ver* value with locally stored *ver* value of that data to check the correctness of the data stored in the cloud. DVS updates the *ver* value in the local index. The method of proof of storage-correctness is given in algorithm 3.

In our framework, we are generating *Did* as a keyword for accessing the encrypted data stored in the cloud. *Did* is unique and the cloud provider cannot learn anything from it. The generation of *Did* is shown in algorithm 1, which ensures confidentiality and integrity.

Algorithm 1. Generating Data Identifier (Did)

```
1:   Procedure
2:     Choose Parameters N, i, Uid, Date, Did, n
3:     N ← Random.nextInt(99999)
4:     for i←0 to n-1 do
5:       if N already generated then
6:          goto step 3
7:       end if
8:     end for
9:     Did ← Append (Uid, Date, N)
10: end Procedure
```

The search operation is shown in algorithm 2. This is composed of three critical operations, i.e., authentication, authorization, and search. Whenever the user wants to update (modify, append, insert), he provides the *Did* to get the data from the cloud and updates it dynamically. Note that the update operation can be performed only by the owner of the data.

Algorithm 2. Search Operation

```
1:   Procedure
2:     Choose Parameters Uid, kw, T, G, n, k,
       CGrade,ver
3:     Identify the user details provided
//Authentication
4:     if grade(Uid) == G then
5:       T ← Enc(kw, k)
6:       for i←0 to n-1 do
7:         if T == secureindex(Enkws) then // Aided
     Keyword Search
8:           CGrade←secureindex(grade)
9:             if G == CGrade then // Authorization based
       on GAC
10:              print secureindex(Did)
11:            end if
12:          end if
13:       end for
14:     To send a request select the Did from the list
15:     for i←0 to n-1 do
16:       if Did == cloudindex(Did) then // Precise Key-
         word Search
17:         EnData← repository(Did)
18:         update cloudindex(ver=ver+1 of Did)
19:         return EnData
20:       end if
21:     end for
22:     update secureindex(ver=ver+1 of Did)
23:     print Data ← Dec(EnData, k)
24:     else restart Procedure
25:   end if
26: end Procedure
```

The proof of storage correctness is shown in algorithm 3. DVS verifies the correctness of the data by checking *ver* value stored locally and in the cloud. If any unauthorized views happen to user data, the *ver* value automatically increases in the cloud index but not in the local index. In such cases, DVS informs the user and the cloud provider. Thus, it achieves the integrity of the user data stored in the cloud storage server.

Algorithm 3. Proof of Storage-Correctness

```
1:   Procedure
2:     Choose Parameters n, i, Did, ver, v, ver1
3:     Did ← secureindex(Did)
4:     send(Did) to cloud
5:     ver1← cloudindex(ver of Did)
6:     update cloudindex(ver=ver+1 of Did)
5:     v ← return ver1
4:     for i←0 to n-1 do
5:        if secureindex(Did) then
6:            ver ← secureindex(ver of Did)
7:        end if
8:     end for
9:     if ver == v then
10:       Data stored correctly and Not viewed by any
11:       else Alert User and Cloud provider
12:    end if
13:    ver ← ver+1
14:    update secureindex(ver)
15: end Procedure
```

5.7 Experimental Evaluation and Discussions

We implemented SecDSIM in Java over the Java cryptography architecture (JAC) API [44]. The standard 128-bit and 192-bit AES [45] algorithms are used to implement the searchable encryption techniques under the Cipher-Block-Chaining mode. Data created by users are encrypted and stored in a text file. All these text files are stored in a repository located in the cloud server.

5.7.1   Results Analysis

To analyse the data storage in the cloud, we created a set of text files that are less than or equal to 1 Mb and another set of text files that are greater than 1 Mb. For example, different sizes of text files including 25, 57, 72, 95, 115, 130, 162, 192, and 225 kb in set I and 1.24, 2.52, 4.2, and 6.03 Mb in set II.

Figure 5.6 shows encryption and storage timings in milliseconds for different data sizes starting from 25 kb to 225 kb by using AES 128-bit key and 192-bit key algorithms in SecDSIM framework.

Figure 5.7 shows encryption and storage timings in milliseconds for large data sizes ranging from 1.2 to 6.03 Mb by using AES 128-bit key and 192-bit key algorithms in SecDSIM framework. By observing Figs. 5.6 and 5.7, we can notice that the encryption and storage timings for different sizes of data sets in SecDSIM framework are linear in nature.

Figure 5.8 presents the difference in data sizes before encryption and after encryption for data set I by using AES 128-bit key and 192-bit key algorithms. Figure 5.9 shows the different data sizes for data set II by using AES 128-bit key and 192-bit key.

Table 5.2 compares encryption timings and data file sizes after encryption using AES 128-bit key algorithm and AES 192-bit key algorithm in set I. Table 5.3 compares encryption timings and data file sizes after encryption using AES 128-bit key algorithm and AES 192-bit key algorithm in set II.

Table 5.4 compares the decryption timings of Set I data files using AES 128-bit key algorithm and AES 192-bit key algorithm. Table 5.5 compares the decryption timings of Set II data files using AES 128-bit key algorithm and AES 192-bit key algorithm.

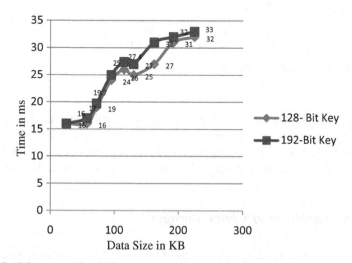

Fig. 5.6 Set I data encryption timings

Fig. 5.7 Set II data encryption timings

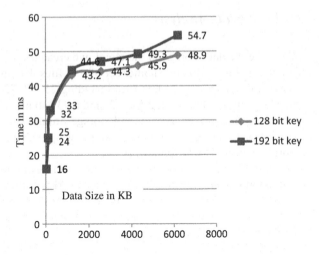

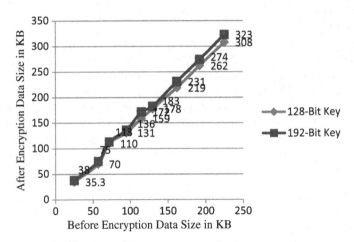

Fig. 5.8 Set I data size after encryption

By observing Tables 5.2 and 5.3, we can identify that the encrypted data sizes in SecDSIM framework are in linear in nature. We also observe that there is a small difference in AES 128-bit key algorithm and AES 192-bit key algorithm for data encryption, storing and decryption timings as well as for encrypted data sizes.

5.7.2 Comparison of Cloud Storages

Table 5.6 compares the encryption results of the SecDSIM framework with broker cloud communication paradigm (BCCP) model [46]. Figure 5.10 shows the data

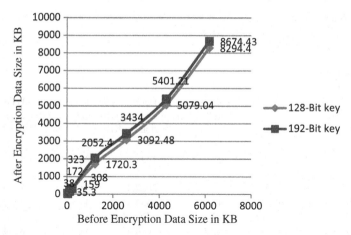

Fig. 5.9 Set II data size after encryption

Table 5.2 Summary of set 1

S. No.	Set I data/file size before encryption (in KB)	No. of words	AES(I92)		AES(128)	
			Time (In milliseconds)	Data/file size after encryption (in KB)	Time (in milliseconds)	Data/file size after encryption (in KB)
1	25	4623	16	38	16	35.3
2	57	9824	17	75	16	70
3	72	14,447	19.7	113	19	110
4	95	17,213	25	136	24	131
5	115	20,927	27.4	172	26	159
6	130	23,392	27	183	25	178
7	162	25,857	31	231	27	219
8	192	34,334	32	274	31	262
9	225	40,444	33	323	32	308

AES advanced encryption standard

encryption timings (in seconds) for different data sizes starting from 25 to 225 kb by using AES 128-bit key algorithm in SecDSIM framework and in BCCP model. Figure 5.11 shows the encrypted data sizes (in kb) for different data sizes using AES 128-bit key algorithm in SecDSIM framework and in BCCP model. In BCCP, we observe that cloud data exchange between a user and cloud storage requires more communications, thereby increasing the encryption and storage timings.

Table 5.7 shows different cryptographic techniques used in different cloud storage schemes and their role in achieving security properties. Our proposed SecDSIM framework achieves many security properties compared to other cloud storage schemes proposed by other reserchers.

Table 5.3 Summary of set II

S. no.	Set II data/file size before encryption (in KB)	No. of words	AES(192)		AES(128)	
			Time (in milliseconds)	Data/file size after encryption (in KB}	Time (in milliseconds)	Data/file size after encryption (in KB)
1	25	4623	16	38	16	35.3
2	115	20,927	25	172	24	159
3	225	40,444	33	323	32	308
4	1224	219,433	44.6	2052.4	43.2	1720.3
5	2581	462,258	47.1	3434	44.3	3092.48
6	4301	771,206	49.3	5401.21	45.9	5079.04
7	6175	107,384	54.7	8674.43	48.9	8294.4

AES advanced encryption standard

Table 5.4 Comparison of set I description timings

S. No.	Set 1 Data/File Size after Decryption (in KB)	AES (192)	AES (128)
		Time (in milliseconds)	Time (in milliseconds)
1	25	13.1	13
2	57	13.7	13
3	72	14.2	13.4
4	95	15	13.9
5	115	15.7	15
6	130	16.4	15.3
7	162	17.1	16
8	192	17.9	16.8
9	225	18.4	17.6

AES advanced encryption standard

Table 5.5 Comparison of set II description timings

S.No.	Set II data/file size after decryption (in KB)	AES (192)	AES (128)
		Time (in milliseconds)	Time (in milliseconds)
1	25	13	13
2	115	15.6	15
3	225	18.4	17.6
4	1224	31.01	27.7
5	2581	35.23	32.5
6	4301	46	42.7
7	6175	51.9	46.3

AES advanced encryption standard

Table 5.6 SecDSIM versus BCCP

S.No.	Data/file size before encryption (in KB)	AES (128)		AES (128)	
		Time (in seconds)	Data/file size after encryption (in KB)	Time (in seconds)	Data/file size after encryption (in KB)
1	25	0.5	129.04	0.016	35.3
2	57	0.7	129.04	0.016	70.01
3	72	0.9	221.65	0.019	110
4	95	0.9	222.65	0.027	131
5	115	0.9	376.18	0.022	159
6	130	1.0	406.25	0.025	178
7	162	1.2	471.47	0.027	219
8	192	1.5	477.0	0.031	262
9	225	1.9	477.15	0.032	308

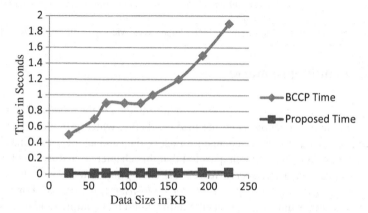

Fig. 5.10 Comparison of encryption timings with broker cloud communication paradigm (BCCP)

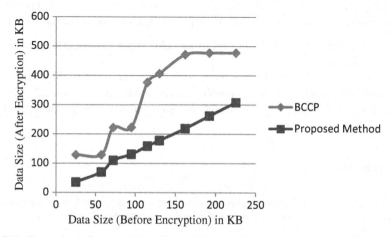

Fig. 5.11 Comparison of encrypted data sizes with broker cloud communication paradigm (BCCP)

Table 5.7 Role of cryptography in the cloud storage schemes

Cloud storage scheme	Cryptographic technique	Security properties and techniques achieved
Kamara et al. [31]	Searchable encryption, attribute-based encryption	Confidentiality
Kamara et al. [32]	Searchable encryption, search authenticator	Confidentiality, global integrity, verifiability, and searchability
Barua et al. [23]	Attribute-based encryption, identity-based encryption	Access control, confidentiality
Zarandioon et al. [25]	Attribute-based encryption and signature	Access control
Chow et al. [47]	Group signature, identity-based broadcast encryption	Access control, confidentiality
Seiger et al. [48]	Symmetric encryption with IDAs and CMAC	Confidentiality, integrity, and availability
SecDSIM	*Multi-user searchable symmetric encryption, grade-based access control*	*Confidentiality, integrity, efficient retrieval, data sharing, and verifiability*

IDAs Information Dispersal Algorithms; *CMAC* Cipher based Message Authentication Code

5.8 Concluding Remarks

In this chapter, we addressed the problem of storing data in the cloud and retrieving data securely and efficiently using the mSSE scheme, which provides an efficient isolation and secure storage mechanism for users' data and an identity management scheme using GAC. The research question that this chapter addresses is as follows: *Can we develop a provably secure searchable encryption scheme with efficient secure cloud storage which is supportable for multi-user applications?* For this, we constructed a secure data storage scheme in the cloud that comprises two steps:

- Create a secure index also called a local index for user data and create a unique data identifier for the user data.
- Encrypt and encode the user data and data identifier and store encrypted user data in the cloud as well as a data identifier in the cloud index for further access.

We implemented identity management using GAC when a user performs a search on own/other's data.

In our future work, we will attempt to further enhance our SecDSIM model for multimedia data and to address searchable symmetric encryption with wild card support and proximity-based keyword search on a local index to improve the efficiency.

References

1. Brodkin J (2 July 2008) Gartner: seven cloud-computing security risks. http://h3compuvision. com/yahoo_site_admin/assets/docs/Cloud_Computing_Security_Risk.276113314.pdf. Accessed July 2013

2. Chandramouli R, Mell P (March 2010) State of security readiness. Crossroads Plugging Cloud 16(3):23–25
3. Subashini S, Kavitha V (Jan 2001) A survey on security issues in service delivery models of cloud computing. J Netw Comput Appl 34(1):1–11
4. Zissis D, Lekkas D (March 2012) Addressing cloud computing security issues. Future Gener Comp Sy 28(3):583–592. doi:10.1016/j.future.2010.12.006
5. Khatibi V, Khatibi E (2012) Issues on cloud computing: a systematic review. International conference on computational techniques and mobile computing (ICCTMC'2012), Singapore, 14–15 Dec
6. Cloud Security Alliance (2011) Security guideline for critical areas of focus in cloud computing v3.0. Cloud Security Alliance, Singapore
7. Mell P, Grance T (Sept 2011) The NIST definition of cloud computing. NIST special publication 800-145. National Institute of Standards and Technology (NIST), Gaithersburg
8. Jansen W, Grance T (2011) Guidelines on security and privacy in public cloud computing. National Institute of Standards and Technology (NIST), Gaithersburg
9. Fiat A, Naor M (1994) Broadcast encryption. In: Stinson DR (ed) Advances in cryptology—CRYPTO '93. Lecture notes in computer science, vol 773. Springer, Berlin, pp 480–491
10. Garay JA, Staddon J, Wool A (2000) Long-lived broadcast encryption. In: Bellare M (ed) Advances in cryptology—CRYPTO 2000. Lecture notes in computer science, vol 1880. Springer, Berlin, pp 333–352
11. Halevy D, Shamir A (2002) The LSD broadcast encryption scheme. In: Yung M (ed) Advances in cryptology—CRYPTO 2002. Lecture notes in computer science, vol 2442. Springer, Berlin, pp 47–60
12. Boneh D, Gentry C, Waters B (2005) Collusion resistant broadcast encryption with short ciphertexts and private keys. Advances in cryptology—CRYPTO 2005. Lecture notes in computer science, vol 3621. Springer, Berlin, pp 258–275
13. Kumbhare A, Simmhan Y, Prasanna V (2012) Cryptonite: a secure and performant data repository on public clouds. Proceedings of the IEEE 5th international conference on cloud computing, Honolulu, 24–29 June, pp 510–517
14. Popa RA, Lorch JR, Molnar D, Wang HJ, Zhuang L (2010) Enabling security in cloud storage SLAs with CloudProof. Microsoft Tech Rep 46:1–12
15. Shamir A (1985) Identity-based cryptosystems and signature schemes. In: Blakley GR, Chaum D (eds) Advances in cryptology—proceedings of CRYPTO'84. Lecture notes in computer science, vol 196. Springer, New York, pp 47–53
16. Boneh D, Franklin M (2001) Identity-based encryption from the Weil pairing. In: Kilian J (ed) Advances in cryptology—CRYPTO 2001. Lecture notes in computer science, vol 2139. Springer, New York, pp 213–229
17. Canetti R, Halevi S, Katz J (2003) A forward-secure public-key encryption scheme. In: Biham E (ed) Advances in cryptology—EUROCRYPT 2003. Lecture notes in computer science, vol 2656. Springer, Berlin, pp 255–271
18. Boneh D, Boyen X (2004) Efficient selective-id secure identity based encryption without random oracles. In: Cachin C, Camenisch JL (eds) Advances in cryptology—EUROCRYPT 2004. Lecture notes in computer science, vol 3027. Springer, Berlin, pp 223–238
19. Sahai A, Waters B (2005) Fuzzy identity based encryption. In: Cramer R (ed) Advances in Cryptology—EUROCRYPT 2005. Lecture notes in computer science, vol 3494. Springer, Berlin, pp 457–473
20. Nali D, Adams C, Miri A (2005) Using threshold attribute-based encryption for practical biometric-based access control. Int J Netw Secur 1(3):173–182
21. Goyal V, Pandey O, Sahai A, Waters B (2006) Attribute-based encryption for fine-grained access control of encrypted data. Proceedings of the 13th ACM conference on computer and communications security, Alexandria, 30 Oct–3 Nov, pp 89–98
22. Bethencourt J, Sahai A, Waters B (2007) Cipher text-policy attribute-based encryption. Proceedings of the IEEE symposium on security and privacy, Berkeley, 20–23 May. IEEE computer society, Los Alamitos, pp 321–334

23. Barua M, Liang X, Lu R, Shen X. (2011) ESPAC: enabling security and patient-centric access control for eHealth in cloud computing. Int J Secur Netw 6(2/3):67–76. doi:10.1504/IJSN.2011.043666

24. Waters B (2011) Cipher text-policy attribute-based encryption: an expressive, efficient, and provably se-cure realization. Public key cryptography—PKC 2011. Lecture notes in computer science, vol 6571. Springer, Berlin, pp 53–70

25. Zarandioon S, Yao D, Ganapathy V (2012) K2C: cryptography cloud storage with lazy revocation and anonymous access. Security and privacy in communication networks. Lecture notes of the institute for computer sciences, vol 96. Springer, Berlin, pp 59–76

26. Goldreich O, Ostrovsky R (1996) Software protection and simulation on oblivious RAMs. J ACM 43(3):431–473

27. Song D, Wagner D, Perrig A (2000) Practical techniques for searching on encrypted data. Proceedings of the IEEE symposium on research in security and privacy, Berkeley, 14–17 May, pp 44–45

28. Boneh D, Crescenzo GD, Ostrovsky R, Persiano G. Public key encryption with keyword search. In: Cachin C, Camenisch JL (eds) Advances in cryptology—EUROCRYPT 2004. Lecture notes in computer science, vol 3027. Springer, Berlin, pp 506–522

29. Goh E-J (2003) Secure indexes. Tech Rep 216. IACR ePrint Cryptography Archive

30. Curtmola R, Garay J, Kamara S, Ostrovsky R (2006) Searchable symmetric encryption: improved definitions and efficient constructions. Proceedings of the 13th ACM conference on computer and communications security, Alexandria, 30 Oct–3 Nov, pp 79–88

31. Kamara S, Lauter K (2010) Cryptographic cloud storage. In Sion R, Curtmola R, Dietrich S, Kiayias A, Miret JM, Sako K, Sebé F (eds) Proceedings of the 14th international conference on financial cryptography and data security. Lecture notes in computer science, vol 6054. Springer, Berlin, pp 136–149

32. Kamara S, Papamanthou C, Reader T (2011) CS2: a searchable cryptographic cloud storage system. Microsoft Res Tech Rep MSR-TR-2011-58

33. Kamara S, Papamanthou C, Roeder T (2012) Dynamic searchable symmetric encryption. Proceedings of the 2012 ACM conference on computer and communications security (CCS '12), pp 965–976. doi:10.1145/2382196.2382298

34. Li M, Yu S, Cao N, Lou W (2011) Authorized private keyword search over encrypted data in cloud computing. Proceedings of the 31st IEEE international conference on distributed computing systems (ICDCS), pp 383–392. doi:10.1109/ICDCS.2011.55

35. Liu C, Zhu L, Wang M, Tan Y (2013) Search pattern leakage in searchable encryption: attacks and new constructions. Cryptology ePrint Archive, report 2013/163

36. Islam MS, Kuzu M, Kantarcioglu M (2012) Access pattern disclosure on searchable encryption: ramification, attack and mitigation. ePrint Archive. https://www.internetsociety.org/sites/default/files/06_1.pdf

37. Zhu Y, Ahn GJ, Hu H, Wang H (2010) Cryptographic role-based security mechanisms based on role-key hierarchy. Proceedings of the 5th ACM symposium on information, computer and communications security (ASIACCS '10), pp 314–319

38. Zhou L, Varadharajan V, Hitchens M (2011) Enforcing role-based access control for secure data storage in the cloud. Comp J 54(10):1675–1687. doi:10.1093/comjnl/bxr080

39. Zhou L, Varadharajan V (June 2011)Crypto-based access control schemes. INSS Technical Report, INSS-TechReport-2011.06. http://www.comp.mq.edu.au/research/inss/publications/. Accessed July 2013

40. Torres J, Nogueira M, Pujolle G (2013) A survey on identity management for the future network. Comm Surv Tutor IEEE 15(2):787–802. doi: 10.1109/SURV.2012.072412.00129

41. Celesti A, Tusa F, Villari M, Puliafito A (2010) Security and cloud computing: intercloud identity management infrastructure. Proceedings of the 19th IEEE international workshops on enabling technologies: infrastructures for collaborative enterprises (WETICE), pp 263–265

42. NIST (26 Aug 2009) A survey of access control models, working draft. http://csrc.nist.gov/news_events/privilege-management-workshop/PvM-Model-Survey-Aug26-2009.pdf. Accessed July 2013

43. Tygar JD (Dec 2002) Security with privacy. Briefing from the Information Science and Technology Study Group on Security and Privacy. http://www.cs.berkeley.edu/~tygar/papers/ISAT-final-briefing.pdf. Accessed Feb. 2013

44. Java Cryptography Architecture (JAC) (n.d.) API specification and reference. http://docs.oracle.com/javase/1.4.2/docs/guide/security/CryptoSpec.html. Accessed Feb 2013

45. National Institute of Standards and Technology (NIST) (2001) FIPS 197, Advanced Encryption Standard (AES)

46. Singh N, Raj G (July 2012) Security on BCCP through AES encryption technique. Int J Eng Sci Adv Technol 2(4):813–819

47. Chow SSM, Chu CK, Huang X, Zhou Y, Deng RH. Dynamic secure cloud storage with provenance. Cryptography and security: from theory to applications. Lecture notes in computer science, vol 6805. Springer, Berlin, pp 442–464

48. Seiger R, Stephan G, Schill A (Sept 2011) SecCSIE: a secure cloud storage integrator for enterprises. Proceedings of the 13th IEEE conference on commerce and enterprise computing (CEC), pp 252–255

20.

21.

22.

23.

24.

25.

26.

Chapter 6
CloudReports: An Extensible Simulation Tool for Energy-Aware Cloud Computing Environments

Thiago Teixeira Sá, Rodrigo N. Calheiros and Danielo G. Gomes

Abstract The cloud computing paradigm integrates several technological models to provide services to a large number of clients distributed around the world. It involves the management of large data centers that represent very complex scenarios and demand sophisticated techniques for optimization of resource utilization and power consumption. Since the utilization of real testbeds to validate such optimization techniques requires large investments, simulation tools often represent the most viable way to conduct experimentation in this field. This chapter presents CloudReports, an extensible simulation tool for energy-aware cloud computing environments to enable researchers to model multiple complex simulation scenarios through an easy-to-use graphical user interface. It provides report generation features and a simple API (Application Programming Interface) that makes possible the development of extensions that are added to the system as plugins. CloudReports is an open-source project composed of five mandatory modules and an optional extensions module. This chapter describes all these modules, their integration with the CloudSim toolkit, and a case study that demonstrates an evaluation of power consumption of data centers with a power model that is created as a CloudReports extension.

Keywords Cloud computing · Simulation tools · Energy-aware distributed systems · Energy-aware cloud computing · Infrastructure virtualization · Data center · Infrastructure management

---

D. G. Gomes (✉) · T. Teixeira Sá
Group of Computer Networks, Software Engineering and Systems (GREat),
Universidade Federal do Ceará, Av. Mister Hull, s/n, Campus do Pici,
bloco 942-A, Fortaleza—CE 60455–760, Brazil
e-mail: danielo@ufc.br

T. Teixeira Sá
e-mail: thiagosa@great.ufc.br

R. N. Calheiros
Department of Computing and Information Systems, The University of Melbourne,
Parkville, VIC 3010, Australia
e-mail: rnc@unimelb.edu.au

© Springer International Publishing Switzerland 2014
Z. Mahmood (ed.), *Cloud Computing,* Computer Communications and Networks,
DOI 10.1007/978-3-319-10530-7_6

6.1   Introduction

The cloud computing paradigm proposes the integration of different technological models to provide hardware infrastructure, development platforms, and applications as services available worldwide. It involves complex scenarios composed of multiple large data centers that provide services to clients located around the world and with different sets of requirements. The management of such complex environments demand new system architectures, protocols, and policies in order to enable optimization of resources utilization and power consumption. Since the utilization of real testbeds to validate experiments on this field requires large investments and makes replication and control of experiments harder, simulation alternatives have been broadly used. However, simulation tools either generate a large amount of data as output or force researchers to develop their own techniques to collect data, which demands an extra effort to organize and extract useful results. Thus, a tool that combines the flexibility and extensibility of simulation frameworks with functionalities that facilitate modeling and data collection would represent a significant contribution to the cloud computing research field.

Aiming to provide this contribution, CloudReports has been developed as an extensible simulation tool for energy-aware cloud computing environments. CloudReports uses the CloudSim toolkit [1] as its simulation engine and enables researchers to model multiple complex simulation environments through an easy-to-use graphical user interface. CloudReports also provides report generation features which automatically organizes simulation results and presents them with a high level of details. Additionally, it provides an API that enables the creation of extensions that are loaded as plugins using the Java Reflection API. CloudReports is an open-source project designed with multiple modules. This chapter describes all these modules and how they are integrated with CloudSim. Moreover, it presents a case study that demonstrates an evaluation of power consumption of two data centers with different power models, one of which is created as a CloudReports extension.

The rest of the chapter is organized as follows. Section 6.2 reports the state-of-the-art simulation tools aimed at distributed systems and energy-aware cloud computing environments. Sections 6.3 and 6.4 provide an overview of the CloudSim toolkit; describe the proposed CloudReports thoroughly and suggest how simulation environments are modeled to depict the software architecture with all its modules. Section 6.5 presents a case study that uses reports generation and data exporting features and demonstrates its application on the evaluation of power consumption aspects of cloud data centers. Finally, Section 6.6 presents conclusions and future work opportunities.

6.2   Related Works

A fair amount of simulation tools aimed at distributed systems and grid computing can be found, but alternatives for simulating energy-aware cloud computing environments are still very scarce. For example, the SimGrid framework [2] provides means to simulate parallel and distributed large-scale systems, and the GridSim toolkit [3] offers a flexible way to model distributed environments, applications, resources, and scheduling algorithms. However, these tools lack the key cloud computing concept of resource virtualization, thus creating the need of extensions or entirely new simulators. A toolkit that exemplifies such extensions is presented by Sulistio et al. [4], notwithstanding it is not specifically focused on cloud computing environments.

Regarding cloud computing simulation tools, the iCanCloud platform [5] is an open-source project written in C++ that aims to model and simulate cloud computing systems. It is based on the OMNET network simulation framework and offers a POSIX-based API for modeling applications. However, it does not provide means to model or simulate any aspect related to power consumption.

The GreenCloud simulator [6] is an extension to the network simulator ns2 with additional features to analyze cloud computing environments. It offers power consumption modeling for servers and network elements such as switches and links. However, it does not support virtual machines representation and application-level aspects such as job scheduling policies.

The CloudSim framework [1], which is described in the next section, is a simulation engine that supports virtual machines representation, creation of scheduling algorithms, and power consumption modeling. CloudReports is a tool that uses CloudSim as its simulation engine and manages all the data created during experiments. Furthermore, it provides a graphical user interface for modeling and managing environments to be simulated.

Aksanli et al. [7] performed a comparative study where they analyzed data center simulation tools in order to evaluate green computing performance. The study highlights the features of eight simulators according to the types of resources that are simulated, how workloads are modeled, the queuing model that is used, the ability to simulate power models, the support to virtual machines simulation, the licensing applied to the project, and the type of information that each simulator generates as output. It also introduces a new simulator (GENSim) and evaluates its use to analyze different green energy integration methods in a data center in order to find the most energy-efficient solution. Additionally, Kocaoglu et al. [8] explore some of the key aspects of green computing and communications as it stresses the importance of simulation tools for evaluating new system architectures and protocols. Finally, opportunities and challenges that arise with the advent of energy-aware cloud computing environments simulators are discussed by Buyya et al. [9], and results obtained from the use of these tools are presented in the derived works [1, 10, 11].

6.3   CloudSim Toolkit

CloudSim is a toolkit for modeling and simulation of cloud computing environments. It offers abstractions representing physical hosts, data centers, virtual machines, and costumers of cloud services. Latest versions of the tool also support modeling of internal data center networks and energy consumption of different physical elements.

Abstractions provided by the toolkit support mainly simulation of IaaS-related (Infrastructure as a Service) components, but they can be extended by users to support simulation of PaaS (Platform as a Service), and SaaS (Software as a Service).

A simulation is constituted by the interaction between cloud providers (represented as data centers) and cloud users (modeled in the form of brokers, that may represent one or more users generating requests for the cloud providers). Users can query data center about its capabilities, request creation of virtual machines, and submit requests for execution of applications (named *Cloudlets* in CloudSim). The decision about how the requested virtual machines are mapped to the data center's hosts is defined by a *provisioning policy*. Similarly, decisions on how the host resources are divided among VMs (Virtual Machines) running on the host, and how resources assigned to a VM are divided among applications running on it are defined by *VM scheduling* and *Cloudlet scheduling* policies, respectively. A few default policies are part of CloudSim, and users can develop and evaluate their own policies for these purposes.

The modeling of application execution is achieved with a field *length* in the Cloudlet object that represents the amount of computing instructions required to complete the execution of the Cloudlet. CPU cores, which are other characteristic of hosts, have a processing capacity expressed in instructions per second. Notice that both the properties are generic in the sense that no specific unit for measuring the processing capacity and processing requirement is specified. Therefore, cores can either be modeled based on well known CPU benchmarks, such as the SPEC CPU, or can assume a user-defined arbitrary value to represent relative computing capacity among different processors and relative execution time among Cloudlets. When a Cloudlet is scheduled to a specific VM, an estimation of the required execution time is computed based on the amount of resources allocated to the VM, the specific scheduling policy in place, and the number of other Cloudlets executing on the same machine. Once the estimation is calculated, an internal event is generated in the data center entity and scheduled for the estimated finish time. When such an event is triggered, executions of Cloudlets are updated, and the number of instructions already computed is updated. When all the instructions of a Cloudlet are computed, the Cloudlet is considered completed. At each update round, the expected completion time of Cloudlets is also recalculated and update events are generated accordingly because the number of Cloudlets in a VM may have changed, and thus more resources might have become available for other Cloudlets, that might have reduced the expected time for completion.

Besides abstractions to model cloud-related entities, CloudSim contains a discrete-event simulation core that coordinates interactions between cloud providers and cloud users. The core receives messages from the entities, controls clock advance, and delivers messages to the destination entities respecting event delivery time stamps. In the earlier versions of CloudSim, the SimJava [12] library provided the simulation core. However, the utilization of such a library imposes restrictions on the scalability and performance of CloudSim. This is because the SimJava engine is based on threads, and in fact, three threads were generated for each entity: one for the input channel (to receive messages from other entities), the second for the output channel (to send messages to other entities) and the third for the entity itself (to control the entity operation). As threads are scarce resources that are managed by operating systems, there is a limit on the maximum number of threads that can run in the operating system at any moment. This indirectly limits the scalability of the simulation, as the number of users and data centers are bounded by such a limit. Furthermore, utilization of threads generates inefficiencies at the operating system scheduling process because, eventually threads that have no operation to perform will receive CPU time.

To counter the above factors limiting the scalability of the simulator, CloudSim, since its version 2.0, contains a single-threaded simulation core that replaced the SimJava library. In order to keep backward compatibility with simulations written with earlier versions of CloudSim, the new core implements the same APIs than SimJava and contains equivalent objects that are accessible by user-generated code. Therefore, data centers and users still extend a *SimEntity* class whose message passage is controlled by the simulation core; and messages are *SimEvents* that contain a destination, tag, send time, and a generic payload, which is unpacked and interpreted by each entity. The new core also adds new features to the simulation engine such as the possibility of defining predicates that enable filtering events based on their characteristics, such as source, destination, and type. Filtered events can be handled in a different way by the system, if required for meeting particular demands of CloudSim users.

At the end of a simulation, information about execution time of Cloudlets, cost related to resource usage, and other user-defined information are available in objects generated during the execution. CloudSim users are responsible for writing the code for extracting such information from objects and presenting them. Nevertheless, the only type of output offered by CloudSim toolkit is printing in a command line terminal. Similarly, the only native way offered to CloudSim users to write a simulation is writing the corresponding Java code. Therefore, if richer visualization or more intuitive methods for expression of simulations are required, they have to be written by users. This motivated the design and development of CloudReports, which is detailed in the next section.

6.4 CloudReports Simulation Tool

CloudReports is a highly extensible simulation tool for energy-aware Cloud Computing environments. The tool uses the CloudSim toolkit as its simulation engine and provides features such as a graphic user interface, reports generation, simulation data exportation, and an API that enables researchers to develop their own policies by creating extensions. CloudReports simplifies the creation and configuration of simulation environments which can be manipulated and saved for later use. Researchers can create multiple data centers with different amount of resources and configure each of their hosts individually. Moreover, client behavior can be customized by setting the amount of virtual machines to be deployed and specifying the applications (Cloudlets) that will run on them. The resources required by each virtual machine is also entirely customizable.

CloudReports allows simulations to be executed in batches, which means that researchers can determine how many realizations must be executed and the amount of time that will be simulated. After completion of all simulations, the tool generates a full report composed of a log of operations and several charts with detailed information related to resources usage, virtual machine allocations, Cloudlet execution, and data center energy consumption. Furthermore, additional files are created to enable output data to be exported to third-party applications such as MATLAB and Octave.

As previously mentioned, CloudSim uses scheduling policies and provisioning policies to make decisions during the simulation process. CloudReports provides an API that enables researchers to develop new policies which are loaded during execution time using the Java Reflection API. In order to develop an extension, researchers do not need to make any modifications to the CloudReports source code whatsoever. Notwithstanding, due to the modular characteristics of CloudReports architecture, new scheduling and provisioning algorithms can be created separately without loss of generality while making use of all CloudSim features. The following subsections address CloudReports simulation environments, its core entities, the extensions functionalities, how simulations are managed, the persistence layer, the reports manager, and the graphical user interface.

6.4.1 Simulation Environments

CloudReports manages one or more simulation environments simultaneously. These environments reproduce the interaction between IaaS providers and cloud users. As depicted in Fig. 6.1, the provider owns a cloud with an arbitrary number of data centers, which are modeled according to their operating systems, processors architecture, hypervisors, available network bandwidth, utilization costs, and virtual machines allocation policies. Moreover, each data center is composed of a customizable number of hosts that are configured according to their available RAM, network bandwidth, storage capacity, processing power, virtual machine schedulers, and energy consumption models.

Clients are modeled through a resource utilization profile and settings regarding their virtual machines that will be deployed on hosts located at the provider's infrastructure. The resource utilization profile describes the clients' applications and a high-level policy that selects data centers to deploy virtual machines. This policy is represented by a simulation entity called broker that also defines how Cloudlets will be managed, and in which virtual machine they will be executed.

Cloudlets are modeled using characteristics such as necessary amount of processor cores, size in million instructions per second (MIPS), length of input and output files that are transferred between clients and providers, and utilization models for CPU, bandwidth, and memory. A virtual machine configuration includes its image size, number of processors, processing capacity in MIPS, amount of RAM and bandwidth, type of hypervisor, and Cloudlet scheduling policy.

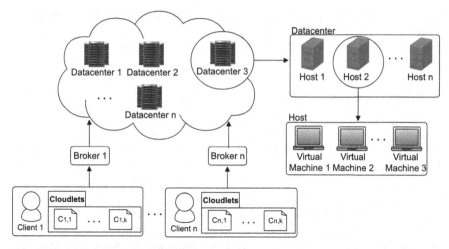

Fig. 6.1 CloudReports' simulation environment

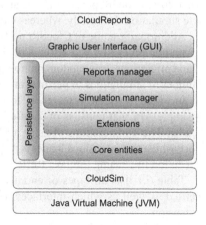

Fig. 6.2 Modular software architecture of CloudReports

6.4.2 Software Architecture

The CloudReports software architecture follows a modular design as depicted in Fig. 6.2. It currently contains five mandatory modules and an optional extensions module. The next sections describe in detail the functionalities of each of these elements and how they interact with each other.

6.4.2.1 CloudReports Core Entities

The core entities define the basic structure supporting CloudReports operation. They consist of classes that represent entities such as customers, data centers, physical

Table 6.1 List of enumerations, classes, and interfaces used to develop CloudReports extensions

CloudReports enumeration	Extensions	
	Must inherit from	Must implement
AllocationPolicy	VmAllocationPolicy	VmAllocationPolicy—Extensible
BrokerPolicy	Broker	–
BwProvisioner	BwProvisioner	–
RamProvisioner	RamProvisioner	–
PeProvisioner	PeProvisioner	–
VmScheduler	VmScheduler	–
CloudletScheduler	CloudletScheduler	–
UtilizationModel	–	UtilizationModel
PowerModel	–	PowerModel

machines, virtual machines, networks, and storage area networks. Although being a part of CloudReports, these classes work in tandem with the Simulation Manager module to translate environments created through the graphical user interface into CloudSim entities, which are the only entities that are used during simulation time. Therefore, CloudReports works as an abstraction layer that helps users to manipulate simulation data easily, whereas CloudSim remains as the simulation engine.

Additionally, some of CloudReports core entities help in the management aspect of simulation events and settings of the software itself. These include virtual machine migrations, true random number generation, reports data, and settings such as number of simulations to perform and e-mail notifications.

In order to enable researchers to create new policies, CloudReports provides a simple API that consists of a set of enumerations, interfaces, and an extensions loader. The enumerations classify all kinds of extensions that CloudReports support, whilst the extensions loader is responsible for loading all extensions during the execution time using the Java Reflection API.

Table 6.1 lists all types of enumerations and shows which classes must be inherited as well as which interfaces must be implemented in order to develop an extension.

The AllocationPolicy extension extends VmAllocationPolicy and implements VmAllocationPolicyExtensible. It determines how data centers allocate virtual machines among servers. The BrokerPolicy extends the Broker class and describes a set of rules that clients make use to define how virtual machines are sent to allocation and how Cloudlets are sent to execution considering all the available data centers. The BwProvisioner, RamProvisioner, and PeProvisioner extensions inherit from CloudSim's namesake classes and define how servers provide bandwidth, RAM, and processing elements to the virtual machines they allocate. Moreover, the VmScheduler extension inherits from CloudSim's VmScheduler and describes how servers schedule the execution of these virtual machines. The CloudScheduler inherits from CloudSim's CloudletScheduler that determines how virtual machines schedule the Cloudlets they run. The UtilizationModel extension implements CloudSim's UtilizationModel interface and enables defining how Cloudlets make use of the resources provided to them. Finally, the PowerModel extension implements CloudSim's PowerModel interface and makes it possible to create new CloudSim power models.

6.4.2.2   Extensions

The extensions module is entirely composed of user-implemented code. Although its existence is not mandatory, it represents one of the main features of CloudReports, as it enables researchers to simulate their own algorithms without modifying CloudSim or CloudReports source code. By following a small set of rules, researchers can add new virtual machine allocation policies, data center brokers, Cloudlet schedulers, resource utilization models, virtual machine schedulers, processing elements, RAM, and bandwidth provisioners. Moreover, this module also enables the development of new power consumption models. CloudSim 3.0 already offers over a dozen types of power consumption models including options with specific hardware specifications. Researches can either extend these models or create entirely new ones as long as they follow the rules set by the extensions API provided by CloudReports.

In order to create a new extension, the researcher first needs to identify which of the aforementioned extension categories better models the algorithm that needs to be simulated. For instance, if the researcher needs to simulate a new broker policy, Table 6.1 states that it is necessary to implement a new class that inherits from CloudReport's Broker class. This new class will only contain code that is related to the new broker policy. Therefore, the researcher will be able to focus entirely on creating the new algorithm instead of having to deal with code that is related to simulator configuration. After creating this new class, a JAR (Java Archive) file needs to be created with the implementation of the new broker policy including all possible code dependencies it may have. Finally, a descriptive XML (Extensible Markup Language) file is created with all information that is necessary for CloudReports to load the new extension. Technically detailed information regarding development of extensions can be found in CloudReports project's official repository on GitHub.

6.4.2.3   Simulation Manager

The simulation manager module consists of two basic elements, namely an entity factory and a simulations handler. The entity factory is responsible for turning CloudReports environments into a set of CloudSim entities, which will then be used during simulation time. The simulations handler retrieves all settings related to simulation execution and starts the simulation process. After the execution of each simulation instance, it triggers the generation of the respective report and then starts the next realization. The module is also responsible for sending e-mail notifications and handling simulation time errors.

6.4.2.4 Persistence Layer

The persistence layer stores all application and simulation data in a single SQLite database file per environment. This approach facilitates the management of multiple environments as each file can be used independently and handled without execution of the application for means of backup. Moreover, since each environment makes use of a different database, it prevents tables from getting too large and keeps data access time reasonably low. However, since SQLite databases are not suitable for applications that need to process very large amounts of data, it is recommended that researchers replace the persistence layer module with more robust database solutions if they wish to perform highly scalable data-intensive simulations and keep data access time at low levels.

6.4.2.5 Reports Manager

The reports manager collects, organizes, and processes simulation data from database files and generates simulation reports. The reports are composed of HTML (HyperText Markup Language) and raw data files. The HTML files contain general information about data centers and customers, which include overall and per host power consumption. The report manager uses all simulation data to generate charts automatically and include them in the HTML report files. Raw data files consist of a compilation of simulation data in a single text file that is ready to be imported by third-party applications such as MATLAB and Octave. This module acts every time the simulation manager triggers a report generation. After completing a report, it notifies the simulation manager so the next simulation realization can take place.

6.4.2.6 Graphical User Interface

As the topmost module, the graphical user interface provides a simple way for researchers to manage environments and keep track of simulation progress. The GUI (Graphical User Interface) allows creation and manipulation of data centers, hosts, storage area networks, customers, virtual machines, and network links. Furthermore, researchers can set data centers' costs of operation, modify application settings, select scheduling and provisioning policies, and resource utilization models, and also determine which environments should be used during the next simulations batch. This module is written using the Swing Java GUI widget toolkit, thus, it is also platform-independent and highly customizable. Figure 6.3 shows a screenshot of CloudReports GUI.

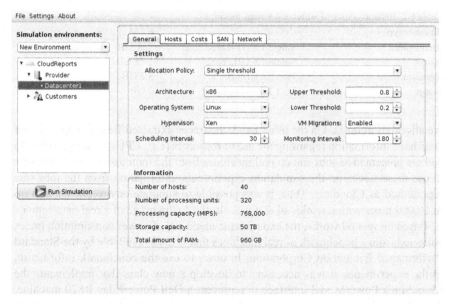

Fig. 6.3 A screenshot of CloudReports graphical user interface

6.5   Case Study

The simulation environments created using CloudReports are composed of an IaaS provider and an arbitrary amount of cloud users. The IaaS provider may have one or more data centers, each of which are modeled independently with characteristics such as virtual machines allocation policies, operational costs and resource utilization thresholds. Moreover, it is possible to configure every data center's host individually. The cloud users are modeled as a set of virtual machines to be allocated by the infrastructure managed by the IaaS provider and a utilization profile. Each virtual machine can be configured using characteristics such as CPU and memory demand, type of hypervisor, and a Cloudlet scheduler. The utilization profile determines how Cloudlets are going to behave regarding resource utilization once they are executed. Furthermore, it provides a brokering policy through which it is possible to determine which data center is going to deploy a specific virtual machine.

As workload modeling plays a decisive role on the results of simulation experiments, it is necessary to use a model that is as similar as possible to real data center environments. Therefore, the experiments presented in this case study made use of data collected from the Google Cluster Data project which makes publicly available a set of resource utilization traces from a real cluster with approximately 12,000 machines managed by Google.

The workload applied to the simulated environments is modeled in CloudSim as tasks which are represented by the Cloudlet class, to be run on virtual machines that

Table 6.2 Instance types of simulated virtual machines

Instance type	CPU	RAM
Extra-small	Single 1 GHz shared core	768 MB
Small	Single 1.6 GHz core	1.75 GB
Medium	Two 1.6 GHz cores	3.5 GB
Large	Four 1.6 GHz cores	7 GB

are allocated in hosts. On the other hand, the traces extracted from Google Cluster Data have information regarding the use of resources (e.g., CPU, memory, and disk) and are presented as jobs run on real machines from the monitored cluster. In order to use these traces on the simulation experiments, information from the jobs was represented as Cloudlets. Thus, it was possible to simulate environments with up to 10,000 hosts with a workload that was similar to the usage of a real data center.

Based on related works, the experiments made use of power consumption traces collected from a benchmark of real machines that is made available by the Standard Performance Evaluation Corporation. In order to use the benchmark information in the experiments, it was necessary to develop a new class that implements the CloudSim's PowerModel interface to represent a Dell PowerEdge R820 machine. Therefore, all data centers represented in the experiments of this case study are composed of a set of machines of the same model. As the benchmark data provides power consumption information in Watts based on discrete levels of load applied to a machine, creating this new power consumption model on CloudSim was straight-forward as the framework already deals with power consumption based on load levels applied to the simulated hosts.

Four different virtual machine allocation policies were used in the experiments. These policies determine how the controller node should distribute virtual machines among all the available hosts. Therefore, such policies play a decisive role on the overall power consumption of the data center. The simulated policies are listed below:

- *Single Static Threshold (SST)*: this policy has a single utilization threshold that determines if a host is overloaded.
- *Double Static Threshold (DST)*: this policy has two utilization thresholds. The first determines if a host is overloaded and the second is used to identify under-used hosts.
- *Median Absolute Deviation-Minimum Migration Time*: this policy has dynamic utilization thresholds and was extracted from a related work [13].
- *Local Regression-Minimum Migration Time*: this policy also has dynamic utilization thresholds and, such as the previous policy, was extracted from a related work [13].

Regarding the virtual machines configuration, the experiments used four types of profiles based on services from a real IaaS provider. Table 6.2 shows detailed information about computing capacity and available memory for each of the four profiles. All experiments made use of equal amounts of virtual machines for each of the profiles.

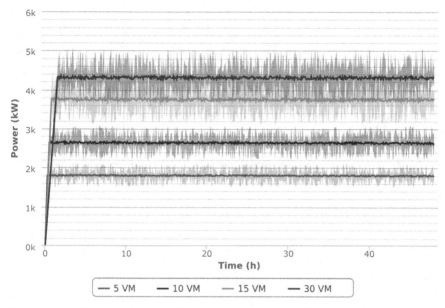

Fig. 6.4 Power consumption of a 10,000 nodes data center with a Single Static Threshold allocation policy

Figure 6.4 shows the power consumption of a data center with 10,000 hosts during a 48 h period of operation with the Single Static Threshold allocation policy. Each line represents a different rate of virtual machines allocated per host. The shaded areas around the lines represent a 90 % level confidence interval. The chart shows that power consumption increases proportionally with the amount of virtual machines allocated per host. Such behavior was expected, since, the higher the load applied to the system, the higher will be the level of resource usage, which increases the overall power consumption of the data center.

Figure 6.5 shows simulation results for an environment similar to the aforementioned but using the Double Static Threshold allocation policy. In this case, it is possible to identify a nearly linear relation between the amount of virtual machines allocated per host and the Consumption Stabilization Interval (CSI), which is defined as the period of time from the beginning of the simulation setup interval until the moment when the power consumption of the data center reaches a stable level. For the specific rate of 30 virtual machines per host, the DST policy performance is very similar to the SST policy. This happens because this rate of virtual machine allocation always keeps the data center with overloaded hosts, which undermines the DST capacity to identify underused hosts and reallocate virtual machines appropriately. This type of reallocations define what is commonly called consolidation techniques. For all other rates of virtual machines allocated per host, it is noticeable that immediately after the simulation setup time, virtual machines start to be consolidated which decreases the power consumption levels significantly.

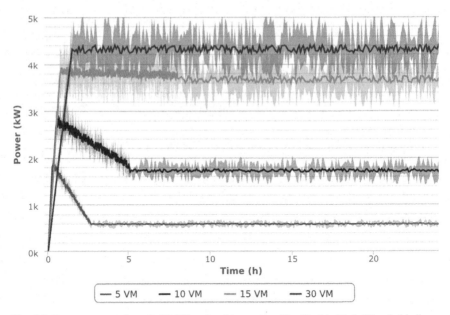

Fig. 6.5 Power consumption of a 10,000 nodes data center with a Double Static Threshold allocation policy

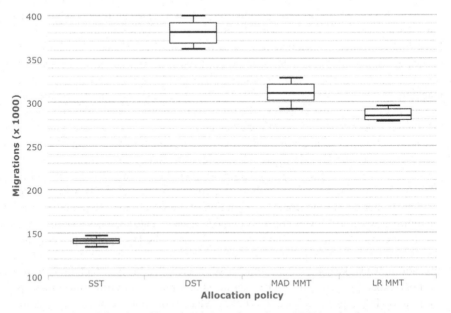

Fig. 6.6 Number of virtual machine migrations performed on a 10,000 nodes data center

The boxplot in Fig. 6.6 shows the number of virtual machine migrations performed for each of the allocation policies. The lowest levels are shown for the SST policy due to the lack of consolidation techniques as this policy cannot identify underused hosts. Hence, despite the low amount of migrations for the SST policy, the previous charts showed that the lack of consolidation techniques has a negative impact on the power consumption of the data center. On the other hand, all the other allocation policies present higher amounts of migrations, which result in lower levels of power consumption. It is important to notice that virtual machine migrations have a significant impact on the Quality of Service (QoS) provided to the end user. Therefore, there is a trade-off relationship between power consumption and QoS that must be considered while deciding which allocation policy should be applied in order to manage virtual machine migrations in a data center.

6.6   Conclusion

This chapter presented CloudReports as a tool aimed at facilitating the modeling of energy-aware cloud computing environments and data collection of simulation results from the CloudSim simulation toolkit. Related works were discussed in order to provide an overview of existing options for simulating energy-aware cloud computing environments. Moreover, some of CloudSim's key functionalities were addressed. As CloudSim represents the core simulation engine used by CloudReports, a description of how its components work and their evolution to the current version of the project was provided. Then, the architecture of CloudReports was fully described. In order to provide a clear and complete understanding of how the simulator works, the core entities were discussed, followed by descriptions on how to create new extensions and how CloudReports' modules work together. Moreover, the chapter presented a case study that used CloudReports and a power model extension to evaluate the power consumption of a data center with 10,000 machines. The case study applied different virtual machine allocation policies and showed that there is a trade-off between the QoS offered to the end user and the total power consumption of the data center. Furthermore, it also became clear that the virtual machine allocation policy applied in the data center has a great influence is this trade-off.

As the future work, we intend to add statistical analysis to the reports and integrate new CloudSim features to the graphic user interface such as intra-data center networks and the utilization of real workloads. As CloudReports is an open-source project, its source code is available online on GitHub, what enables researchers to create feature branches that can later be integrated to CloudReports' main project.

References

1.   Calheiros RN, Ranjan R, Beloglazov A, De Rose CAF, Buyya R (2011) Cloudsim: a toolkit for modeling and simulation of cloud computing environments and evaluation of resource provisioning algorithms. Softw Pract Exp 41:23–50
2.   Casanova H, Legrand A, Quinson M (2008) SimGrid: a generic framework for large-scale distributed experiments. Proceedings of the tenth international conference on computer modeling and simulation, UKSIM'08. IEEE Computer Society, Washington, DC, pp 126–131

3. Buyya R, Murshed M (2002) Gridsim: a toolkit for the modeling and simulation of distributed resource management and scheduling for grid computing. Concurr Comput Pract Exp 14:1175–1220
4. Sulistio A, Cibej U, Venugopal S, Robic B, Buyya R (2008) A toolkit for modelling and simulating data grids: an extension to gridsim. Concurr Comput Pract Exp 20:1591–1609
5. Nez A, Vzquez-Poletti A, Caminero A, Casta G, Carretero J, Llorente I (2012) iCanCloud: a flexible and scalable cloud infrastructure simulator. J Grid Comput 10:185–209. doi:10.1007/s10723-012-9208-5
6. Kliazovich D, Bouvry P, Audzevich Y, Khan S (2010) Greencloud: a packet-level simulator of energy-aware cloud computing data centers. In: Global Telecommunications Conference (GLOBECOM 2010), IEEE, pp 1–5
7. Aksanli B, Venkatesh J, Rosing T (2012) Using datacenter simulation to evaluate green energy integration. Computer 45:56–64
8. Kocaoglu M, Malak D, Akan O (2012) Fundamentals of green communications and computing: modeling and simulation. Computer 45:40–46
9. Buyya R, Ranjan R, Calheiros RN (2009) Modeling and simulation of scalable cloud computing environments and the cloudsim toolkit: challenges and opportunities. Proceedings of the international conference on high performance computing & simulation (HPC & S'09), IEEE Computer Society, Leipzig, pp 1–11
10. Beloglazov A, Buyya R (2010) Energy efficient allocation of virtual machines in cloud data centers, 2010. In: 10th IEEE/ACM international conference on cluster, cloud and grid computing (CCGrid), Melbourne, pp 577–578
11. Kim KH, Beloglazov A, Buyya R (2009) Power-aware provisioning of cloud resources for real-time services. Proceedings of the 7th international workshop on middleware for grids, clouds and e-science, MGC'09, ACM, New York, 1:1–1:6
12. Howell F, Mcnab R (1998) SimJava: a discrete event simulation library for java. Proceedings of the first international conference on web-based modeling and simulation, SCS, San Diego, pp 51–56
13. Beloglazov A, Buyya R (2012) Optimal online deterministic algorithms and adaptive heuristics for energy and performance efficient dynamic consolidation of virtual machines in cloud data centers. Concurr Comput Pract Exp 24:1397–1420

Chapter 7
Cloud Computing: Efficient Congestion Control in Data Center Networks

Chi Harold Liu, Jian Shi and Jun Fan

Abstract Today's data center networks (DCNs) are expected to support large number of different bandwidth-hungry applications with increased amounts of data for purposes such as real-time search and data analysis. As a result, significant challenges are imposed to identify the cause of link congestion between any pair of switch ports that may severely damage the overall network performance. Generally, it is expected that the granularity of the flow monitoring to diagnose network congestion in DCNs needs to be down to the flow level on a physical port of a switch in real time with high estimation accuracy, low computational complexity, and good scalability. In this chapter, motivated by a comprehensive study of a real DCN trace, we propose two sketch-based algorithms, namely "α-CU" and "P(d)-CU," which are based on the existing conservative update (CU) approach. The α-CU algorithm adds no extra implementation cost to the traditional CU, and also successfully trades off the achieved error with time complexity. The P(d)-CU algorithm fully considers the amount of skew for different types of network services to aggregate traffic statistics of each type of network traffic at an individual and horizontally partitioned sketch. We also introduce a way to produce the real-time moving average of the reported results. By theoretical analysis and sufficient experimental results on a real DCN trace, we extensively evaluate the proposed and existing algorithms on their error performance, recall, space cost, and time complexity.

Keywords Data center networks · Flow monitoring · Flow analysis · Sketching techniques · Streaming algorithms · Trace study · sFlow

C. H. Liu (✉) · J. Shi · J. Fan
School of Software, Beijing Institute of Technology, 100081 Beijing, P.R. China
e-mail: chiliu@bit.edu.cn

J. Shi
e-mail: mirroer@gmail.com

J. Fan
e-mail: jfan@bit.edu.cn

© Springer International Publishing Switzerland 2014   143
Z. Mahmood (ed.), *Cloud Computing,* Computer Communications and Networks,
DOI 10.1007/978-3-319-10530-7_7

7.1 Introduction

Recent years have been witnessing the evolving trend of data center networks (DCNs) [2] from relatively a small-scale to lining up tens of thousands of servers and harnessing petaflops of computation power with petabytes of storage in a cost-efficient manner [8]. The analysis of massive data sets is a major driver for today's data centers. For example, the web-based information retrieval highly relies on the continuous collection and mining countless web pages and click-stream data to build fresh indexes and improve search quality. To support a variety of distinct applications and manage the exploding data, adequate bandwidth ultimately becomes the most critical part for the smooth running of many distributed infrastructures, e.g., GFS, BigTable [19, 23], Yahoo's Hadoop, PIG [13, 33], and Microsoft's Cosmos Scope [4]. Furthermore, these bandwidth-hungry applications in a DCN are (mostly) running distributed algorithms, such as MapReduce [12], which shuffles the data with growing size from one virtual machine to the other sitting across potentially different server rack. DCNs are typically constructed as a tree-based hierarchical topology, as shown in Fig. 7.1, where top-of-rack (ToR) switches, switches in the aggregation layer, and routers in core layers form a multiroot tree. As the number of core layer routers is far smaller than that of the servers at the bottom, the root nodes can easily become the bottleneck of the entire network performance. The flows, generated by applications, usually come and go very quickly and dynamically, and thus the unexpected sudden traffic increase may cause some links between a pair of switch port in a DCN to be highly congested and cause bandwidth overuse.

Although, various redundant topologies and routing algorithms [2] have been proposed to optimize the DCN architecture so that the potential congestion can be alleviated, they all rely on the accurate and efficient flow monitoring and analysis method to identify the cause of congestion on a physical port of a switch. It is then expected to infer a taxonomy of network traffic and classify flows as "elephant" and "mice" [24], where the elephant's bursty behavior may cause network congestion. To facilitate the flow monitoring and analysis in an efficient manner, protocols such as NetFlow [25] and IFPIX [10] are proposed to collect IP traffic information from switches, and later sFlow [31] is instrumented to sample packets (typically, 1 in 1000) from the switch hardware so that only a subset of packet headers from overall huge volume of data are transferred to the flow analyzer. Even so, the aggregated amount of records in a short period of time is still overwhelming and growing over time. Thus, it is impractical to store all of them in a persistent database and further identify elephants via database querying. Then, application-oriented [30] and per-flow based approaches [27] are proposed, but the former type of methods needs specific application support, and the latter suffers from the scalability issues.

Towards this end, streaming algorithms [32] are used as runtime solutions. The input items to the algorithm are the key–value pairs as a stream, where the key can represent the distinct pair of source–destination IP addresses, and the value is the amount of carried workload in that flow. Therefore, the same key may appear randomly and repetitively many times when time passes by; and the goal of the algorithm is to identify a set of IP pairs carrying most of the workload within a time

Fig. 7.1 An illustrative example of the commodity hierarchical DCN architecture

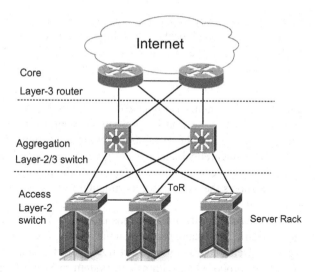

period, as elephants. The algorithms can be implemented in different kinds of data structures. The first category of methods are the counter-based algorithms, which use a one-dimensional array of counters to track a small portion of inputs. Some examples are Lossy Counting (LC) [11] and Space Saving (SS) [14]. For limited storage space, they decide whether to store the newly arrived item or not, but unfortunately fail to provide estimations for any particular flow from the entire inputs with satisfactory accuracy. The second category is the sketch-based algorithms [5], which uses a fixed two-dimensional array of counters to track/summarize a large number of statistics over time (while none of the inputs are lost track of). Some examples are Count-Min (CM) and Conservative Update (CU) [3, 6]. Although, streaming algorithms are easy to implement and show good scalability, current proposals have not sufficiently considered the trade-off between error performance, memory cost, and time complexity. Especially, SS and LC suffer from the scale of inputs, CM achieves good time complexity but with inevitable estimation error, and CU improves the error performance with the sacrifice of running time.

Motivated by these facts, we reexamined the performance of existing streaming techniques to profile the DCN performance and explicitly made the following five contributions in this chapter:

We also provide a comprehensive analysis of a real DCN traffic data set on the carried workload and traffic classifications which provides insights to enhance the existing sketch-based streaming algorithms.

- We propose "α-CU" to trade-off the estimation accuracy and time complexity between CM and CU algorithms with zero implementation cost to existing approaches.
- We propose "P(d)-CU" to partition CU along the vertical dimension of the sketch, while fully considering the amount of skew for different network services to achieve both high accuracy and low computational complexity.

- We propose a way to perform real-time moving average on the reported results for sketch-based algorithms with high accuracy.
- We show extensive experimental results on a real DCN trace against the space cost, update, recall, average relative error (ARE), and compute time, compared with existing approaches.

The rest of the chapter is organized as follows. Section 7.2 highlights the related research activities. Section 7.3 presents the insights to DCN traffic by a real trace. Section 7.4 presents the existing sketching algorithms. Enhanced CU algorithms and detailed theoretical analysis are given in Sects. 7.5 and 7.6. Section 7.7 provides the end-to-end system architecture of the proposed analysis algorithms, and Sect. 7.8 shows the extensive experimental results. Finally, conclusions are drawn in Sect. 7.9.

This chapter significantly extends the approch discussed in [1], by providing a more specific and detailed survey on the related research activities in Sect. 7.2, giving a comprehensive analysis of a real DCN traffic data set to introduce the motivation of our proposed algorithms and system in Sect. 7.3, presenting entire system architecture for DCN traffic monitoring and analysis (in Sect. 7.7), and demonstrating more extensive performance evaluation results and corresponding analysis in Sect. 7.8.

7.2 Related Works

Much research efforts have been expanded to identify the elephant flows [16–18] consisting of three categories: application-oriented approaches [9, 30], per-flow based traffic monitoring [15, 27], and streaming algorithms [3, 6, 11, 14, 20–22, 32].

In the application-oriented approaches, the research reported in [30] focuses on giving higher priority to latency and throughput-sensitive flows like voice and video applications, which is impractical for traffic management in data centers because it needs the modification of each application. Another approach is to classify traffic by the source applications which initiates them using stochastic machine learning techniques [9]. Nevertheless, it suffers from the difficulty in obtaining flow traces to train the classification algorithms.

The per-flow based approaches, e.g., Hedera [27] and Helios [15], monitor each flow at the ingress switch. Then, the controller will pull the statistical data from switches at regular intervals to further classify the elephant flows. However, this approach does not scale to large networks due to its significant consumption of switch resources. Moreover, the limited bandwidth between switches and the controller also becomes the bottleneck for network traffic management.

The streaming algorithms [32] can generally be classified into two categories. The first category consists of the counter-based algorithms, which track a subset of items from the inputs and monitor counts associated with these items. Demaine et al. [21] proposed the Frequent algorithm to solve the Hot Items problem that keeps counters to monitor elements. If a monitored element is observed, its counter is incremented, else all counters are decremented. In case any counter reaches 0, it is assigned the next observed element. Manku and Motwani [11] proposed the LC, which splits an input stream of elements into fixed-size windows and processes each window sequentially. For each element in a window, it inserts an entry into a table, or, if the element is already in the table, it updates its frequency. At the end of each window, the algorithm removes elements of small frequency from the table. In [14], the authors proposed SS, where (item, count) pairs are stored, initialized by the first distinct items and their exact counts. When the next item in the sequence corresponds to a monitored item, its count is incremented. But, when the next item does not match a monitored item, the (item, count) pair with the smallest count has its item value replaced with the new item and the count incremented. Unfortunately, LC and SS are only applicable when tracking a very small amount of items from the input stream but fail to provide aggregated statistics for any particular flow.

The second category consists of the sketch-based algorithms. Sketch-based techniques do not monitor a subset of elements but rather provide frequency estimation for all elements by using bit-maps of counters with less-stringent guarantees. Usually, each element is hashed into the space of counters using a family of hash functions, and the hashed-to counters are updated for every hit of this element. Cormode and Muthukrishnan [20] proposed the GroupTest algorithm that maintains a small space data structure that monitors the transactions on the relation, and when required, quickly outputs all hot items without rescanning the relation in the database. Estan and Varghese [22] proposed the Multistage filters approach by hashing every element to a number of counters which are updated every time the element is observed in the stream. Other well-known approaches are CM [6] and CU [3], as detailed in Sect. 7.4. They aim to use a fixed two-dimensional array of counters to summarize a large number of statistics over time. Nevertheless, CM always overestimates the exact value, and although CU improves it by conservatively updating a counter, it comes with a huge time complexity to perform the point query for each update.

Finally, Cormode et al. [5] reported that the workload distribution of different network services (DNS, HTTP, etc.) can exhibit significant and different amount of skew defined as a measure of the asymmetry to the probability distribution of the carried workload. This amount can be well modeled by the Zipfian parameter. However, none of these algorithms successfully capture this property during the analysis phase.

7.3 Motivation from a Real DCN Trace

We performed a trace study on a real DCN hosting a trial-running commercial airline travel booking service in 2008. It is composed of four BLADE Network Technologies (BNT) virtual fabric 10 G switches that periodically export sFlow packets to a commercial server. From the packet header of sFlow packets, we extract useful information including the source and destination IP addresses, workload of that flow, destination port number, and time. For every extracted information from a packet header, we save it in a CSV format record line. In this way, we received 29,614,720 record lines that represent the traffic flow of the DCN during the monitoring phase. The results are computed offline by database queries.

First, we analyze the distribution of workload exchanged between all source–destination IP pairs and plot the probability distribution function (PDF) and cumulative distribution function (CDF), for both the entire DCN and on each switch. Then, we show the evolving trend of the workload over time and analyze its composition by different types of network services. As shown in the following, the results demostrate that the amount of traffic moving between different IP pairs are unevenly distributed and most of the traffic is highly concentrated on only a small fraction of the IP pairs. Furthermore, bursty traffic is observed that may incur significant temporal link congestion to a DCN. Therefore, we need to design an efficient congestion identifcation algorithm. As our study also confirms the existence of Zipf's law for different types of network services, as presented originally by [5], the accuracy of CM algorithm is not only related to the space of the sketch but also the parameters indicate that different network services may use different space of the sketch to achieve the same error performance; it inspires a new way to enhance the existing sketch-based approaches. We aim to provide a new way to enhance the existing sketch-based approaches, reducing the computational complexity and estimation error at the same time.

7.3.1 Overall Workload Analysis

To investigate the traffic conditions between the communicating parties via the DCN, we extract all source–destination IP pairs with their workload from the obtained trace data. Figure 7.2 shows the logarithmic amount of workload exchanged between all source–destination IP pairs during the day. For illustration purposes, we anonymize their actual IP addresses and arbitrarily set a unique number ranging from 0 to 6481, i.e., in total we have 6481 IP addresses (or users in the network). It is observed that the amount of traffic moving between different IP pairs are unevenly distributed, and most traffic are highly concentrated on a small fraction of the IP pairs. This implies different user behaviors that some users may generate larger amount of traffic as "elephants" while most of the users behave as "mice."

Figure 7.3 shows the workload for both the entire DCN (in Fig. 7.3a, b), and on each switch (in Fig. 7.3c, d). Observing the PDF and CDF of the reported workload flowing through the entire DCN, we see that a flow of less than 10 KB eventually occupies more than 80 % of the entire traffic, since the considered network provides travel booking services where HTTP and DNS flows dominate. Additionally, we see that the workload on two switches are quite similar to the overall DCN traffic behavior, which implies that this is a relatively load-balanced network from the switch's perspective.

To visualize the evolving trend of traffic over time, we show both its magnitude and normalized difference which is defined as $|M(t+\tau)-M(t)|/|M(t)|$, where

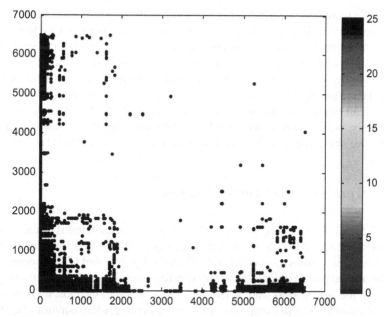

Fig. 7.2 Workload exchanged between all source–destination IP pairs during the day

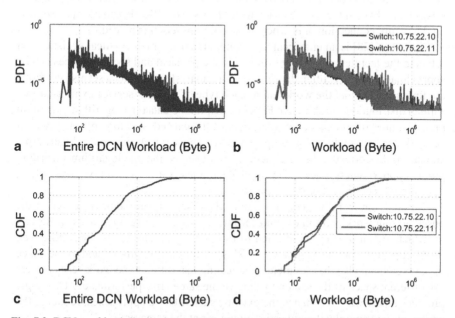

Fig. 7.3 DCN workload distribution. **a** *PDF* of entire DCN workload. **b** *CDF* of entire DCN workload. **c** *PDF* of per-switch workload. **d** *CDF* of per-switch workload

$M(t)$ is the workload magnitude at time t and τ is the step size for both the entire DCN (see Fig. 7.4a, b) and on each switch (see Fig. 7.4c, d). It is expected to observe that results comply well with the users' daily routine. That is, traffic is quite low early in the morning between 12:00 and 6:00 am (most people are asleep); it starts to increase after 12:00 pm and reaches the top after 6 pm. Besides, we observe four spikes that are mainly caused by the switch 10.75.22.11 (see Fig. 4c, d), distributing at 2:10–2:30 am, 3:00–3:30 am, 5:00–5:50 am and 10:00–10:40 am local time, respectively, which may cause significant network congestion and bandwidth overuse. We shall further analyze the cause of these spikes in the next section.

7.3.2 Workload Composition Analysis

Figure 7.5 analyzes the composition of the carried workload in terms of the type of network services. Figure 7.5a shows the percentage of appearance frequency where HTTP occupies the most portion of 48 %, followed by DNS and HTTPs, consistent with the offered travel booking service by web browsing. Figure 7.5b shows the percentage of the carried workload, where HTTP also occupies the most by more than 50 %, followed by Secure Computing Sidewinder Remote Administration (SCSRA, a protocol for secure connections) and HTTPs. Specially, we can conclude that the magnitude of each SCSRA flow is relatively large compared with HTTP, DNS, and HTTPs, as SCSRA occupies a considerable amount of total workload but it appears less frequently than the rest. This is due to the nature of SCSRA that helps users set up the secure connection only when an actual transaction is placed.

Zipf's law [28] is an empirical law formulated using mathematical statistics that refers to the fact that many types of data in the physical and social sciences can be approximated with a Zipfian distribution. Our analysis on this data set also confirms the finding in [5] that the workload of each type of network service exhibits strong Zipfian distribution. As shown in Fig. 7.6, we plot the data on a logarithm-logarithm plot. The horizontal axis denotes the rank of the carried workload by each type of network service, ranking by the packet size. The vertical axis is the logarithmic amount of the corresponding frequency. It is observed that the logarithm-logarithm plot is approximately linear. The fitted Z parameters are $z_{\text{HTTP}} = 1.53$, $z_{\text{DNS}} = 1.93$, $z_{\text{others}} = 1.02$ (coefficient 0.95), respectively.

Our study on workload composition analysis shows that the main source of the observed four workload spikes comes from only a small category of network services, which are empirically confirmed to follow the Zipfian distribution. Moreover, in [5], it proves that the accuracy of CM algorithm is not only related to the space of the sketch but also the parameters, indicating that different network services may use different space of the sketch to achieve the same error performance. This angle provides a new way to enhance the existing sketch-based approaches, reducing the computational complexity and estimation error at the same time.

Spike Analysis In each CSV format record line, we can get the time, workload, and the port numbers of that traffic record. Distinguishing flows via TCP destination port numbers, we analyze the cause of spikes in terms of their associated type

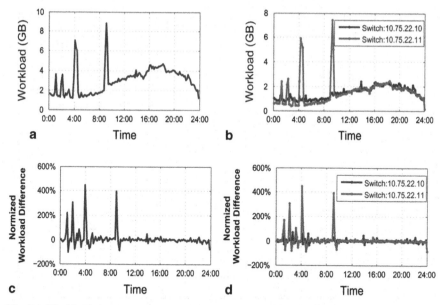

Fig. 7.4 Workload changing curve over time for 24 h. **a**, **b** Entire DCN workload and its normalized difference. **c**, **d** Per-switch workload and its normalized difference

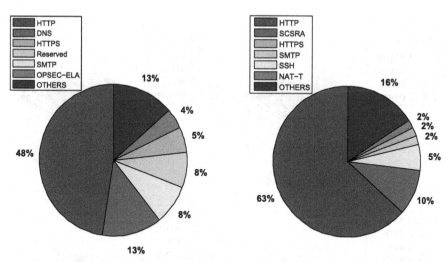

Fig. 7.5 Workload composition analysis for entire traffic, where (*left*) appearance frequency of a type of network service, and (*right*) workload of a type of network service

of network service. As shown in Fig. 7.7, for four spikes, 44, 37, 18, and 30% of total workload comes from HTTP and HTTPs protocol, respectively, and 40, 47, 72, and 53% of total workload comes from the SCSRA protocol to establish the secure connection (for real booking transactions).

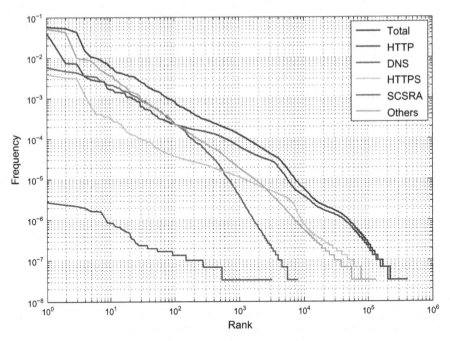

Fig. 7.6 Zipf distribution for different types of network services in the considered data set

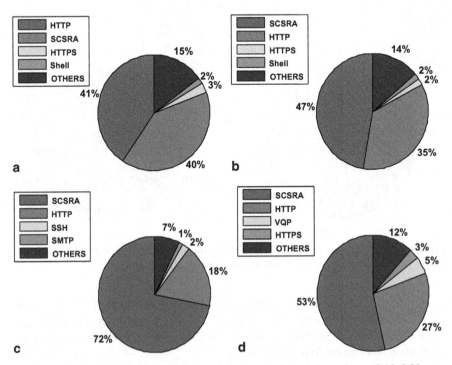

Fig. 7.7 Spike analysis in terms of the associated type of network service. **a** 2:10–2:30 am. **b** 3:00–3:30 am. **c** 5:00–5:50 am. **d** 10:00–10:40 am

To summarize, in a DCN, there exists a few workload spikes over time which may cause bandwidth overuse and degrade the network performance, and the traffic between any pair of source–destination IP addresses are also unevenly distributed. Therefore, it is necessary and also possible to extract the high-traffic sources by carefully designing the flow monitoring/analysis techniques to ultimately avoid the network congestion. One interesting application is to retrieve the top K records from all packets received on a list of physical ports of a specific switch in the past T seconds, grouped by specified fingerprint information which can uniquely identify a flow. The fingerprint information can be the source/destination IP addresses, source/destination port numbers, etc. The output top-K records can be ranked by the sum of flow workload, or counting the number of appearances (i.e., heavy hitters).

7.4 Existing Sketching Algorithms

To illustrate the existing sketching algorithms, we consider the following congestion management application (which can provide key results for many commercial flow analysis software like IBM Security QRadar QFlow Collector [29]): *providing estimations when retrieving the top-K (e.g., default 100) source–destination IP pairs sorted by their carried sum of workload, on a specific physical port of a switch in the lastT (e.g., default 5000) seconds.* Without loss of generality, we denote the distinct input items as a *vector* $\underline{a}$ with dimension m, presented in an implicit, incremental fashion, where for each element $a_i \geq 0, \forall i = 1, 2, \ldots, m$. Its current state at time t is denoted by $\underline{a}(t) = [a_1(t), \ldots, a_i(t), \ldots, a_m(t)]$. In the above example, $a_i(t)$ represents a distinct IP pair, and the value denotes the aggregated amount of the carried workload within a time period T. For convenience, we shall usually drop t and refer only to the current "state" of the vector, and when time evolves it behaves identically in the same process. Initially, $\underline{a}$ is the zero vector. Updates to individual entries of the vector are presented as a stream of pairs, as (item, update) or (a_i, c_i). In practice, update c can be the newly carried workload on an IP pair, or $c = 1$ if the application aims to count the number of appearances of that IP pair, or heavy hitters. We next describe the existing sketching algorithms to produce the vector estimate $\underline{a}$ of dimension m.

7.4.1 CM Sketch

CM sketch [6] is named after the two basic operations used to handle the updates to individual entries, i.e., counting first and computing the minimum next. Initially, $\underline{a}$ is a zero vector. Updates to individual entries of the vector are presented as a stream of pairs (i, c), e.g., the ith IP pair's total workload is increased by amount c. As shown in Fig. 7.8a, the data structure of a CM sketch is represented by a two-dimensional array of counters with width w and depth d: $cell[1,1] \ldots cell[d,w]$. Each counter is initially zero. Additionally, we choose d hash functions $h_1 \ldots h_d : \{1 \ldots m\} \rightarrow \{1 \ldots w\}$

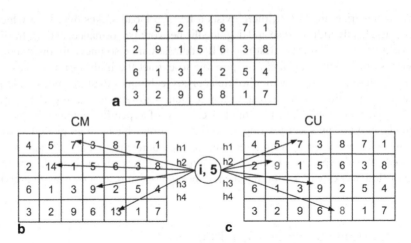

Fig. 7.8 An illustrative example of CM sketch and CU algorithms, where: **a** sketch before update, **b** sketch after the CM update, and **c** sketch after the CU update

uniformly at random from a pairwise-independent family, hashing the ith element d times to d different cells $[j, h_j(i)]$, $\forall 1 \le j \le d$ of each row in the data structure. When the new updates arrive, all hashed cells are increased with the according amount c. The ideal case is that each cell only stores a unique input element, however as in practice $m \gg w$, each cell may store the aggregated values of multiple items which will inevitably cause collisions. Fortunately, this collision rarely repeats in *all* rows *simultaneously* due to the different hash functions chosen. Then, the estimation $\hat{a}_i$ from the structure is given by $\hat{a}_i = \min_{1 \le j \le d} cell\,[j, h_j(i)]$, i.e., the minimum of d hashed cells. Note that the size of sketch is related to the estimation accuracy, where $w = \lceil e/\varepsilon \rceil$ and $d = \lceil -\ln \delta \rceil$ can produce ε estimation accuracy with probability of at least $1 - \delta$:

$$Pr\{\hat{a}_i - a_i > \varepsilon \| \underline{a} \|_1\} \le \delta, \tag{7.1}$$

where $\| \underline{a} \|_1 = \sum_{i=1}^{n} a_i$. An example is illustrated in Fig. 7.8a, b, where the new arrival update item $(i, 5)$ gets mapped by four hash functions, and finally updates the counts from $(2,9,4,8)$ to $(7,14,9,13)$. For the query operation, the estimation for a_i is given by 7 as the minimum over $(7,14,9,13)$.

Obviously, given a data type in each cell, the space cost of CM sketch is $O(wd)$. The update process only takes $O(1)$ by hashing to one cell, thus for a data stream of n records, its update complexity is $t_{CM} = O(nd)$.

7.4.2 CU Sketch

As discussed earlier, since m is sufficiently larger than w, one hash function may hash multiple items to the same cell, and this collision would cause erroneous aggregation of streaming updates from different items. Therefore, CM always *overestimates* the exact value of the vector. Estan and Varghese introduced the idea of conservative update [3] in the context of networking, and later extended in [7] to further improve the estimation accuracy. In CU, counters are conservatively updated according to:

$$\begin{cases} updateby(\hat{a}_i + c), & if cellvalue < (\hat{a}_i + c) \\ remainthesamecellvalue, & otherwise. \end{cases}$$

This means that we will update a counter only if it is necessary as indicated by the above equation. This heuristic approach avoids the unnecessary updates of counter values and thus reduces the estimation error. An example is also illustrated in Fig. 7.8a, c, where the counts (2,9,4,8) are updated to (7,9,9,8) by performing conservative update.

Since, CU needs to perform the point query (of complexity $O(d)$ among d independent cells) whenever there is a new update arrival, and thus, its time complexity is $t_{CU} = O(2nd)$ for n input records. To this end, we have identified the trade-off between time complexity and error performance between CM and CU, and in the following, we aim to enhance CU's performance.

7.5   Enhanced CU Algorithms

In this section, first we introduce two enhanced CU algorithms, namely: α-CU and partitioned CU. The α-CU maintains all basic features of CU, but only performs CU process probabilistically for an arrival update. Partitioned CU algorithms maintain a new data structure compared with CU that performs sketch partition along the horizontal or vertical dimension.

7.5.1   α-CU

As the CM algorithm sacrifices its error performance with time complexity, one immediate improvement is to "probabilistically" perform CU for an arrival update. Without loss of generality, we use parameter $\alpha \in (0,1]$ to denote this switching probability between CM and CU processes. That is, at any time when a new update arrives at the sketch, e.g., a particular IP pair's carried workload is incremented, we probabilistically decide whether to adopt the CU with probability α. We call this improvement method as "α-CU". Note that the realization of this switching probability can be different, but none of them eventually adds any extra implementation cost to existing CU and CM. For simplicity reasons, we assume that this switching probability is a uniformly distributed random variable. It is clear that when $\alpha = 1$, α-CU approach is identical to the CU approach. The smaller the α, higher is the probability of CM used. To this end, it is expected that the error performance and time complexity is trading off by α, as $t_{\alpha-CU} = O(2\alpha nd + (1-\alpha)nd) = O((1+\alpha)nd)$.

7.5.2 Partitioned CU

Although, α-CU can reduce the time complexity (compared with the classic CU approach), it proportionally sacrifices the error performance when CM is adopted more frequently. Furthermore, it does not explicitly consider the amount of skew for different types of network services, e.g., HTTP, DNS, etc. According to the observations that different types of network services in the network conform to different Zipf's law, and more importantly, in [5], it proves that to answer point queries (or estimations) by CM with ε accuracy with probability at least $1 - \delta$ needs space $O(\varepsilon^{-\min\{1,1/z\}} \ln 1/\delta)$, and thus different types of network services may use distinct space cost of the sketch to achieve the *same* error performance. Therefore, we aim to propose an enhanced algorithm to reduce the computational complexity and estimation error from this angle.

We reduce the computational complexity of CU by requesting *different* sketch sizes for each type of network services, while satisfactorily guaranteeing the error performance of each individual sketch. It is obvious that the partition can be performed either along the horizontal or vertical dimension of the sketch, denoted as "P(d)-CU" and "P(w)-CU" algorithms, respectively, while preserving the other dimension as constant. For the sake of comparison fairness, we guarantee equal space cost of the sketch before (i.e., the original one) and after the partition (as the sum of the sizes for individual sketch). Let w and d denote the width and depth of the original sketch before partition, respectively. Then, after the partition along either dimension, $d_k (d = \sum_{k=1}^{\wedge} d_k)$ denotes the depth of the kth partition, and $w_k (w = \sum_{k=1}^{K} w_k)$ denotes the width of the kth partition. Finally, let $n_k (n = \sum_{k=1}^{K} n_k)$ denote the size of the input stream to the kth sketch, while K is the number of partitions in total. The updates of each type of network services are performed at the corresponding individual sketch, respectively, and for one type of network service, its associated updates will not be sent and processed in two sketches. To better explain the process, Fig. 7.9 shows an illustrative example. Note that the similar process can be applied for P(w)-CU, where the only difference is to partition the sketch along the horizontal dimension.

The processing steps of P(d)-CU are illustrated in Fig. 7.9a, b as an example. The entire sketch of $w = 7, d = 6$ is horizontally divided into $K = 3$ sketches, each of which has $2,1,3$ rows to process flows from HTTP, DNS, and other types of network services, respectively. As shown in Fig. 7.9a, assume items a_1, a_2, a_3 (representing different source/destination IP pairs exchanging different types of network services) from three categories are monitored, they are hashed into cells of different sub-sketches, and the stored counts before update were $(2,9)$, 4, and $(2,3,9)$, respectively. Then, to return the estimation of a_1, a_2, a_3, we perform the point query on three sketches and the results are $\hat{a}_1 = \min\{2,9\} = 2, \hat{a}_2 = 4, \hat{a}_3 = \min\{2,3,9\} = 2$, i.e., the minimum of all counts in the hashed cells. Now suppose new updates arrive $c_1 = 5, c_2 = 9, c_3 = 6$. In this particular case, the update rule increases the cell value, only if its stored value is less than sum of estimation result and new update, i.e., $\hat{a}_1 + c_1 = 7, \hat{a}_2 + c_2 = 13, \hat{a}_3 + c_3 = 8$. As a result, Fig 7.9b shows the cell values after the update which become $(7,9)$, 13, and $(8,8,9)$, respectively.

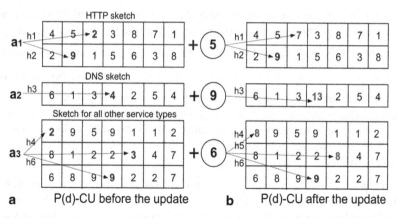

Fig. 7.9 An illustrative example of P(d)-CU algorithm, where: **a** sketch before update, **b** Sketch after update

7.5.3 Performance Analysis

The implementation of these K sketches can either be parallel or serial, and we next show its superiority even if *serialized* approach is adopted.

Compute/Update Time When considering the time complexity, we refer to the time, when performing all n updates in a sketch, of P(w)-CU is the same as CU since the width w does not control the update time: $t_{P(w)-CU} = O\left(2\sum_{k=1}^{K} n_k d\right) = O(2nd)$. The proposed P($d$)-CU exhibits the time complexity as the sum of K CU algorithms, or $O\left(2\sum_{k=1}^{K} n_k d_k\right)$. Through simple derivations, we show that it is far lower than that of CU approach:

$$2nd = 2\sum_{k=1}^{K} n_k d_k + 2\sum_{k=1}^{K} n_k (d - d_k) \gg 2\sum_{k=1}^{K} n_k d_k. \tag{7.2}$$

Theorem 5.1 A CU sketch with width w and depth d is able to achieve the minimum computational complexity $O(2nd / K)$ if partitioned into K sketches, irrespective of how the partition is performed as long as the input data stream (with size n) is equally fed into K sketches.

Proof We form the following optimization problem, i.e., to minimize the update time of P(d)-CU given the constraint of the sum of partitioned sketch depths equals the original sketch:

$$\{d_k\} = \arg\min_{d_k} \sum_{k=1}^{K} n_k d_k \quad s.t. \quad \sum_{k=1}^{K} d_k = d, \tag{7.3}$$

where $n = \sum_{k=1}^{K} n_k$. It is a classic constrained optimization problem which could be solved by using the Lagrangian multiplier λ. We take the gradient $\partial L / \partial d_k = 0$, where $L(\lambda) = \sum_{k=1}^{K} n_k d_k - \lambda(\sum_{k=1}^{K} d_k - d)$, and we have $\lambda = n_k, \forall k$ (since $\sum_k n_k = \sum_k \lambda = n, n_k = n / K, \forall k$). Therefore, it is clear that irrespective of how the partition is performed, the lowest computational complexity is always achieved if the input data stream is equally fed into each of the K sketches. Replace $n_k = n / K$ into the objective function, we complete the proof. As the width w does not control the update time, we conclude that P(w)-CU is the same as CU on time complexity.

Finally, We have $t_{CM} \le t_{P(d)-CU} \ll t_{CU} = t_{p(w)-CU}$.

Error Performance The error performance of all sketching algorithms depends both on the width and depth of a sketch. This is because the width decides the collision probability when a hash function maps different items into the same cell. The smaller the width, higher the probability that any of the two items will collide. As a result, a cell will store the wrongly aggregated values of different items. Furthermore, when the output is generated from the sketch, the point query returns the minimum value of d hashed cells, and thus larger depth will spread out the collisions and as a result to decrease the estimation error. Therefore, the estimation error is inversely proportional to width and depth. Meanwhile, width has a higher impact on the derived error than depth, since it directly controls the collision probability, and thus P(w)-CU would not yield any better performance, and can be even worse than CM due to its significantly less allocated width (more erroneous aggregated results). α-CU's error performance depends on the value of switching probability α P(d)-CU achieves better error performance than the traditional CU, since the reduction of the input data size has larger impact than the reduced data structure. This is because we feed different types of network services to different sketches, and thus potentially each small sketch will produce less collision when hashing and this is confirmed at a later section of this chapter.

7.6   Real-Time Moving Averages

In this section, we propose an approach to produce the real-time moving average of workload using only one sketch without any implementation cost.

In all previous analysis, we drop the time notation and focus on estimating item counts *periodically* from the sketch. However, reports may be generated by a "sliding window" whose length is T and moving speed is l ($l \ll T$). A typical example in a DCN is to report results every 10 s while always considering the summarized statistics in the past 300 s. Unfortunately, none of the existing streaming algorithms is applicable for this domain.

The problem can be solved by using $\lceil T/l \rceil$ sketches of the same size. That is, each sketch stores the aggregated statistics within a period of l. When time evolves, the sketch storing the most outdated statistics beyond the time window T is reset to zero, and starts to collect newly arrived ones in the current time frame.

Meanwhile, all other $\lceil T/l \rceil - 1$ sketches remain the same. When reporting the result, each sketch exports the summarized statistics individually, and then combined together. Although, this approach is straightforward and accurate by nature, it requires significant space cost (from one single sketch to $\lceil T/l \rceil$ separate sketches of the same size), and imposes implementation complexities like sketch coordination, result merge, and sort.

We propose a "real-time exponential moving average" approach that maintains only *one* sketch without any implementation cost to P(d)-CU. Every l when a update arrives, we first exponentially discount the stored value of all cells by a factor of γ, which is defined as the ratio between the speed of sliding window movement l and the looking-back interval T, i.e., $\gamma = 1 - l/T \in (0,1)$. Then, we add the new update value to the discounted cells. The intuition is that smaller step size l results in the slow historical forgetting effect (bigger γ), and the smaller observation window size T results in faster forgetting effect (smaller γ).

The main advantage of this approach is to save the space cost. Also, it exhibits exponential behaviors in the long-run, given that each cell stores all arrived data (i.e., none of them is discarded) but they are added up together after exponentially discounted in a scale proportional to its lifetime in the data structure. For example, most recent update is only discounted once in contrast with the first update, so that the effect of the historical measurements is mitigated from time being, and abrupt changes like spikes can be tracked.

7.7 System Architecture

To facilitate the above designs as a part of the software in real DCN management, in this section, we present the entire system design. For the sake of simplicity, we take the sFlow datagram as an illustrative example to implement the end-to-end system. However, it is worth noting that the proposed sketching techniques are not constrained in the sFlow standard, but have wide applicability to any data stream inputs exported from the switches in a data center. The principle is this [31]: sFlow packets contains the IP packet length information of that sampled packet and the sampling rate enforced in the hardware, so that one is able to compute the total amount of workload before sampling. If further grouped by different soruce/destination IP pairs, and/or switch port, we can estimate the aggregated traffic load after the sketch processing.

Figure 7.10 shows the system flow for both implementing a single sketch (i.e., SS, CM, CU, and α-CU, as shown in Fig. 7.10a) and partitioned sketch (i.e., P(d)-CU and P(w)-CU, as shown in Fig. 7.10b). The considered inputs to the analyzer can be either the real-time streaming packets like sFlow datagram generated by any compatible switch, or the historical flow records stored in a persistent database (and here we consider the .csv format). Having both real-time and historical data as inputs can satisfy the requirements of different applications, and they both serve as the inputs to a First-In-First-Out (FIFO) queue. The queue successfully caches the input data to decouple from the actual sketch computations. Take real-time inputs

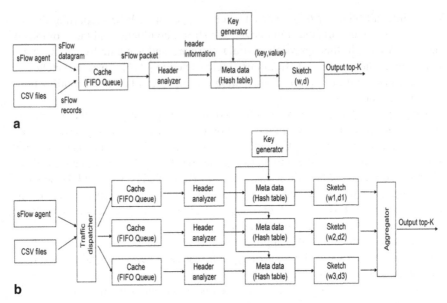

Fig. 7.10 System architecture of the flow monitoring and analysis. **a** Single sketch. **b** Partitioned sketch

sFlow datagram as an example, packets dequeued from the cache are used for header analysis, where all needed information are included, e.g., the source/destination IP/MAC addresses, source/destination port numbers, flow workload, the port of the exported switch, connection type, etc. Then, according to the user-specified ranking criterion in the output, a key generator module is employed to hash those ranking information (potentially of multiple fields) to a single unique identifier, which is used to update the sketch. For example, if one is interested in identifying which particular pairs of source/destination IP addresses exchanging packets become the cause of link congestion on a switch, we hash their IP addresses (i.e., in this case we have two fields) together into one single unique key, and later all arrival packets belonging to that IP pair are updated in the sketch accordingly. Finally, the sketch module is the core of the entire system, which may vary from different employed techniques. In general, it is a two-dimensional array with width w and depth d, and its output are the sorted list of records satisfying different application requirements.

As for the partitioned sketching algorithms, the only two differences are the dispatcher module before the FIFO queue, distinguishing their associated type of network service, and the aggregator module after the results are produced by each individual sketch to generate an entire list of records, irrespective of their associated type of network service. The implementation of these two modules at both ends can be in many classic ways.

Finally, it is worth noting that the reduced processing supported by the two sketch-based algorithms means that they could be implemented in NetFPGA [26] or other programmable switches, which would (potentially) be a good way to offload that work from the end hosts, and just give input to the load balancers, flow scheduling-ers (or Explicit Congestion Notification (ECN) to Multipath TCP weights if being used).

7.8 Performance Evaluation

In this section, we first conducted a comprehensive study of the performance produced by existing three streaming techniques, namely: SS, CM, and CU. Then, we compared our proposed α-CU and Partitioned CU approach in terms of compute time and estimation error. Finally, we showed the effects of performing real-time moving average on P(d)-CU under different settings.

To assess the performance of different algorithms, we use the same data trace as in Sect. 7.3, because it provides a good diversity of $m = 6482$ distinct source–destination IP pairs, which is satisfactory to testify the sketch-based algorithms since the larger m would potentially cause more collisions in the data structure. Therefore, the algorithms' estimation accuracy can be verified. The considered application is to retrieve the estimated workload of all IP pairs. We received $n = 29,614,720$ records. All results are computed on an ordinary laptop Thinkpad x220i with hardware configurations of Intel(R) Core(TM) i3–2310M, CPU@2.10 GHz and 4 GB RAM. Specially, we aim to study the performance of the existing/new proposed algorithms in term of the following:

- Space cost: the size of memory needed to perform the streaming algorithm (measured in bytes).
- Update : the processed number of updates per second.
- Recall: measured in the total number of true workload/heavy hitters reported over the number of true workload/heavy hitters given by an exact approach (e.g., database query).
- Compute time: the period of time generating the estimations of the reported workload/heavy hitters.
- Average relative error (ARE) of the reported workload/heavy hitters, as:

$$\frac{1}{m} \sum\nolimits_{i=1}^{m} \frac{|\hat{a}_i - a_i|}{a_i},$$ where m is the dimension of $\underline{a}$.

7.8.1 Existing Approaches: SS, CM, and CU

Workload Ranking Figures. 7.11 and 7.12 show the experimental results for space cost, update, recall, and ARE of SS, CM, and CU algorithms, when ranking the exchanged workload between any source/destination IP pair. We vary the parameters of width w, depth d, and the number of output records K, respectively.

Specifically, Fig. 7.11a shows the space cost of these three algorithms. To track the inputs and perform stream estimations, both CM and CU need a two-dimensional array of counters of size wd, while SS uses a one-dimensional array of counters of size w. Figure 7.11b illustrates that, unlike storing data in a database with growing size, all three algorithms consume a fixed size of memory although different amount of output records are produced, showing good scalability with the increase of the amount of top-K outputs. Figure 7.11c shows the change of update versus the size of array. For SS, it is clear that the update decreases when increasing the array size (also confirmed in Fig. 7.11d by three red lines). This is because, in SS, if a new arrival item does not match any monitored items in the array, the item with smallest count will be replaced; hence, a larger size of array needs more time to find the smallest count and consequently increases the time of item replacement. For CM and CU, they behave consistently with our analyzed update time complexity, i.e., $t_{CM} = O(nd)$, $t_{CU} = O(2nd)$, in Sect. 7.4. Figure 7.11c shows that the update for CM and CU is inversely proportional to depth d while it remains unchanged when varying w (which is also confirmed in Fig. 7.11d, as three blues/green lines representing CM and CU with different w overlap), and CM performs always faster than CU. Figure 7.11c also indicates that SS is much slower than CM and CU in terms of running time, especially when the utilized memory size is relatively large. Finally, from Fig. 7.1d we see that increasing the desired number of output records has no impact on the update, since time complexity is only related to the size of array and the size of input data stream.

For the recall performance, as shown in Fig. 7.12a, increasing the array size can promote the obtained recall for all three algorithms, since a larger allocated memory decreases the probability of item replacement for SS and lowers the collision probability of CM/CU while performing the item hashing. It is worth noting that with a small piece of memory ($w = 1000, d = 6$) the algorithms has already achieved more than 95 % recall when handling a huge amount of input data stream. Figure 7.12b shows that the recall performance suffers from the increasing of desired number of output records, especially for SS. However, CU always achieves the highest recall by conservatively updating the counters to avoid overestimations.

For ARE, as shown in Fig. 7.12c, SS slightly outperforms CM around 3 % less ARE, but CU achieves the least error always lower than 0.2 % and only 1/10th of the SS and CM algorithms, when $d = 14$. This gain becomes weak when the w increases and after $w = 2500$, all three algorithms succeed in achieving almost 0 % ARE. Furthermore, when increasing the sketch depth, CM performs better, e.g., when $w = 512$ with doubled depth, its ARE can be halved. Therefore, among existing streaming algorithms, CU's error performance is the best. This is also confirmed in Fig. 7.12d. Although ARE decreases when the number of top-K records increase, CU still achieves the least estimation error using the same size of memory.

7.8.2 α-CU and Partitioned CU

We next demonstrate both the ARE and compute time of the proposed α-CU and Partitioned CU algorithms, while varying different α, w, and d values. In Fig. 7.13a, for the fixed sketch depth, when α increases from 0.1–1.0, i.e., with higher

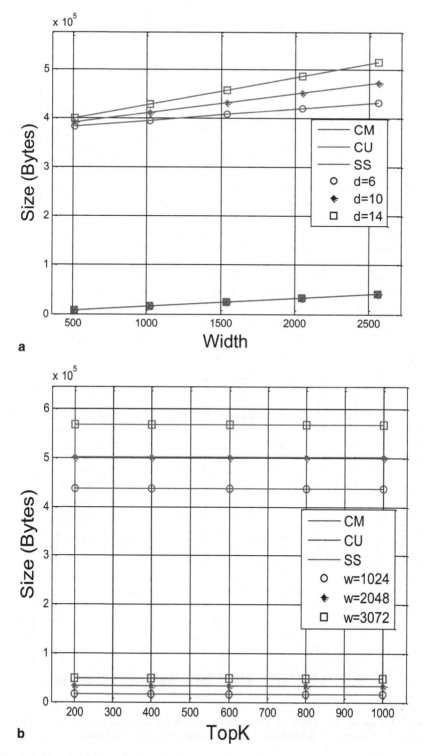

Fig. 7.11 Experimental results for space cost of SS, CM and CU algorithms, when ranking the workload. **a** Space versus width and depth. **b** Space versus top-K and width

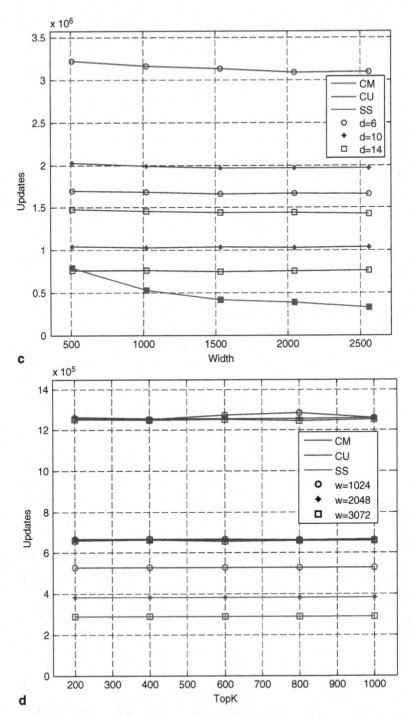

Fig. 7.11 Experimental results for space cost of SS, CM and CU algorithms, when ranking the workload. **c** Updates versus width and depth. **d** Updates versus top-K and width.

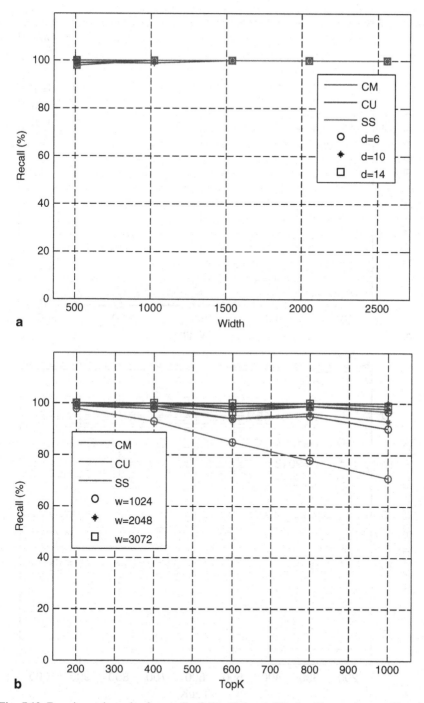

Fig. 7.12 Experimental results for recall of SS, CM and CU algorithms, when ranking the workload. **a** Recall versus width and depth. **b** Recall versus top-K and width

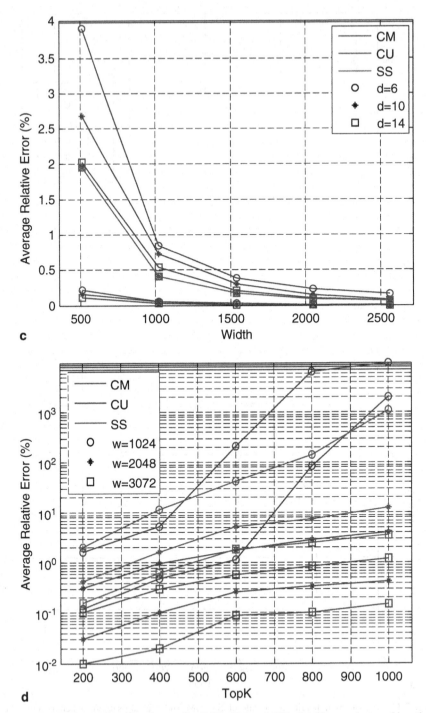

Fig. 7.12 Experimental results for recall of SS, CM and CU algorithms, when ranking the workload. **c** ARE versus width and depth. **d** ARE versus top-K and width

probability to perform CU, the achieved ARE decreases gradually. Meanwhile, with the increase of the depth, the error also decreases, and after $d = 33$, its value can reach as low as 1.5%. As for the time complexity shown in Fig. 7.13b, when α increases by 30%, the amount of time required for processing all updates increases by around 16%, which clearly confirms the trade-off between time and error performance of CM and CU algorithms. Figure 7.13c, d shows the results when varying the sketch width, and it clearly confirms that w has no relationship with compute time, and ARE decreases with the growing size of the data structure to reduce the collision probability when processing the input items.

To facilitate the sketch partition, we use the TCP destination port number to distinguish the HTTP and DNS flows. Then, based on the inverse ratio of the fitted Z parameters (for Zipfian distribution) from the trace (where we have $z_{\mathrm{HTTP}} = 1.53$, $z_{\mathrm{DNS}} = 1.93$, $z_{\mathrm{others}} = 1.02$ with fitting coefficient 0.95), we partition the sketch into three small sketches, whose depth ratio is 3:2:4 between HTTP, DNS, and all other service types.

Figures 7.14a and 7.12b show both the ARE and compute time versus the depth of the sketch d, while setting $w = 8192$ as a constant. It can be seen that P(d)-CU successfully reduces the estimation error by at least 50% when compared to CU when $d = 12$, and this effect continuously holds when d increases as the lowest to 0%. The curve of P(w)-CU further confirms that partitioning the horizontal dimension of the sketch would not yield extra benefits of lower ARE since width strictly controls the amount of collisions. As for time complexity, P(d)-CU shows its superiority over CU approach and very close to CM algorithm. This gain becomes clearer when d increases and the complexity reduction can reach up to 18% when $d = 36$. As an overall trend, the time complexities of four algorithms conform to the strict linearity showing good scalability with the space cost of the sketch. The effect of changing the width of sketch is depicted in Fig. 7.14c, d. Bigger w will decrease the ARE for all four approaches and P(d)-CU always achieves the best error performance and good time complexity compared with CM. We also perform an evaluation while processing 70 and 35% of total data by P(d)-CU, and found that when $w = 2560$ it only requires 52 and 17% of compute time showing that the algorithm itself contributes 18% less time consumption apart from the help in the reduction of data size.

7.8.3   Real-Time Moving Averages

Finally, we arbitrarily pick up some specific IP pairs and show the effects of performing real-time moving average on P(d)-CU, while setting the looking-back interval at $T = 300$ s and moving speed at $l = \{10, 100\}$ s and comparing with the exact value from database querying. We show the results obtained from three different IP pairs whose moving average curve of the workload exhibit different shapes over time. Case 1 has a curve with an early peak happened before 8:30 am in the morning as shown in Fig. 7.15a, b. Figure 7.15c, d of Case 2 both have a late peak that

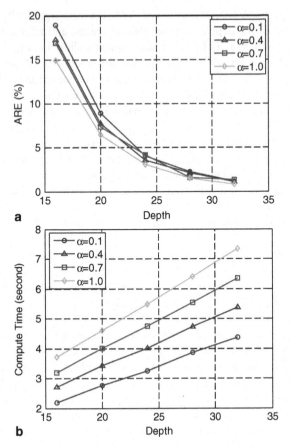

Fig. 7.13 Experimental results for ARE versus depth (**a**). **b** Compute time versus depth of α-CU algorithm.

appears after 8:30 am. For the last case in Fig. 7.16a, b, there are two peaks of workload

Figures 7.15b, d and 7.16b show the result when $l = 100$s or $\gamma = 0.67$, where the estimated value successfully tracks the exact value when the workload slowly changes. Meanwhile, when abrupt changes like spikes occur we observe certain amount of latency in tracing the change. This is primarily because that the historical data out of 300 s still have certain impacts on the aggregated statistics, although they have been exponentially discounted. Figures 7.15a, c and 7.16a show the result when $l = 10$s, or $\gamma = 0.97$, which is expected to be more fine-grained (i.e., the window move slower) and the effect of historical observations are more obvious. From the three cases, we confirm that the proposed moving average approach successfully tracks the abrupt changes with satisfactory response time. It is also worth noting that the performance of our proposed approach behaves stably under different scenarios when the peak of workload appears arbitrarily.

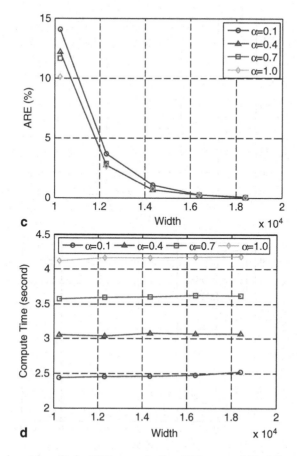

Fig. 7.13 Experimental results for ARE versus depth. **c** ARE versus width. **d** Compute time versus width of α-CU algorithm

Finally, Fig. 16c, d shows the compute time for all IP pairs during the simulation period from 8:00 to 9:00 am, plotting under different l values. We can see that the curve of Fig. 7.16c is much more fine-grained than Fig. 7.16d. This is because a small moving speed indicates more calculating counts and avoids the possible severe jitter of compute time, forming a more smooth curve accordingly.

7.9   Conclusion

Emerging bandwidth-hungry applications in DCNs impose significant challenges to identify the cause of congestion and bandwidth overuse. In this chapter, at first, we provide a comprehensive study of a real DCN traffic data set and analyze its operational characteristics. Then, motivated by the analysis results, we reexamine various streaming techniques to approximate the DCN traffic characteristics in real-time, and propose two enhanced algorithms, α-CU and P(d)-CU, based on existing CU

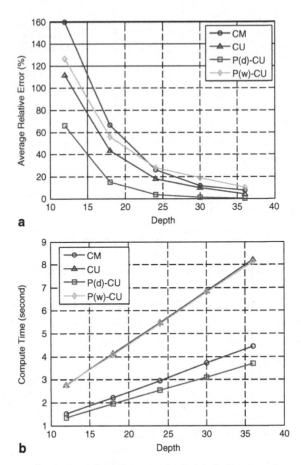

Fig. 7.14 Experimental results for ARE versus depth (**a**). **b** Compute time versus depth of P(d)/P(w)-CU algorithms

algorithm, together with the end-to-end system architecture. α-CU targets to serve as a zero-cost alternative to the existing flow analyzers that already run CM and CU, providing a configurable trade-off between the error performance and time complexity. P(d)-CU, which successfully improves both accuracy and time complexity, is a significant enhancement to any existing sketching techniques that requires the known Zipfian parameter for different network services at the configuration phase. Further, we propose a way to produce real-time moving average of the reported results. Finally, sufficient experiments by a real DCN trace verify the effectiveness of the proposed algorithms on error performance, space cost, and time complexity.

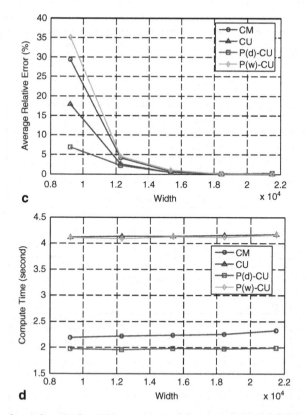

Fig. 7.14 Experimental results for ARE versus depth **c** ARE versus width. **d** Compute time versus width of P(*d*)/P(*w*)-CU algorithms

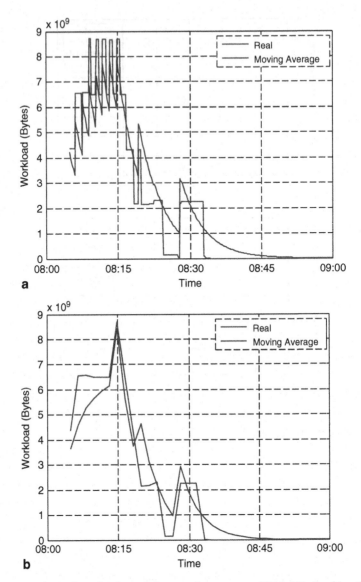

Fig. 7.15 Experimental results for real-time moving average of P(d)-CU algorithm (Case 1). **a** 10 s interval. **b** 100 s interval. Experimental results for real-time moving average of P(d)-CU algorithm (Case 2)

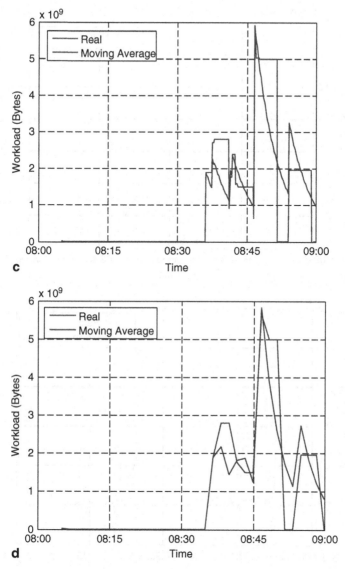

Fig. 7.15 Experimental results for real-time moving average of P(d)-CU algorithm (Case 1). **c** 10 s interval. **d** 100 s interval

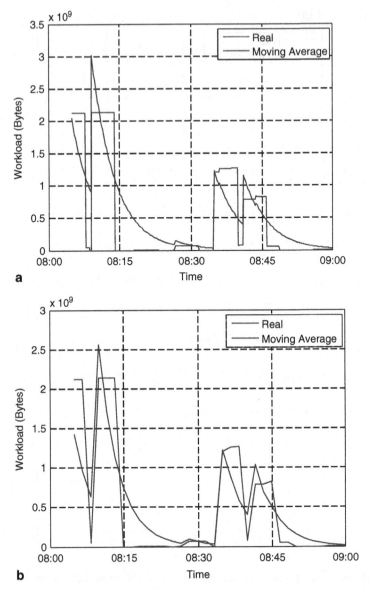

Fig. 7.16 Experimental results for real-time moving average of P(d)-CU algorithm (Case 3). **a** 10 s interval. **b** 100 s interval. Experimental results for compute time of real-time moving average of P(d)-CU algorithm (Compute time)

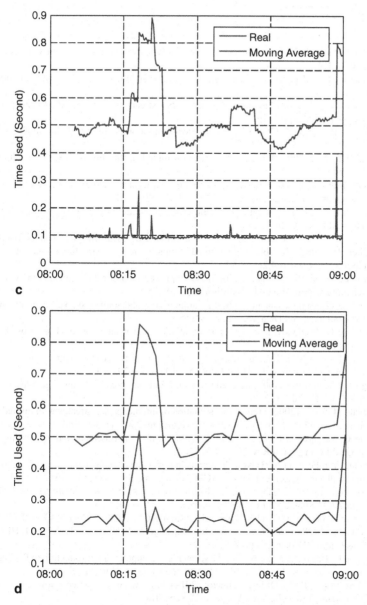

Fig. 7.16 Experimental results for real-time moving average of P(d)-CU algorithm (Case 3). **c** 10 s interval. **d** 100 s interval

References

1. Al-Fares M et al (2008) A scalable, commodity data center network architecture. In: ACM SIGCOMM'08, pp 63–74
2. Al-Fares M et al (2010) Hedera: dynamic flow scheduling for data center networks. In: NSDI, 2010, pp 19–19
3. Babcock B et al (2002) Models and issues in data stream systems. In: ACM Principal Database System, 2002, pp 1–16
4. Babcock B, Olston C (2003) Distributed top-k monitoring. In: ACM SIGMOD'03, 2003, pp 28–39
5. Barakat C et al (2005) Ranking flows from sampled traffic. In: ACM CoNEXT'05, 2005, pp 188–199
6. Braden R et al (1994) Integrated services in the internet architecture: an overview. IETF IETF RFC1633, http://tools.ietf.org/html/rfc1633, June 1994
7. Chaiken R et al (2008) SCOPE: easy and efficient parallel processing of massive data sets. VLDB Endow 1(2):1265–1276
8. Chang F, Dean J, Ghemawat S, Hsieh WC, Wallach DA, Burrows M, Chandra T, Fikes A, Gruber RE (2008) Bigtable: a distributed storage system for structured data. ACM Trans Comput Sys 26(2):4:1–4:26
9. Cormode G, Muthukrishnan S (2005) An improved data stream summary: the count-min sketch and its applications. J Algorithm 55(1):58–75
10. Cormode G, Muthukrishnan S (2005) Summarizing and mining skewed data streams. In: SIAM Conference on Data Mining, pp 44–55
11. Cormode G, Muthukrishnan S (2005) What's hot and what's not: tracking most frequent items dynamically. ACM Trans Database Syst (TODS) 30(1):249–278
12. Curtis AR et al (2011) Mahout: low-overhead datacenter traffic management using end-host-based elephant detection. In: IEEE Infocom, 2011, pp 1629–1637
13. Dean J, Ghemawat S (2008) Mapreduce: simplified data processing on large clusters. Commun ACM 51(1):107–113
14. Demaine ED et al (2002) Frequency estimation of internet packet streams with limited space. In: 10th Annual European Symposium on Algorithm, 2002, pp 348–360
15. Estan C, Varghese G (2002) New directions in traffic measurement and accounting. ACM SIGCOMM Comp Com Rev 32(4):323–336
16. Estan C, Varghese G (2003) New directions in traffic measurement and accounting: focusing on the elephants, ignoring the mice. ACM Trans Comp Syst (TOCS) 21(3):270–313
17. Farrington N et al (2011) A hybrid electrical/optical switch architecture for modular data centers. ACM SIGCOMM Comput Commun Rev 41(4):339–350
18. Ghemawat S et al (2003) The Google file system. ACM SIGOPS Oper Sys Rev 37(5):29–43
19. Goyal A et al (2010) Sketching techniques for large scale NLP. In: The NAACL HLT Sixth Web as Corpus Workshop, pp 17–25
20. Hoelzle U, Barroso LA (2009) The datacenter as a computer: an introduction to the design of warehouse-scale machines, 1st edn. Morgan and Claypool, San Rafael
21. IBM Security QRadar QFlow Collector (2014). http://www–03.ibm.com/software/products/us/en/qradar-qflow-collector/. Accessed 22 Feb 2014
22. Liu CH et al (2013) Sketching the data center network traffic. IEEE Netw 27(4):33–39
23. Manku GS, Motwani R (2002) Approximate frequency counts over data streams. In: VLDB Conference, 2002, pp 346–357
24. Metwally A et al (2005) Efficient computation of frequent and top-k elements in data streams. In: International Conference on Database Theory, 2005, pp 398–412
25. Muthukrishnan S (2005) Data streams: algorithms and applications. Found Trends Theor Comp Sci 1(2):2005, pp 1–136
26. NetFPGA. http://netfpga.org/. Accessed 2010
27. Network Working Group (2014) Cisco systems netflow services export version 9. http://www.ietf.org/rfc/rfc3954.txt. Accessed 22 Feb 2014

28. Network Working Group (2014) Evaluation of candidate protocols for IP flow information export (IPFIX). http://www.ietf.org/rfc/rfc3955.txt. Accessed 22 Feb 2014
29. Olston C et al (2008) Pig latin: a not-so-foreign language for data processing. In: ACM SIGMOD'08, 2008, pp 1099–1110
30. Pietronero L et al (2001) Explaining the uneven distribution of numbers in nature: the laws of Benford and Zipf. Physica A 293(1):297–304
31. Roughan M et al (2004) Class-of-service mapping for QOS: a statistical signature-based approach to IP traffic classification. In: ACM IMC, pp 135–148
32. sFlow. http://www.sflow.org/. Accessed 2010
33. Shvachko K et al (2010) The Hadoop distributed file system. In: IEEE Symposium on Mass Storage System Technology (MSST), 2010, pp 1–10

Chapter 8
Energy-Aware Virtual Machine Consolidation in IaaS Cloud Computing

Md Hasanul Ferdaus and Manzur Murshed

Abstract With immense success and rapid growth within the past few years, cloud computing has been established as the dominant paradigm of IT industry. To meet the increasing demand of computing and storage resources, infrastructure cloud providers are deploying planet-scale data centers across the world, consisting of hundreds of thousands, even millions of servers. These data centers incur very high investment and operating costs for the compute and network devices as well as for the energy consumption. Moreover, because of the huge energy usage, such data centers leave large carbon footprints and thus have adverse effects on the environment. As a result, efficient computing resource utilization and energy consumption reduction are becoming crucial issues to make cloud computing successful. Intelligent workload placement and relocation is one of the primary means to address these issues. This chapter presents an overview of the infrastructure resource management systems and technologies and detailed description of the proposed solution approaches for efficient cloud resource utilization and minimization of power consumption and resource wastages. Different types of server consolidation mechanisms are presented along with the solution approaches proposed by the researchers of both academia and industry. Various aspects of workload reconfiguration mechanisms and existing works on workload relocation techniques are described.

Keywords Cloud computing · Energy-awareness · Virtualization · Server consolidation · Reconfiguration · Virtual machine migration · Combinatorial optimization

M. H. Ferdaus (✉)
Faculty of Information Technology, Monash University, Churchill, VIC 3842, Australia
e-mail: md.ferdaus@monash.edu

M. Murshed
School of Information Technology, Faculty of Science, Federation University Australia, Churchill, VIC 3842, Australia
e-mail: manzur.murshed@federation.edu.au

© Springer International Publishing Switzerland 2014
Z. Mahmood (ed.), *Cloud Computing,* Computer Communications and Networks,
DOI 10.1007/978-3-319-10530-7_8

8.1   Introduction

With the rapid development of computing and storage technologies and the extreme
success of the Internet, computing resources have become more powerful, cheaper,
and ubiquitously available than ever before. This technological shift has enabled
the realization of a new computing paradigm called *Cloud Computing*. Technically
speaking, clouds are large pool of easily accessible and readily usable virtualized
resources, such as hardware (e.g., CPU, memory, storage), development platforms
(e.g., Java,.NET, Go), and services (e.g., Email, CRM, HR) that can be dynamically
reconfigured to adjust to a variable load in terms of scalability, elasticity, and load
balancing, and thus allow opportunities for optimal resource utilization. This pool
of resources is typically provisioned as a pay-per-use business model in which very
high availability and guarantee (e.g., 99.99 % for Amazon S3) are offered by the
cloud infrastructure provider by means of service level agreements (SLAs) [49].
Consumers of cloud can access resources and services based on their requirements
without any regard of the location of the consumed resource and service. A similar
concept of delivering computing resources has been termed *Utility Computing* in
the arena of information technology for a few decades. Recent advancement in technologies like high-speed internet, virtualization, and web 2.0, and high availability
of commodity computing equipment have paved the way of cloud computing to a
quick success.

According to the National Institute of Standards and Technology (NIST) definition [32], the five essential elements of cloud computing are:

- On-demand computing service
- Broad network access
- Resource pooling
- Rapid elasticity, and
- Measured service

In addition to these five essential characteristics, the cloud community has extensively used the following service models to categorize the cloud services [49]:

- Infrastructure as a service (IaaS): Cloud provides provision for computing resources (e.g., processing, network, storage) to cloud customers in the form of
  virtual machines (VM), for example Amazon EC2 and Google compute engine.
- Platform as a service (PaaS): PaaS providers offer a development platform (programming environment, tools, etc.) that allows cloud consumers to develop
  cloud services and applications as well as a deployment platform that hosts those
  services and applications, thus supports full software lifecycle. Examples include Google App Engine and Windows Azure.
- Software as a service (SaaS): Cloud consumers release their applications on a
  hosting environment fully managed and controlled by SaaS cloud providers and
  the applications can be accessed through internet from various clients (e.g., web
  browser and smartphones). Examples are Google Apps and Salesforce.com.

To respond to the rapid growth of customer demands for processing power and storage, cloud providers like Amazon, Microsoft, and Google are deploying large number of planet-scale power-hungry data centers across the world. Cloud giants like Microsoft and Google individually have more than 1 million servers in their data center infrastructures, as recent report shows [35]. As a consequence, a huge amount of energy is required to run the servers and keep the cooling systems operating for these gigantic data centers. As per the Data Center Knowledge report [42], power is one of the critical total cost of ownership (TCO) variables in managing data centers, and servers and data equipment are responsible for 55 % of energy used by the data center followed by 30 % for the cooling equipment.

Large data centers are not only expensive to maintain, but also have enormous effects on environment. According to McKinsey report [25], world data centers consume 0.5 % of world's electricity and drive in more carbon emission than both Argentina and the Netherlands. The reason behind this extremely high energy consumption is not just the amount of computing resources used and the power inefficiency of the hardware, but also lies in inefficient use of these resources. Data collected from more than 5000 production servers over 6-month period showed that on average servers operate only at 10–15 % of their full capacity most of the time, leading to expenses on overprovisioning of resources [4]. Narrow dynamic power range of server further aggrandizes the problem: even completely idle servers consume about 70 % of their peak power usage [17]. As cloud promises unlimited resources through elastic provisioning, absolute reliability and availability, as well as customer demands show high dynamics, overprovisioning of resources in cloud data centers is a common phenomenon.

Among all the service models, the key for the success of cloud computing is the IaaS substrate that enables cloud service providers to provision the computing infrastructure needed to deliver the services simply by renting resources as long as needed without even buying a single component. Cloud infrastructures depend on one or more data centers, either centralized or distributed and on the use of various cutting-edge resource virtualization technologies, which enable the same physical resource (computing, network, or storage) to be shared among multiple application environments. Virtualization technologies allow data centers to address resource and energy inefficiency by creating multiple VMs in a single physical machine, each of which representing a runtime environment completely isolated from one another and by live migrating VMs [11] from one server to another, and thus improving resource utilization. Reduction of energy consumption can be achieved by switching idle physical servers to lower power states (suspended or turned off) while still preserving customers performance requirements. Thus, monitoring server utilization, making appropriate workload relocation decision, and by this process, improving data center resource utilization and energy consumption, technically termed *VM Consolidation (or Server Consolidation or Workload Consolidation)* is an essential part of resource management of virtualized data centers [54], including cloud data centers.

Higher resource utilization and energy efficiency in cloud data centers through server consolidation come with the associated overhead or cost of reconfiguration of the workloads. Relocation of VM from one machine to another using VM live migration consumes nonnegligible amount of computing and network resources [11]. Also, VM live migration may lead to significant performance issues for the hosted applications depending on the current resource utilization conditions in the physical servers, network traffic, types of applications, and other colocated workloads [1, 24, 55]. The most obvious effect of VM live migration that hosted applications perceive is the VM downtime when the applications will be unavailable to the clients. The domain of applications that leverages the cloud platforms is broad, including high performance computing (HPC), video processing, scientific simulation, and web applications. With the wide adaptation of Web 2.0 technologies, modern web applications such as social networking and e-commerce websites exhibit highly dynamic and interactive characteristics and thus, resulting in particular client/server communication patterns, write patterns, and server load compared with traditional static web applications. Proper estimation of the total cost or overhead of reconfiguration through VM live migration techniques in a cloud setting is essential to guide server consolidation, VM multiplexing and scheduling schemes so that trade-off between VM packing efficiency that gives measure of server resource utilization and reconfiguration overhead that impacts customer SLA can be performed. As a response, research community has contributed to the appropriate design, modeling, and validation techniques to estimate realistic reconfiguration costs considering both system parameters and application characteristics.

The rest of the chapter is organized as follows: Sect. 8.2 presents a brief overview of the architectural components and underlying technologies of IaaS cloud infrastructure. Resource management issues and challenges of IaaS clouds including server resource utilization and energy management along with the solution approaches in existing works are described in Sect. 8.3. Finally, Sect. 8.4 summarizes the content of the chapter.

8.2   IaaS Cloud Management Systems

While the number and scale of cloud computing services and systems are continuing to grow rapidly, significant amount of research is being conducted both in academia and industry to determine the directions to the goal of making the future cloud computing platforms and services successful. As most of the major cloud computing offerings and platforms are proprietary or depend on software that is not accessible or amenable to experimentation or instrumentation, researchers interested in pursuing cloud computing infrastructure questions as well as future cloud service providers have very few tools to work with [41]. Moreover, data security and privacy issues have created concerns for enterprises and individuals to adopt public cloud services [2]. As a result, several attempts and ventures of building open-source cloud computing solutions came out of both academia and industry collaborations including

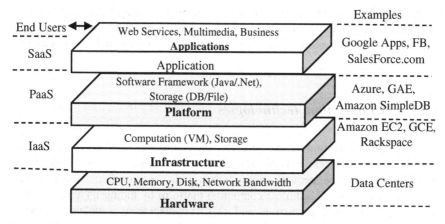

Fig. 8.1 Cloud computing architecture

Eucalyptus [41], OpenStack, OpenNebula [44], and Nimbus[1]. These cloud solutions provide various aspects of cloud infrastructure management such as:

- Management services for VM life cycle, compute resources, networking, and scalability.
- Distributed and consistent data storage with built-in redundancy, failsafe mechanisms, and scalability.
- Discovery, registration, and delivery services for virtual disk images with support of different image formats (VDI, VHD, qcow2, VMDK).
- User authentication and authorization services for all components of cloud management.
- Web and console-based user interface for managing instances, images, cryptographic keys, volume attachment/detachment to instances, and similar functions.

From the architectural perspective, the cloud computing environment is divided in to four layers as presented in Fig. 8.1, as follows:

- *Hardware layer*: This layer is responsible for managing the physical resources of the cloud, including physical servers, routers, switches, power, and cooling systems.
- *Infrastructure layer*: This layer (also known as *Virtualization layer*) creates a pool of computing and storage resources by partitioning the physical resources using virtualization technologies such as Xen [3] and VMware.
- *Platform layer*: Built on top of the infrastructure layer, this consists of operating systems and application frameworks and minimizes the burden of deploying applications directly on the VM containers.

---

[1] Nimbus Project. http://www.nimbusproject.org/.

- *Application layer*: This layer consists of the actual cloud applications, which are different from traditional applications and can leverage the automatic-scaling feature of cloud to achieve better performance, availability, and lower operating cost.

8.2.1 Virtualization Technologies

One of the main enabling technologies that paved the way of cloud computing toward its extreme success is *virtualization*. Cloud leverages various virtualization technologies (machine, network, storage) to provide users an abstraction layer that provides a uniform and seamless computing platform by hiding its hardware heterogeneity, geographic boundaries, and internal management complexities [59]. It is a promising technique by which resources of physical servers can be abstracted and shared through partial or full machine simulation by time-sharing and hardware and software partitioning into multiple execution environments each of which runs as complete and isolated system. It allows dynamic sharing and reconfiguration of physical resources in cloud computing infrastructure that makes it possible to run multiple applications in separate VMs having different performance metrics. It is virtualization that makes it possible for the cloud providers to improve utilization of physical servers through VM multiplexing [33] and multitenancy (i.e., simultaneous sharing of physical resources of same server by multiple cloud customers). It also enables on-demand resource pooling through which computing resources, like CPU and memory, and storage resources are provisioned to customers only when needed [27]. This feature helps avoid static resource allocation based on peak resource demand characteristics. In short, virtualization enables higher resource utilization, dynamic resource sharing, and better energy management, as well as improves scalability, availability, and reliability of cloud resources and services [9].

Virtualization in modern computing has been implemented using different approaches. Two significant techniques that have been heavily deployed in cloud computing infrastructures are full virtualization and paravirtualization:

- *Full virtualization* [3] provides a complete VM enabling unmodified guest operating systems (guest OS) to run in isolation. It provides flexibility to run different versions of different operating systems and the guest OS does not know that it is being virtualized. However, full virtualization requires Hardware Virtualization support (e.g., Intel-VT, AMD-V) from underlying host server.
- *Paravirtualization* [14] provides a complete but specialized VM to each guest OS allowing modified guests to run in isolation. It provides a lightweight and near native speed, and allows the guest OS to cooperate with hypervisor to improve performance. However, this technology is only limited to open source guest OS.

Hypervisor, also termed *Virtual Machine Monitor* (VMM), is the piece of software that multiplexes hardware among the VMs that it provides, the way traditional operating systems multiplexes hardware among the various processes [43]. Among the various virtualization systems, VMware, Xen, and KVM (Kernel-based Virtual Machine) [26], as listed below, have proved to be the most successful by combing features that make them uniquely well suited for many important applications:

- VMware Inc. is the first company to offer commercial virtualization technology. It offers a hypervisor called ESXi[2] server that supports full virtualization. Para-virtualization can also be supported by using VMI [31].
- Xen [15] is one of a few Linux hypervisors that support both full virtualization and paravirtualization. Each guest OS (termed domain in Xen terminology) uses a preconfigured share of the physical server. A privileged domain called Domain0 is a bare-bone OS that actually controls physical hardware and create, configure, migrate, or terminate other VMs.
- KVM [26] also supports full virtualization. It is a modification to the Linux kernel that actually makes Linux into a hypervisor on inserting a KVM kernel module. One of the most interesting KVM features is that each guest OS running on it is actually executed in user space of the host system. This approach makes each guest OS look like a normal process to the underlying host kernel.

8.2.2 VM Migration Techniques

One of the most prominent features of the virtualization systems is the VM *Live Migration* [11], which allows for the transfer of a running VM from one physical machine to another, with little downtime of the services hosted by the VM. It transfers the current working state and memory of a VM across the network while they are running. This has been already a built-in feature for both Xen and KVM. VMware also added live migration feature called VMotion [39]. Other architectures including Microsoft Hyper-V, Oracle VirtualBox, and OpenVZ also support this feature.

Another approach for VM migration is *Cold* or *Static Migration* [47] in which the VM to be migrated is shut down and a configuration file is sent from the source machine to the destination machine. The same VM can be started on the target machine by using the configuration file. This is a much faster and convenient way to migrate a VM with negligible increase in network traffic, but static VM migration incurs high downtime.

8.3 Energy-Aware VM Consolidation and Reconfiguration in IaaS Cloud Data Centers

Resource allocation in cloud has been challenging because of the unique service features that cloud claims to provide; on-demand resource provisioning and pay-as-you-go pricing policy not only create flexible and attractive business models, but also intricate the resource management functions and operations. To support

---

[2] vSphere ESX and ESXi, VMware Inc. http://www.vmware.com/au/products/esxi-and-esx/.

such service models, cloud providers need to deploy dynamic resource management systems that would maximize resource utilization while minimizing energy
consumption and operating costs. Cloud provides elasticity and high scalability of
resources that require autonomous and self-configured management systems [59].
To ensure constant high resource utilization, clouds allow multitenancy and shared
resource pooling where workloads and VMs from different users and possibly of
different application environments can colocate on the same physical servers [8].
Clouds leverage virtualization technologies [14] that allow integration of flexible
and efficient resource management strategies into cloud infrastructure. Resource
management policies and algorithms in the arena of public clouds are not disclosed
due to business reason. Moreover, the current open-source cloud management systems like OpenStack and Eucalyptus take simplistic views on resource management
and provide very basic algorithms such as random, round-robin, or uniform with
primary focus on load balancing.

8.3.1 Energy-Efficient VM Consolidation

While cloud computing provides many advanced features, it still has some short-
comings such as the relatively high operating costs for both public and private
clouds. The area of *Green Computing* is also becoming increasingly important in
a world with limited energy resources and an ever-rising demand for more computational power. As pointed out before, energy costs are among the primary factors that contribute to the TCO and its influence will grow rapidly due to the ever
increasing demands of resources and continuously increasing electricity costs [21].
As a consequence, optimization of energy consumption through efficient resource
utilization and management is equivalent to operating cost reduction in data center
management. To optimize the energy consumption of the physical devices, different
techniques have been proposed and used, including server consolidation, energy-
aware resource management frameworks and design strategies, and energy-efficient
hardware devices.

Resource management and optimization is getting more challenging day-by-
day for large-scale data centers like cloud data centers due to their rapid growth,
high dynamics of hosted services, resource elasticity, and guaranteed availability
and reliability. Static resource allocation techniques used in traditional data centers are simply inadequate to address these newly immerged challenges [23]. With
the advent of virtualization technologies, server resources are now better managed
and utilized through server consolidation by placing multiple VMs hosting several
applications and services in a single physical server, and thus ensuring efficient
resource utilization. Energy-efficiency is achieved by consolidating the running
VMs in minimum number of servers and transitioning idle servers into lower power
states (i.e., sleep or shut down mode).

VM consolidation techniques provide VM placement decisions that indicates
the mapping of each running VM to appropriate server. Depending on the initial

condition of data centers that VM consolidation techniques start with, it is categorized into two variants: *Static* and *Dynamic VM Consolidation.*

8.3.1.1   Static VM Consolidation

The static VM consolidation techniques start with a set of fully empty physical servers, either homogenous or heterogeneous with specific resource capacity and a set of workloads in the form of VMs with specific resource requirements. Thus, such consolidation mechanisms require prior knowledge about all the workloads and their associated resource demands. Such techniques are useful in situations like initial VM placement phase or migration of a set of workload from one data center to another. Static consolidation does not consider the current VM-to-server assignments and thus unaware of the associated VM migration overheads on both the underlying network traffic and hosted application performance [19]. Considering the predominant energy-costs of running large data centers and low utilization of servers resulted by traditional resource management technologies, and through the blessings of virtualization techniques, VM placement strategies like server consolidation have become a hot area of research [18, 20, 22, 40, 48, 50].

8.3.1.2   Dynamic VM Consolidation

Consolidation mechanisms that consider the current VM-to-server assignments for the consolidation decision fall in the category of dynamic consolidation. Contrary to static consolidations where the current allocations are disregarded and whole new solution of VM placement is constructed without considering the cost of reallocation of resources, dynamic consolidation techniques include the cost or overhead of relocation of existing workloads into the modeling of consolidation and try to minimize relocation overhead and maximize consolidation. Such server consolidation mechanisms employ VM live or cold migration techniques [11, 39] to move around workloads from servers with low utilization and consolidate them into minimum number of servers, thus improving overall resource utilization of the data center and minimizing power consumption.

As clouds offer an on-demand pay-as-you-go business model, customers can demand any number of VMs and can terminate their VMs when needed. As a result, VMs are created and terminated in the cloud data centers dynamically. This causes resource fragmentation in the servers, and thus leads to degradation in server resource utilization. However, efficient resource management in clouds is not a trivial task, as modern service applications exhibit highly variable workloads causing dynamic resource usage patterns. As a result, aggressive consolidation of VMs can lead to degradation of performance when hosted applications experience an increasing customer demand resulting in a rise in resource usage. As cloud providers ensure reliable quality of service (QoS) defined by SLAs, resource management systems in cloud data centers need to deal with the energy-performance trade-off.

To estimate the cost of relocation of workloads by the dynamic VM consolidation techniques, several system and network level metrics and parameters are used as modeling elements, such as the number of VM live migrations required to achieve the new VM-to-server placement [19], VM active memory size, speed of network links used for the migration [1, 23, 51], page dirty rate [52], and application-specific performance model [24].

8.3.1.3   VM Consolidation Modeling Techniques

Cloud data centers consist of hundreds or thousands, or even millions of high-end servers, for example rack-mount servers and blade servers with virtualization enabled to allow on-demand creation and termination of VMs on them. Popular cloud providers (e.g., Google, Amazon, and Rackspace) offer their customers different categories of VM instances to run with specification for each type of resource like the number of CPU cores, amount of memory, network bandwidth, and storage capacity. According to modern data center architectures[3], data storage is implemented as storage area network (SAN) or network attached storage (NAS) and is architecturally separate from compute servers. This type of architectural separation provides IaaS cloud providers the flexibility to offer on-demand storage blocks (e.g., Amazon EBS) to their customers. As a consequence, most of the recent works on VM placement considers compute (CPU and memory) and network resource (network I/O) that are relevant to the physical servers and the VMs running on them.

Moreover, VM instances offered by public cloud providers differ in their individual resource capacities: some instances are larger than others (e.g., AWS EC2 instances: small, large, extra-large, etc.) whereas some instances have relatively higher capacity for one type of resource compared with their other resources (e.g., Google instances: High CPU, High Memory, etc.). Such diverse range of VM instances are offered to match the workload characteristics of the hosted cloud applications that range from web and enterprise business applications to HPC, scientific, and complex workload applications.

As cloud VM in stances host various types of applications, the active VMs in cloud data centers exhibit dynamic resource demands during run-time. This dynamic nature of VMs can be captured and intelligently used to perform workload prediction and estimation mechanisms [57]. Because of the various types of VM instances offered by the providers with emphasis on size and types of resources and dynamic change in workload demands, it is very common that they will have random and nonuniform resource demands in difference resource dimensions of CPU, memory, and network I/O. To appropriately capture the various types of resource capacities of physical servers and the different types of resource requirements of hosted VMs, the VM consolidation problem is usually modeled as a variant of multi-dimensional vector packing problem (mDVPP) [20, 36] and multi-dimensional bin

---

[3] Cloud-ready Data Center Reference Architecture. Juniper Networks, Inc. http://www.juniper.net/us/en/local/pdf/reference-architectures/8030001-en.pdf.

packing problem (mDBPP) [18, 19, 23], and sometimes as multiple knapsack problem (MKP) [40, 48]. In [36], the authors argued that VM consolidation is in fact an instance of mDVPP rather than mDBPP and some analysis is presented in their work. All of the aforementioned problems fall in the broad category of Discrete Combinatorial Optimization and from computational complexity perspective, these problems are NP-hard in nature and the best known algorithms that guarantee to identify an optimal solution have exponential time worst case complexity [13].

Most of the research works on VM consolidation consider the cloud data center environment consisting of homogeneous physical servers (or PMs) having same types of resources (e.g., CPU, memory, and network I/O) with different capacity represented as 2-tuple (CPU, MEM)or 3-tuple (CPU, MEM, IO). Resource demands of active VMs are also represented in a similar fashion. It is assumed that individual VM resource demand does not exceed individual PM resource capacity; otherwise the VM request is rejected. Given the set of servers with their respective resource capacities and the VM with their respective resource demands, the VM consolidation algorithms try to find VM-to-server placement mappings with some defined objective function that they try to minimize or maximize while maintaining the physical servers' resource capacity constraints. In the case of static VM consolidation, the objective function is very often modeled as a minimization function that tries to minimize the number of active servers that are used for VMs assignments [18, 23, 40, 48]. On the other hand, in the case of dynamic VM consolidation, the objective function is often formulated as a combination of maximization of the number of released servers (i.e. servers that are made empty and turned to power saving states) and resource utilization of active servers, as well as minimization of the number of VM migrations required for the new VM placement [19].

Depending on the modeling technique, static VM consolidation is often regarded as a *single-objective problem* where dynamic VM consolidation is considered as a *multiobjective problem* [19]. However in [20], the authors modeled the static VM consolidation problem as a multi-objective combinatorial optimization problem with the goal of simultaneously optimizing the total resource wastage and power consumption.

Server Resource Utilization and Wastage Modeling Depending on the VM placement decisions, the remaining resources available to use in physical servers may vary greatly. As different VMs have different resource demands along multiple resource dimensions, server resource utilization and wastage models need to capture the level of imbalance in utilization for particular VM-to-server assignments. A simple approach of capturing the utilization of multidimensional resources of a server as presented in [18] that uses L_1 norm based mean estimator, is:

$$U = U^{\text{CPU}} + U^{\text{MEM}} + U^{\text{IO}},$$

where U^{CPU}, U^{MEM}, and U^{IO} represent the normalized CPU, memory, and network I/O utilization (i.e. the ratio of used resource to total resource) after the VM assignments.

As the goal of static VM consolidation is to minimize the number of active servers by placing as many VMs as possible in those servers, minimization of resource wastage along every possible resource dimension is essential to improve the VM packing efficiency of the consolidation algorithm. Focusing on this goal, authors in [20] presented server resource wastage model by the following formulation (considering CPU and memory resources only):

$$W = \frac{\left| L^{\mathrm{CPU}} - L^{\mathrm{MEM}} \right| + \varepsilon}{U^{\mathrm{CPU}} + U^{\mathrm{MEM}}},$$

where U^{CPU} and U^{MEM} represent the normalized CPU and memory resource usage, and L^{CPU} and L^{MEM} denote the normalized remaining CPU and memory resource, and ε is a very small positive real number that is set to be 0.0001. The key point of the above resource wastage modeling is to make effective use of the server resources along each dimension and balance the left out resources across different dimensions.

Power Consumption Modeling It has been shown experimentally that power consumption of physical servers is dominated by their CPU utilization and increases linearly [17]. As a result, the electricity energy drawn by a server is usually represented as a linear function of its current normalized CPU utilization U^{CPU}:

$$E = \begin{cases} \left(E_{\max} - E_{\mathrm{idle}} \right) \times U^{\mathrm{CPU}} + E_{\mathrm{idle}}, & if\ U^{\mathrm{CPU}} > 0 \\ 0, & \mathrm{otherwise} \end{cases},$$

where $E_{\max}$ and E_{idle} are the average electrical power drawn when the server is fully utilized and idle, respectively.

Finally, the estimate of the total energy consumed by a VM placement decision is computed as the sum of the individual energy consumption of the active servers [18, 20]. Due to the nonproportional power usage (i.e. high idle power) of commodity servers, the idle servers (i.e., servers that do not host any running VM) are turned off or put in suspended or sleep mode after the new VM placement and are not considered in the total energy consumption model. If a data center consists of n servers, the overall energy consumption of a VM placement decision x is formulated as follows:

$$E(x) = \sum_{p=1}^{n} E(p).$$

8.3.1.4   Taxonomy and Survey of VM Consolidation Mechanisms

With the increasing adoption of virtualization technologies and rapid success of hosting services, and very recently of cloud computing, VM consolidation techniques have been very attractive to reduce energy costs and increase data center resource utilization. As resource management mechanisms of public clouds (such as Amazon AWS) are not known in the public domain due to business policies, several open-source cloud projects (such as Eucalyptus [41], OpenStack, and Open-Nebula [44]) have emerged as a means of alternative solutions to the proprietary cloud infrastructures. However, one of the major limitations of these current cloud frameworks is the absence of efficient energy-aware workload consolidation mechanisms. As a result, a good amount of research works have been conducted and published within the past few years with focus on different aspects of consolidation ranging from energy saving and resource usage optimization to minimization of VM migration overhead and SLA violations.

To analyze, assess, and compare among the various research works, taxonomy and characterization have been established as proven methodologies in any research area. The proposed research works on VM consolidation have incorporated state-of-the-art technologies in data center management, including virtualization, autonomic data center management platforms, cloud management systems, and various types of simulated and real-world workloads and benchmarking tools. A brief description of the identified aspects of the research works used in the course of taxonomy is given below:

1. *System assumption:* Server resources in data center or IT infrastructure are primarily modeled as either homogeneous or heterogeneous. Homogeneous cluster of servers normally represent servers with same capacity for certain fixed types of resources (e.g., CPU, memory, and storage), whereas heterogeneous cluster of servers can represent either mean servers having different capacities of resources or different types of resources (e.g., virtualized servers powered by Xen or VMWare hypervisor, and servers with graphics processing units (GPUs)).

2. *Server resource:* Generally, optimization across different ranges of resources (i.e. CPU, memory, network I/O, storage, etc.) is harder than single resource optimization. Often various mean estimators (such as L1 norm, vector algebra, etc.) are used to compute equivalent scalar estimation while trying to optimize across multiple types of server resources. This aspect has direct influence on the modeling techniques applied in the research works and also on the consolidation performance.

3. *Modeling technique:* As for any research problem, the solution approach varies depending on the modeling (mathematical, analytical, or algorithmic) applied for the addressed problem. The characteristics of VM consolidation problem make it most resemble to the general mDBPP/mDVPP. Furthermore, depending on the objectives/goals set in the research projects, modeling can vary across other theoretical problems such as multiple multidimensional knapsack problem, constraint satisfaction problem (CSP), and multiobjective optimization problems.

4. *Objective:* Most of the works set objective as to minimize the overall power consumption of the data center and maximization of server resource utilization by increasing the VM/workload packing efficiency using minimum number of active/running servers. With the consolidation process comes the tradeoff between application performance (and hence, SLA) and power consumption. With given importance on SLA violations, some of the works consider the cost

of reconfiguration primarily due to VM live migrations, and thus incorporate this cost in the objective function modeling. Moreover, some the works further focus on automated and co-ordinated management frameworks with the VM consolidation as an integral component of the proposed frameworks.

5. *Solution approach/Algorithm:* Considering the fact that the VM consolidation is a strictly NP-hard problem, algorithmic approaches in the research works vary from simple greedy approaches to metaheuristic strategies and local search methods. Greedy approaches such as First Fit Decreasing (FFD) and Best Fit Decreasing (BFD) are very fast in producing results but are not guaranteed to produce optimal solutions. Metaheuristics such as Ant Colony Optimization (ACO), Genetic Algorithms (GA), and Simulated Annealing (SA) work on initial or existing solutions and refine them to improve on objective function value. Exhaustive search methods (e.g., Constraint Programming (CP)) normally fix the domain of possible values for the model variables to compute the optimal solution within a reasonable amount of time; however, in this process these methods effectively limit the size of the data center (in terms of the number of servers) or the volume of the workload (in terms of the number of VMs).

6. *Evaluation/Experimental platform:* Evaluation methodologies have direct impact on the performance and practicality of the research works, most importantly in the competency analysis. Proposals that primarily have theoretical contributions mostly apply simulation based evaluation to focus highly on the algorithmic and complexity aspects, whereas works involving various workload patterns and application characteristics conduct their performance evaluation on real test beds or experimental data centers, or even on emulated platforms.

7. *Workload:* Depending on the experimental environment, the workload data used as input for the evaluation of various consolidation techniques varies from synthetic data to real-time application/VM workloads. Simulation-based evaluation primarily relies on synthetic workload data generated using various statistical models such as random, Gaussian, or Poisson distribution, or on workload dataset collected from real data centers. Evaluations based on experimental test beds mostly use real time workload data generated from the applications that are deployed and run in the test bed servers. Such test beds though capture realistic behaviors of applications and systems suffer from scalability issues in the domain of VM consolidation.

Analysis of VM Consolidation Solution Approaches Table 8.1 illustrates the most significant aspects of the notable recent research works in the area of energy-aware VM consolidation based on the contents and description found in the published materials. Depending on the analytical modeling techniques used in the existing works, various algorithmic and problem solving techniques are applied to solve server consolidation and related energy management problems [20], e.g.:

• *Greedy algorithms:* mDVPP and mDBPP as well as various knapsack problems have been well studied over the past few decades, and as a result a good amount of greedy heuristics have been proposed for both bin packing and knapsack problems in the fields of computer science and operations research. First-fit (FF),

Table 8.1 Aspects of notable recent research works on workload and server consolidation

Research project	System assumption	Server resources	Modeling technique	Objectives	Solution approach/ algorithm	Evaluation/experimental platform	Workload
Adaptive threshold-based approach for energy-efficient consolidation of virtual machines in cloud data centers	Heterogeneous	CPU, memory, IO, and storage	Bin Packing problem	Threshold-based dynamic VM consolidation, minimization of energy consumption, SLA, and number of VM migration	Greedy Approach, Modified Best Fit Decreasing algorithm	CloudSim-based simulation	CPU utilization data from CoMon monitoring project for PlanetLab
EnaCloud: an energy-saving application live placement approach for cloud computing environments	Homogeneous	CPU and memory	Bin Packing problem	Energy-aware application scheduling and placement	Greedy heuristic based on First Fit and Best Fit algorithms	EnaCloud framework implemented in iVIC virtual computing environment and running on cloud server pool powered by Xen	Randomly generated workloads Web and database servers, compute-intensive applications, and common applications
pMapper: power and migration cost aware application placement in virtualized systems	Heterogeneous	CPU	Bin Packing problem	Power consumption minimization under performance constraints	Greedy Approach, Modified First Fit Decreasing	Simulation based on pMapper framework running on VMWare ESX-based testbed	Server utilization trace data from server farm
A mathematical programming approach for server consolidation problems in virtualized data centers	Homogeneous	CPU, memory, and bandwidth	Multi-dimensional Bin Packing problem, Linear Programming Relaxation	Server consolidation through workload data pre-processing and resource usage optimization	Greedy heuristic based on Branch and Bound, First Fit, and First Fit Decreasing, LP-relaxation-based heuristic	Open source solver lp_solve 5.5.0.9 and COIN-OR CBC branch-and-cut IP solver, as well as ad hoc simulator for First Fit and First Fit Decreasing heuristics	Workload traces from Web, application, and database servers, as well as ERP applications from industry partner

Table 8.1 (continued)

Research project	System assumption	Server resources	Modeling technique	Objectives	Solution approach/ algorithm	Evaluation/experimental platform	Workload
Entropy: a consolidation manager for clusters	Heterogeneous	CPU and memory	Instances of 2-dimensional Bin Packing and Knapsack Problem. Modeled as Constraint Satisfaction Problem	Dynamic VM consolidation, Minimization of the number of active servers and VM migrations	Exhaustive search (depth first) based on Constraint Programming	Simulation and Xen-powered Grid'5000 experimental testbed	Randomly generated synthetic data and NASGrid benchmark data
Autonomic virtual resource management for service hosting platforms	Heterogeneous	CPU and memory	Instance of Knapsack Problem. Modeled as Constraint Satisfaction Problem	Optimization of global utility function through maximization of SLA fulfilment and minimization of operating costs (number of servers)	Time-bound exhaustive search using Constraint Programming	Simulation based on Choco constraint solver	Synthetic Web workload distributed in a round-robin fashion
Performance and power management for cloud infrastructures	Homogeneous	CPU and memory	Instance of Multiple Knapsack Problem. Modeled as Constraint Satisfaction Problem	Utility maximization and energy cost minimization	Choco constraint programming sol-ver based brute-force search	Xen-powered testbed running cluster of Apache servers and farm of rendering applications controlled by Condor Grid scheduler	Web workload generated by CLIF load injector and batch workload using constant stream of jobs

Table 8.1 (continued)

Research project	System assumption	Server resources	Modeling technique	Objectives	Solution approach/ algorithm	Evaluation/experimental platform	Workload
SLA-aware virtual resource management for cloud infrastructures	Homogeneous	CPU and memory	Instance of Multiple Knapsack Problem. Modeled as Constraint Satisfaction Problem	Autonomic dynamic VM provisioning and placement with utility maximization, active server minimization, and reduction of reconfiguration cost due to VM live migrations	Self-optimization through the combination of utility functions and constraint programming	Simulation environment based on 4 servers running cluster of web servers and multiplayer online game. The simulation relies on the Choco constraint solver	Synthetic workload distributed in a round-robin algorithm
Energy-aware ant colony based workload placement in clouds	Homogeneous	CPU, memory, IO, and storage	Multidimensional Bin Packing Problem	Energy consumption minimization through optimization of server resource utilization and minimization of the number of active servers	Ant Colony Optimization-based algorithm	Ad hoc simulation toolkit	Randomly generated VM resource demands

Table 8.1 (continued)

Research project	System assumption	Server resources	Modeling technique	Objectives	Solution approach/algorithm	Evaluation/experimental platform	Workload
A case for fully decentralized dynamic VM consolidation in clouds	Heterogeneous	CPU, memory, and IO	Decentralized system based on unstructured P2P network of servers	Maximization of VM Packing efficiency and scalability, as well as minimization of the number of associated VM live migrations	Decentralized dynamic VM consolidation schema based on Cyclon membership protocol and Ant Colony Optimization-based algorithm	Python-based Cyclon P2P system emulator running on Grid'5000 experimental testbed	Randomly generated VM resource demands
A multiobjective ant colony system algorithm for virtual machine placement in cloud computing	Heterogeneous	CPU and memory	Multi-objective optimization and Multi-dimensional Vector Packing Problem	Minimization of power consumption and server resource wastage	Ant Colony Optimization-based algorithm	Ad hoc simulation toolkit	Randomly generated VM resource demands

best-fit (BF), next-fit (NF), FFD, BFD, choose pack (CP), and permutation pack (PP) are among the widely used greedy approaches [18]. A survey on the existing greedy solutions on single-dimensional bin packing problem can be found in [12]. In [5], the authors have presented a modified version of the BFD algorithm for the workload placement problem and have reported substantial energy saving based on simulation-driven results. Similarly in [29], a framework called EnaCloud is presented where a modified version of the BF algorithm is used. In [51], Verma et al. proposed pMapper, a VM placement scheme that models the workload placement as an instance of single-dimensional bin-packing problem and applies a modified version of the FFD heuristic to perform server consolidation. Further works on greedy algorithm based energy-aware VM placement approaches can be found in [30] and [46].

• *Linear programming:* This is a popular and traditional analytical approach to solve combinatorial optimization problems. Such linear programming formulations for server consolidation problems are presented in [6] and [45]. The authors also described constraints for limiting the number of VMs to be assigned to a single server and the total number of VM migrations, ensuring that some VMs are placed in different servers and placement of VMs to specific set of servers that has some unique properties. To minimize the cost of solving the linear programming problem, the authors further developed an LP-relaxation-based heuristic. Based on linear and quadratic programming model, Chaisiri et al. [10] presented an algorithm for finding optimal solutions to VM placement with the objective of minimizing the number of active servers.

• *CP:* VM placement and packing problem is also modeled as CSP, which is defined as a set of variables, a set of domains that represent the set of possible values for each variable and a set of constraints that denote the required relations between the values of the variables [48]. A solution of the CSP is a variable assignment that tries to maximize or minimize the value of a particular variable while maintain all the defined constraints. Based on CP, Hermenier et al. [23] proposed Entropy, a dynamic server consolidation manager for clusters that finds solutions for VM placement with the goal of active server minimization and tries to find any reconfiguration plan of the proposed VM placement solution with objective to minimize the necessary VM migration costs. Both the problems are solved using CP solver CHOCO [37]. The authors have provided detailed analysis and experimental results of the impacts of VM activity and VM memory size on the necessary VM migration duration and VM performance. Furthermore, several optimizations for the constraint solver are also suggested. Authors in [40] and [50] proposed an autonomic virtual resource management framework that separates the VM provisioning and VM packing phases. The VM provisioning phase takes resource level utility function [56] for each application environment as input and determines the necessary VMs from a list of predefined VM classes while maximizing a global utility function. The VM packing phase determines the best possible placement for all the VMs in the servers with the goal of minimizing the number of active servers. Both the phases resort to CHOCO CP solver [37]. Later in [48], the authors proposed extensions to their framework with multiple components for modeling performance of applications, costs of provisioned VMs, and scheduling the VM provisioning and placement (with packing) phases. However, the proposed analysis does not allow scaling-up of VMs in terms of resources and does not consider multiplexing of VMs in a time-sharing manner, which is very often used as an efficient way to improve resource utilization in virtualized environments, especially in clouds.

- *Evolutionary algorithms:* Evolutionary algorithms like GA have already been proven as efficient techniques for solving optimization problem including combinatorial problems. Jing et al. [58] formulated the VM placement problem as a multiobjective optimization problem with objective of minimizing power consumption, total resource wastage, and thermal dissipation costs. As a solution, the authors proposed a modified GA with fuzzy multiobjective evaluation to search the large solution space efficiently and combining possibly conflicting objectives. In [34], the authors proposed GABA, a GA based adaptive and self-reconfiguration mechanism for VMs in cloud data centers that consist of heterogeneous servers. Based on time-varying requirements and dynamic environmental conditions, GABA can efficiently decide the optimal VM placements.

- *Swarm intelligence:* Swarm Intelligence is a relatively new approach to problem solving that takes inspiration from the social behaviors of insects and animals. Within the past two decades, ants have inspired a number of methods and techniques among which the most studied and the most successful is the general purpose optimization technique known as ACO [16]. In ACO, multiple artificial agents work independently within its local search space in a random, decentralized fashion with indirect form of interaction, and after multiple interactions the produced solutions converge to near optimality. ACO metaheuristics have been proven to be efficient in different problem domains and so far it has been tested on more than 100 different NP-hard problems, including discrete optimization problems. First work on solving single-dimensional bin-packing problem based on ACO metaheuristics was proposed in [28]. The authors argued that the complementary nature of ACO metaheuristics and local search can benefit from each other and presented experimental results and showed that their proposed algorithm can compete with the contemporary best known solutions. In [7], the authors have proposed AntPacking, an improvement over the previous algorithm shown to perform as good as the best known GA. In [18], Feller et al. first proposed a single-objective static VM consolidation algorithm based on a variant of ACO, namely Max-Min Ant System and presented improved performance over FFD greedy algorithm. Later in [19], the authors presented a multiobjective dynamic VM consolidation schema using appropriate adaptation of ACO metaheuristics. They proposed decentralized approach to solve the problem based on an unstructured peer-to-peer network of servers to address the issues of scalability and improved packing efficiency. Another ACO based multi-objective static VM consolidation algorithm is presented in [20] where the authors have developed models for server resource wastage and power consumption with focus on balanced resource utilization across multiple resource dimensions. The algorithm simultaneously tries to minimize the power consumption and total resource wastage of the servers that host running VMs.

8.3.1.5   Advantages and Disadvantages of VM Consolidation

Virtualization technologies have revolutionized the IT management works and opened up a new horizon of opportunities and possibilities. It has enabled application environments to be compartmentalized and encapsulated within VMs. By the use of VM and VM live migration techniques, virtualized data centers have emerged as highly dynamic environments where VMs hosting various applications are created, migrated, resized, and terminated instantaneously as required. Utilizing virtualization, IT infrastructure management has widely adapted VM consolidation techniques to reduce operating costs and increase data center resource utilization. The most notable advantages of adopting VM consolidation techniques are mentioned below:

1. *Reduction in physical resources:* By the help of efficient dynamic VM consolidation, multiple VMs can be hosted in single physical server without compromising hosted application performance. As a result, compared with static resource allocations where computing resources such as CPU cycles and memory frequently lay idle, through dynamic VM consolidation fewer numbers of physical machines can provide the same QoS and maintain SLAs, and thus effectively cut the TCO. Reduction in the number of servers also implies reduction in the cooling equipment necessary for the cooling operations in data centers.
2. *Energy consumption minimization:* Unlike other approaches of energy efficiency (e.g., implementing efficient hardware and operating systems), VM consolidation is a mechanism under the disposal of data center management team. If same level of service can be provided by fewer servers through VM consolidation, it implies minimization of energy costs both for the running servers and the operating cool systems. As energy costs continue to escalate, this implies a significant saving that will continue during the course of the data center operation.
3. *Environmental benefits:* World data centers contribute a significant portion of CO_2 emission and thus have enormous effects of environment. With recent trend toward *Green Data Centers*, VM consolidation is a major business drive in IT industry to contribute to the Green Computing.
4. *Minimization of physical space:* Reduction in the number of hardware implies reduction in the space needed to accommodate the servers, storage, network, and cooling equipment. Again, this contributes to the reduction of the TCO, as well as the operating costs.
5. *Decreased labor cost:* A major portion of the TCO of data centers is derived from administrative, support, and outsourced services, and thus VM consolidation can help trim down these costs significantly by reducing the maintenance effort.
6. *Automate maintenance:* By incorporating autonomic and self-organizing VM consolidation and VM migration techniques, much of the administrative and support tasks can be reduced and automated; and therefore, it can further reduce the maintenance overhead and costs.

With all the above mentioned benefits, if not managed and applied appropriately, VM consolidation can be detrimental to the services provided by the data center in at least the following ways:

1. *System failure and disaster recovery:* VM Consolidation puts multiple VMs hosting multiple service applications in a single physical server, and therefore can create single-point-of-failure (SPOF) for all the hosted applications. Moreover, upgrade and maintenance of a single server can cause multiple applications to be unavailable to users. Proper replication and disaster recovery plans can effectively remedy such situations. Since VMs can be saved in storage devices as disk files, virtualization technologies provide tools for taking snapshots of running VMs and resuming from saved checkpoints. Thus, with the help of shared storages such as NAS or SAN, virtualization can be used as convenient disaster recovery tool.

2. *Effects on application performance:* Consolidation can have adverse effects on hosted application performances due to resource contention, as they would share the same physical resources. Delay sensitive applications such as voice-over-IP (VoIP) and online audio-visual conferencing services as well as database management systems that require heavy disk activity need to be given special consideration during resource allocation phase of VM consolidation. Such applications can be given dedicated resources whereas delay-tolerant and less resource hungry applications can be scheduled with proper workload prediction and VM multiplexing schemes.

3. *VM migration and reconfiguration overhead:* Performing VM consolidation dynamically requires VM live migrations that have overheads on network links of the data center as well as on the CPU cycles of servers executing the migration operations. As a consequence, VM migrations and postmigration reconfigurations can have non-negligible impact on application performance. Experimental results [53] show that applications that are being migrated as well as colocated applications can suffer from performance degradation due to VM live migrations. As a consequence, VM consolidation mechanisms need to minimize the number of VM live migrations and its effects on applications.

Despite all the drawbacks of VM consolidation, due to its benefits in continuous reduction in energy and operating costs and increasing resource utilizations data center owners are increasing adopting VM consolidation mechanisms, especially for large data centers. As VM consolidation can have adverse effects on application performance, various characteristics and features of data center resources and hosted applications need to be taken into account during the design and implementation of VM consolidation schemes, such as heterogeneity of servers and storage devices, system software and tools, middleware and deployment platforms, physical and virtual network parameters, as well as application types, workload patterns, and load forecasting.

8.3.2   VM Migration and Reconfiguration

Dynamic reconfiguration of workloads in virtualized data centers is achieved through VM resizing and VM live migration techniques [11, 39]. While VM resizing overhead in modern hypervisors is negligble, anecdotal evidence and experimental findings [24, 55] identified the VM live migration as reconfiguration mechanism with significant performance impact both on application and system resources. Thus, achievement of high packing efficiency with large number of VM migrations can effectively null and void the benefit of workload consolidation with the risk of possible high number of SLA violations of hosted applications and high resource wastage due to handling the migrations. However, the number of VM migrations alone does not represent the true overhead of the reconfiguration, as the total migration time and total VM downtime primarily depend on the Active Memory size of VM and speed of the network links used for the migration [1].

Moreover, both the source server and destination server experience extra CPU overhead during live migration, mostly due to the successive precopying phases [11, 39], which is an essential part of the state-of-the-art live migration subsystems in modern hypervisors like Xen [3], KVM [26], and VMWare ESXi. As multitenancy in cloud infrastructures is a common characteristic in today's clouds where VMs (and also applications) from different cloud customers can colocate in a single physical server, VM live migration overhead can have adverse effects on other customers' applications. Current cloud-hosted application domain is dominated by web applications, especially multitier web applications, and it is shown experimentally in [24] that the different J2EE-based tiers of RUBiS[4], a widely used multitier benchmark, experience 40% to more than 200% change in their end-to-end mean response time due to live VM migrations. Furthermore, an extra amount of network bandwidth is consumed due to live migration, potentially affecting the responsiveness of hosted internet applications. Last but not the least, a slowdown of VM performance is also expected due to the cache warm-up at the destination server after the migration [38].

8.3.2.1   Reconfiguration Cost Modelling Principles

To design an efficient and pragmatic workload consolidation mechanism, it is important to properly estimate the associated overall cost of the reconfiguration plans, which is mostly dominated by cost of VM migrations. Several existing approaches for dynamic consolidation consider migration cost to be a function of single system parameter, like VM active memory size [23, 51], page dirty rate [52], or use an application-specific model [24], and thus being oblivious to server resource utilization levels, other colocated workloads, and resource usage characteristics as well as the demands of the hosted applications. The importance of considering such aspects in migration overhead estimation is evident from the report [51], which shows that the duration of a live migration for an application running identical workloads can vary by 50% or more depending on server utilization and other colocated VMs. Therefore, a usable model for live migration not only needs to be aware of application

---

[4] RUBiS Benchmark, OW2 Consortium. http://rubis.ow2.org/.

and system parameters like active memory and write rate, but also take into account other colocated VMs, physical server utilization, as well as network parameters. A practical and accurate model of live migration is needed to complement dynamic consolidation schemes and provide an estimate of the cost of reconfiguration in cloud data centers.

Technically, live migration at the level of an entire VM refers to the process of transferring the active memory and execution state from the source server to the destination server. As in a typical cloud data center, the secondary memory or storage is implemented by SAN/NAS connected to compute servers through Internet small computer system interface (iSCSI), network file system (NFS), or server message block (SMB) protocols, VM disks are not transferred during migration. The most important aspect in terms of the performance impact of a live migration activity is the copying of in-memory state, as pre- and postmigration overheads (e.g., reattaching device drivers, advertising moved IP addresses) are pretty static [1, 11]. Among the several techniques for live migration in modern hypervisors, *Pre-copy Migration* is proven to be the most effective in terms of VM. Precopy migration involves two phases:

1. *Push phase* when Active Memory pages of running VM are copied from source to the target server in multiple rounds until some stop condition is fulfilled (e.g., the number of dirty pages during the last pre-copy iteration is less than some constant, like 50 for Xen) and
2. *Stop-and-copy phase* when the stop condition is met and the VM is stopped (and also its application) and all the remaining dirty pages are copied to the target server.

Two obvious temporal parameters are defined to measure the performance of a live migration, viz:

1. *Total migration time:* The total time required to move the VM between physical servers and
2. *Total downtime:* The portion of total migration time when the VM is not running.

Generally, the stop-and-copy phase is comparatively small for typical applications, usually between 1 to 3 s [55] and the push phase is much longer and increases with the size of memory being copied, page write patterns of applications, server resource utilization levels, and network link speed. As VM live migration requires significant amount of spare CPU, current resource utilization and the resource demands from colocated workloads, it can have significant effects on the total migration time and hosted application performance.

8.3.2.2   Related Works

Though the designers of the VM live migration technology do provide empirical evidence that suggests that the performance impact of live migration is manageable

[11, 39], recent experiments on live migrating VMs hosting different applications indicates that live migration can have significant impact on application performance and system resources [24, 55].

In [1], Akoush et al. addressed reconfiguration overhead solely in terms of the migration times and provided analytical derivation to define the upper and lower bounds of migration times, with particular emphasis on the Xen virtualization platform [3] and its live migration subsystem [11]. They have identified that link speed and page dirty rates are the major factors impacting migration behavior (in terms of migration times) and have a nonlinear effect on migration performance largely because of the hard stop conditions of Xen live migration algorithm that forces the migration to its final stop-and-copy phase. They also provided two migration simulation models based on average memory page dirty rate and historical data on page modification to predict migration times. The authors have also presented the effects of the following system and network parameters:

- *Network link bandwidth*: It is perhaps the most influential parameter on migration performance. Total migration time and VM downtime are inversely proportional to the migration link capacity.
- *Page dirty rate*: It is the rate at which memory pages of each VM are modified that directly affects the number of pages transferred in each push phase of the precopy migration. Higher page dirty rate causes more data to be sent per iteration leading to longer total migration time. Moreover, higher page dirty rates results in longer VM downtime, as more pages need to be sent in the final transfer round.
- *VM memory size*: In the precopy migration, the first iteration tries to copy across the entire VM allocated memory to the destination. As a result, on average the total migration time increases linearly with VM memory size.
- *Pre- and postmigration overhead*: It refers to operations that are not part of the actual transfer process. These are operations related to initializing a container on the destination host, mirroring block devices, maintaining free resources, etc.

In [38], an autonomic and transparent mechanism for proactive fault tolerance for arbitrary message passing interface (MPI) application has been studied and implemented using Xen live migration technology. In their research, the authors have given a general overview on the total migration time and possible parameters that affects it, but emphasis was given primarily on the amount of memory allocated to guest VMs.

In [24], Jung et al. have shown that runtime reconfiguration actions such as VM replication and migration can impose significant performance costs in multitier applications running in virtualized data center environments and proposed a middleware for generating cost-sensitive adaptation actions using a combination of predictive models and graph search techniques.

Voorsluys et al. in [55] showed experimental results of VM live migration on Internet applications using Web 2.0 benchmarking tool. They have shown that the average response times of typical multitier web application increases rapidly during the live migration period, especially due to the postmigration overhead. Their results also demonstrate that in an instance of a nearly oversubscribed system, live migration causes a significant downtime (up to 3 s), a larger value than expected. The work presents valuable and realistic insights on the effects of VM live migration on SLA violations of today's web applications. However, the work lacks proper characterization and modelling of the factors and parameters that contribute to the migration cost.

In [52], Verma et al. presents a study on the cost of reconfiguration of cloud-based IT infrastructure with response to workload variations. Their study suggests that VM live migration requires a significant amount of spare CPU capacity on the source server. The study also suggests that if space CPU cycles are not available, it impacts both the duration of migration and the performance of the hosted application. Later, in [53], the authors designed CosMig model that predicts (1) the total VM migration time, (2) performance impact of migration on the migrating VM, and (3) performance impact of migration on other colocated VMs. This model is based on CPU utilization and active memory size as these two parameters are normally monitored in large data centers. The authors also showed that by the use of selected microbenchmarks and representative applications, CosMig model has been able to accurately estimate the impact of live migration in a cloud environment. The following parameters were used in CosMig to determine the performance impact of migrating VM V_i:

- *Duration*: Time duration for the full migration completion.
- *VM self-impact*: Ratio between the drop in throughput of the hosted application of V_i during the migration period and the throughput without migration.
- *VM coimpact*: Ratio between the drop in throughput of any other application in colocated VM V_j during the migration period of V_i and the throughput of the same without migration of V_i.

8.4   Conclusions and Future Research Directions

Cloud computing is quite a new computing paradigm and from the very beginning it has been growing rapidly in terms of scale, reliability, and availability. Because of its flexible pay-as-you-go business model, virtually infinite pool of on-demand resources, guaranteed QoS, and almost perfect reliability, consumer base of cloud computing is increasing day-by-day. As a result, cloud providers are deploying large data centers across the globe. Such gigantic data centers not only incur huge energy costs, but also have environmental effects. Power consumption of such data centers can be improved by employing efficient resource allocation and management strategies through better server resource utilization. This chapter has discussed various virtual resource management technologies used in virtualized data centers including cloud data centers, as well as algorithms and mechanisms for achieving higher resource utilization and optimization of energy consumption through VM consolidation and data center reconfiguration. An in depth analysis on the different approaches proposed by the recent research works has also been presented.

Virtual resource allocation and VM placement strategies play significant roles in resource management and optimization decisions in data centers. Modern cloud applications are composed of multiple compute and storage components, and such components exhibit communication correlations among themselves. Incorporation of the communication correlations during VM placement decisions is a very important area of research that is not yet explored enough. A typical objective for network-aware VM placement and relocation would be keeping the heavily communicating VMs in the same server so that inter-VM communication would take place through memory or in near proximity under the same edge switch, and thus keeping the overall network overhead minimum on the physical network infrastructure. Development of realistic power consumption models for network devices and VM placement and reallocation policies with power management capabilities are areas of potential optimization in data center management.

VM consolidation and resource reallocation through VM migrations with focus on both energy-awareness and network overhead is yet another area of research that requires much attention. VM placement decisions focusing primarily on server resource utilization and energy consumption reduction can produce data center configurations that are not traffic-aware or network optimized, and thus can lead to higher SLA violations. As a consequence, VM placement strategies utilizing both VM resource requirements information and interVM traffic load can come up with placement decisions that are more realistic and efficient.

Cloud environments allow their consumers to deploy any kind of applications in an on-demand fashion, ranging from compute intensive applications such as HPC and scientific applications, to network and disk I/O intensive applications like video streaming and file sharing applications. Colocating similar kinds of applications in the same physical server can lead to resource contentions for some types of resources while leaving other types under-utilized. Moreover, such resource contention will have adverse effects on application performance, thus leading to SLA violations and profit minimization. Therefore, it is important to understand the behavior and resource usage patterns of the hosted applications to efficiently place VMs and allocate resources to the applications. Utilization of historical workload data and application of appropriate load prediction mechanisms need to be integrated with VM consolidation techniques to minimize resource contentions among applications and increase resource utilization and energy efficiency of data centers.

Centralized VM consolidation and placement mechanisms can suffer from the problems of scalability and SPOF, especially for cloud data centers. One possible solution approach would be replication of VM consolidation managers; however, such decentralized approach is nontrivial, as VMs in the date centers are created and terminated dynamically through on-demand requests of cloud consumers, and as a consequence consolidation managers need to have updated information about the data center. As initial solution, servers can be clustered and assigned to the respective consolidation managers and appropriate communication and synchronization among the managers need to be ensured to avoid possible race conditions.

References

1. Akoush S, Sohan R, Rice A, Moore A, Hopper A (2010), Predicting the performance of virtual machine migration, in Modeling, Analysis & Simulation of Computer and Telecommunication Systems (MASCOTS), 2010 IEEE International Symposium on, pp 37–46
2. Armbrust M, Fox A, Griffith R, Joseph A, Katz R, Konwinski A, Lee G, Patterson D, Rabkin A, Stoica I et al (2010) A view of cloud computing. Communications of the ACM 53(4):50–58
3. Barham P, Dragovic B, Fraser K, Hand S, Harris T, Ho A, Neugebauer R, Pratt I, Warfield A (2003) Xen and the art of virtualization, in ACM SIGOPS operating systems review, pp 164–177
4. Barroso L, Holzle U (2007) The case for energy-proportional computing. Computer 40(12):33–37
5. Beloglazov A, Buyya R (2010) Adaptive threshold-based approach for energy-efficient consolidation of virtual machines in cloud data centers, in proceedings of the 8th international workshop on middleware for grids, clouds and e-science, p 4
6. Bichler M, Setzer T, Speitkamp B (2006) Capacity planning for virtualized servers, in workshop on information technologies and systems (WITS), Milwaukee, Wisconsin, USA
7. Brugger B, Doerner K, Hartl R, Reimann M (2004) AntPacking-an ant colony optimization approach for the one-dimensional Bin Packing problem, evolutionary computation in combinatorial optimization, pp 41–50
8. Buyya R, Yeo CS, Venugopal S, Broberg J, Brandic I (2009) Cloud computing and emerging IT platforms: vision, hype, and reality for delivering computing as the 5th utility. Future Generat Comput Syst 25(6):599–616
9. Buyya R, Broberg J, Goscinski, AM (2011) Cloud computing: principles and paradigms. Wiley Online Library
10. Chaisiri S, Lee B-S, Niyato D (2009) Optimal virtual machine placement across multiple cloud providers, in services computing conference, 2009. APSCC 2009. IEEE Asia-Pacific, pp 103–110
11. Clark C, Fraser K, Hand S, Hansen J, Jul E, Limpach C, Pratt I, Warfield A (2005) Live migration of virtual machines, in proceedings of the 2nd conference on symposium on networked systems design & implementation, vol 2, pp 273–286
12. Coffman EG Jr, Garey MR, Johnson DS (1996) Approximation algorithms for Bin Packing: a survey, in approximation algorithms for NP-hard problems, pp 46–93
13. Cormen T, Leiserson C, Rivest R, Stein C (2001) Introduction to algorithms. MIT press, Cambridge
14. Crosby S, Brown D (2006) The virtualization reality. Queue 4(10):34–41
15. David C (2008) The definitive guide to the Xen Hypervisor. Prentice Hall, Upper Saddle River
16. Dorigo M, Stutzle T (2004) Ant colony optimization. Mit Press, Cambridge
17. Fan X, Weber W, Barroso L (2007) Power provisioning for a warehouse-sized computer. ACM SIGARCH Comput Archit News 35(2):13–23
18. Feller E, Rilling L, Morin C (2011), Energy-aware ant colony based workload placement in clouds, in proceedings of the 2011 IEEE/ACM 12th international conference on grid computing, pp 26–33
19. Feller E, Morin C, Esnault A (2012) A case for fully decentralized dynamic VM consolidation in clouds, in cloud computing technology and science (CloudCom), 2012 IEEE 4th international conference on, pp 26–33.
20. Gao Y, Guan H, Qi Z, Hou Y, Liu L (2013) A multi-objective ant colony system algorithm for virtual machine placement in cloud computing. J Comput Syst Sci 79(8):1230–1242
21. Guazzone M, Anglano C, Canonico M (2011) Energy-efficient resource management for cloud computing infrastructures, in cloud computing technology and science (CloudCom), 2011 IEEE third international conference on, pp 424–431
22. He S, Guo L, Guo Y (2011) Real time elastic cloud management for limited resources, in cloud computing (CLOUD), 2011 IEEE international conference on, pp 622–629

23. Hermenier F, Lorca X, Menaud J-M, Muller G, Lawall J (2009) Entropy: a consolidation manager for clusters, in proceedings of the 2009 ACM SIGPLAN/SIGOPS international conference on virtual execution environments, ACM, New York, NY, USA, pp 41–50
24. Industry Perspectives (2013) Using a total cost of ownership (TCO) model for your data center. http://www.datacenterknowledge.com/archives/2013/10/01/using-a-total-cost-of-ownership-tco-model-for-your-data-center/. Accessed 2 Jan 2014
25. Jung G, Joshi K, Hiltunen M, Schlichting R, Pu C (2009) A cost-sensitive adaptation engine for server consolidation of multitier applications, Middleware 2009, pp 163–183
26. Jussien N, Rochart G, Lorca X (2008) The CHOCO constraint programming solver, in CPAIOR'08 workshop on open-source software for integer and constraint programming (OS-SICP'08)
27. Kaplan J, M Forrest W, Kindler N (2008) Revolutionizing data center efficiency. McKinsey & Company
28. Kivity A, Kamay Y, Laor D, Lublin U, Liguori A (2007) Kvm: the Linux virtual machine monitor, in proceedings of the Linux Symposium, pp 225–230
29. Kusic D, Kephart JO, Hanson JE, Kandasamy N, Jiang G (2009) Power and performance management of virtualized computing environments via lookahead control. Clust Comput 12(1):1–15
30. Levine J, Ducatelle F (2004) Ant colony optimization and local search for Bin Packing and cutting stock problems. J Oper Res Soc 55(7):705–716
31. Li B, Li J, Huai J, Wo T, Li Q, Zhong L (2009) EnaCloud: an energy-saving application live placement approach for cloud computing environments, in cloud computing, 2009. CLOUD'09. IEEE international conference on, pp 17–24
32. Lim MY, Rawson F, Bletsch T, Freeh VW, (2009), Padd: power aware domain distribution, in distributed computing systems, 2009. ICDCS'09. 29th IEEE international conference on, pp 239–247
33. Lo J (2005) VMware and CPU virtualization technology. World Wide Web electronic publication
34. Mell P, Grance T (2011) The NIST definition of cloud computing (draft). NIST special publication vol 800, pp 145
35. Meng X, Isci C, Kephart J, Zhang L, Bouillet E, Pendarakis D (2010) Efficient resource provisioning in compute clouds via VM multiplexing, in proceedings of the 7th international conference on autonomic computing, pp 11–20
36. Mi H, Wang H, Yin G, Zhou Y, Shi D, Yuan L (2010) Online self-reconfiguration with performance guarantee for energy-efficient large-scale cloud computing data centers, in services computing (SCC), 2010 IEEE international conference on, pp 514–521
37. Miller R (2013) Ballmer: Microsoft has 1 million servers. http://www.datacenterknowledge.com/archives/2013/07/15/ballmer-microsoft-has-1-million-servers/. Accessed 2 Jan 2014
38. Mishra M, Sahoo A (2011) On theory of VM placement: anomalies in existing methodologies and their mitigation using a novel vector based approach, in cloud computing (CLOUD), 2011 IEEE international conference on, pp 275–282
39. Nagarajan A, Mueller F, Engelmann C, Scott S (2007) Proactive fault tolerance for HPC with Xen virtualization, in proceedings of the 21st annual international conference on supercomputing, pp 23–32
40. Nelson M, Lim B, Hutchins G et al (2005) Fast transparent migration for virtual machines, in proceedings of the annual conference on USENIX annual technical conference, pp 25–25
41. Nguyen Van H, Dang Tran F, Menaud J-M (2009) Autonomic virtual resource management for service hosting platforms, in proceedings of the 2009 ICSE workshop on software engineering challenges of cloud computing, IEEE Computer Society, Washington, DC, USA, pp 1–8
42. Nurmi D, Wolski R, Grzegorczyk C, Obertelli G, Soman S, Youseff L, Zagorodnov D (2009) The eucalyptus open-source cloud-computing system, in cluster computing and the grid, 2009. CCGRID'09. 9th IEEE/ACM International Symposium on, pp 124–131
43. Smith J, Nair R (2005) Virtual machines: versatile platforms for systems and processes. Morgan Kaufmann, Burlington

44. Sotomayor B, Montero R, Llorente I, Foster I (2009) Virtual infrastructure management in private and hybrid clouds. Internet Comput IEEE 13(5):14–22
45. Speitkamp B, Bichler M (2010) A mathematical programming approach for server consolidation problems in virtualized data centers. IEEE Trans Serv Comput 3(4):266–278
46. Srikantaiah S, Kansal A, Zhao F (2008) Energy aware consolidation for cloud computing, in proceedings of the 2008 conference on power aware computing and systems
47. Takemura C, Crawford L (2009) The book of Xen: a practical guide for the system administrator. No Starch, San Francisco
48. Van Hein N, Tran F, Menaud J-M (2009) SLA-aware virtual resource management for cloud infrastructures, in computer and information technology, 2009. CIT '09. Ninth IEEE international conference on, pp 357–362.
49. Van Hein N, Tran F, Menaud J-M, (2010), Performance and power management for cloud infrastructures, in cloud computing (CLOUD), 2010 IEEE 3rd international conference on, pp 329–336.
50. Vaquero L, Rodero-Merino L, Caceres J, Lindner M (2008) A break in the clouds: towards a cloud definition. ACM SIGCOMM Comput Commun Rev 39(1):50–55
51. Verma A, Ahuja P, Neogi A (2008) pMapper: power and migration cost aware application placement in virtualized systems, in proceedings of the 9th ACM/IFIP/USENIX international conference on middleware, Springer-Verlag New York, Inc., New York, NY, USA, pp 243–264
52. Verma A, Kumar G, Koller R (2010) The cost of reconfiguration in a cloud, in proceedings of the 11th international middleware conference industrial track, pp 11–16
53. Verma A, Kumar G, Koller R, Sen A, (2011), Cosmig: modeling the impact of reconfiguration in a cloud, in modeling, analysis & simulation of computer and telecommunication systems (MASCOTS), 2011 IEEE 19th international symposium on, pp 3–11
54. Vogels W (2008) Beyond server consolidation. Queue 6(1):20–26
55. Voorsluys W, Broberg J, Venugopal S, Buyya R (2009) Cost of virtual machine live migration in clouds: a performance evaluation, Cloud Computing, pp 254–265
56. Walsh W, Tesauro G, Kephart J, Das R, (2004), Utility functions in autonomic systems, in autonomic computing, 2004. Proceedings international conference on, pp 70–77
57. Wood T, Shenoy P, Venkataramani A, Yousif M (2009) Sandpiper: Black-box and gray-box resource management for virtual machines. Comput Netw 53(17):2923–2938
58. Xu J, Fortes JA (2010) Multi-objective virtual machine placement in virtualized data center environments, in Green Computing and Communications (GreenCom), 2010 IEEE/ACM Int'l conference on & int'l Conference on Cyber, Physical and Social Computing (CPSCom), pp 179–188
59. Zhang Q, Cheng L, Boutaba R (2010) Cloud computing: state-of-the-art and research challenges. J Internet Serv Appl 1(1):7–18

Chapter 9
Software-Defined Networking (SDN) for Cloud Applications

Lin Lin and Ping Lin

Abstract One of the key requirements of cloud computing is the dynamic provisioning and configuration of communications networks that interconnect dynamically provisioned and configured computing and storage elements. Traditional networking approaches are often not optimal for this type of usage since these tend to build and tune the network infrastructure based on information available at the lower networking layers only, without tying into the time-varying communication needs of the mix of applications that are currently running. These, then, lack the programmability needed to directly control the network based on higher-layer information or a more global view of network resource utilization. Software-defined networking (SDN), which separates the control plane of a network from its data plane and enables programmability of network behavior, is a new architecture that aims to support flexible application-driven networking. This chapter introduces the architecture of SDN, and gives a brief overview of its development including the key previous works, the current state of the art, and implementation challenges. The chapter also illustrates what SDN can do for infrastructure-as-a-service (IaaS) cloud computing through a number of open-source technology examples including Open-Stack, OpenFlow, and Floodlight. After examining some cloud datacenter usage scenarios in the areas of network virtualization, network functions virtualization, and traffic engineering, we conclude by looking at how SDN techniques may be applied to unified communications cloud applications which depend on the integration of voice and data networking.

Keywords Software-defined networking · SDN · OpenFlow · OpenStack · SDN controller · Software-defined data center · SDDC · Cloud computing · Infrastructure-as-a-service · IaaS · Unified communications · UC

P. Lin (✉) · L. Lin
Avaya Canada, 250 Sidney Street, Belleville, ON, K8P 3Z3, Canada
e-mail: linping@avaya.com

L. Lin
e-mail: linlin@avaya.com

© Springer International Publishing Switzerland 2014
Z. Mahmood (ed.), *Cloud Computing,* Computer Communications and Networks,
DOI 10.1007/978-3-319-10530-7_9

209

9.1 Introduction

Cloud computing requires dynamic provisioning, configuration, and reconfiguration of not only computing elements but also the communications networks that interconnect these elements. For example, a virtual machine that runs an application which needs to communicate with end-user devices or other applications needs to "bring its networking configuration along" when it is first set up or when it is relocated. As another example, an application that provides audio/video conferencing with shared whiteboarding may require varying amounts of bandwidth for the different media flows involved at different times depending on the number of users served, their locations, and the types of media that they choose to use.

In many cases, building and tuning the network infrastructure based on information available at the network level only—without tying into the time-varying communications requirements of the mix of applications that are currently running—will result in high overhead in coordinating applications with the networking configurations that they need, as well as nonoptimal usage of network resources. Since the quantity and nature of computing tasks in a cloud environment change constantly, what is often needed to achieve greater efficiency is a way of programmatically setting up/ tearing down networks and controlling network flows based on information from above the network layer or a more global view of network resource utilization, rather than "simply letting distributed networking algorithms converge."

Software-defined networking (SDN), a technology that separates the control plane of a network from its data plane and enables programmability of network behavior, can potentially provide useful solutions to the problems described above.

This chapter aims to explore how SDN techniques can be used in cloud computing and applications. It is divided into the following sections:

- SDN architecture. This section gives an overview of the concept of SDN, common architectural approaches to SDN, and the architecture of OpenFlow/ SDN which is currently the more prevalent approach in the industry.
- The IaaS cloud—SDN software stack. The OpenStack platform is described as an example of an IaaS cloud framework, and the OpenFlow protocol and SDN controllers are introduced in this context.
- The software-defined data center. This section discusses some of the ways in which SDN techniques can be used to build a flexible software-defined cloud data center in which networking is provisioned, configured, and reconfigured programmatically from a logically centralized point that has a global view of the network and can leverage information about the data center's current application workload.
- SDN implementation challenges. This section discusses some of the key issues that current SDN implementations face and what is being/could potentially be done about these issues.
- SDN for unified communications applications. Two use cases are examined in this section to illustrate some ways in which a specific type of application, unified communications (UC), can make use of SDN. A high-level interaction model between UC and SDN is also presented.

9.2   SDN Architecture

SDN is a new networking paradigm that offers: (1) Decoupling of the control plane of a network from its data plane; (2) Direct programmability of network control; as well as (3) Standardized application programming interfaces (APIs).

The control plane of a network consists of functions that control the behavior of the network, such as network paths or forwarding patterns, while the data plane consists of functions that are responsible for the actual forwarding (or not forwarding) of traffic, which are usually instantiated as flow tables in network switches, routers, and middleboxes (e.g., firewalls, network address translators, etc.).

By decoupling the control plane from the data plane, an SDN enables administrators to dynamically adjust network-wide traffic flow to meet changing requirements. It is also this decoupling that makes direct programmability of network control possible, so that applications can interact programmatically with the SDN control plane and control the operation of the network through standardized APIs.

9.2.1   SDN Architectural Approaches

The Internet Research Task Force's SDN Research Group identified three common architectural approaches to SDN [1], based on distinctions including centralized vs. distributed control, different degrees of separation of control and data planes, and different programmability points. These approaches are:

- OpenFlow/SDN (OF/SDN), which is characterized by complete separation of control and data planes, open programmable interfaces to the data plane, and logically centralized control.
- Control Plane/SDN (CP/SDN), which aims to make existing distributed control planes programmable.
- Overlay/SDN (OL/SDN), which overlays a new programmable control plane (or in some cases a new programmable data plane) on top of existing control and data planes.

Instead of being cut-and-dried, these three approaches are actually points in a continuous architectural feature space, and it is possible to mix and match the features that the three approaches represent.

Currently in the industry (at the time of writing in 2014), OF/SDN and OL/SDN are the more prevalent approaches and the two are often used together, with OF/SDN occupying the primary position and leveraging OL/SDN through its centralized control capability. The SDN discussed in the rest of this chapter will be this blend of OF/SDN and OL/SDN.

9.2.2 OF/SDN Architecture

In the OF/SDN architecture, applications and cloud operating environments interact programmatically with the SDN controller, which (logically) centralizes network intelligence and maintains a global view of the network, and appears to the applications as a single, logical switch. The controller presents a northbound interface to the application layer, and a southbound interface to the network devices that it controls.

Network administrators can configure, manage, secure, and optimize network resources dynamically using programs which they can write themselves to interact with the controller. Some of these tasks can also be delegated to business logic residing in the applications or embedded in cloud operating environments when it is desirable to do so for efficiency reasons (i.e., when "the application knows its requirements best" and can achieve efficient utilization of network resources more readily and rapidly by directly controlling the network).

When implemented through open standards, SDN simplifies network design and operation by presenting a single controller interface to the application layer instead of multiple vendor-specific device-level interfaces. This effectively abstracts the network infrastructure for ease of utilization by applications and services.

Figure 9.1 presents a high-level view of OF/SDN architecture.

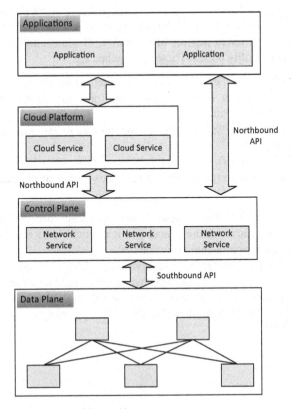

Fig. 9.1 Software-defined networking architecture

9.2.3   A Brief Overview of SDN Developments

Although the field of SDN is relatively new, the basic ideas of network programmability and control plane decoupling have actually been discussed at length in the industry since at least the mid−1990s. For example, the Open Signalling Workgroup [2] held workshops as early as 1995 with the goal of "making ATM, Internet and mobile networks more open, extensible, and programmable." Research in the area of active networking [3] around the same timeframe also led to mechanisms for sending remote code capsules and performing local programming on switches, although they were not adopted in practice due to the lack of compelling use cases at the time.

The concept of OF/SDN started around 2004 from the SANE [4] and Ethane [5] projects which defined an architecture that employs a centralized controller to manage security policies in a network. In this architecture, the controller, which is responsible for deciding if a packet should be forwarded or not, instructs the simple Ethernet switches to modify their flow tables, thereby directly implementing the security policy.

SANE and Ethane were the immediate predecessors of OpenFlow [6], which is currently (as of 2014) the most widely adopted mechanism for SDN programmability. The first version of the OpenFlow protocol specification was published in 2009. In 2011, the Open Networking Foundation (ONF) was formed by a group of service providers to commercialize, standardize, and promote the use of OpenFlow in production networks. A number of vendors, including Brocade, HP, Juniper, IBM, NEC, and others, have implemented support for OpenFlow in their physical switches. In addition, there are several software-based virtual switches available, such as Open vSwitch and VMware's virtual switch.

Quite a few SDN controllers have been developed, including both open-source and commercial implementations. Some examples include NOX and POX by Nicira, Floodlight by Big Switch, and OpenDaylight by multiple contributors. Further information on various available controllers can be found in [7]; while [8] describes the operation of the NOX controller in some detail.

Although, OpenFlow is a standardized protocol for the southbound SDN controller interface, it should be recognized that SDN controllers can use a variety of other open or proprietary interfaces to communicate with switches, and it is necessary to do so from a practical point of view so that SDN can work with existing switches without requiring a complete upgrade.

As for the northbound SDN controller interface, there is currently no standardization, although standards are likely to be formulated as usage of SDN increases.

9.3   The IaaS Cloud—SDN Software Stack

9.3.1   OpenStack

We start by examining an IaaS cloud to identify what an SDN would be called upon to implement. To be specific, we will look at OpenStack [9]. Its feature set is very similar to that of the commonly-used Amazon Elastic Compute Cloud (EC2) and Simple Storage Service (S3), but being open-source, one can readily see how SDNs fit in.

OpenStack originated from compute code from NASA and storage code from Rackspace. It is now managed by the nonprofit OpenStack Foundation and released on a 6-month cycle. The discussion that follows is based on the Havana release that is current at the time of writing.

As shown in Fig. 9.2, OpenStack consists of a set of interacting services:

- Nova: Virtual machines (VMs)
- Neutron: Virtual networks
- Cinder: Block storage
- Swift: Object storage
- Glance: VM images
- Keystone: Identity management
- Ceilometer: Usage metering
- Horizon: Web-based dashboard
- Heat: Orchestration

Many of the services use external components to do the actual work, and only provide the APIs themselves and offer choice in component selection through the use of plugins and drivers. In this sense, OpenStack is really cloud middleware. The relevant services are now briefly described below:

Server Virtualization Nova provides virtual machines. It manages a set of physical compute nodes; in particular, it picks the server on which to instantiate a VM. It uses an actual hypervisor such as Kernel-based Virtual Machine (KVM) or Xen to implement VMs. VMs come in different flavors that differ by the amount of processor, memory, disk space, and network bandwidth.

A VM can be migrated from one physical server to another. This can be used, for example, to dynamically consolidate active VMs onto fewer servers, thus allowing a data center to save on electricity and cooling.

Glance provides disk images containing the guest operating system and application for a VM. It is a catalogue; the actual images are stored in file systems or object stores.

Storage Virtualization Three types of storage are available to a VM, viz:

- Ephemeral storage: that behaves like a disk, except that its contents are lost when the VM is deleted. Typical uses include hosting the root file system that holds a copy of the VM image and providing temporary directories.

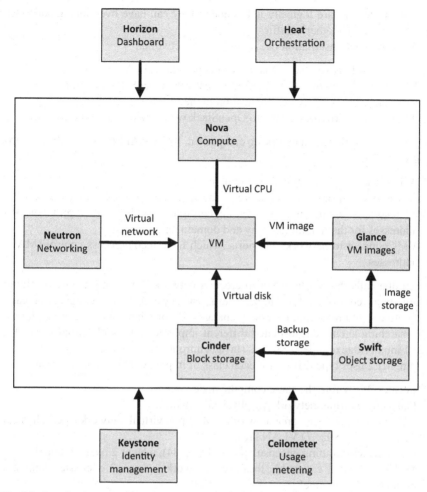

Fig. 9.2 OpenStack services

- Block storage: that also behaves like a disk, but its lifetime is independent of VMs. It comes in the form of volumes that may be attached and detached from VMs. Cinder provides volumes by calling on an actual volume manager such as the Linux Logical Volume Manager (LVM). A VM accesses a volume using the Internet small computer system interface (iSCSI). A typical use of block storage is to hold a database.
- Object storage: that provides highly scalable and reliable storage for files. It is not a traditional file system; files are uploaded and downloaded in their entirety over HTTP. It is typically slower than ephemeral or block storage. Swift implements object storage by distributing replicas of a file over a set of storage nodes.

Network Virtualization VMs are connected to virtual networks. Every tenant of an OpenStack cloud can define its very own set of virtual networks. Networks belonging to different tenants are logically independent; they can have overlapping addresses and do not see each other's traffic.

An OpenStack installation has four physical networks:

- Data network: Hosts the virtual networks populated by VMs.
- Management network: Communication between OpenStack components.
- External network: Provides connection to the Internet.
- API network: Provides access to OpenStack web services from the Internet.

Neutron is OpenStack's networking component. Its base API has three abstractions as given below:

- A network is a layer 2 broadcast domain.
- A network can have one or more subnets, which are blocks of IPv4 or IPv6 addresses. A subnet may further be configured with Internet protocol (IP) addresses for the default gateway and domain name servers.
- VMs connect to networks via ports, which have media access control (MAC) addresses.

When one calls the Neutron API to create a network, for example, one is talking to a network controller. The latter, in turn, uses a plugin to direct agents on each compute node to make the necessary changes. Before the Havana release, plugins and matching agents encapsulated different implementations of virtual networks, e.g., Linux bridge or Open vSwitch. Havana introduced the Modular Layer 2 (ML2) plugin. ML2 uses type drivers for each class of implementation. The types are:

- Local: VMs within the same compute node.
- Flat: Single virtual network per physical network.
- VLAN: Virtual local area network—Multiple virtual networks per physical network using 802.1Q VLAN tags.
- GRE: Generic routing encapsulation (RFC 2784), a layer 2 over IP tunnel.
- VXLAN: Virtual extensible local area network, a layer 2 over user datagram protocol (UDP) tunnel.

ML2 mechanism drivers are specific to each implementation and communicate with the agents.

The Neutron API has a growing number of extensions. Provider networks are virtual networks that map to a specific physical network. They are used to provide connectivity to the Internet or to parts of a tenant's private network outside of the cloud.

Virtual routers are used to connect virtual networks. They can also perform network address translation. A floating IP address can be assigned to a port in a network. When the router (as the network's default gateway) receives a packet from the port's fixed address, it rewrites the source address to the floating address before forwarding. The destination is similarly rewritten in the opposite direction.

Network Functions Virtualization Neutron's security groups extension controls what network traffic is allowed into and out of a VM. A group contains rules which specify filtering by protocol, port, and source address. A VM can be a member of one or more groups. Firewall functionality is distributed across compute nodes.

Havana introduced an experimental firewall as a service extension. A virtual firewall attaches to one or more networks, either at layer 2 or 3. A firewall carries out a policy, which is a set of filtering rules. In this sense, a firewall policy is similar to a security group.

Load balancing as a service is another extension. The reference implementation wraps the HAProxy load balancer.

9.3.2   OpenFlow

OpenFlow is a widely-implemented protocol between the controller and the network devices in an SDN for the purposes of enabling network programmability from a centralized viewpoint.

The OpenFlow switch specification [10] covers the components and basic functions of an (abstract) OpenFlow switch, and the protocol for an external controller to control the switch's operation by adding, updating, and deleting rules in the switch for forwarding and packet modification.

Support for OpenFlow switches can be plugged in to OpenStack Neutron as mechanism drivers for the ML2 plugin (preferred) or as their own plugins. The mechanism driver for Open vSwitch, a software switch that implements OpenFlow, is included with the Neutron distribution.

9.3.2.1   OpenFlow Switch

Figure 9.3 presents a model of an OpenFlow switch, which consists of the following:

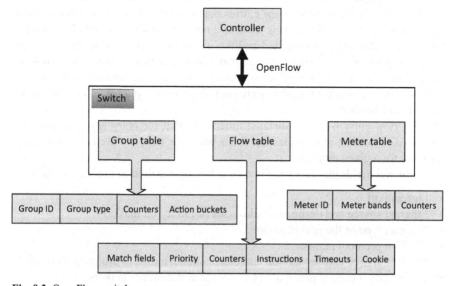

Fig. 9.3 OpenFlow switch

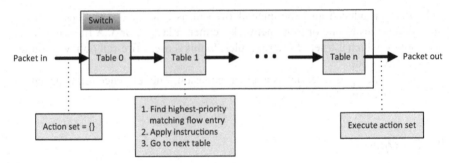

Fig. 9.4 OpenFlow pipeline processing

- One or more flow tables: Each flow table contains a set of flow entries; each flow entry consists of match fields, counters, and a set of instructions to apply to matching packets.
- A group table that contains group entries; each group entry contains a list of action buckets. The actions in one or more action buckets are applied to packets sent to the group.
- A meter table that contains meter entries; each meter entry defines a per-flow meter used to measure packet rate and enable rate limiting or other similar operations.
- An OpenFlow channel to an external controller.

The controller uses the OpenFlow protocol to add, update, and delete entries in the flow and group tables, both proactively and reactively (in response to packets).

The tables in the OpenFlow switch form a pipeline for processing incoming packets, as shown in Fig. 9.4.

When a packet arrives at a switch, the header fields are matched against the entries in the first flow table. Flow entries match packets in priority order, and the first matching entry in the table is used. If a matching entry is found, the counters indicated in that entry are updated and the instructions specified are executed. If no match is found in a flow table, the instructions specified by the table-miss flow entry are executed. A variety of actions may be taken such as forwarding the packet to the controller over the OpenFlow channel, dropping the packet, or continuing on to the next flow table.

Each flow entry has an associated timeout so that the entry is either removed after a fixed amount of time, or after it has been idle (i.e., not used to process any packets) for a given duration.

The match fields that all OpenFlow switches are required to implement include:

- Ingress port
- Ethernet source and destination addresses (arbitrary bit masks)
- Ethernet type of the packet payload
- IP v4/v6 protocol number
- IP v4/v6 source and destination addresses (subnet masks or arbitrary bit masks)
- Transmission control protocol (TCP) source and destination ports
- UDP source and destination ports

It can be seen that OpenFlow matching enables forwarding and packet modification actions to be based on more fields compared to traditional destination-based forwarding.

Counters are intended to provide readings (e.g., on a per-flow or per-port basis) that enable the controller to measure and optimize network traffic.

Instructions associated with each flow entry either contain actions or modify pipeline processing by directing the packet to a higher-numbered flow table. The actions may be executed immediately if so specified, or accumulated in the packet's action set to be executed at the end of the pipeline. The types of actions include:

- Required actions that must be supported by every implementation
  - Output: Forwards the packet to a port, which may be a physical port, a switch-defined logical port (used to represent, e.g., link aggregation groups, tunnels, or loopback interfaces), or a reserved port (used to represent, e.g., sending to the controller, flooding, etc.).
  - Drop: Drops the packet (this is actually represented by a lack of actions to execute).
  - Group: Sends the packet to the specified group for processing.

- Optional actions
  - Set-queue: Sets the queue identifier that determines which of the queues associated with a port is used for scheduling and forwarding the packet.
  - Set-field: Rewrites a header field in the packet.
  - Push-tag/Pop-tag: Push or pop tags such as VLAN headers, etc.
  - Change-TTL: Changes the time-to-live or hop limit of the packet.

When the group action is used, it directs packets to a group in the switch's group table. Groups are used to implement operations such as multicast and broadcast forwarding, load sharing, IP forwarding to a common next hop, etc.

Switch designers are free to implement the internals of an OpenFlow switch in any way as long as the correct match and instruction semantics are realized. Also, some OpenFlow switches may support hybrid operation and implement both an OpenFlow pipeline and a traditional packet forwarding mechanism.

9.3.2.2 OpenFlow Protocol

The controller communicates with the OpenFlow switch over a connection that is typically secured with transport layer security (TLS). The OpenFlow protocol used for this communication supports the three types of messages shown below along with the main messages of each type:

- Controller-to-switch
  - Features: Find out the identity and basic capabilities of a switch.
  - Configuration: Set and query configuration parameters in the switch.
  - Modify-state: Add, update and delete flow/group table entries, and set switch port properties.

- Read-state: Obtain information from the switch including current configuration, statistics and capabilities.
- Packet-out: Used by the controller to send packets out of a specific port of the switch, or to forward a packet received via a Packet-in message earlier on.

• Asynchronous (switch-to-controller, unsolicited)
- Packet-in: Transfer the control of a packet to the controller.
- Flow-removed: Inform the controller of the removal of a flow table entry.
- Port-status: Inform the controller of a change on a port, e.g., up/down.

• Symmetric (controller-to-switch or switch-to-controller, unsolicited)
- Hello: Exchanged at connection start-up time.
- Echo: Used to ascertain liveness of the connection.
- Error: Inform the other side of an error condition.

A number of messages can be packaged together into a bundle so that they are treated as a single operation, i.e., either all of the changes are applied or none are applied.

9.3.3   SDN Controllers

Having looked at OpenFlow as a concrete example of protocols between SDN controllers and switches, we are now in a position to examine what a controller does in more detail.

An SDN controller is typically comprised of the following components:

• A database or other repository of information needed to facilitate management and distribution of network state. The contents of the database includes information obtained from network devices as well as information associated with SDN applications.
• A high-level data model that captures the relationships between managed resources, policies and other services provided by the controller.
• A northbound API that exposes the controller services to applications. Some controllers also allow expansion of core capabilities and publishing of APIs for new plugin modules.
• A secure control session between the controller and the associated agents on the network devices within the controller's scope.
• One or more protocols for provisioning application-driven network state on devices.
• A device, topology, and service discovery mechanism.
• A path computation mechanism.
• Other network services that may be needed.

The SDN controller is the main area where vendors compete to differentiate their SDN capabilities, and therefore there are many products and open-source implementations available. As one example, the Floodlight open-source controller [11] is structured as shown in Fig. 9.5.

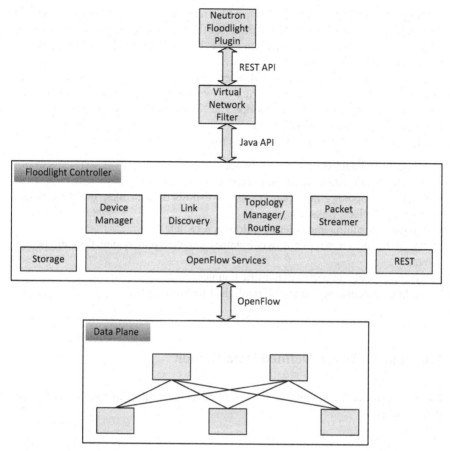

Fig. 9.5 Floodlight controller

Floodlight is written in Java and organized into modules. The core modules are as follows:

- OpenFlow services provide an API over OpenFlow. Incoming messages are turned into Floodlight events that other modules can obtain by subscription.
- The device manager monitors packets referred to the controller via OpenFlow to discover what devices are connected to the network. It tracks each device's MAC address, IP address, and attachment points (i.e., switch and port).
- Link discovery uses link layer discovery protocol (LLDP) and broadcast domain discovery protocol (BDDP) packets to infer the connectivity between switches.
- The topology manager extracts islands of OpenFlow switches from link discovery data. The routing function uses Dijkstra's algorithm to compute the shortest path between two devices.
- The packet streamer is used to examine the conversation between the controller and a switch.

Floodlight modules may provide a Java API, a representational state transfer (REST) API, or both. The northbound API is therefore the union of all the individual module APIs. Applications that need access to events have to use the Java API, and run as additional modules alongside the controller.

A pair of applications is involved when Floodlight is used to provide network virtualization to OpenStack. The virtual network filter is a module that exports a REST API for creating virtual networks. The Neutron Floodlight plugin consists of Python code that calls this API.

The Floodlight APIs include functions for:

- Creating and deleting a virtual network
- Attaching and removing a host to/from a virtual network
- Obtaining topology information such as listings of networks, switches, switch clusters, devices, links, etc.
- Proactively adding and deleting a flow in a switch
- Retrieving different types of switch statistics such as port, queue, flow, aggregate, etc.
- Listing global and per-switch traffic counters
- Adding and deleting a rule in Floodlight's firewall module

9.4   The Software-Defined Data Center

We now consider, by way of examples, how SDN techniques are used in IaaS cloud data centers.

9.4.1   Network Virtualization

Cloud workloads frequently consist of multiple communicating VMs, e.g., a business application might consist of separate web, application, and database tiers, making virtual networks an essential part of a cloud service offering. Enterprise software that populates these tiers often uses broadcasting or multicasting to implement clustering. Implementing a layer 2 abstraction enables these schemes to continue working in the virtual network.

A multi-tenant cloud brings additional requirements including:

- Isolation: Different tenants should not be able to see each other's traffic.
- Independent addressing: The cloud may be an extension of a tenant's existing data center, and VMs would have to follow the data center's addressing scheme.
- Automatic provisioning: Virtual networks need to be brought up and down within minutes. Manual procedures are too slow and error-prone.

802.1Q VLAN is one way to implement virtual networks that satisfies the first two requirements. One problem is that the 12-bit VLAN ID limits the number of networks possible to at most 4096. A more serious concern is that the entire physical

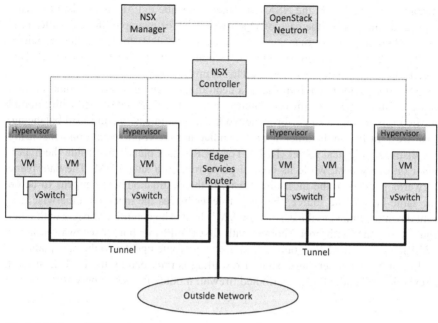

Fig. 9.6 VMware NSX

network that underpins the cloud has to be layer 2. This has some undesirable consequences, e.g.:

- Lack of address summarization: The number of VMs is potentially large, and they come and go all the time.
- Inefficiencies in spanning tree protocol: Instead of utilizing all available links between switches, many links have to be disabled in order to avoid loops in the topology.

Layer 3 tunnels such as VXLAN are therefore favored for implementing virtual networks. They support a larger number of networks; e.g., VXLAN has a 24-bit network ID. They can take advantage of the spine-leaf network topology used for east-west traffic between VMs; tunnels can be distributed to different links using equal-cost multipath routing.

This is the context for VMware's NSX network virtualization offering. NSX is a merger of VMware's vCloud Network and Security (vCNS) with Nicira's Network Virtualization Platform (NVP), which is an SDN controller. As such, it can operate in either a pure vSphere environment (VMware ESXi hypervisor only) or a mixed environment (Xen, KVM, and ESXi).

Figure 9.6 shows the generic architecture of NSX. There are three types of virtual switch: vSphere distributed switch (for ESXi in a vSphere environment), Open vSwitch (for Xen and KVM), and NSX vSwitch (for ESXi in a mixed environment).

Virtual layer 2 networks are realized using layer 3 tunnels between machines hosting participating VMs. When a network is created, either at the behest of NSX manager or OpenStack, the NSX controller's northbound API is invoked to create a mesh of tunnels. In the case of Open vSwitch, for example, the controller uses open vSwitch database management protocol (OVSDB) to define the tunnels at each switch and OpenFlow to set up the mapping from IP address to tunnel ID. This means that multicasting is not needed to set up VXLAN.

NSX routes north-south traffic in a centralized manner using the edge services router (ESR), which is a software router in a VM. The ESR is designed with external traffic in mind, and also performs network address translation and load balancing. East-west traffic, on the other hand, is handled in pure vSphere environments using the distributed logical router (DLR). The DLR's data plane runs inside the hypervisor on every host, while its control plane runs in a single VM. The data plane forwards packets in the most direct way. If the destination VM happens to be on the same host as the source, the packet never leaves the machine; otherwise it is sent down the tunnel to the destination VM's host. The control VM peers with other routers as usual with open shortest path first (OSPF) or border gateway protocol (BGP), but uses the NSX controller to distribute route updates to the data planes.

In a similar manner, north-south firewalling is provided by the ESR. East-west firewalling is handled by a distributed firewall module in each hypervisor.

9.4.2 Network Functions Virtualization

In addition to interconnected VMs, most cloud applications need to access the Internet or some other external network, filter network traffic, and distribute requests among VMs. In other words, virtual machines also need virtual routers, firewalls, and load balancers. These may be realized by using multitenant functionality in physical devices or by introducing service VMs into tenant networks. On the other hand, the flow level primitives from which these functions can be built are available in Open vSwitch and are being added to OpenFlow over time. A third implementation is thus to distribute the work amongst hypervisor-based virtual switches.

Midokura's MidoNet is an example of this approach. It provides virtual layer 2 and layer 3 networks, as well as virtual load balancers and firewalls. Every machine hosting VMs runs an Open vSwitch controlled by a MidoNet agent. Gateway machines are used to interface to external layer 2 and layer 3 networks; they also contain an Open vSwitch plus a MidoNet agent. Finally, network state is maintained in a distributed database.

Logically, a packet may traverse several nodes and be transformed in the process as it heads towards its destination. For example, when a packet is sent from a VM to a client on the Internet, it would go from a virtual tenant router to a gateway router. It might also undergo source network address translation (NAT). Physically, the first packet of a flow would be sent up to a MidoNet agent, which would look up the virtual network topology from the database, and add flow table entries to modify the source IP address, decrement time-to-live (TTL), and forward along a GRE tunnel to the gateway machine.

Similarly, when a packet comes in from the Internet for a VM, it would go through a virtual tenant firewall, destination NAT, and a virtual tenant router before arriving at the VM. For the first packet of a flow, the MidoNet agent on a gateway would check if the packet is allowed under the rules configured for the tenant in the database, and if so, add flow table entries to modify the destination IP address, decrement TTL, and forward along a GRE tunnel to the machine hosting the VM.

MidoNet uses a distributed synchronization service and a distributed database to propagate state to all agents.

Network topology is kept in Apache Zookeeper. Zookeeper's data model is that of a tree to which nodes bearing data can be added or deleted. Clients watch nodes for changes and are notified when they occur; this allows topology changes to take effect immediately. Physically, the tree is replicated over a set of servers, one of which is elected as leader. Any server may handle read requests, but writes must go through the leader and require quorum.

Session state, e.g., the IP address translation for a flow, is kept in Apache Cassandra. Cassandra is essentially a persistent distributed hash table; a row key calls up a set of key-value pairs. The data associated with a row key is replicated to a configurable number of servers chosen from a pool of servers. Any server may handle requests. The number of servers that must respond positively in order for a read or write request to be considered successful can be varied on a per-request basis in order to tradeoff between consistency and latency.

9.4.3 Traffic Engineering

Integrating information about application intent with global network state can lead to better choices in packet forwarding. VM relocation is one such case. When a VM is moved from one compute node to another, its entire memory image has to be transferred within seconds to avoid an outage at the application level.

Cloud data centers typically have a spine-leaf network topology. Compute nodes attach to leaf routers, and every leaf router is in turn linked to every spine router. If all such links have the same bandwidth, there are as many equivalent paths between two compute nodes as there are spine routers.

Equal cost multipath (ECMP) routing is usually used to distribute traffic across the paths by hashing on packet headers; this ensures that all packets belonging to a TCP connection take the same route. This works reasonably well when there are many small flows; however, there is no guarantee that several large flows from VM relocation will not end up on one path at the same time.

With an SDN, one can query the link utilization along all paths leading from the source to the destination compute node, and set up a flow to use the least loaded path. When no path of sufficient capacity is available, the memory transfer can be split up into several parallel transfers.

Taking this one step further, bandwidth availability (based on actual measurement) can be factored into the decision to make a particular VM move. If there is insufficient bandwidth leading from the source compute node, any move has to be postponed. On the other hand, insufficient bandwidth heading to a candidate destination compute node might be worked around by picking another candidate.

9.5   SDN Implementation Challenges

The usage of SDN is still in its early days, and a number of implementation challenges have been identified [12, 13], including:

How to build a high-performance programmable switch?

- When it comes to hardware implementations of switches, there is a trade-off between programmability/flexibility and performance. General purpose processors are the most flexible but offer lower performance and dissipate more power, while application-specific integrated circuits are the least flexible but provide the highest performance, power and cost benefits. There are technologies in between these two extremes, such as network flow processors, programmable logic devices, and application-specific standard products.
- It appears that given the programmability/performance trade-off, a hybrid approach where SDN functions are decomposed into sub-functions, each implemented using higher-performance or higher-flexibility technologies as best suited to its purpose, would be more effective.

How to build a scalable SDN controller that provides a global network view?

- SDN controller scalability is challenging due to factors such as the latency introduced in exchanging network information between multiple network devices and the controller, interactions between multiple (physical) controllers, and the size of the controller backend database.
- Some of the approaches for increasing controller scalability include consistent state sharing mechanisms for multiple controllers such as HyperFlow [14] and resolving some queries locally on the network device in order to reduce the amount of information exchanged with the controller and keep its database to a more manageable size.

How to ensure the security of a software-defined network?

- Given its privileged position in the network, the SDN controller makes for a very attractive target for malicious activity such as unauthorized modification of flow rules and denial of service attacks.
- Common security measures including mutual authentication, role-based authorization, transport layer security and intrusion detection are certainly applicable, but the SDN controller's programmability and open interfaces increase the "attack surface." On the positive side, one of the original usages of OF/SDN when the concept first appeared on the scene was to implement security policies in the network, and the advancements in this area that have taken place since then can be leveraged.

How to integrate SDN solutions into existing networks?

- In practice, SDN solutions are almost always deployed into an environment that already has a lot of existing network equipment and infrastructure. Even in greenfield situations, SDN solutions would likely need to work with switches and other equipment that are not SDN-enabled.

- Further development of backward-compatible interfaces, protocols and mechanisms is required to achieve interoperability between the SDN and non-SDN portions of a network in more than an ad-hoc manner.

How to make SDN solutions serve the needs of applications better?

- Although the main goal of the SDN architecture is to provide open programmability of the network to applications, current implementations of, e.g., SDN controller APIs, still have very low-level semantics that reflects the entities and relationships at the network level but not so much the ways in which applications formulate their requirements. Also, SDN efforts have so far been focused mostly on layer 3 (network layer) and below, and there has not been as much work on application traffic flows and configuration of applications in this context.
- SDN technology can actually be extended to manage application traffic above layer 3. For an example of a research project pursuing this direction, refer to [15]. There is also starting to be some work towards providing programming interfaces that better match the level of semantics needed by applications. Indeed, application- and policy-driven networking are the current thrust of several vendors in the telecommunications industry such as Avaya, Cisco and others.

9.6   SDN for UC Applications

As mentioned in the previous section, one of the key directions in which SDN is evolving is towards application-driven networking (ADN). In our view, studying the interactions between specific types of applications on the one hand and SDN on the other is a fruitful way to bring in more experience to inform the research that furthers this evolutionary trend. To this end, we will look at two use cases in this section to illustrate some ways in which a particular type of application—unified communications—can make use of SDN, and describe a high-level interaction model between UC and SDN.

Others in the industry are interested in the topic of SDN for UC applications as well. For example, the UC Interoperability Forum (UCIF) has signed an agreement with ONF in November 2013 to define a framework and API that capture the interaction of UC with various SDN functions, which will likely build upon related work from ONF.

9.6.1   UC Applications

UC applications integrate real-time communications such as telephony, audio/video conferencing, presence and instant messaging with non-real-time functionality such as web browsing, email, voice mail and directories to provide a unified user experience across multiple media and device types. These applications are increasingly being hosted in the cloud. For example, public cloud service providers may offer IP telephony, instant messaging, web access to email/voice mail and other UC functionality to consumers and small/medium enterprise users, while private cloud data centers may provide larger enterprises with cost-effective ways to work across sites via audio/video conferencing, multimedia collaboration, etc.

Why are we discussing UC applications in the context of this chapter? In our view, UC is a particularly interesting application category because it represents the integration of voice and data networking.

With a lot of voice communication taking place over IP these days, the distinction between voice and data networking may have blurred to some extent, but voice and other forms of real-time communication such as video continue to place stringent requirements on the underlying data network. Fulfilment of these requirements is fundamental to providing a high-quality end user experience for UC.

In addition, a single UC application often involves coordination between multiple services each responsible for a different aspect of its functionality, and these services can have correlated networking requirements. For example, a user of a collaboration application may have a voice call, a text chat session and a shared whiteboard running simultaneously.

In any UC deployment, there can be many network elements, such as switches, routers, reverse proxies, firewalls, session border controllers, etc., that all need to be configured correctly for optimal media flow. Instead of having to configure all of these elements discretely, SDN can provide a single policy-based method of operation driven by the UC application.

9.6.2 Some Use Cases

Here, we present two use cases that aim to show a few of the ways in which UC applications can leverage SDN capabilities.

9.6.2.1 Automating Quality of Service Configuration

One of the key tasks in ensuring a high-quality end user experience for UC applications is the proper configuration of quality of service (QoS) in the underlying network. As part of its work on defining a UC SDN framework and API, the UCIF is publishing a number of use cases of which the first involves automating QoS configuration [16].

In this use case, a UC infrastructure component (acting on behalf of an endpoint or application) interacts with an automated QoS network service application (referred to as "QoS service" below), which in turn interacts with an SDN controller through its northbound interface. The QoS service maps QoS treatments requested by the UC infrastructure into actual QoS capabilities of the underlying network, e.g., by translating class of service specifications into differentiated services code point (DSCP) or wireless multimedia extensions (WMM) markings.

The use case's interactions can be divided into two parts which relate to signalling and media traffic respectively:

Signaling Traffic

1. When the UC infrastructure starts up, it authenticates with the QoS service.
2. The UC infrastructure then interacts with the QoS service to request that UC signaling traffic, e.g., session initiation protocol (SIP) traffic on TCP port 5061, be processed with the appropriate class of service. The QoS service configures the corresponding QoS policy on the network elements involved, e.g., re-mark TCP port 5061 traffic going from/to the IP address(es) of the UC infrastructure to DSCP class selector 3.
3. When a user starts a UC user agent (e.g., a physical or soft phone, conferencing client, etc.), the user agent exchanges signaling messages with the UC infrastructure to register itself.
4. When the user initiates a UC session (e.g., an audio or video call, conference, collaboration session, etc.), the user agent exchanges signaling messages with the UC infrastructure to request that a session be started. In response, the UC infrastructure exchanges signaling messages with the destination endpoint specified by the session initiator.
5. Once a session has been established, the UC endpoints involved in the session may exchange additional signaling messages to manage or terminate the session.

The signaling messages in steps 3, 4 and 5 are all re-marked to the appropriate priority based on the QoS policy configured on the network elements in step 2.

Media Traffic

6. The UC user agents in the session exchange signaling messages through the UC infrastructure to negotiate media flows. Typically there will be at least one flow in each direction. In addition, a session may include more than one media type (e.g., audio and video) and some media types may involve more than one media stream (e.g., live camera video and presentation video). Often media traffic is sent directly between the user agents without going through the UC infrastructure.
7. Each media flow can be uniquely identified by a 5-tuple consisting of its source IP address and port, destination IP address and port, plus network protocol. The UC infrastructure extracts this 5-tuple for each of the media flows involved in the session by looking at the signaling messages exchanged, and makes a request to the QoS service to set up the QoS policies needed to provide each flow with the appropriate treatment.
8. The QoS service determines the ingress and egress network elements involved in each media flow, and configure the corresponding QoS policies on these network elements. This causes the media flows to be re-marked to the appropriate

priority, including any flows that have already started before the QoS policies were set and were previously processed on a best effort basis.

9. Once the session completes, the UC infrastructure sends a request to the QoS service to remove the associated QoS policies from the network elements.

The description above applies to scenarios where the interacting endpoints and all of the intermediate network elements are in the same SDN administrative domain, i.e., within the scope of the same (logical) SDN controller. In the more general case where multiple SDN domains are involved, federation between the domains is needed to configure QoS end-to-end.

The main value of the automated QoS service application is in ensuring that only authentic UC media flows can be given higher-priority treatment as indicated by the policies that the QoS service configured on the network elements, rather than relying on markings provided by various endpoints which may or may not comply with overall network usage guidelines.

9.6.2.2 Providing Diagnostics to Facilitate Prioritization of Real-Time Wi-Fi Traffic

Microsoft Lync is a UC system that provides a single interface for the user to communicate via voice and video calls, conferences, presence, instant messaging, and persistent chat. In Lync server deployments, the end user experience can be adversely impacted by poor network performance that results in dropped calls, jittery audio or choppy video.

Microsoft has made a Lync SDN API available to facilitate real-time media traffic monitoring and QoS optimization. (It should be pointed out that this API is better described as an API to inform SDNs, rather than an SDN API in the sense of a controller API). The Lync SDN API has been applied by Aruba Networks to a use case involving its Wi-Fi solution. Building a Wi-Fi network to handle-real time voice and video traffic requires the ability to distinguish real-time from non-real-time traffic in order to prioritize and protect the former from disruption. Also needed is the ability to report quality problems with real-time traffic and identify possible causes. One constraint, however, is that since Wi-Fi traffic is often encrypted, it is not directly visible to observation.

In this use case, the Aruba Mobility Controller receives Lync network diagnostic information about voice, video, desktop sharing and file transfer through the SDN API. The Lync server sends information to the mobility controller when a call is initiated, which is used to identify clients in the call and prioritize their real-time traffic streams. When the call completes, the Lync server sends information (based on data from its quality-of-experience database containing reports sent in by Lync clients) to the mobility controller to provide visibility into call quality, which is correlated with the health of wireless devices and access points.

9.6.3   UC-SDN Interaction Model

The model shown in Table 9.1 identifies areas in which UC applications may interact with SDN, including some examples of usage scenarios in each area:

When defining a higher-level northbound API that matches the level of semantic abstraction needed by UC applications, rather than the lower level of detail that current SDN controller APIs offer, it would be useful to examine the areas in an interaction model such as this one, and include functions for each of the areas. Below we make some general observations related to this model:

- UC communication flows are generally not limited to the data center, but can "reach out" from the cloud to end user devices and "reach in" from the reverse direction. Although one could say that the same is true of web applications being accessed by web browsers, the difference in the UC case is that control of real-time communication flows goes right down to the end user device level.
- UC communication flows often involve explicit call setup, which provides a natural opportunity for configuring network-level flows.
- If network level flows and QoS settings are proactively configured as part of call setup, the configuration settings need to follow the end user device or UC application as it moves.
- IP-based voice networking can actually been seen as a parallel layer to data networking, and SIP telephony servers as well as other voice networking equipment such as media gateways, etc. can be viewed as the equivalent of data networking switches in the voice network.
- One could visualize a picture in which an application delivery controller is controlling flows at the application layer, while an SDN controller is controlling

Table 9.1 A UC–SDN interaction model

Interaction area	Sample usage scenario(s)
Device discovery and inventory	Automatically discovering an IP phone when it is plugged into the network (in a private cloud environment), and making its network attachment point/device capabilities known
Network topology configuration	Setting up an IP telephony trunk
Network flow configuration	Proactively setting up network flows as part of voice/video call setup
Quality of service	Prioritizing real-time traffic generated by a UC application
Traffic engineering	Adjusting network flows based on "big picture" knowledge of application activity such as multiple ongoing video conferences
Performance monitoring and diagnostics	Measuring latency, loss and jitter; identifying/localizing causes of quality issues
Security and access	Opening a port on the firewall that is required for specific UC application flows; assigning a class of service based on user role, access location, access method, etc.

flows at the networking layer and below, with the two controllers interworking with each other. The application layer flows have dependencies on the networking layer flows, which could be in the sense that the latter need to be set up once before the former can take place, or in the sense that the two are tied together dynamically and the presence of one or more application layer flows induces the corresponding networking layer flows.

9.7 Conclusions

In this chapter, we have suggested that software-defined networking brings open programmability, a more global network view and logically centralized control to satisfy the dynamic networking requirements of applications in a cloud computing environment. Of the challenges that need to be overcome in order to further the adoption of this technology, one of the most important is how SDN may be able to evolve from its current relatively low-level "bits-and-pipes" orientation to become more application-oriented, i.e., easier for applications to use its capabilities and for it to work directly with higher-level application flows. The end goal of this evolution can be termed application-defined networking.

We are of the opinion that studying the interactions between specific types of applications on the one hand and SDN on the other can bring in more experience to inform the research needed to make the SDN-to-ADN transition happen, and are working specifically with unified communications applications, which represent the integration of voice and data networking.

Two use cases—automating quality of service configuration, and providing diagnostics to facilitate prioritization of real-time Wi-Fi traffic—were considered in this chapter to illustrate some of the ways in which UC applications can leverage SDN capabilities. A high-level interaction model between UC and SDN was then sketched out. It was observed that SDN can provide a single policy-based method to configure multiple network elements involved in a UC deployment. Further, if one were to consider IP-based voice networking as a parallel layer to data networking, one could construct a model where an application delivery controller controls UC flows at the application layer while an SDN controller controls flows from the networking layer downwards, with the two controllers interworking with each other.

Given the interest in the telecom and computer industries in providing cloud-based UC applications such as voice/video calling, business collaboration, distance education, etc., we believe that there is potential for new fruitful work in this area that would make a substantial new contribution to ADN research.

Acknowledgements The authors are grateful to Prof. Alberto Leon-Garcia of the Dept. of Electrical and Computer Engineering, University of Toronto, and Mr. Ravi Palaparthi, Senior Director, Avaya Networking for reviewing this chapter, as well as to the anonymous referees for their helpful comments to improve the manuscript.

References

1. Meyer D (2013) The software-defined-networking research group. IEEE Internet Comput 17(6):84–87
2. Campbell A et al (1999) Open signaling for ATM, Internet and mobile networks (OpenSIG '98). ACM SIGCOMM Comput Commun Rev 29(1):97–108
3. Tennenhouse DL et al (1997) A survey of active network research. IEEE Commun Mag 35(1):80–86
4. Casado M et al (2006) SANE: a protection architecture for enterprise networks. USENIX security symp, August 2006
5. Casado M et al (2007) Ethane: taking control of the enterprise. ACM SIGCOMM Comput Commun Rev 37(4):1–12
6. McKeown N et al (2008) OpenFlow: enabling innovation in campus networks. ACM SIGCOMM Comput Commun Rev 38(2):69–74
7. Mendonca M et al (2014) A survey of software-defined networking: past, present, and future of programmable networks. IEEE Commun Surv Tutor PP(99):1–18
8. Gude N et al (2008) NOX: towards an operating system for networks. ACM SIGCOMM Comput Commun Rev 38(3):105–110
9. OpenStack cloud administrator guide—Havana, OpenStack Foundation, 2013
10. OpenFlow switch specification, version 1.4.0, Open Networking Foundation, 2013
11. Project Floodlight [web site], http://www.projectfloodlight.org
12. Sezer S et al (2013) Are we ready for SDN? Implementation challenges for software-defined networks. IEEE Commun Mag 51(7):36–43
13. Kuklinski S, Chemouil P (2014) Network management challenges in software-defined networks. IEICE Trans Commun E97-B(1):2–9
14. Tootoonchian A, Ganjali Y (2010) HyperFlow: a distributed control plane for OpenFlow. Proc. 2010 Internet network management conference on research on enterprise networking
15. Paul S, Jain R (2012) OpenADN: mobile apps on global clouds using OpenFlow and software-defined networking. International workshop on management and security technologies for cloud computing, Dec 2012
16. Automating QoS, UC SDN use case, version 1.2, Unified Communications Interoperability Forum, Feb 2014

Part III
Advances in Cloud Technologies and Future Trends

Chapter 10
Virtualization and Cloud Security: Benefits, Caveats, and Future Developments

Flavio Lombardi and Roberto Di Pietro

Abstract The Cloud computing paradigm allows for fast provisioning and deprovisioning of a large variety of, in most cases, preconfigured services. This would not have been possible without certain supporting technologies enabling rapid deployment and release of services. Virtualization technologies have been the solution to the service management requirements. In particular, hardware virtualization technology has speeded up the deployment of possibly a large number of virtual machines (VM) on multiple hosts. These achievements enable a far more efficient usage of physical resources which can be shared among multiple tenants in order to benefit from cost savings and ease of management. Multitenancy is a fundamental feature of Cloud computing. However, multitenancy and in general resource sharing increases the exposure to security threats. In particular, timing attacks can infer information from sibling VMs running on the same physical host. Furthermore, security and privacy issues are due to the present architecture of virtualization-based services in the Cloud. In particular, platform-as-a-service (PaaS) and infrastructure-as-a-service (IaaS) on both Public and Hybrid Clouds potentially allow the Cloud host administrators to get access to service provider (SP) and service consumer data. This way, service execution time and outcome reliability can be affected. Enterprises are mostly aware of the risks involved with multitenancy. As such, they often opt for a Private or Hybrid Cloud approach that is more costly and usually less scalable than a Public Cloud. In this context, novel Cloud approaches are required to enhance monitoring and security auditing of VMs and services. At the same time, a better privacy for both the SP and the service user (SU) should be guaranteed. The objective of this chapter is to shed light on virtualization technologies that empower the Cloud and that will be increasingly relevant for the evolution of Cloud services, together with the associated frameworks and principles. It also reviews present and possible future approaches to security for Cloud resources.

Keywords Virtualization · Security · Isolation · Introspection · Monitoring · Execution · Modeling

F. Lombardi (✉) · R. Di Pietro
SPRINGeR Research Group, Maths and Physics Department, Roma Tre University,
Rome, Italy
e-mail: lombardi@mat.uniroma3.it

R. Di Pietro
e-mail: dipietro@mat.uniroma3.it

© Springer International Publishing Switzerland 2014
Z. Mahmood (ed.), *Cloud Computing,* Computer Communications and Networks,
DOI 10.1007/978-3-319-10530-7_10

10.1 Introduction

Cloud computing would not have been possible without the virtualization technology advances of the past decade which have opened up the possibility of dynamically sharing the increasing number of processing cores among different tenants. In particular, the infrastructure-as-a-service (IaaS) layer adopts and exposes advanced virtualization technologies. These advances have induced relevant cost savings, but they have also created new security concerns within the Cloud. Some issues stem from the adoption of immature virtualization approaches as the basis for scalability and isolation. The underlying technologies adopted by different Clouds (such as Amazon, Microsoft, IBM, Rackspace, and SalesForce) hide potential security issues. At present, Cloud service integrity, confidentiality, and availability concerns are still open problems that call for effective and efficient solutions. Cloud nodes are inherently more vulnerable to cyber-attacks than traditional physical server solutions, as their underlying complexity brings an unprecedented exposure of services and interfaces to third parties. As a consequence, guaranteeing an adequate protection level to Cloud nodes is a challenging task, for which it is crucial to recognize the possible threats and to establish security processes to protect services and hosting platforms (HPs) from attacks.

Cloud computing aims at massive scalability. It offers clear benefits as regards efficiency, availability, and high utilization which, in turn, result in reduced capital expenditure and operational costs, further promising agility, innovation, flexibility, and simplicity. Most of these benefits are due to virtualization. The offerings from Cloud service vendors, in terms of software (SaaS), platform (PaaS), and infrastructure (IaaS) services are continuing to mature and the cost savings are becoming particularly attractive in the current competitive economic climate. Another broader aim of Cloud technology is to make *supercomputing* available to the general public and, in particular, to enterprises and to the scientific community.

Cloud deployment approaches adopt specific types of virtualization. The way the Cloud delivers services (i.e., software, platform, and infrastructure as *services*) is depended onto the implemented virtualization approach. The virtualization environment generally consists of three core components, namely: hypervisor, management tools, and VMs. Here are some examples of how Cloud services may be tied to virtualization approaches:

- Multi-tenant virtualization—software-as-a-service (SaaS)
- Container-based virtualization—platform-as-a-service (PaaS)
- Hardware virtualization—infrastructure-as-a-service(IaaS)
- Storage virtualization—data storage-as-a-service (dSaaS)

In this chapter, we provide a survey of various aspects of Cloud service security, availability, isolation, loss of physical control, and secure virtualization. In particular, Sect. 10.2 will provide some technology background where existing virtualization technologies for x86 architectures (e.g., Xen, KVM, VMWare, and VirtualBox) will be discussed, with an attempt to highlight advantages and disadvantages of each of them. This section will also present potential security flaws of virtualization approaches when deployed in a Cloud environment. In Sect. 10.3, the main security issues of Cloud computing are discussed, especially with respect to isolation, denial of service and information leakage. Moreover, confidentiality issues will be discussed showing that it is possible to infer information from a target VM on the same physical host machine. Relevant research on virtualization and Cloud security will be introduced in Sect. 10.4. In Sect. 10.5, future Cloud trends, of interest to practitioners, will be detailed and discussed. Latest advances in service modeling, monitoring, and control will be described in Sect. 10.6. Future research trends and directions will be discussed in Sect. 10.7. Finally, conclusions will be presented in Sect. 10.8.

10.2 Technology Background

A large variety of heterogeneous virtualization technologies are currently deployed in the Cloud for mainstream x86_64 architectures (e.g., Xen, KVM, VMWare, VirtualBox, and HyperV). They have proven vulnerable in the past to different exploits that could potentially be used in a Cloud. In addition, a vast number of Cloud management platforms have been deployed, both open source and proprietary. Vulnerabilities have been discovered through the years for these platforms as well. In the following, we offer a perspective on the main players of both the virtualization and the Cloud management systems.

10.2.1 Cloud Frameworks

Many Cloud middleware platforms have been introduced during the first pioneering years. Few are still actively maintained. Most relevant Cloud platforms are depicted in Table 10.1.

Some features that are common to the above systems are as follows:

- On-demand deployment of virtual resources both under web request load and when required by the Cloud service client. Management/billing interface exposed to the Cloud service client, allowing easy monitoring, controlling, and reporting.
- Multitenancy and resource pooling that allows combining heterogeneous computing resources (e.g., hardware, software, servers, and network) to serve multiple customers.
- Rapid elasticity and scalability that allows resources to be elastically and automatically scaled out or in, following the demand.

It is worth noting that these surviving Cloud management platforms are backed and supported by companies (e.g., Microsoft), scientific agencies (e.g., NASA) or large hardware/software resource providers (e.g., Red Hat, Amazon). The reason why is that maintaining and evolving such complex software systems has inherently high costs. Nonetheless, complex hardware/software architectures also induce larger exposure to vulnerabilities, as shown in the last columns of Tables 10.1 and 10.2.

Table 10.1 Most relevant Cloud platforms (Cloud middleware)

Cloud	Open source	VM format type	Vuln./exploit	Vuln. Ref.
OpenStack	Yes	VHD, VMDK, VDI, QCOW2, RAW, OVF, OVA, AMI	KVM, Xen	[18]
CloudStack	Yes	QCOW2, RAW, OVA	KVM, Xen	[19]
OpenNebula	Yes	QCOW2, RAW, OVA	KVM, Xen	[10]
VMWare vSphere	No	VHD, VMDK, VDI	Proprietary VMware	[15, 40]
MS Azure	No	VHD	Proprietary Hyper-v	[11]
Amazon	No	AMI	Xen	[13]

Table 10.2 Virtualization frameworks and tools

Virt. frameworks	Full/para Virt	Open source	Main features	Vuln. Ref.
Xen	Both	Yes	Small codebase, pure hypervisor, mature	[12, 17]
KVM	Full	yes	Integrated in Linux kernel	[16]
MS Hyper-v	Unknown	No	Proprietary, supports Windows and Linux guests	[2]
Virtualbox	Para	Partly	Supports Linux and Windows both as guest and host	[20]
VMware vSphere	Full	No	Mature costly solution. Scalability and performance	[15]
Parallels/Virtuozzo	Mostly para	No	Supports Mac OS	[9]

10.2.2 Virtualization Frameworks

The essential characteristics of most widespread virtualization environments are summarized in Table 10.2. It is worth noting that most hypervisors support full virtualization, as it offers relevant isolation benefits. In fact, full virtualization allows the CPU to intercept possibly malicious or unauthorized access to data in memory. The specific configuration and behavior of the virtualization framework is however different and it can be tuned according to the requirements of the Cloud platform. However, no existing virtualization framework is immune to software bugs that potentially expose the virtualization platform itself (and, as a consequence, the Cloud) to the referenced exploits. In the following section, we discuss some of these vulnerabilities by introducing a general model for Cloud services.

10.3 Cloud Security

A generic Cloud security scenario and model can be described as follows [29]: a service provider (SP) runs one or more service instances (SI) on the Cloud, which can be remotely accessed by a group of final service users (SU). For this purpose, the SP hires HP resources from the Cloud provider (CP). It is worth noting that the SU and the SP do not have any physical control over Cloud physical server machine, whose status cannot be observed. The SU and the CP enter into a service level agreement that describes how the Cloud is going to run service instance SI (See Fig. 10.1).

A taxonomy of possible attacks against Cloud systems follows:

1. Resource attacks against CPs
2. Resource attacks against SPs
3. Data attacks against CPs
4. Data attacks against SPs
5. Data attacks against SUs

Resource attacks 1 and 2 target resources, such as stealing virtual resources to mount a large-scale attack (e.g., botnet). Data attacks 3 and 4 steal or modify service or node configuration data (that can be used later to perform a different attack). Data attacks against SU (Attack 5) usually lead to leakage of sensitive data. Classes 1 and 3 involve an attack to Cloud infrastructure components. Virtualization technologies underlying Cloud computing infrastructure are of themselves liable to security vulnerabilities. In addition, the Cloud computing middleware potentially allows some novel attacks that have not been addressed yet.

In the typical Cloud scenario described above, we can observe the following major security issues:

- *Privileged user access control*: access to sensitive data in the Cloud has to be restricted to a subset of trusted users (to mitigate the risk of abuse of high privilege roles)
- *Data isolation*: one instance of customer data has to be fully isolated from data belonging to other customers
- *Privacy*: exposure of sensitive information stored on a Cloud implies its legal liability and loss of reputation
- *Bug Exploitation*: an attacker can exploit a software bug to steal data or to gain access to resources that allow for further attacks
- *Reliability/Availability*: the CP has to setup an effective replication and recovery mechanism to restore services, should an outage/disaster occur
- *Accountability:* even though Cloud services are difficult to trace for accountability purposes, in some cases this is a mandatory application requirement

In particular, service accountability can increase security and reduce potential risks for both the SU and the SP [23].

A trade-off exists between privacy and accountability, since the latter produces a record of events/actions that can be analyzed by a third party in case something goes wrong. Nevertheless, such investigation might expose faulty components or internal Cloud configuration details. This way, any Cloud customer might be able to learn information about the internal configuration of the Cloud that could be used later to perform an attack. A possible solution lies with the use of obfuscation and anonymization/detail-preserving techniques to limit the information the VM exposes to the Cloud. However, encryption cannot fully protect the user from malicious or curious CP, as the computing resources (central processing unit (CPU) and

Fig. 10.1 A typical Cloud
scenario

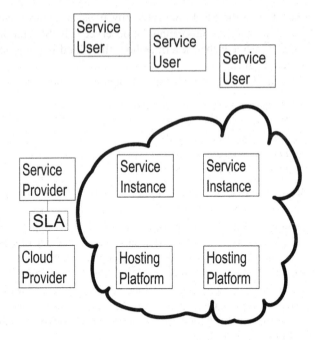

graphics processing units (GPU) cores) are fully controlled by them and therefore, keys are exposed to the privileged hypervisor administrator. In fact, current CPU technology cannot prevent a virtual machine monitor (VMM) from accessing guest raw memory. This limitation produces confidentiality issues with respect to the SP (or with respect to an attacker that manages to compromise the host platform).

One of the key aspects of Cloud computing is loss of control. As a prime example, the SU does not usually know for sure where its data are stored and processed in the Cloud. Moreover, it is unclear what happens to data and information held on a Cloud resource when the company that manages the Cloud goes out of business. How (and if) this data will be retrieved and returned to the owner organization is not clear. On a Cloud, computation and data are remote and potentially mobile. As such, they can be migrated to systems the SU cannot directly control. Over the internet, data are free to cross borders and reach countries where privacy enforcement is not considered relevant, which in turn can expose to further security threats. A second example of loss of control is that the CP gets paid for running a service it does not know the details of. This is one of the most relevant risks of the "Infrastructure as a Service" model, but also of other "as a Service" approaches. To date, even though misuse problems tend to be regulated by a service contract, such an agreement has to be enforced and controlled by monitoring tools.

10.3.1 Requirements for Cloud Monitoring

A core set of requirements that a security monitoring system for the Cloud [29] should meet can be summarized as follows:

- *Effectiveness*: *the system should be able to detect attacks and integrity violations.*
- *Accuracy*: the system should be able to (ideally) avoid false-positives, i.e, mistakenly detecting malware attacks where authorized activities are taking place.
- *Transparency*: the system should minimize detectability from VMs, i.e., SP, SU, and potential intruders should not be able to detect the presence of the monitoring system.
- *Robustness*: the host system, Cloud infrastructure and the sibling VMs should be protected from attacks proceeding from a compromised guest and it should not be possible to disable or alter the monitoring system itself.
- *Deployability*: the system should be deployable on the vast majority of available Cloud middleware and hardware/software configurations.
- *Dynamic Reaction*: the system should detect an intrusion attempt over a Cloud component and, if required by the security policy, it should take action against the attempt and against the compromised guest and/or notify remote middleware security-management components.
- *Accountability*: the system should not interfere with Cloud and Cloud application actions, but collect data and snapshots to enforce accountability policies.

However, it is not possible to satisfy all these requirements at the same time. As an example, there is a trade-off between transparency and dynamic reaction. This problem can be addressed by:

- *Hiding reaction*: reacting using regular guest maintenance actions, e.g., halting the guest, restarting it from a fresh image, and migrating the VM instance.
- *Delaying reaction*: snapshot the current status and delay reaction: this way the adversary may be able to perform further activity before being stopped. However, once traced, the effect of these activities can be reverted.

The above actions are, from the point of view of the SU or SP, virtually indistinguishable from regular load-balance based VM operations.

A possible approach to achieve integrity protection is to actively monitor key components that would most probably be targeted by attacks. This would allow to better protect the VMs and the Cloud infrastructure. By either actively or passively monitoring key kernel or middleware components, it is in fact possible to detect any possible modification to kernel data and code, thus guaranteeing that kernel and middleware integrity have not been compromised. Furthermore, Cloud entry points (application and network interfaces), behavior and integrity can be controlled via logging and periodic checksum verification of executable files and libraries. A further requirement, especially when the guest image is not trusted by the CP, is ensuring that an attacker-run application cannot detect that an external intrusion detection system is in place. Note that, as it happens with introspection techniques, they can potentially be detected by the target VM. In fact, the presence of a monitoring system can be probed by measuring the execution time of specific function calls. In order to address this issue, an asynchronous monitoring system can be a viable solution [27]. A monitoring system can also be useful when managing the reliability and replication of Cloud services, which suffer from specific problems as detailed in the following.

10.3.2 Replication and Cloud Reliability

The availability and reliability of Cloud services is enabled by the possibility to deploy a large number of identical (cloned) services. However, such replication does not by itself guarantee reliability as there are some issues that have to be addressed:

- *Vendor shut-down*: the Cloud service should be able to (ideally) resist a server shut down or large scale failure. In order to do so not all resources and services have to be deployed on a single provider. A Cloud of Clouds can help achieve this result.
- *Vendor lock-in*: The possibility of deploying the same service over different providers is tied to the support of standards that allow interoperability and migration of workload across different CPs. Unfortunately large providers (Amazon, Microsoft Azure) tend to offer specialized application programming interfaces (APIs) that trade-off additional functionality with increased vendor lock-in.
- *Denial of Service (DoS)*: As often experienced in the past [42], having a single host and guest architecture replicated over large arrays renders them massively exposed to even a single vulnerability and/or service disruption. In this case also, a smart monitoring tool over a federated Cloud of Clouds would be of help.

The following section further surveys the state-of-the-art approaches that aim at securing virtual resources and as a consequence, aim at improving the Cloud security.

10.4 Related Work

Secure virtualization approaches have been proposed during the past few years, taking into account that the most relevant deployment scenario is Cloud computing. This section compares these approaches and describes on how proposed techniques are used in existing Clouds. Further, it defines the basis of the components that can be actively used to increase security, privacy, and robustness of Cloud services.

In the past, privacy issues in Clouds have been the objective of much work [32]. Some interesting security issues are discussed in [3], while an almost complete survey of security in the context of Cloud storage services is provided by Cachin [5]. An exhaustive Cloud security survey has been presented in [23, 37].

A fundamental reference for Cloud security is the work on colocation by Ristenpart [34]. This work shows that it is possible to instantiate an increasing number of guest

VMs until one is placed coresident with the target VM. Once successfully achieved coresidence, attacks can extract information from a target VM on the same machine using timing measurements [14]. An attacker might also actively trigger new victim instances exploiting Cloud auto-scaling systems. Ristenpart shows that it practical to hire additional VMs whose launch can produce a high chance of coresidence with the target VM. He also shows that determining coresidence is quite simple.

Most integrity monitoring and intrusion detection solutions can be successfully applied to Cloud computing. File system integrity tools and intrusion detection systems such as Tripwire [25] and AIDE [1] can also be deployed in VMs, but are exposed to attacks possibly coming from a malicious guest machine user. Furthermore, when an attacker detects that the target machine is in a virtual environment, it may attempt to break out of the virtual environment through vulnerabilities in the VMM. Most present approaches leverage VMM isolation properties to secure VMs by using various levels of virtual introspection. Virtual introspection is a process that allows to observe the state of a VM from the VMM. Syringe [7] makes use of virtualization to observe and monitor guest kernel code integrity from a privileged VM or from the VMM. However, a number of solutions are available for the guest code to realize it is running in a honeypot VM by Pek [33] and Kapravelos [24]. BVMD [30] aims at detecting kernel rootkits by monitoring the integrity of kernel code. However, BVMD does not protect against kernel data attacks. Most proposals have limitations that prevent them from being used in distributed computing scenarios (e.g., supports for only one guest per each host) or just do not consider the special requirements or peculiarities of distributed systems. In an effort to make nodes resilient against long-lasting attacks, self-cleansing intrusion tolerance (SCIT) [4] treats all servers as potentially compromised (since undetected attacks are extremely dangerous over time). SCIT restores servers from secure images on a regular basis. The drawback of such a system is that it does not support long-lasting sessions required by most Cloud applications. Similarly, PipeCloud [43] creates redundant server copies which can periodically be refreshed to increase the resilience of the server. This approach combines proactive recovery with services that allow correct replicas to react and be recovered when there is a sufficient probability that they have been compromised. Along with the many advantages brought by virtualization, there are additional technological challenges that virtualization presents, which include an increase in the complexity of digital forensics investigations and questions regarding the forensics boundaries of a system.

Transparent Cloud protection system (TCPS) [28] introduces fundamental requirements for a VM monitoring system [31]. In particular, the monitoring system is protected inside the hypervisor in order to be as transparent as possible to guests. ACPS [29] extends TCPS and enjoys unique features, such as a synchronous warning asynchronous delayed response (SWADR) approach, where the increased decoupling of action and reaction, the increased immunity and integrity of the platform, and the support for accountability help achieving effectiveness and efficiency of active monitoring of Cloud resources.

Most of the solutions described in this section is general enough to be applied the present and future Cloud scenarios. In the light of the state-of-the-art solutions presented here, in the following section we briefly introduce and discuss relevant new trends that will be increasingly common in the future.

10.5 Visionary Thoughts for Practitioners

This section introduces concepts that will be increasingly common in the years to come; together with novel security issues (see Table 10.3). One relevant topic is mobile virtualization for small devices such as smartphones, smart watches, and tablets, that are carried everywhere by its owner. As such, they are often referred to as bring your own device (BYOD) since their owner usually carries them even inside a company's secure perimeter or in general at work. Present section also shows the practitioner how to make use of VMs for controlling applications' behavior. Further, this section highlights the usage of Cloud virtualization honeypots for malware collection and for forensics purposes. In fact, malware can be analyzed and dissected based on the interaction with the emulated virtual environment.

Reports from different market analysts predict that PCs will no longer be the primary digital device for most users in the next few years [39]. This implies that most users will make use of thin lightweight devices to access digital information stored and computed in the Cloud. Some more pervasive broader device perspectives that include smartphones and tablets and many other consumer devices that render the Cloud a fundamental resource. Emerging Cloud services will become the glue that connects heterogeneous devices that users choose to access during the different aspects of their daily life. The trends that Gartner foresees for the Cloud also induce novel security issues, as indicated below:

This new approach in computing will have a relevant impact on the client computing, both as regards users' personal digital life and business activity.

10.5.1 BYOD and Virtualization

The mobile devices that are pervasively present in the personal life of everybody also enter the company/enterprise boundaries. As such they can hide malware or eavesdrop sensitive data to the outside world. Unfortunately, the enterprises have little or no control over their personnel's mobile device data and application content and integrity. One possible approach is to ban such devices altogether from within enterprise boundaries. Another, less drastic novel approach is to remotely attest integrity and compliance of the employee's mobile device via novel secure virtualization mechanisms.

While software integrity attestation is quite advanced in the x86 PC technology, the ARM architecture that is the most widespread on mobile devices still offers fewer guarantees as regards software integrity and compliance. However, the perspective is good as ARM is increasingly supporting smart virtualization extensions that enable the implementation of reliable VM hypervisors that can run trusted VMs even on mobile/handheld devices [36].

Lightweight virtualization systems will be able to control the execution mode of the mobile device by imposing the exclusive execution of a specific VM when the device is inside the enterprise boundaries. The same VM will not be able to operate outside such boundaries. This way relevant sensitive information would transparently be kept under control.

Table 10.3 Cloud trends and induced security issues

Trend	Security issues
Virtualization. Virtualization allows users to make use of heterogeneous devices to access the same or novel services at a reduced cost	The isolation level allowed by virtualization is far from perfect and potentially induces integrity and DoS issues
BYOD-ification. Handheld or wearable devices are carried everywhere by (un?)aware users	Untrusted devices with a wide range of sensors can pervasively eavesdrop information
Personal Cloud. Personal, self-service Clouds allow users to create tailored virtual workspaces, pervasively available on multiple devices [38]	The ease of creation of self service Clouds exposes to security issues in case resources are shared and are not properly and constantly managed
Mobility. Improved mobile devices allow performing traditionally PC-based tasks pervasively on different devices	Mobile devices are more exposed to vulnerabilities that traditional PCs as protection mechanisms are less advanced
Remotization. Apps can be used to allow legacy applications work on a larger range of devices and platforms	Migrating legacy applications to the Cloud moves the data away from the user to the Cloud. As such it is exposed to eavesdropping

10.5.2 Virtual Mobile Honeypots and Forensics

More and more often, smartphones are relevant targets of civil and criminal investigations. Currently, there are several tools available to acquire forensic evidence from smartphones. Most of these tools require a destructive physical access or physical connection to the device. However, secure virtualization can be used to access live data without interfering with regular phone activity and thus allowing live mobile forensics. LiveSD Forensics [6] is an example of ondevice live data acquisition of the RAM and the EEPROM of Windows mobile devices. LiveSD Forensics uses a standard SD-card equipped with tailored code to perform the data acquisition. Unfortunately, LiveSD generates a memory alteration, albeit small.

Virtualization allows to study and classify malware in a controlled way by means of mobile honeypots. In fact, similarly to mobile forensics, mobile virtualization will be used extensively to attract malware and study its behavior [41] at the same time protecting the device integrity through isolation features. As future mobile hardware will be powerful enough to allow the concurrent execution of multiple VMs, different levels of security can be associated to different VMs as to block malware spreading.

10.5.3 ARM CPUs for the Cloud

The virtualization extensions of ARM CPUs provide the basis for addressing the needs of both client and server devices for the partitioning and management of complex software environments into VMs. ARM CPUs have been wildly successful in embedded applications, cell phones and in tablet devices, but now the recent ARM server market is flourishing. Cloud computing and other data or content oriented solutions increase the demand on the physical memory system from each

VM. This is the main reason why ARM has extended the 32-bit Architecture to support 40-bit physical addressing and now by introducing a 64-bit ARM architecture. This happens with the introduction of the new AArch64 execution state in version 8 of the ARM architecture. AArch64 is a new architecture state complete with a new A64 instruction set. The price-performance and power-per-watt convenience of novel 64-bit ARM CPUs suggests that many future Cloud servers will be built upon such technology, thus shifting the focus away from traditional x86 architectures. This will have an impact on Cloud services as virtualization software will have to adapt to the new instruction set architectures (ISA), possibly introducing new bugs and security issues. Further, the ARM CPUs will feature a much higher number of cores that present x86 CPUs, thus rendering multithreading issues vital for both security and performance Cloud services.

10.5.4 A Way Forward

Because of the huge savings and computing agility that novel Cloud environments offer, large enterprises are starting to experiment with heterogeneous multicore Cloud computing into their existing IT systems and resources. For the newcomers aiming to consider leveraging future Cloud trends, the following best practices can be seen as a way forward. As regards, the perspective and the guidelines that can be followed in order to better exploit and manage future Cloud trends, the following best practices can be suggested:

- Evaluate technology internally—start deploying on premise as much as possible in order to gain experience and evaluate solutions without bias.
- Learn from others' mistakes—adopting the practices that have been successful elsewhere but also keeping an eye on latest research results.
- Avoid vendor lock-in—aim towards open standards as they eventually lead to reduced migration costs as the technology evolves.
- Ensure security of data and information—This on of the major concerns on any nonprivate Cloud.

When deciding whether to deploy existing resources on a traditional Cloud or on novel approaches and technologies such as those introduced above, the following suggestions hold:

- Consider the enterprise applications, other systems and IT resources and explore new technology incrementally but pervasively.
- Leverage Public Cloud, together with Private Cloud technology in order to limit information exposure and guarantee reliability and scalability with an hybrid approach.
- Pay particular attention on how sensitive data is managed. Especially as regards novel technologies and approaches, the CP can be held responsible for any security incident might happen on untrusted platforms.

10.6   Semantic Introspection and Modeling VM Behavior

Monitoring key Cloud components that would be targeted or affected by attacks is vital in order to protect the VMs and the Cloud infrastructure [26]. By either actively or passively monitoring key VM components any possible modification to VM data and code can be traced and recorded.

The approach depicted in Fig. 10.2 is an example of advanced transparent passive tracing and recording of VM events from the hypervisor [29]. Any relevant event or status change is recorded by an event interceptor (IWR) and it is then stored in a pool of recorder warnings (WP) where the collected information is asynchronously evaluated (evaluator) and, if needed, a reaction is triggered (act) according to a chosen policy (it can be merely passive and transparent or blocking and more visible). This approach enables a deeper evaluation of the relationship among events to better detect the cause of anomalies. Further it can be extended by making use of additional computing resources.

Providing an adequate level of resilience to Cloud services is a challenging problem due to the complexity of the environment and the need for efficient solutions that could preserve Cloud benefits over other solutions. A novel interesting approach is to make use of virtualization to effectively build a live model of the VM and of its applications. CloRExPa [21] provides a customizable resilience service solution for Cloud guests, using an execution path analysis approach. In particular, CloRExPa can trace, analyze and control live VM activity, and intervened code and data modifications, possibly due to either malicious attacks or software faults. Execution path analysis allows the VMM to trace the VM state and to prevent such a guest from reaching faulty states. CloRExPa makes use of scenario graphs.

Figure 10.3 shows a small scenario graph that has been automatically inferred node by node using a monitoring tool to infer state changes and activity from a real VM. Later such high level information can be used to foresee if a pattern or execution path leads to a fault. In this case a wide range of countermeasures can be adopted, according to the relevance of the protected VM and to the status of the system/monitoring tool.

This trend towards semantic introspection of VM activity is a very active field also as regards mobile devices in the Cloud [7]. This is the way to go for enabling control over possibly untrusted mobile Cloud nodes/applications. In fact, as discussed above also for BYOD untrusted devices, either they have to be banned altogether from the enterprise or enhanced semantics-aware introspection has to be put in place to prevent them from leaking sensitive information. Outside of the enterprise, semantic introspection allows legitimate users to regain control over their device internals. This approach will help detect and react to malware and to backdoors that are put in place even by trusted software or apps [36].

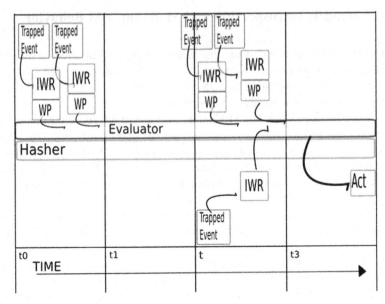

Fig. 10.2 SWADR approach to VM and service monitoring [29]

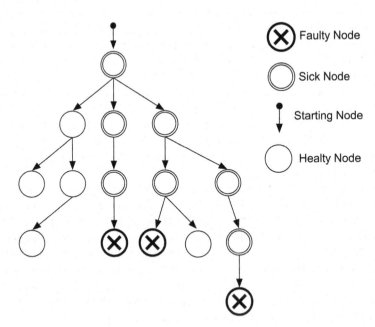

Fig. 10.3 Modeling resource activity and status through scenario graphs

10.7   Future Research Directions

This section highlights the future trend of virtualization approaches in the Cloud. In particular, it introduces the novel technological opportunity of virtualization support for the ARM CPU platforms that is gaining momentum in the server and Cloud market. In addition, a perspective over novel multicore technologies in the Cloud is depicted. An overlook is given on at the emerging GPU-Cloud trend to summarize its potential security issues. This allows to suggest solutions to the security issues of such new platforms, especially as regards hardware virtualization support. Finally, this section also introduces the issues related to effective randomness in the Cloud that are due to the reuse of VM images.

10.7.1   Manycore Computing for the Cloud

Apart from ARM multicore CPUs a rich set of massively multicore (also known as manycore) computing devices will be increasingly present in the future Clouds. GPU feature hundreds of processing cores that allow speeding up parallel tasks. GPUs usually support their own ISA. Another relevant architecture, proposed by Intel, is the Intel many integrated core architecture (MIC) featuring hundreds of simplified x86 cores. This choice should ease portability and compatibility with legacy Cloud applications.

Some of the most relevant opportunities that the practitioner will be able to leverage in the future heterogeneous multicore Cloud are:

- Efficiently Exploiting Virtualization: securely and efficiently sharing of new Cloud resources is not easy. However, efficiently virtualizing distributed heterogeneous computing in the Cloud is an opportunity to improve Cloud security and reliability.
- Easing Access to Resources: allowing seamless access to novel technologies is vital for their success. Novel technological contributions are still to come that will ease distributed computing inside the Cloud.
- Monitoring Shared Resources: in order to allow efficient and secure usage of multicores, such resources have to be constantly monitored for usage patterns and abuse/misconfiguration, since sharing resources also induces security and privacy issues.
- Exploiting Redundancy: the availability of a much larger quantity of computing resources allows using them for a number of novel applications, such as computation replication for reliability and availability or proactive computing [22] for most different possible scenarios.

10.7.2 Effective Randomness for the Cloud

Cloud SaaS and PaaS providers, but also IaaS usually deploy identical clones of the same VM. The lifecycle of VMs involves freezing and reviving the very same images for the same or different tenants. As a consequence, the internal random pool for clone VMs is most probably the same for different VMs [35]. This issue can be exploited by an adversary to guess the value of generated keys for cryptographic protocols. In order to address such issue, the CP or SP should try to increase the number of events fed to the entropy pool of VM operating systems as soon as they are deployed, so as to provide an adequate level of security.

10.7.3 Novel Cloud Application Scenarios

Personal Cloud approaches where resources are contributed to the Cloud pervasively from distributed remote locations [38] such as Clouds@Home [8] provide means for the creation of open, interoperable Clouds for supporting scientific purposes and other general purpose Clouds. Volunteer computing benefits can be experienced in public administration and open communities (e.g., social networks, peer-to-peer). Enterprises would also partly benefit from Clouds@Home: computing infrastructures would be available on demand especially in small and medium enterprises. It would be possible to implement a datacenter with local, existing, and off the shelf, resources. This would help reduce and optimize business costs according to quality of service (QoS)—service level agreement (SLA) policies, improving performances and reliability. For example, this paradigm will allow to deal with request peaks: Clouds@Home data centers could be sized for the regular workload, whereas worst cases (peaks) could be managed by renting computing resources from large CPs.

10.8 Conclusion

Cloud computing was born out of the evolution of virtualization technology. As such, it offers similar benefits and suffers from similar issues, mostly regarding security, privacy, and isolation. Advantages are many but there are also challenges and issues, related to service management, process monitoring, infrastructure reliability, information security, data integrity, and business continuity. The way forward for CPs is to integrate transparent auditing and monitoring of Cloud resources. This addition requires devising and deploying further enhanced virtualization approaches as well as making use of additional computing resources such as novel multicore CPUs and GPUs. These ones will possibly ease the management of integrity and security of Cloud resources. Once this is achieved, enterprises will be more confident about migrating to Cloud environments and they will be able to fully leverage the benefits of such technology in the next few years.

The way forward for the enterprise is to plan a strategy for integrating novel resources into Cloud offerings, to have appropriate internal knowledge of Cloud mechanisms, to correctly align the IT resources with applications, to follow best practices and, strategically to think in terms of moving towards distributed heterogeneous computing. Once, these steps are taken, the enterprise will be well on its way to achieve benefits that the Cloud paradigm offers and enjoy the new opportunities that novel Cloud technologies offer.

References

1. AIDEteam (2005) Advanced intrusion detection environment. Advanced intrusion detection environment
2. Anonymous (2012) Vulnerability in Hyper-V could allow denial of service. http://technet. microsoft.com/en-us/security/bulletin/ms11-047. Accessed 1 Sept 2014
3. Balduzzi M et al (2012) A security analysis of Amazon's elastic compute Cloud service. ACM, New York, NY, USA, 2012 SAC 12
4. Bangalore AK, Sood AK (2009) Securing web servers using self cleansing intrusion tolerance (SCIT). DEPEND
5. Cachin C, Keidar I, Shraer A (2009) Trusting the Cloud. ACM, 2009. SIGACT News 40:81–86
6. Canlar ES, Conti M, Crispo B, Di Pietro R (2013) Windows mobile LiveSD forensics. J Netw Comput Appl 36(2):677–684
7. Carbone M, Conover M, Montague B, Lee W (2012). Secure and robust monitoring of virtual machines through guest-assisted introspection. RAID'12
8. Clouds@home http://clouds.gforge.inria.fr/pmwiki.php. Accessed 1 Sept 2014
9. CVE-2008-6478 (2008) Cross-site request forgery (CSRF) vulnerability in the file manager in the VZPP web interface for Parallels Virtuozzo. http://www.cvedetails.com/cve/CVE-2008-6478/. Accessed 1 Sept 2014
10. CVE-2009-1877 (2009) OpenNebula XSS vuln. http://cve.mitre.org/cgi-bin/cvename. cgi?name=CVE-2013-4492. Accessed 1 Sept 2014
11. CVE-2011-1068 (2011) Microsoft Windows Azure SDK vulnerability. http://www.cvedetails. com/cve/CVE-2011-1068/. Accessed 1 Sept 2014
12. CVE-2012-0217 (2012) Vulnerability of the x86-64 kernel system-call functionality in Xen 4.1.2 and earlier. http://www.cve.mitre.org/cgi-bin/cvename.cgi?name=CVE-2012-0217. Accessed 1 Sept 2014
13. CVE-2012-5781 (2012) Amazon EC2 man-in-the-middle attack vulnerability to spoof SSL. http://www.cvedetails.com/cve/CVE-2012-5781/. Accessed 1 Sept 2014
14. CVE-2013-0169 (2013) "Lucky Thirteen" vulnerability. http://web.nvd.nist.gov/view/vuln/ detail?vulnId=CVE-2013-0169. Accessed 1 Sept 2014
15. CVE-2013-1405 (2013) vSphere authentication vulnerability. http://cve.mitre.org/cgi-bin/ cvename.cgi?name=CVE-2013-1405. Accessed 1 Sept 2014
16. CVE-2013-1796 (2013) Buffer overflow vulnerability. http://www.securityfocus.com/ bid/58607. Accessed 1 Sept 2014
17. CVE-2013-1964 (2013) Local guest administrators to cause a denial of service. http://www. cvedetails.com/cve/CVE-2013-1964/. Accessed 1 Sept 2014
18. CVE-2013-2096 (2013) OpenStack Compute Nova does not verify the virtual size of a QCOW2 image. http://www.cvedetails.com/cve/CVE-2013-2096/. Accessed 1 Sept 2014
19. CVE-2013-2136 (2013) Apache CloudStack Cross-site scripting (XSS) vulnerabiliity. http:// cve.mitre.org/cgi-bin/cvename.cgi?name=CVE-2013-2136. Accessed 1 Sept 2014

20. CVE-2013-3792 (2013) Unspecified vulnerability in the Oracle VM VirtualBox component in Oracle Virtualization. http://www.cve.mitre.org/cgi-bin/cvename.cgi?name=CVE-2013-3792. Accessed 1 Sept 2014
21. Di Pietro R, Lombardi F, Signorini M (2012) CloRExPa: Cloud resilience via execution path analysis. Future Generation Computer Systems
22. Engel Y, Etzion O (2011) Towards proactive event-driven computing. In: Proceedings of the 5th ACM international conference on distributed event-based system (DEBS '11). ACM, New York, NY, USA, pp 125–136
23. Enisa (2009) Cloud computing risk assessment
24. Kapravelos A, Cova M, Kruegel C, Vigna G (2011) Escape from monkey island: evading high-interaction honeyclients. DIMVA'11
25. Kim GH, Spafford EH (1994) The design and implementation of tripwire: a file system integrity checker. CCS '94: proceedings of the 2nd ACM conference on computer and communications security, p 18–29
26. Li Q et al (2008) VM-based architecture for network monitoring and analysis. ICYCS '08: proceedings of the 2008 the 9th international conference for young computer scientists, p 1395–1400
27. Lombardi F, Di Pietro R (2009) KvmSec: a security extension for Linux kernel virtual machines. SAC '09: proceedings of the 2009 ACM symposium on applied computing, p 2029–2034
28. Lombardi F, Di Pietro R (2010) A security management architecture for the protection of Kernel virtual machines. IEEE Computer Society, Washington, DC, USA 2010 TSP 10
29. Lombardi F, Di Pietro R (2011) Secure virtualization for Cloud computing. J Netw Comput Appl 34(4):1113–1122
30. Oyama Y, Giang TTD, Chubachi Y, Shinagawa T (2012). Detecting malware signatures in a thin hypervisor. SAC '12
31. Payne BD et al (2008) Lares: an architecture for secure active monitoring using virtualization. SP '08: proceedings of the 2008 IEEE symposium on security and privacy (sp 2008), p 233–247
32. Pearson S (2009) Taking account of privacy when designing Cloud computing services. CLOUD '09: proceedings of the 2009 ICSE workshop on software engineering challenges of Cloud computing, p 44–52
33. Pek G, Bencsath B, Buttyan L (2011) nEther: in-guest detection of out-of-the-guest malware analyzers. EUROSEC '11
34. Ristenpart T et al (2009) Hey, you, get off of my Cloud: exploring information leakage in third-party compute Clouds. New York, NY, USA, ACM, 2009. CCS '09: proceedings of the 14th ACM conference on computer and communications security, p 103–115. ISBN:978-1-60558-352-5
35. Ristenpart T, Yilek S (2010) When good randomness goes bad: virtual machine reset vulnerabilities and hedging deployed cryptography. Network and distributed systems security—NDSS 2010
36. Russello G, Conti M, Crispo B, Fernandes E (2012) MOSES: supporting operation modes on smartphones. In: Proceedings of the 17th ACM symposium on access control models and technologies (SACMAT '12). ACM, New York, NY, USA
37. Somorovsky J, Heiderich M, Jensen M, Schwenk J, Gruschka N, Lo Iacono L (2011) All your Clouds are belong to us: security analysis of Cloud management interfaces. (CCSW). s.l., ACM
38. Srivastava A, Butt S, Ganapathy V, Lagar-Cavilla A (2012) Self-service Cloud computing. ACM, CCS 2012
39. Vasudevan A, Owusu E, Zhou Z, Newsome J, McCune JM (2012) Trustworthy execution on mobile devices: what security properties can my mobile platform give me?. In: Proceedings of the 5th international conference on trust and trustworthy computing (TRUST'12), Springer-Verlag, Berlin, Heidelberg

40. VMSA-2013-0002 (2013) VMware privilege escalation vulnerability. http://www.vmware. com/security/advisories/VMSA-2013-0002.html. Accessed 1 Sept 2014
41. Wählisch M, Trapp S, Keil C, Schönfelder J, schmidt TC, Schiller J (2012) First insights from a mobile honeypot. SIGCOMM Comput Commun Rev 42(4):305–306
42. Whitney L (2013) Gmail, Google Docs hit by service disruption. http://news.cnet.com/8301-1023_3-57604178-93/gmail-google-docs-hit-by-service-disruption/. Accessed 1 Sept 2014
43. Wood T, Lagar-Cavilla HA, Ramakrishnan KK, Shenoy P (2011) PipeCloud: using causality to overcome speed-of-light delays in Cloud-based disaster recovery. SOCC, 2011, pp 17:1–17:13

Chapter 11
Quality-of-Service Data Warehouse for the Selection of Cloud Services: A Recent Trend

Ahmad Karawash, Hamid Mcheick and Mohamed Dbouk

Abstract Cloud Computing presents an efficient, on-demand and scalable way to integrate computational resources. However, existing Cloud paradigm is increasingly transforming the information technology landscape, and organizations and businesses are exhibiting strong interest in software-as-a-service (SaaS) delivery model. This enables application service providers to lease data centre capabilities for deploying applications depending on quality of service (QoS) requirements. However, it still remains a challenging task to provide QoS assured services to serve customers with best quality, while also guaranteeing the maximization of the business objectives to service provider and infrastructure provider within certain constraints. To address these issues, this chapter proposes building a data warehouse of QoS to achieve better service matching and enhance dynamic service composition. The proposed QoS data warehouse (QoSDW) model supports the following: ensures a deep analysis of the service's interior structure and properties through online database analysis; facilitates reasoning about complex service weakness points; supports visual representation of analysis results; and introduces a new QoS factor for study.

Keywords Cloud service · Data warehouse · QoS · Quality of service · Analysis · Composition · Service selection

A. Karawash (✉) · H. Mcheick
Department of Computer Science, University of Quebec at Chicoutimi (UQAC),
555 Boulevard de l'Université, Chicoutimi G7H 2B1, Canada
e-mail: ahmad.karawash1@uqac.ca

A. Karawash · M. Dbouk
Ecole Doctorale des Sciences et de Technologie, Lebanese University,
Rafic-Hariri Campus, Hadath-Beirut, Lebanon

H. Mcheick
e-mail: hamid_mcheick@uqac.ca

M. Dbouk
e-mail: mdbouk@ul.edu.lb

© Springer International Publishing Switzerland 2014   257
Z. Mahmood (ed.), *Cloud Computing*, Computer Communications and Networks,
DOI 10.1007/978-3-319-10530-7_11

11.1 Introduction

Cloud computing is a model for allowing expedient, on-demand network access to a shared collection of configurable computing resources (e.g. networks, servers, storage, applications and services) that can be rapidly released with minimal management effort or service provider interaction. Cloud computing promotes availability and is composed of three service models. These services in industry are referred to as infrastructure-as-a-service (IaaS), platform-as-a-service (PaaS) and software-as-a-service (SaaS), respectively. Cloud environments aim to power the next generation data centres by exposing them as a network of virtual services (hardware, database, user-interface and application logic) so that users are able to access and deploy applications from anywhere in the world on demand at competitive costs depending on users' QoS requirements [1].

Cloud computing presents an efficient managerial, on-demand and scalable way to integrate computational resources. However, existing Cloud architecture lacks the layer of middle-ware to enable dynamic service composition. Service composition provides a current technology for developing complex applications from existing service components. Prediction of the QoS of composite services makes it possible to determine whether the composition meets the non-functional requirements [2]. Previous researches have focused on service composition and integration in terms of services, orchestration and choreography.

As SaaS gains greater acceptance, user cloud expectations start moving from best-effort service to guaranteed service. Hence, it is foreseen the development of QoS as a dominant consideration for cloud service adaptation. QoS has many facets which depend on the aspect that is crucial for the user. Application specific performance includes, e.g. response time or throughput, application security varying from data integration and consistency to privacy and service availability, which are some of the QoS considerations that clouds need to address. Such qualities are of interest to service providers and service consumers alike. They are of interest to service providers when implementing multiple service levels and priority-based admission mechanisms. The agreement between the customer and the service provider is referred to as the Service Level Agreement (SLA). An SLA describes agreed service functionality, cost and qualities [3]. This work proposes building a data warehouse of QoS to manage the matching between customer and service provider. The obtained data warehouse gives a better analysis level, reasoning and decision-taking before selecting a cloud service.

This chapter is organized as follows. Section 11.2 describes some previous methods of service selection. Section 11.3 discusses the service selection structure. In Sect. 11.4, quality of service data warehouse (QoSDW) model components are introduced, and Sect. 11.5 highlights the benefits that this model promises. The model simulation and the results are shown in Sect. 11.6. In the last section on conclusions, the main ideas of this chapter are summarized and the future perspectives considered.

11.2 Background

QoS has received much interest in cloud service research because of the rapid increase of the number of services and the approximate equal qualities of the discovered services. Several research activities focused on how to benefit from the
QoS in the service selection process. Some of these studies sought to extend the
Universal Description, Discovery and Integration (UDDI) Registry to support service consumers by comprehensible QoS information. Firstly, it is relevant to mention the service selection algorithms used by the *QoS broker* for sequential composite flow models with only one QoS constraint (i.e. *Throughput*). There are two
main approaches we can use to select the optimal services for each component of a
business process. The first is the combinatorial approach [4], modelling the problem as a Multiple Choice Knapsack Problem (MCKP). To solve the MCKP, three
methods are proposed: exhaustive search, dynamic programming and a minimal
algorithm for MCKP and performance study method. The second approach is the
graph approach, modelling the problem as the constrained shortest path problem in
the graph theory. The proposed methods to solve the shortest path algorithm are:
Constrained Bellman-Ford (CBF), constrained shortest path (CSP) and breadth-
first-search (BFS).

There are also a number of other research studies that dealt with the service
selection problem. Keskes et al. [5] proposed a model of automatic selection of
the best service provider, which is based on mixing context and QoS ontology
for a given set of parameters of QoS. In 2010, Raj and Saipraba proposed a service selection model that selects the best service based on QoS constraints [6].
Squicciarini et al. (2011), furthermore, studied the privacy implication caused by
the exchange of a large amount of sensitive data required by optimised strategies for service selection [7]. Garg et al. proposed the SMICloud framework for
comparing and ranking cloud services by defining a set of attributes for the comparison of mainly IaaS cloud offerings [8], while Hussain et al. proposed a multi-
criteria decision-making methodology for the selection of cloud services [9]. To
rank services, they matched the user requirements against each service offering
for each criterion. Wang et al. proposed a cloud model for the selection of Web
services [10]. This model relies on computing what the authors called QoS un-
certainty and identifies the most appropriate Web services using mixed integer
programming. In 2012, Anita Mohebi proposed a vector-based ranking model to
enhance the discovery process of services [11]. Rehman et al. proposed a cloud
service selection framework that relies on QoS history [12]. A heuristic service
selection method, called 'Bee Algorithm', was proposed by Karry et al., which
helped to optimize the discovery and selection of a service that meets customer
requirements [13].

In this chapter, we adopt the Service Oriented Architecture to build a data warehouse of quality of services. It enables application of an advanced level of analysis
and optimization in discovering cloud services.

11.3   Cloud Service Selection Structure

Cloud computing can be defined as a model for enabling convenient, on-demand network access to a shared pool of resources that can be rapidly provisioned and released with minimal management effort or service provider interaction. A cloud environment is characterized by system level, Cloud Broker level and user middleware level (as shown in Fig. 11.1).

The user Middle-ware level includes the software frameworks such as Web 2.0 Interfaces and provides the programming environments and composition tools that ease the creation, deployment and execution of applications in Clouds. The system level is composed of thousands of servers, each with its own service terms management systems, operating platforms and security levels. These servers are transparently managed by the higher level virtualization [14] services and toolkits that allow sharing their capacity among virtual instances of servers. The Cloud Broker level implements the platform level services that provide runtime environment enabling Cloud computing capabilities to build cloud services. The Cloud Service Broker performs several management operations to deliver personalized services to consumers. These operations are: security and policy management, access and identity management, SLA management, provision and integration management. The security and policy manager is responsible for managing different kinds of policies such as authorization policies and QoS-aware selection policies of service providers. The access and identity manager is responsible for the accessing services and respect the identity rules of services. The SLA manager directs the concession process between a consumer and a selected SaaS provider in order to reach an agreement as to the service terms and conditions. The provision and integration manager is responsible for implementing different policies for the selection of suitable SaaS providers, based on the consumer's QoS requirements and the SaaS providers' QoS offerings. The back-end database stores sustain information about service policies, consumer profiles, SLAs, Registry and dynamic QoS information. Cloud broker layer works to identify the most appropriate cloud resource and maps the requirements of application to customer profile. Its job can also be dynamic by automatically routing data, applications and infrastructure needs based on some QoS criteria like availability, reliability, latency, price, etc. On the Broker side, service properties are stored as a combination of functional and non-functional properties. The functional properties relate to the external behaviour of a service such as: service inputs and outputs, service type and the information required for connecting to the service. However, the non-functional properties are summarized by the QoS.

By dynamically provisioning resources, Cloud broker enables cloud computing infrastructure to meet arbitrary varying resource and service requirements of cloud customer applications. However, there are still imperfections regarding service matching based on available services and customer profile requirements. The services selection problem is identified by an inaccurate QoS dependency and the utility of the imprecise domain of results suggested by QoS broker. As in [19],

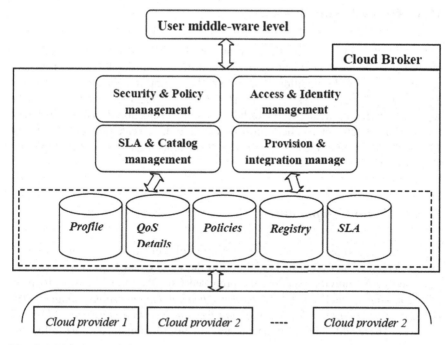

Fig. 11.1 Main layers of cloud service infrastructure

services are ranked in many levels, such as Poor, Good and Excellent. It is based on Web Service Relevancy Function (WsRF), which is measured based on the weighted mean value of the QoS parameters. Services are classified according to user's invocations as follows:

- *Excellent*: Users accept to pay lower cost regarding better service qualities such as: response time, availability … etc.
- *Good*: Users pay normal cost for normal service qualities.
- *Poor*: Users accept worse cost with lower service qualities.

The QoS broker orchestrates resources at the end-points, coordinating resource management across layer boundaries. Based on the available technology, Service consumer is still incapable of a real analysis of the QoS based on the internal structure of complex service. Today's service selection solutions do not focus on QoS support from the service requester view point, but they depend on service provider interpretation. Indeed, the current form of service selection is provider driven [15]. A consumer may interact with a composite service without knowing much about the qualities of the services that underlie it [16].

To improve the selection of a complex service, we propose to analyze the QoS of every sub-service, which shares in the composition of that service, using a QoSDW.

11.4   QoSDW Model

Nowadays, the cloud is full of a large number of cloud services. Some of these services are similar in goal and quality. Therefore, it is difficult to select best service depending on the traditional QoS methods. To improve the service selection process, we propose a QoSDW model. The QoSDW model (described in Fig. 11.2) supports a better analysis of services before taking a selection decision. The QoSDW model extracts details about services stored in the service provider, and gives the service's consumer the ability to discover the hidden facts about the properties of these services.

11.4.1   Main Components

This section describes a model for the selection of a cloud service that can fulfill the service consumer request. In addition to the main cloud framework elements discussed in the previous section, the proposed QoSDW model adds a group of other components such as: *QoSDW parser, schema manager, graph manager, QoSDW analyzer, QoSDW cube, analysis interface, service tree manager and report manager*. These additional components are now briefly explained in the following paragraphs.

QoSDW Parser QoSDW parser is simply a *service business process* parser. Based on the parsers outputs and the QoS at service provider, *QoSDW schema and QoSDW graph* are extracted and transported into the cloud broker to be stored in a specific database. Regarding the database tables, each row entry collects details about service activities. It provides information about the current state name, current state properties (as *My Role, Partner Role*), *PartnerLink*, name of the operation being invoked, condition of a looping structural activity, current state number and next possible state numbers.

Schema Manager This component is responsible for managing the QoSDW schemas. The *QoSDW schema* is a star schema which is composed of a set of organized tables, and which has a main fact table and set dimensional tables. *QoSDW schema* consists of 22 dimensional tables as follows: *Quality, Availability, ResponseTime, Documentation, BestPractice, Throughput, Latency, Successability, Reliability, Compliance, property, ServiceType, ServiceName, ExpiryDate, CreationDate, ServiceFlow, Loop, Sequence, AndSplit, XorSplit, AndJoin and XorJoin table.*

Graph Manager Graph manager ensures transforming the output of parsing the service business into a directed acyclic graph. Also, it converts the obtained graph into a service tree. For example, Fig. 11.3 shows how *SteamBoat* service process diagram is transformed into a service tree. The service tree inserts a semantic layer into the service selection process.

QoSDW Cube This is a data warehouse of quality and structure of both a service and its sub-services. It is accessed as a cloud service and supports users by details about the quality and flow of service through a special analyzer. It maps the idea of

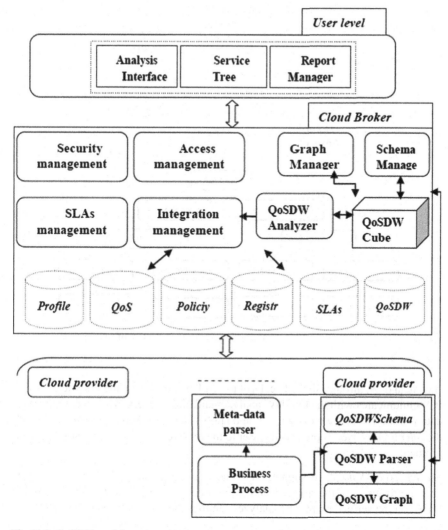

Fig. 11.2 QoSDW model components

the multidimensional data model to service selection model, through which it gives the service's user the ability to apply a multidimensional query on the discovered set of services.

QoSDW Analyzer QosDW analyzer works like an analysis tool. It monitors QoS changes and prepares analytical reports about QoS information stored in the *QoSDW Cube*. It gives the service consumer the right to query the *QoSDW Cube* through its interface.

Analysis Interface It is a user interface application utilized to select cloud services (SaaS). It consists of a statistical form which allows a user to deal easily with large

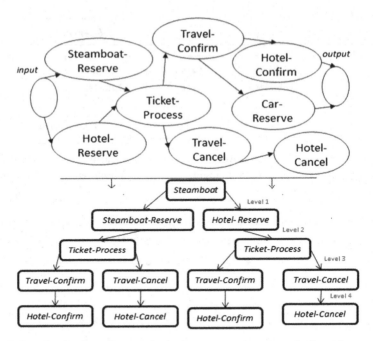

Fig. 11.3 Transforming SteamBoat service business process into a tree of sub-services

statistical data, through slice, dice, Drill Down/Up and Roll-up the statistical results. It communicates with the QoSDW analyzer and allows users to connect to the QoS data warehouse, at the cloud broker, and apply queries. When a service is selected, the *selection interface* connects the user to the required service via the SOAP/HTTP protocol.

Service Tree Manager It supports a visual representation of the service's tree. It communicates with the *graph manager* indirectly through the *QoSDW analyzer*. Based on the service graph, the analyzer supplies the user by the service tree.

Report Manager Sometimes the service's consumer needs ready reports that support their analysis. *Report manager* allows requesting two types of reports: the primary report gives analysis results about the quality of first level sub-services, and the advanced report supports a deep service tree analysis to detect a weak quality subservice (or fatal sub-service). Both reports are requested from the *QoSDW analyzer*.

11.4.2   Formal Definitions

QoSDW is the base for a successful QoS analysis system. The concept of QOSDW starts by creating central locations for QoS storages followed by a permanent storage QoS that feed from various cloud providers. It ends by different levels of analysis, reporting and other Business Intelligence functions.

The main objective of a QoSDW model is to provide efficient analytical reporting on the quality of service. To qualify a service, the QoSDW depends on analyzing the quality of its sub-services. QoSDW depends on the service business process to specify the structure of subservices. The key work in QoSDW model is to establish relations among business processes and qualities of cloud services.

Definition 1 A *service business process* is a tuple $K=(A, E, C, L)$ where:

A is a set of activities,
E is a set of events,
C is a set of conditions and L is a set of control links.

Let $f: A \rightarrow B$ be a function that assigns activities to types, where activities are extracted from the set of activity $A = \{sequence, flow, pick, switch, while, scope, invoke, receive, reply, wait, assign, empty, throw, compensate, exit\}$. Let I be a set of service information, where $I= \{service\ name, service\ type, service\ creation\ date, service\ expiry\ date)$.

Let $g: P \rightarrow I$ be a function which assigns service information to properties.

QoSDW utilizes an on-line analytical processing (OLAP) approach and performs analysis in conjunction with the operational database on a constant basis. The basic concept of OLAP model is to map the initial database schema to a multidimensional model. The *QoSDW schema* is structured as star (or snowflake) schemas.

Definition 2 A QoSDW schema is a tuple $S=(Q, P, B)$ where:

Q is a set of QoS, such that $Q= \{Response\ time, Availability, Throughput, Successability, Reliability, Compliance, Best Practice, Latency, Documentation\}$. Here:

- P is a set of service properties, such that $P= \{ServiceType, ServiceName, ExpiryDate, CreationDate\}$.
- B is a set of activity type, where $B= \{Loop, Sequence, AndSplit, XorSplit, AndJoin, XorJoin\}$.
- Let h be a function which assigns the values of QoS to elements of set Q.

The QoSDW graph adds a type of semantic knowledge when analyzing the quality of sub-services and covers indirectly the hidden service business process vague.

Definition 3 A *QoSDW graph* is a tuple $G=(Ni, Nf, N, F)$, where:

Ni is the node of the input, Nf is the node of output, N is the set of names of subservices and F is the set of service integration models. $F= \{Sequence, ANDSplit, XORSplit, loop, ANDJoin, XORJoin\}$.

Let $m:B \rightarrow F$ be a function that maps service activities to integration models.

The operations which are applied in the analysis phase of the QoSDW model are summarised by: Composition, Pairing, Projection and Restriction.

Composition takes as input two functions f and g, such that $range\ (f) \subset def(g)$, and returns a function $g°f: def(f) \rightarrow range\ (g)$, defined by: $(g°f)\ (x)=g(f(x))$ for all x in $def(f)$.

Pairing takes as input two functions f and g, such that $def(f)=def(g)$, and returns a function $f^\wedge g : def(f) \rightarrow range(g)$, defined by:

$(f^\wedge g)(x) =< f(x), g(x)) >$, for all x in $def(f)$.

Projection is the usual projection function over a Cartesian product. Take function f: $X \to Y$ and g: $X \to Z$ with common domain X, and let πy and πz denote the projection functions over $Y \times Z$:

$$f = \pi y^\circ (f^\wedge g) \ and \ g = \pi z^\circ (f^\wedge g).$$

Restriction takes as argument a functionand a set f: $X \to Y$ and a set D, such that DC X, and returns a function f/D: $D \to Y$ defined by: $(f/D)(x)=f(x)$, for all x in D.

11.4.3 QoSDW Schema

The base of QoSDW schema is a finite labelled diagram whose nodes and connections satisfy the following conditions: there is only one root, at least one path from the root to every other node and all arrow labels are distinct. Our goal from the obtained QoSDW schema is to have an organized store of service qualities, properties and structure in which multidimensional queries can be applied. The proposed *QoSDW schema* consists of the following tables:

Fact table: Fact (service_id*, URI_type);
Table of dimension Quality: Quality (Quality_id*, Quality_value, foreign_ service_id);
Tables of dimension Quality attributes:
Availability: Availability (avail_id*, avail_value, foreign_Quality_id);
Response time: ResponseTime (response _id*, response_time_value, foreign_ Quality_id);
Documentation: Documentation (Doc _id*, Documentation _value, foreign_ Quality_id);
BestPractice: BestPractice (practice_id*, practice _value, foreign_Quality_id);
Throughput: Throughput (throughput_id*, throughput_value, foreign_Quality_ id);
Latency: Latency (Latency_id*, Latency _value, foreign_Quality_id);
Successability: Successability (Successability_id*, Successability _value, foreign_Quality_id);
Reliability: Reliability (Reliability_id*, Reliability_value, foreign_Quality_id);
Compliance: Compliance (Compliance_id*, Compliance_value, foreign_Quality_id);
Table of dimension property: property (property_id*, property_value, foreign_ service_id);
Tables of dimension property attribute:
Type: ServiceType (ser_type_id*, type_value, foreign_property_id)/value: service or sub-service
Name: ServiceName (ser_name_id*, ser_value, foreign_property_id);
ExpiryDate: ExpiryDate (ExpiryDate_id*, ExpiryDate _value, foreign_property_id);

CreationDate: CreationDate (CreationDate_id*, CreationDate_value, foreign_property_id);
Table of dimension flow: ServiceFlow (flow_id*, service_flow_value, foreign_service_id);
Tables of dimensional flow attribute:
Loop: Loop (loop_id*, input_service, output_service, service_stage, foreign_flow_id)/ stages: start node, normal node or end node.
Sequence: Sequence (sequence_id*, input_service, output_service, service_stage, foreign_flow_id);
AndSplit: AndSplit (AndSplit_id*, input_service, output_service, service_stage, foreign_flow_id);
XorSplit: XorSplit (XorSplit_id*, input_service, output_service, service_stage, foreign_flow_id);
AndJoin: AndJoin (AndJoin_id*, input_service, output_service, service_stage, foreign_flow_id);
XorJoin: XorJoin (XorJoin_id*, input_service, output_service, service_stage, foreign_flow_id);

The proposed QoSDW schema, in Fig. 11.4, is a logical description of the entire multi-dimensional database. This schema is designed as a practical part of the proposed QoSDW model. It includes the name and description of some QoS and basic integration types (such as: sequence, loop, … etc).

11.4.4   Service Selection Based on QoSDW

Based on the QoSDW schema, the QoS data warehouse is built. Similar to the traditional discovery method, the service consumer requests a service and the service registry replies by a set of related service. If the QoS is not helpful to select the best service, the service consumer requests an OLAP analysis report about the quality of the discovered set of services. The QoSDW model consists of a special *QoSDW analyzer* which supports two types of reports about QoS. The first type is a preliminary report which provides information about the quality of first level sub-services. Figure 11.5 shows a visual representation given by the *QoSDW analyzer* about QoS of sub-services.

Sometimes the results of the initial report are not beneficial in designing a new composite service of better quality. Thus, the advanced QoS report is demanded by the service designer. As regards building the required report, the QoSDW analyzer applies some queries on data warehouse, which results in a service's tree (refer to Fig. 11.3). Then, the analyzer utilizes a tree search algorithm to detect fatal sub-services (as shown in Algorithm 1).

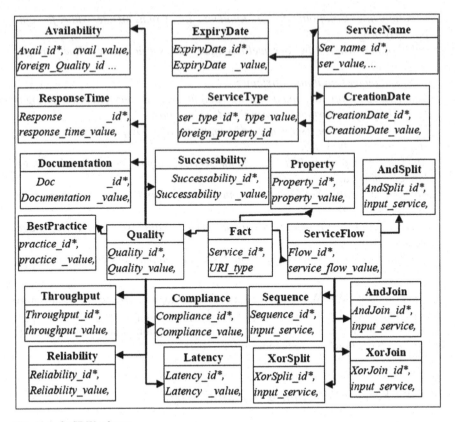

Fig. 11.4 QoSDW schema

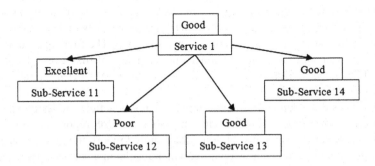

Fig. 11.5 Visual representation of the initial report

Algorithm 1: Detection of infected services

Input: A tree graph,
               A set of start nodes,
Boolean procedure *undercritical (n),* that tests if the *QoS* of a tree node ' *n* 'is
under critical values.
Frontier: = {< *s*>: s is a start node};
Fatalist: = {< *r*>: r is a sub-service of weak *QoS*};
Filter (x): a procedure that removes the node duplications from array list *x.*
   While *frontier* is not empty:
         Select and **remove** path <*n0; ...; nk*> from *the frontier*;
         If *undercritical (nk)*
         Add node *nk* to the *FatalList*
         For every neighbor *n* of *nk*
         Add <n0; ...; nk> to *frontier*;
   End while
   Filter (FatalList)

Output: Return the filtered set of *FatalList*

The fatal service is a weak quality sub-service (its QoS is below the critical values), which causes weakness in the quality of the parent service. The existence of fatal sub service is sufficient for the service consumers not to select the parent service, because they pay their money for utilizing an infected service. Thus, the QoSDW models added a new quality attribute in the selection process—the number of fatal sub-services. Indeed, if there is a group of discovered services of equal QoS level, the service which has the least number of infected sub-services must be selected. In terms of infected services detection, the service designer is capable of rebuilding improved versions of these services, free of fatal sub-services.

Also, if the *QoSDW analyzer* reports are not helpful in selecting the best service, service consumers can apply their own queries on the data warehouse as described in the next section.

11.5   QoSDW Benefits

Services with similar functionality may be accessible at different QoS levels. Thus, to build a service process, decisions must be made based on more specific component at appropriate QoS levels. Consequently, QoSDW model benefits from the quality of every sub-service to qualify a complex cloud service. In the previous approaches, the discovered services are only qualified with no information about their internal flow of sub services. Conversely, the QoSDW model allows studying and

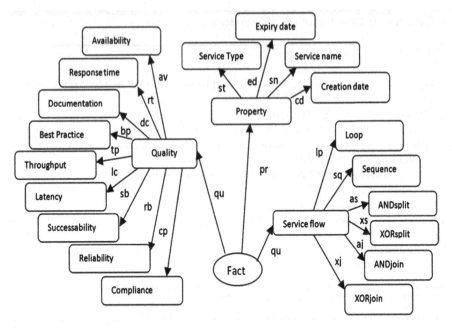

Fig. 11.6 The proposed QoSDW schema

analyzing the weak sub-services which lead to bad qualities of parent service before making a selection decision. Compared with the traditional selection process, QoS-DW is more advanced and both of service consumers and service providers may benefit from its facilities. On one side, service consumers are capable of applying a deep analysis concerning the service component before selection, using QoSDW analyzer reports and OLAP queries. On the other side, the QoSDW is also beneficial for cloud service providers; because service designers are capable of analyzing and detecting fatal sub-services that cause weakness in cloud processes.

To show the advantages of the *QoSDW model* from the queries' prospective, we present an OLAP example, which is simulated as graph and algebraic queries. Consider a schema S, an OLAP query over S is a triple $Q = (x, y, z)$, satisfying the following conditions:

x and y are path expressions such that the source $(x) = $ source $(y) = root\ object$. z is an *operation* over the target of y.

The expression x will be referred to as the classifier of Q and the expression v as the measure of Q.

Figure 11.6 shows the QoSDW schema as an acyclic graph, such that the root is the object of an application, while the remaining nodes model the attributes of the object. Through queries, some functions (such as *av*, *rt* and *dc*) are used when invoking object. Concerning the online QoS analysis through QoSDW, OLAP queries are prepared using paths starting at the root object (Fact).

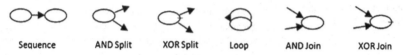

Fig. 11.7 Basic integration models for complex cloud services

Fig. 11.8 Example of interior composition of the steamboat

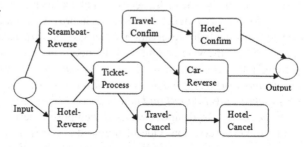

Through OLAP, service consumers can apply an advanced query such as:

- *Q1:* Ask for sub-services which utilise *XORjoin* integration when invoking other services and their *Response Time* greater than 80 (*ms*) sorted by name of service. Let us divide the query *Q1:*
  - Ask for sub-services: **pr o st.value=='sub-service'**
  - Which utilizes *XORjoin* integration when invoking other services: **qu o xj**
  - Their *Response Time* greater than 80 (ms): **qu o rt. value>80**
  - Sub-services are sorted by name of service: **(pr o sn)^ (pr o st.value== 'service')**
- *Q1=<(pr o sn)^ (pr o st.value=='service'), ((pr o st.value=='sub-service') ^ (qu o xj) ^ (qu o rt. value>80)), sum>*

Considering the SteamBoat service (Sect. 11.3), the answer of the query *Q1* is: *Ticket_Process.* For more details about the algebraic base of OLAP refer to [17].

11.6 Simulation and Results

To facilitate understanding of the model, we discuss in this part an example of service selection and simulation of selecting service based on the fatal service property.

11.6.1 Service Selection Example Based on QoS

QoS consists of a group of properties, but for the purpose of simplicity, the example, in this section, examines just two of these properties (the service *cost* and service *response* time). For complex services, six basic integration models (Fig. 11.7) are considered and they are compatible with the business process of a service.

Table 11.1 QoS (cost and response time) of three services

Service name	Cost ($)	Response time (ms)	Class
Steamboat	0.088	106	Good
Travel via steamboat	0.012	130	Good
Manage steamboat	0.18	183	Poor

Suppose a client is looking for a service to make a steamboat travel reservation (Fig. 11.8). Firstly, she or he needs to make a steamboat and hotel reservation and then apply for a visa ticket. If the visa is approved, he can buy the steamboat ticket and confirm the hotel reservation, otherwise, he will have to cancel both reservations. Also, if the visa is approved, he needs to make a car reservation. To complete its job, this complex service (*steamboat service*) invokes other services such as: *steamboat-reserve, hotel-reserve, ticket-process, travel-confirm, hotel-confirm, car-reserve, travel-cancel and hotel-cancel.*

A cloud service designer wants to compose a service that serves all types of online travel reservation. One of the used services in this composition is *Steam-Boat* service, which serves an online boat reservation. However, several cloud providers support such type of boat service (Table 11.1). In this case, the service consumer depends on the QoS (or QoSBroker) to select the best service. While, services are divided into three classes: *Excellent*; users accept to pay lower cost (*0.001 $ < Cost < 0.009 $*) for better service qualities, *Good*; users pay the regular cost (*0.01 $ < Cost < 0.09 $*) for normal service qualities, and *Poor*; users accept worse costs (*0.1 $ < Cost < 0.9 $*) with lower service qualities.

Based on the service properties mentioned in Table 11.1, the service consumer will choose the steamboat service because it is evaluated as best service (Class: *Good*) by *QoSBroker*. But how was the QoS calculated?

The QoS calculations are based on Cardoso's QoS formulas [18]. This provides insights into computational details about the estimation of some QoS in the service selection process such as, Response Time and Cost where:

- *Response Time* (*T*): refers to the time taken by a request to be processed by a task. For sequential tasks, two tasks *ti* and *tj*, which are in sequence, may be reduced to a single task *tnew*, so that: $T(tnew) = T(ti) + T(tj)$. In a parallel system, multiple tasks (*ti, tj,…, tn*) are reduced to their maximum according to the formula: $T(tnew) = Maxi_e(0,1,…,n)\{T(ti)\}$.
- *Cost* (*C*): is considered as a cost incurred by the service provider when a task is executed. For sequential tasks *ti* and *tj*, the new task is calculated according to the following formula: $C(tnew) = C(ti) + C(tj)$. While in parallel tasks *ti* and *tj*, the cost is obtained using this formula: $C(tnew) = \sum_{1 \le i \le n} C(ti)$.

The evaluation of a service depends on its entire structure and the quality of the other sub-services invoked to compose such service. In our example, the properties of the steamboat service are based on the properties of its sub-services such as *Steamboat-Reserve and others* (as shown in Table 11.2).

Table 11.2 QoS (cost and response time) of steamboat sub-services

Service name	Cost ($)	Response time (ms)	Class
Steamboat-reserve	0.21	190	Poor
Hotel-reserve	0.019	112	Good
Ticket-process	0.015	125	Good
Travel-confirm	0.009	122	Excellent
Hotel-confirm	0.007	99	Good
Car-reserve	0.012	84	Good
Travel-cancel	0.003	114	Excellent
Hotel-cancel	0.002	119	Excellent

11.6.2 QoSDW Simulation

This section explains the results of the QoS data warehouse simulation based on the proposed QoSDW model. To implement this simulation, we use *SQL server 2012, Eclipse indigo, Apache Tomcat Server (v.7), Microsoft visual studio 2012 and windows Azure.*

This simulation discusses selection of a SteamBoat service, which was described in Sect. 11.5.1 above, based on the fatal service property that resulted from the application of QoSDW model.

The service consumer requests a *steamboat* service and the *cloud broker* reply by a list of three discovered services: *SteamBoat, TravelViaSteamboat* and *ManageSteamboat* (see Table 11.1 in Sect. 11.5.1). In the traditional service selection process, the *QoSBroker* calculates the QoS of the discovered set service, based on the service provider measures. Figure 11.9 shows the variation of QoS *(Response-Time, Availability, Throughput, Successability, Reliability, Compliance, BestPractice, Latency, Documentation)* of a three services (*SteamBoat, TravelViaSteamboat and ManageSteamboat*) given by the *QoSBroker.*

As a result, the *QoSBroker* marks services *SteamBoat* and *TravelViaSteamboat* as *Good* services. However, it marks *ManageSteamboat* as a *Poor* service. Based on the QoS primary results, the weak service is excluded, while the QoS of the two other good services is studied, in order to select the best of them. Indeed, the traditional selection method shows that the QoS of the two good services is approximately equal. Thus, it is difficult to decide which service is better.

Based on the QoSDW model, the service consumer is capable of requesting more analysis details about the discovered services. Indeed, the QoSDW analyzer supports the consumer by a preliminary report, which analyses the QoS of first sub-service level of the discovered set of services.

Figures 11.10 and 11.11 show, respectively, the variation of quality of sub-services of both *SteamBoat* and *TravelViaSteamboat* services.

Sometimes, the first report is not beneficial in selecting the best service, so a more advanced report is requested from the *QoSDW analyzer.* In our example, the *QoSDW analyzer*, in its second report, detects a fatal sub-service in the tree of *TravelViaSteamboat* service (as shown in Fig. 11.11, the *SteamBoatTravel* service suffers from weak qualities in which: Response Time=65 ms, Throughput=17

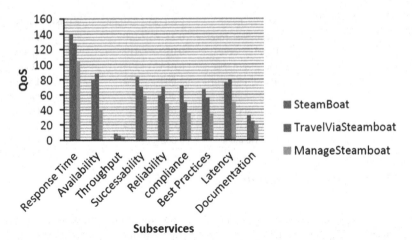

Fig. 11.9 Difference in QoS values among three cloud services (*SteamBoat*, *TravelViaSteamboat* and *ManageSteamboat*)

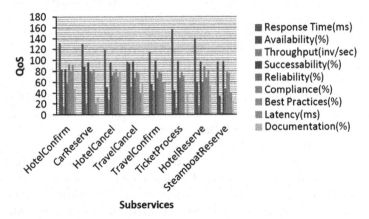

Fig. 11.10 QoS of the sub-services of *SteamBoat* service

invokes per second, Latency=34 ms, Availability=53 %, Reliability=40 % and Best Practice=43 %). The final report concludes that the *SteamBoat* service is the best service to be selected. However, if sometimes results are not convincing, a service consumer can query the *QoSDW analyzer*, using OLAP queries, and build a much advanced cloud service analysis (as discussed in Sect. 11.4).

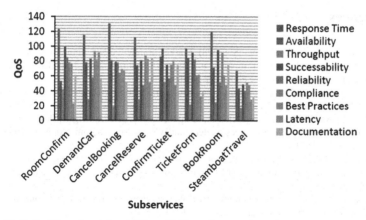

Fig. 11.11 QoS of the sub-services of *TraveVialSteamboat* service

11.7   Conclusion

Clouds aim to control the next generation data centres by exposing them as a network of virtual services. Cloud users are able to access and deploy applications from anywhere in the world on demand at competitive costs depending on user requirements. With the volatile growth of the number of cloud services published over the web, it is difficult to select a suitable service among the candidate cloud services which offer similar functionalities. QoS is considered as the main non-functional criterion for service selection. However, there are still some limitations face QoS-based cloud service selection process. Indeed, improving these limitations need much time and research efforts to modify the cloud processing infrastructure. Smartly, this chapter introduces a QoSDW model that improves the service selection process without altering Cloud standards. A QoSDW is a centralized storage that combines QoS information from various Cloud sources. Mainly, it helps solve the Cloud service selection problem through processing of large numbers of historical QoS of complex Cloud services in a highly-efficient manner. QoSDW provides an environment that supports Cloud infrastructure since it is completely designed for QoS analytical-reporting and decision-support. As a summary of the flow QoSDW model, the service business processes are mapped into star relational database schemas at the Cloud provider side. At the Cloud broker, an OLAP Cube is implemented using the stored QoSDW schemas. Based on advanced analysis levels of Cube content, the *QoSDW analyzer* monitors Cloud services and returns up-to-date reports about any modification occurs in their qualities. As a future work, our goal is to achieve a logic layer of cloud services, which support service autonomy in case of selection and composition procedures.

Acknowledgement This work is supported by the Department of Computer Science at the University of Quebec at Chicoutimi, the Ecole Doctorale des Sciences et des Technologies at the Lebanese University and the AZM association.

References

1. Buyya R, Yeo C, Venugopal S (2008) Market-oriented cloud computing: vision, hype, and reality for delivering IT services as computing utilities. 2008 10th IEEE international conference high performance computer communication
2. Wu J, Yang F (2007) QoS prediction for composite web services with transactions, LNCS, vol. 4652. Springer, Berlin, pp 86–94
3. Dan A, Davis D, Kearney R, Keller A, King A, Kuebler D, Ludwig H, Polan M, Spreitzer M, Youssef A (2004) Web services on demand: WSLA-driven automated management. IBM Syst J 43(1):136–158
4. Yu T, Lin K (2004) Service selection algorithms for Web services with end-to-end QoS constraints. In: Proceedings of IEEE international conference on e-commerce technology CEC 2004
5. Keskes N, Lehireche A, Rahmoun A (2010) Web services selection based on context ontology and quality of services. Int Arab J e-Technol 1(3):98–105
6. Raj RJ, Sasipraba T (2010) Web service selection based on QoS Constraints. In Trendz in Information Sciences & Computing (TISC), IEEE
7. Squicciarini A, Carminati B, Karumanchi S (2011) A privacy-preserving approach for web service selection and provisioning. 2011 IEEE international conference on web service, pp 33–40
8. Garg S, Versteeg S, Buyya R (2011) SMICloud: a framework for comparing and ranking cloud services. 2011 fourth IEEE international conference on utility cloud computing, pp 210–218
9. Rehman Z, Hussain O, Hussain F (2012) Iaas cloud selection using MCDM methods. 2012 IEEE Ninth international conference on e-business engineering, pp 246–251
10. Wang H, Lee C, Ho T (2007) Combining subjective and objective QoS factors for personalized web service selection. Expert Syst Appl 32:571–584
11. Anita M (2012) An efficient QoS-based ranking model for web service selection with consideration of user's requirement. Thesis and dissertations, Ryerson University, Canada
12. Nallur V, Bahsoon R (2012) A decentralized self-adaptation mechanism for service-based applications in the cloud. IEEE Trans Softw Eng. doi:10.1109/TSE.2012.53
13. Karray A, Teyeb R, Ben Jemaa M (2013) A heuristic approach for web-service discovery and selection. Int J Comput Sci Inf Technol (IJCSIT) 5(2). doi:10.5121/ijcsit.2013.5210
14. Smith J, Nair R (2005) Virtual machines: versatile platforms for systems and processes, book. Morgan Kaufmann, Boston
15. Liu W (2005) Trustworthy service selection and composition—reducing the entropy of service-oriented Web. INDIN '05. 2005 3rd IEEE international conference on industrial informatics
16. Yu Q, Bouguettaya A (2010) Guest editorial: special section on query models and efficient selection of web services. IEEE Trans Serv Comput 3(3):161–162. doi:10.1109/TSC.2010.43
17. Spyratos N (2006) A functional model for data analysis, lecture notes in computer science, vol 4027. Springer, Berlin, pp 51–64
18. Cardoso J (2002) Quality of service and semantic composition of workflows. Ph.D thesis, University of Georgia, Athens, GA
19. Al-Masri E, Mahmoud QH (2007) Discovering the best web service. Proceedings of the 16th international conference on World Wide Web, pp 1257–1258. http://dx.doi.org/10.1145/1242572.1242795

Chapter 12
Characterizing Cloud Federation Approaches

Attila Kertesz

Abstract Cloud Computing offers on-demand access to computational, infra-structure and data resources operated from a remote source. This novel technology has opened new ways of flexible resource provisions for businesses to manage IT applications and data responding to new demands from customers. In this chapter, we provide a general insight to the formation and interoperability issues of Cloud Federations that envisage a distributed, heterogeneous environment consisting of various cloud infrastructures by aggregating different Infrastructure-as-a-Service (IaaS) provider capabilities coming from both the commercial and academic area. These multi-cloud infrastructures are also used to avoid provider lock-in issues for users that frequently utilize different clouds. We characterize and classify recent solutions that arose from both research projects and individual research groups, and show how they attempt to hide the diversity of multiple clouds and form a unified federation on top of them. As they still need to cope with several open issues concerning interoperability; we also provide guidelines to address related topics such as service monitoring, data protection and privacy, data management and energy efficiency.

Keywords Cloud computing · Cloud Federation · InterCloud · Interoperability · Data protection · Energy efficiency · IaaS

12.1 Introduction

Cloud computing is a diverse research area that encompasses many aspects of sharing software and hardware solutions, including computing and storage resources, application runtimes or complex application functionalities. The concept of Cloud

A. Kertesz (✉)
MTA SZTAKI, Budapest, Hungary
e-mail: keratt@inf.u-szeged.hu

Software Engineering Department, University of Szeged, Szeged, Hungary

© Springer International Publishing Switzerland 2014   277
Z. Mahmood (ed.), *Cloud Computing,* Computer Communications and Networks,
DOI 10.1007/978-3-319-10530-7_12

computing has been pioneered by successful commercial companies with the promise to allow elastic construction of virtual infrastructures, which attracted users early on. Its technical motivation has been introduced in [1, 2]. Cloud solutions enable businesses with the option to outsource the operation and management of IT infrastructure and services, allowing the business and its employees to concentrate on their core competencies. As new products and technologies are offered in the near future, Gartner estimates that $112 billion will be spent by the year 2015 by businesses and individuals on Cloud Computing offerings from service providers such as Amazon, IBM and Microsoft [3].

In this chapter, we first gather relevant architectural views of Clouds to give an insight where interoperation could be enabled to form federations, and then focus on and characterize existing solutions of Cloud Federations that envisage a distributed, heterogeneous environment consisting of various cloud infrastructures by aggregating different Infrastructure-as-a-Service (IaaS) provider capabilities coming from both the commercial and academic area. Nowadays, cloud providers operate geographically diverse data centers as user demands like disaster recovery and multisite backups became widespread. These techniques are also used to avoid provider lock-in issues for users that frequently utilize multiple clouds. By this work we aim at revealing the important properties and capabilities of recent cloud reports and solutions dealing with federations. These approaches try to hide the diversity of multiple clouds and form a unified federation on top of them. Today's large systems need new, interoperable approaches to allow their efficient operation in terms of cost, energy consumption and balanced resource utilization, which have also been emphasized by the European Commission [4]. Therefore, we also highlight the open issues concerning the interoperability of the participants of these federative approaches, such as service monitoring, data protection and privacy, data management and energy efficiency. Finally, we provide hints where future research should be driven to achieve the final goal of interoperable Cloud Federations.

The remainder of this chapter is organized as follows: Section 12.2 introduces and analyzes the architectural views of standardization bodies and relevant projects, while Sect. 12.3 summarizes and classifies state-of-the-art approaches aiming at Cloud federations. Section 12.4 introduces four relevant interoperability research issues of federations with possible solutions towards practical realizations. Finally, Sect. 12.5 summarizes and concludes the chapter.

12.2   Architectural and Deployment Models of Clouds

In this section, we gather the relevant views on the architectural and deployment models of Cloud environments defined and published by standardization bodies from all around the world and by corresponding European research projects.

Fig. 12.1 Cloud Architec-
tures derived from the Cloud
Computing Expert Working
Group report

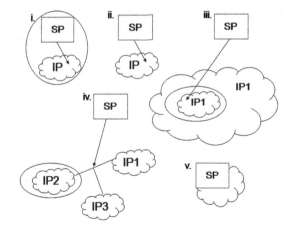

12.2.1 Definitions of Standardization Bodies

The View of the European Commission An expert group set up by the European
Commission published their view on Cloud Computing in [4, 5]. These reports
categorize Cloud architectures into five groups as follows and as shown in Fig. 12.1:

- Private Clouds (i): these consist of resources managed by an infrastructure
  provider (IP) that are typically owned or leased by an enterprise from a service
  provider (SP). Usually, services with "Cloud-enhanced" features are offered,
  therefore this group includes Software as a Service (SaaS) solutions like eBay
  [6].
- Public Clouds (ii): these offer their services to users outside of the company and
  may use Cloud functionality from other providers. In this solution enterprises
  can outsource their services to such Cloud providers mainly for cost reduction.
  Examples of these providers are Amazon [7] or Google Apps [8].
- Hybrid Clouds (iii): these consist of both private and public Cloud infrastructures
  to achieve a higher level of cost reduction through outsourcing by maintaining
  the desired degree of control (e.g., sensitive data may be handled in private
  Clouds). The report states that hybrid Clouds are rarely used at the moment.
- Community Clouds (iv): these different entities contribute with their (usually
  small) infrastructure to build up an aggregated private or public Cloud. Smaller
  enterprises may benefit from such infrastructures, and a solution is provided by
  Zimory [9].
- Special Purpose Clouds (v): This variety provides more specialized functionalities
  with additional, domain specific methods, such as the distributed document management by Google's App Engine. This group is an extension or a specialization
  of the previous Cloud categories.

Fig. 12.2 Cloud
Architectures derived from
ENISA reports

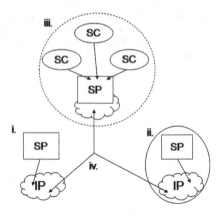

The View of ENISA The European Network and Information Security Agency (ENISA) differentiates between four architectures [10], as shown in Fig. 12.2, viz: (1) A Public Cloud—that is a publicly-available infrastructure to which any organization may subscribe and use (also called service consumers (SC)), (2) Private Clouds—that offer services built on Cloud Computing principles, but accessible only within a private network, (3) Partner Clouds—that are operated by a provider to a limited and well-defined number of parties, and (4) Cloud Federation—that may be built up by aggregating two or more other varieties of Clouds.

Cloud Architectures Defined by NIST The National Institute of Standards and Technology (NIST) defines four deployment models [11, 12] as depicted in Fig. 12.3. According to their definition, (i) A Private Cloud is an infrastructure operated solely for an organization that may be managed by either the organization or a third-party and located locally or remotely; (ii) A Community Cloud is a distributed computing environment shared by several organizations and individuals, and supports a specific community that has similar concerns (e.g., mission, security requirements, policy, and compliance considerations). It may be managed by organizations or third parties, and may exist on premises or off premises; (iii) A Public Cloud infrastructure is made available to the general public or a large industry group, and is owned by an organization selling Cloud services; and finally, (iv) A Hybrid Cloud is a composition of two or more Clouds (private, community, or public) that remain unique entities but are bound together by standardized or proprietary technology that enables data and application portability (e.g., Cloud bursting for load balancing between Clouds).

The Cloud Computing Use Case Discussion Group [13] adopts the NIST models. They extend the view on Hybrid Clouds by stating that "multiple Clouds work together, coordinated by a Cloud broker that federates data, applications, user identity, security and other details." Though a brokering mechanism is needed for federating Clouds, no specific guidelines are given how to achieve this.

The View of DMTF The Distributed Management Task Force (DMTF) Open Cloud Standards Incubator view [14] has also adopted the NIST models and defined different scenarios showing how Clouds may interoperate (depicted in Fig. 12.4).

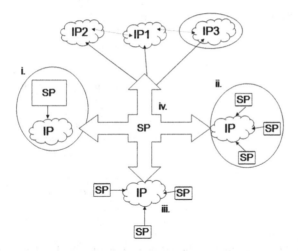

Fig. 12.3 Cloud deployment models of NIST

Fig. 12.4 Cloud architectures
by DMTF

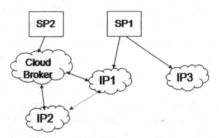

These scenarios explain how data centers interact with Cloud providers and differentiate three cases:

- If a datacenter, run by Service Provider 1 (SP1) and hosted by Infrastructure Provider 1 (IP1), exceeds the available capacity limits then IP2 provides extra computing capacity for IP1 and SP1 is unaware of this provisioning.
- In a multiple Cloud scenario, SP1 may operate services in both IP1 and IP3 Clouds, therefore a datacenter may request services from both providers since they may support different services or Service-level Agreement (SLA) parameters.
- A provider may act as a Cloud broker to federate resources from other providers (e.g., IP1 and IP2) to make them available to its consumers transparently without using any of its own resources.

12.2.2   Cloud Models in European Research Projects

The View of OPTIMIS The OPTIMIS project [15] identified that commercial solutions in the field of Cloud Computing have mainly focused on providing

Fig. 12.5 The OPTIMIS
cloud architectures

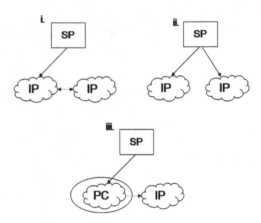

functionalities at levels close to the infrastructure, and higher-level solutions, like Platform as a Service (PaaS) environments are limited to a single infrastructure provider. Their goal is to build an improved cloud service ecosystem that supports higher-level concerns and non-functional aspects to achieve a wider adoption of Cloud Computing. The project follows a holistic approach for multiple coexisting cloud architectures and they target cloud service life-cycle optimization including cost, trust, risk, and economic goals. They also plan to enable market-oriented multi-cloud architectures with clarified legislative background. The architectural views of the OPTIMIS project [16] are shown in Fig. 12.5. The project has three basic architectural scenarios. In (i) a Federated Cloud Architecture, a Service Provider (SP) assesses an Infrastructure Provider (IP). IPs can share resources among each other. In (ii) a Multi-Cloud Architecture, different infrastructure providers are used separately by a service provider. Finally in (iii) a Hybrid Cloud Architecture, a Private Cloud (PC) is used by the SP, which can utilize resources of different IPs.

The View of Reservoir The Reservoir project [17] claims that small and medium Cloud providers cannot enter the Cloud-provisioning market due to the lack of interoperability between Clouds. Their approach is exemplified by the electric grid approach: "for one facility to dynamically acquire electricity from a neighboring facility to meet a spike in demand." Disparate datacenters should be federated to provide a "seemingly infinite service computing utility." Regarding the architectural view, a Reservoir Cloud consists of different Reservoir Sites (RS) operated by different IPs. Each RS has resources that are partitioned into isolated Virtual Execution Environments (VEE). Service applications may use VEE hosts from different RSs simultaneously. Each application is deployed with a service manifest that formally defines its SLA contract. Virtual Execution Environment Managers (VEEM) interact with VEEs, Service Managers and other VEEMs to enable federations to be formed. A VEEM gathers interacting VEEs into a VEE group that serves a service application. This implies that a Reservoir service stack has to be present on the resources/sites of IPs. Their specialized Cloud architecture is depicted in Fig. 12.6.

Fig. 12.6 The Reservoir
cloud architecture

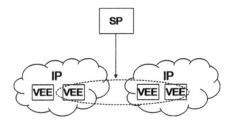

The View of Contrail The Contrail project [18] proposes an SLA-centered federated approach for Clouds. Its goal is to minimize the burden on the user with eliminating provider lock-in by exploiting resources belonging to different cloud providers regardless the kind of technology they use, and to increase the efficiency of using Cloud platforms by performing both a vertical and a horizontal integration. It follows an open-source approach toward technology and standards, and supports user authentication and applications deployment by providing extended SLA management functionalities. Its federation architecture, shown in Fig. 12.7, acts as a bridge among the users and the cloud providers, and has three layers. The top, interface layer provides ways to interact with the federation. It gathers requests from users and other Contrail components that rely on the federation functionalities. The bottom, Adapters layer contains drivers for external Cloud services, while the middle, Core layer contains modules that fulfill the functional and nonfunctional requirements of the federation. The federation runtime manager operates in this layer, which uses a set of heuristics that consider different aspects to govern the federation, such as to minimize economical cost and to maximize performance levels.

The View of BonFIRE The BonFIRE project [19] aims at exploring the interactions between novel service and network infrastructures. The project was focused on the extension of current cloud offerings towards a federated facility with heterogeneous virtualized resources and best-effort Internet interconnectivity. They have developed a set of procedures to interconnect a multi-cloud environment with advanced facilities for controlled networking. These procedures enable the provisioning of customized network functions and services in support of experiments running in a multi-cloud test-bed. Their aim is to federate three advanced networking facilities within the BonFIRE multi-cloud environment: the interconnections with FEDERICA and GÉANT are already active, and OFELIA planned to be connected soon. The BonFIRE facility (shown in Fig. 12.8) is composed of six geographically distributed cloud test-beds, located at EPCC, INRIA, HLRS, iMinds, HP, and PSNC.

Fig. 12.7 Contrail
architecture

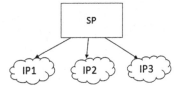

Fig. 12.8 The BonFIRE
facility

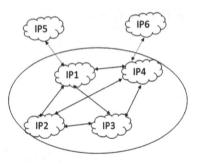

The View of mOSAIC The mOSAIC project [20] offers the specification of service requirements in terms of a cloud ontology via an innovative API. The implementation of this approach will offer a higher degree of portability and vendor independence. It also provides application programming interfaces for building applications using services from multiple cloud providers and plans to realize a self-adaptive distributed scheduling platform composed of multiple agents implemented as intelligent feedback control loops to support policy-based scheduling and expose self-healing capabilities. They plan to foster competition between cloud providers by enabling the selection of best-fitting cloud services to actual user needs and efficiently outsource computations. In its hybrid cloud scenario, they envision multiple clouds working together coordinated by a cloud broker that federates data, applications, user identity, and security, as shown in Fig. 12.9.

The View of EGI Federated Cloud The European Grid Infrastructure (EGI) is a federation of national and domain specific resource infrastructure providers, who use virtualised management environments to improve the local delivery of services. Many of EGI's current and new user communities would also like to access the flexibility provided by virtualisation across the infrastructure resulting in a cloud-like environment. Federating these individual virtualised resources has been a major priority for EGI, therefore it has set up the Federated Clouds Task Force [21]. Its main objectives were to provide guidelines for its resource providers to securely federate and share their virtualised environments as part of the EGI production infrastructure, and to create a testbed to evaluate the integration of virtualised resources within the existing EGI production infrastructure for monitoring,

Fig. 12.9 mOSAIC hybrid
cloud architecture through
APIs

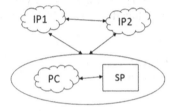

Fig. 12.10 EGI Federated
Cloud

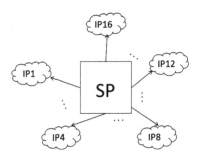

accounting and information services. Their guidelines do not define what hypervisor the participating resource providers should use, and the federation adopts a set of well-defined functionalities and interfaces that every provider is free to implement independently. Currently there are 16 providers participating in the EGI Federated Cloud (FedCloud) testbed using OpenNebula, OpenStack and StratusLab. Their federated architecture is depicted in Fig. 12.10. Currently, the clouds of the participating infrastructure providers can be reached in a centralized way, and utilized separately.

12.2.3   Classification of Research Projects

To compare the previously introduced approaches, we have created a classification of these views concerning their abilities to form federations. We propose four categories in this classification:

- *Hierarchical* type of federations: In this vision there is a usually centralized, higher level management service that is responsible for federation forming and the coordination. This type is also called as a "Multi-Cloud" approach in the literature [22].
- *Horizontal* type of federations: In this vision bi- or multi-lateral resource renting is the main goal of the participating providers, mainly for optimizing resource utilization and reducing operation costs. This type is generally named as "Federation" in the literature [22].
- *Heterogeneity* of participating providers: With this category we represent the variety of IaaS software stacks available in the federation (where "No" means that the same software stack need to be used in order to participate in a federation).
- *Specialty* of federation forming: Here we named one of the unique capabilities of the appropriate solution.

The actual categorization is shown in Table 12.1. The introduced categories reveal the most important properties of the surveyed solutions.

Table 12.1 Classification of federative approaches of research projects

	Hierarchical	Horizontal	Heterogeneity	Specialty
OPTIMIS [15]	X	–	Yes	Legislation awareness
Reservoir [17]	–	X	No	Reservoir service stack
Contrail [18]	X	–	Yes	SLA contracts
BonFIRE [19]	–	X	Yes	Controlled networking
mOSAIC [20]	–	X	Yes	Cloud ontology, API
EGI FedCloud [21]	–	X	Yes	Virtualised EGI environments

12.3 InterCloud and Cloud Federation Approaches

Cloud federation refers to a mesh of cloud providers that are interconnected based on open standards to provide a universal decentralized computing environment where everything is driven by constraints and agreements in a ubiquitous, multi-provider infrastructure. Until now, the cloud ecosystem has been characterized by the steady rising of hundreds of independent and heterogeneous cloud providers, managed by private subjects, which offer various services to their clients. In this subsection next to the already overviewed research projects, we gather relevant federative approaches found in the literature. Cloud providers offering PaaS solutions may form "sub-federations" simultaneously to these approaches. Specific service applications may be more suitable for these provisions, and projects like Reservoir [17] and 4CaaSt [23] are working towards such a solution. Our considered federative works targets IaaS-type providers, e.g. RackSpace, the infrastructure services of Amazon EC2, and providers using Cloud middleware such as OpenNebula and Eucaliptus.

InterCloud Vision Buyya et al. [1] envision that one day Cloud Computing will be the fifth utility by satisfying the computing needs of everyday life. Their pioneering paper discusses the current trends in Cloud computing and presents candidates for future enhancements. They emphasize the market-oriented side of Clouds, and introduce a market-oriented cloud architecture, discussing how global cloud exchanges could take place in the future. They further extended this vision [24] by suggesting a federation oriented, just in time, opportunistic and scalable application services provisioning environment called InterCloud. They envision utility oriented federated IaaS systems that are able to predict application service behavior for intelligent down and up-scaling infrastructures. They list the research issues of flexible service to resource mapping, user and resource centric QoS optimization, integration with in-house systems of enterprises, scalable monitoring of system components. They present a market-oriented approach to offer InterClouds including cloud exchanges and brokers that bring together producers and consumers. Producers are offering domain specific enterprise Clouds that are connected and managed within the federation with their Cloud Coordinator component.

Cross-Cloud Federation Approach Celesti et al. [25] proposed an approach for the federation establishment considering generic cloud architectures according to a three-phase model, representing an architectural solution for federation by means

Fig. 12.11 Federated Cloud
Management Architecture

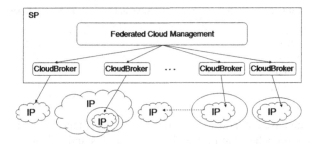

of a Cross-Cloud Federation Manager (CCFM), a software component in charge of executing the three main functionalities required for a federation. In particular, the component explicitly manages: (i) the discovery phase in which information about other clouds are received and sent, (ii) the match-making phase performing the best choice of the provider according to some utility measure, and (iii) the authentication phase creating a secure channel between the federated clouds. These concepts can be extended taking into account green policies applied in federated scenarios.

Multi-Cloud Approach Bernstein et al. [26] define two use case scenarios that exemplify the problems of multi-cloud systems: (i) VM mobility where they identify the networking, the specific cloud VM management interfaces and the lack of mobility interfaces as the three major obstacles, and (ii) storage interoperability and federation scenario in which storage provider replication policies are subject to change when a cloud provider initiates subcontracting. They offer interoperability solutions only for low-level functionality of the clouds that are not focused on recent user demands but on solutions for IaaS system operators.

FCM Approach In the Federated Cloud Management solution [27], interoperability is achieved by high-level brokering instead of bilateral resource renting, as shown in Fig. 12.11. Although, this does not mean that different IaaS providers may not share or rent resources, but if they do so then it is transparent to their higher level management. Such a federation can be enabled without applying additional software stack for providing low-level management interfaces. The logic of federated management is moved to higher levels, and there is no need for adapting interoperability standards by the participating infrastructure providers, which is usually a restriction that some industrial providers are reluctant to undertake.

Classification of Research Approaches To classify the relevant research directions addressing federations reported in the literature, we use the same categorization as in Table 12.2. In this case, we can also observe that both hierarchical and horizontal federation types are represented, and heterogeneity within the participating providers is only present in hierarchical solutions. While most of the projects considered in Section 12.2.2 applied the horizontal approach, smaller research groups are in favor of the hierarchical way. The motivation behind this observation is that research projects lasting for 3–4 years had the manpower to develop own interfaces to enable interoperation among the participating Cloud providers, and also had the ambitious aim to come up with a solution that could be standardized

Table 12.2 Classification of federative approaches of research papers

	Hierarchical	Horizontal	Heterogeneity	Specialty
InterCloud [1]	X	–	Yes	Market-oriented
Cross-Cloud [25]	–	X	Yes/No	Authentication
Multi-Cloud [26]	X	–	Yes	VM mobility
FCM [27]	X	–	Yes	Meta-brokering

and used in industry later on. On the other hand, smaller research groups focused on approaches that utilize already existing standards to avoid provider lock-in, and to enable easier collaboration with industrial solutions.

12.4 Interoperability Issues of Cloud Federations

Not only the interchangeability of user applications in different clouds participating in a federation represents and open issue, but other related interoperability problems concerning the management of such a large distributed ecosystem need to be addressed as well.

As mentioned before, the European Commission has assigned an expert group to publish reports on future research challenges of Clouds [4, 5]. In these reports they also performed a gap analysis of already existing commercial and academic solutions and highlighted the following topics that need further research:

- Manageability: Even though most Cloud solutions handle elasticity, intelligent methodologies are needed to reach optimal resource utilization.
- Data management: Most data flowing to or created in the Cloud need to be supported by meta-data information and new standards are needed to guarantee long-term storing and interoperable sharing among multiple providers.
- Privacy and security: Legislative issues of data distribution should be better addressed, and security holes during resource sharing among multiple tenants should be eliminated.
- Federation and interoperability: Proprietary data structures should be replaced by de facto standards, and new approaches are needed to ensure convergence towards real interoperability eliminating vendor lock-in.
- Virtualization and adaptability: Optimized resource scheduling solutions are needed considering cross-platform executions and migrations taking into account rapidly changing workloads.
- Programming models: Better control on data distribution should be achieved, and new means are needed to enable better application development and deployment.
- Economy: New scheduling policies are needed to enable green resource utilization, more efficient resource utilization with reduced power consumption.

By addressing many of these concerns, we summarize four important research fields that are necessary to be taken into account in building and operating Cloud Federations. These topics represent different facets of interoperability: (i) enhanced monitoring solutions are needed to enable optimized management of participating providers; (ii) legislative regulations need to be considered during multi-tenant data processing; (iii) sustainable and user-friendly data management solutions are needed through standard interfaces; and (iv) energy efficient resource management have to be enabled for future ecosystems.

12.4.1 Monitoring in Cloud Federations

Infrastructure-as-a-service (IaaS) cloud systems provide access to a remote computing infrastructure by allowing their users to instantiate virtual appliances on their virtualized resources as virtual machines. Nowadays, several IaaS systems co-exist, and they are independently offered by several public service providers or by smaller scale privately managed infrastructures. As we have seen before, to enable interoperability of multiple clouds, federations need to handle the differences of various cloud providers and have to negotiate user requirements with multiple parties. Federated clouds aim at supporting these users by providing a single interface on which they can transparently handle different cloud providers, as they would do with a single cloud system. Therefore it is essential to construct federated cloud systems in a way that they not only offer a single interface for their users, but also automatically manage virtual machines (VM) independently from the availably cloud systems.

An efficient cloud selection in a federated environment requires a cloud monitoring subsystem that determines the actual status of available IaaS systems. Since there is only limited monitoring information available for the users or higher-level managers in these clouds, there is a need for a sophisticated service monitoring approach to evaluate basic cloud reliability status, and to perform seamless service provisioning over multiple cloud providers in an interoperable way. We exemplify such an extension to a federation with our Federated Cloud Management solution, where we applied a web service monitoring approach to gather additional and more detailed service quality information from the participating cloud [28]. The FCM approach uses the Generic Meta-Broker Service as the entry point for the users of the cloud federation. This service selects the most suitable cloud provider to perform the service requests of the user by investigating the current state of the participating clouds according to the information stored in a generic service registry and the reliability metrics collected by the integrated SALMon service monitoring framework [29]. The participating clouds are managed by Cloud-Brokers that are capable of handling service requests and managing virtual machines within single IaaS cloud systems.

To enable the meta-brokering service to differentiate between cloud providers, we proposed to use a basic service that is used to cost effectively determine the important characteristics of the available VMs in the federation. As a result, the system is capable to evaluate and choose between both public and private clouds based on the same kind of metrics. We refer to this basic service as the Minimal Metric Monitoring Service (M3S), which is capable of measuring infrastructure reliability together with the integrated SALMon framework in public and private clouds. The M3S service is prepared to run in a virtual machine and it offers three methods to evaluate the basic capabilities of its hosting VM. SALMon uses the response times of these methods to express the reliability of the particular cloud that runs the M3S VM. It has: (i) a generalized ping test to check the availability of the service; (ii) a CPU analyzer method that performs several mathematical calculations in a large loop over a predefined set of variables, consisting on integer and floating point numbers to determine the computational capability of a given VM; and finally (iii) bandwidth analyzer methods, which are used to compute the download and upload transfer speed of the system to determine its inbound and outbound data transfer capabilities.

Our investigations showed that both service reliability and responsiveness do vary over time and load conditions, and these measures can be used by our federated cloud management solution to select better execution environments for achieving a higher level of user satisfaction.

12.4.2 Data Protection in Cloud Federations

Cloud Computing allows the outsourcing of computational power, data storage and other capabilities to a remote third-party. In the supply of any goods and services, the law gives certain rights that protect the consumer and provider, which also applies for Cloud Computing: it is subject to legal requirements and constraints to ensure Cloud services are accurately described and provided to customers with guarantees on quality and fitness-for-purpose.

To exemplify issues arising from data management in Cloud Federations, we have also evaluated the formerly introduced cloud architectures against legal requirements in [30], where we have chosen to perform an evaluation using requirements from data protection law. Data protection legislation is fundamental to Cloud Computing as the consumer looses a degree of control over personal artifacts, when they are submitted to the provider for storage and possible processing. To protect the consumer against the provider misusing their data, data processing legislation has been developed to ensure that the fundamental right to privacy is maintained. However, the distributed nature of Cloud Computing (where cloud services are available from anywhere in the world) makes is difficult to analyze every country's data protection laws for common Cloud architecture evaluation criteria. Therefore, we have chosen a common directive that applies as widely as possible and used the European Data Protection Directive (DPD) [31] as a basis for our investigations. Although it is a European Union (EU) directive, countries that want to collaborate in data transactions with EU Member States are required to provide an adequate level of protection.

The requirements of the DPD are expressed as two technology-neutral actors that have certain responsibilities that must be carried out in order to fulfill the directive. These roles are the data controller and data processor, where a data controller is the natural or legal person which determines the means of the processing of personal data, whilst a data processor is a natural or legal person which processes data on behalf of the controller. However, following these definitions, a special case arises:

if the processing entity plays a role in determining the purposes or the means of processing, it is a controller rather than a processor.

We have also explored Cloud Federations through a series of use cases to demonstrate where legal issues can arise. In these use cases, the relevant actors and their roles were identified and the necessary actions have been stated that should be taken to prevent violations of the directive. We identified that there are complications when personal data is transferred to multiple jurisdictions. For example, considering a service provider (SP) located in the European Union offers services provisioned in a Cloud Federation, which utilizes different infrastructure providers (IPs, usually operating private clouds), and one of which (IP_2) is located in a non-Member State, we arrived to the following conclusion: since SP is the data controller and the participating IPs are processors, the law of the SP's Member State has to be applied, and IP_2 has to provide at least the same level of protection as the national law of SP. Otherwise, if IP_2 cannot ensure an adequate level of protection, the decision making process should rule out IP_2 from provider selection during data management.

As a result of our investigation, we can state that service providers are mainly responsible for complying with the data protection regulation, and when personal data is transferred to multiple jurisdictions, it is crucial to properly identify the controller since this role may change dynamically in specific actions.

12.4.3 Cloud Storage Services in Cloud Federations

One of the most important open issues of Cloud Federations is the interoperable management of data among the participating systems. Retrieving and sharing user data and virtual images among different IaaS clouds is an unsolved issue. Besides concerning data privacy issues, it is also not an easy task to move a user application from one cloud infrastructure to another. Virtualization techniques and virtual image formats different providers support to run on their virtual machines are usually incompatible. Retrieving a user's Virtual Appliance (VA, which is a specialized image hosting the user application) from an IaaS cloud is impossible in most cases, not only in case of commercial providers, but also in academic solutions. Therefore, finding an interoperable way for managing user data among multiple tenants is an important issue.

A popular family of cloud services is called cloud storage services. With the help of such solutions, user data can be stored in a remote location, independent from the infrastructure of cloud providers participating in a federation. Therefore, to exemplify the interoperable utilization of storage and infrastructure clouds, we proposed an approach to retrieve and share user application data among different providers with the help of these online storage services. In this way, VAs running at different cloud infrastructures can manage the same data at the same time, and the users can access these data from their own local devices without the need for accessing any IaaS clouds. Mobile devices can also benefit from Cloud services: the enormous data users produce with these devices are continuously posted to online services, which may require the modification of these data. Nowadays more mobile devices are sold compared to traditional PCs, and Android devices are more and more popular. We have also investigated how user data could be managed in an interoperable way among different IaaS systems participating in a federation. Our aim was to develop a solution that uses cloud storage services together with infrastructure services of cloud federations, which we further used to enhance the capabilities of mobile devices [32]. Though the computing capacity of mobile devices has rapidly increased recently, there are still numerous applications that cannot be solved with them in reasonable time. Our approach is to utilize cloud infrastructure services to execute such applications on mobile data stored in cloud storages.

The basic concept of our solution is the following. Services for data management are running in one or more IaaS systems that keep tracking the cloud storage of a user, and execute data manipulation processes when new files appear in the storage. The services running in the cloud can download the user data files from the cloud storage, execute the necessary application on these files, and upload the modified data to the storage service. Such files can be, for example, photo or video files made by the user with their mobile phone to be processed by an application unsuitable for mobile devices. We have developed an image generator application that interconnects mobile devices, IaaS services and cloud storage services, and evaluated the prototype application using mobile devices and a private IaaS cloud. The evaluation of this application showed that it is worth both in terms of computation time and energy efficiency to move computation-intensive tasks to clouds from mobile devices.

12.4.4 Energy Efficient Management of Cloud Federations

The Cloud Computing technology has created the illusion of infinite resources for use by consumers, however, this vision raises severe issues with energy consumption e.g. the higher levels of quality and availability require irrational energy expenditures. The consumed energy of resources spent for idling represent a considerable amount, therefore the current trends are claimed to be clearly unsustainable with respect to resource utilization, CO_2 footprint and overall energy efficiency. It is anticipated that further growth is objected by energy consumption furthermore, competitiveness of companies will be strongly tied to these issues.

Energy awareness is a highlighted research topic, and there are efforts and solutions for processor level, component level and datacenter level energy efficiency. For instance, new energy efficient approaches were proposed to automate the operation of datacenters behind clouds, so that they help with rearranging the virtualized load from various users. Thus, smaller sized physical infrastructure is sufficient for the actual demand and momentarily unused capacities can be switched off. Nevertheless, these approaches are applicable to single data centers only. On one hand, today's large systems are composed of multiple service providers per se that need new approaches to ensure their overall energy-aware operation. On the other hand, there is an unexplored potential for energy-aware operation in federated and interoperable clouds. Our research in [33] was targeted at examining what new aspects of energy awareness can be exploited in federative schemes.

As small cloud providers and cloud startups are becoming more popular, they soon face user demands that cannot be satisfied with their current infrastructures. Therefore, these providers need to increase the size of their infrastructure by introducing multiple data centers on various locations or join a federation capable of offering unprecedented amount of resources.

Energy consumption is a major component of operating costs. Despite its significance, current IaaS clouds barely provide energy-aware solutions. Providers are restricted to reduce their consumption at the hardware level, independently from the IaaS. These reductions range from the use of more energy efficient computer components to the upgrade of their heating, ventilation and air conditioning systems to increase their power usage efficiency. Although these improvements are crucial, the energy consumption could also be significantly reduced by software means in over-provisioned IaaS systems where more physical resources are available at the provider side than actually requested by users. Over-provisioning is a key behavior at smaller sized providers that offer services for users with occasional peaks in resource demands. To reduce their energy costs, these providers should minimize their over-provisioning while they maintain a fluid experience towards their customers without violating the previously agreed service level. Energy consumption could be reduced with software techniques focusing on intra- and inter-datacenter issues.

To exemplify how energy consumption and CO_2 emissions could be addressed in Cloud Federations, we introduce enhancements in our proposed Federated Cloud Management solution [27]. At the meta-brokering layer, relying on an enhanced monitoring system within the federation, service executions can be directed to data centers of providers consuming less energy, having higher CO_2 emission quotas, or have produced less amount of CO_2 that expected within some timeframe. At the cloud brokering layer, if the energy consumption parameters of a cloud suddenly change, there should be strategies to limit or move around calls and even (if necessary) VMs federation-wise. The changes here may mean the introduction of new hardware, or just switching on/off some parts of the datacenters, or changing the number of VMs. Realigning calls may not have immediate effects, however migration of VMs across the federation is also an energy consuming operation, that needs to be measured and considered when decisions are made, thus this operation should not happen only in case of really drastic changes. An interoperable federation management system should prefer datacenters, where the difference between the highest load and the average load is small because a VM has the smallest impact on those resources.

12.5 Conclusion

In this chapter, we provided a general insight into the formation and interoperability issues of Cloud Federations that envisage a distributed, heterogeneous environment consisting of various cloud infrastructures by aggregating different IaaS provider capabilities coming from both the commercial and academic area. These multi-cloud infrastructures are used to avoid provider lock-in issues for users that frequently utilize different clouds. We have surveyed and characterized recent solutions that attempt to hide the diversity of multiple clouds and form a unified federation on top of them, but they still need to cope with several open issues.

We have shown that these federative approaches, arose from both research projects and individual research groups, *can be categorized into hierarchical and horizontal architecture types*. The hierarchical ones are more favorable by smaller research groups, and have the advantage of supporting more heterogeneous infrastructure providers to avoid vendor lock-in. We have also highlighted *open interoperability issues of federation forming and management* such as service monitoring, data protection and privacy, data management and energy efficiency.

We believe that these research directions can serve as guidelines for researchers in this field, and contribute to fostering further research works on Cloud Federations. By following the guidelines defined by the European Commission, and putting together the pieces of already existing, promising solutions of federation approaches of various research works, we will arrive to such federations that will be able to operate efficient ecosystems attracting thousands of users.

Acknowledgments The research leading to these results has received funding from the CloudSME FP7 project under grant agreement 608886, and it was supported by the European Union and the State of Hungary, co-financed by the European Social Fund in the framework of TAMOP 4.2.4. A/2-11-1-2012-0001 "National Excellence Program."

References

1. Buyya B, Yeo CS, Venugopal S, Broberg J, Brandic I (June 2009) Cloud computing and emerging it platforms: vision, hype, and reality for delivering computing as the 5th utility. Future Gener Comput Syst 25(6):599–616
2. Vaquero LM, Rodero-Merino L, Caceres J, Lindner M (2008) A break in the clouds: towards a cloud definition. SIGCOMM Comput Commun Rev 39(1):50–55
3. Pring B et al (June 2010) Forecast: public cloud services, worldwide and regions, industry sectors, 2009–2014. Gartner report. http://www.gartner.com/Display-Document?ref=clientFriendly-Url&id=1378513. Accessed 12 Jan 2013
4. Schubert L, Jeffery K, Neidecker-Lutz B (2010) The future of cloud computing—report from the first cloud computing expert working group meeting. Cordis (Online), BE: European Commission. http://cordis.europa.eu/fp7/ict/ssai/docs/Cloud-report-final.pdf. Accessed 15 Jan 2013
5. Schubert L Jeffery K (2012) Advances in clouds—research in future cloud computing, report from the cloud computing expert working group meeting. Cordis (Online), BE: European Commission, 2012. http://cordis.europa.eu/fp7/ict/ssai/docs/future-cc-2may-finalreport-experts.pdf. Accessed 12 Jan 2013
6. eBay Inc (2013) Online Shopping Solution, http://www.ebay.com/. Accessed 6 Sept 2013
7. Amazon (2013) Amazon Web Services, http://aws.amazon.com/. Accessed 5 Nov 2013
8. Google (2013) Google Apps for Business, http://www.google.com/apps/. Accessed 12 Jan 2013
9. Zimory GmbH (2013) Cloud infrastructure management. http://www.zimory.com/, Accessed 10 Sept 2013
10. Catteddu D, Hogben G (2009) Cloud computing risk assessment: benefits, risks and recommendations for information security, ENISA report. http://www.enisa.europa.eu/act/rm/files/deliverables/cloud-computing-risk-assessment/at_download/fullReport. Accessed 12 Jan 2013

11. Mell P Grance T (Sept 2011) The NIST definition of cloud computing, NIST special publication 800-145. http://csrc.nist.gov/publications/nistpubs/800-145/SP800-145.pdf. Accessed 12 Dec 2012

12. Liu F, Tong J, Mao J, Bohn RB, Messina JV, Badger ML, Leaf DM (Sept 2011) NIST cloud computing reference architecture, NIST special publication 500–292. Online: http://www.nist.gov/customcf/get_pdf.cfm?pub_id=909505. Accessed 12 Jan 2013

13. Ahronovitz M et al (2010) Cloud computing use cases, a white paper produced by the cloud computing use case discussion group, version 4.0, http://opencloudmanifesto.org/Cloud_Computing_Use_Cases_Whitepaper-4_0.pdf. Accessed 12 Jan 2013

14. DMTF (2009) Interoperable clouds, a white paper from the open cloud standards incubator 1.0, DMTF white paper no. DSP-IS0101. http://www.dmtf.org/sites/default/files/standards/documents/DSP-IS0101_1.0.0.pdf. Accessed 12 Dec 2012

15. OPTIMIS (2010) Cloud legal guidelines, OPTIMIS FP7 project deliverable no. D7.2.1.1. http://www.optimis-project.eu/sites/default/files/D7.2.1.1~OPTIMIS~Clo-ud~Legal~Guidelines.pdf. Accessed 12 Jan 2013

16. Ferrer AJ et al (2012) OPTIMIS: a holistic approach to cloud service provisioning. Future Gener Comput Syst 28:66–77

17. Rochwerger B et al (Apr 2009) The reservoir model and architecture for open federated cloud computing. IBM J Res Development

18. Carlini E, Coppola M, Dazzi P, Ricci L, Righetti G (2012) Cloud federations in contrail, Euro-Par 2011 Workshops, LNCS 7155, pp 159–168

19. Jofre J et al (2013) Federation of the BonFIRE multi-cloud infrastructure with networking facilities, Comput Netw, http://dx.doi.org/10.1016/j.bjp.2013.11.012. Accessed 13 Nov 2013

20. Petcu D et al (2013) Experiences in building a mOSAIC of clouds. J Cloud Comput Adv Syst Appl 2:12.

21. EGI (2013) Federated clouds task force, https://wiki.egi.eu/wiki/Fedcloud-tf:FederatedCloudsTaskForce. Accessed 20 Oct 2013

22. Grozev N Buyya R (2012) Inter-cloud architectures and application brokering: taxonomy and survey. Softw: Pract Exper. doi:10.1002/spe.2168

23. 4CaaSt EU FP7 project (2013) PaaS cloud Platform, http://4caast.morfeo-project.org, Accessed 2 Oct 2013

24. Buyya B, Ranjan R, Calheiros RN (2010) InterCloud: utility-oriented federation of cloud computing environments for scaling of application services, lecture notes in computer science: algorithms and architectures for parallel processing, vol. 6081, 20 pages

25. Celesti A, Tusa F, Villari M, Puliafito A (2010) How to enhance cloud architectures to enable cross-federation. Proceedings of the 3rd international conference on cloud computing (CLOUD 2010), IEEE: Miami, Florida, US, 2010, pp 337–345

26. Bernstein D, Ludvigson E, Sankar K, Diamond S, Morrow M (2009) Blueprint for the Intercloud—protocols and formats for cloud computing interoperability. In Proceedings of the fourth international conference on internet and web applications and services, pp 328–336

27. Marosi AC, Kecskemeti G, Kertesz A Kacsuk P (2011) FCM: an architecture for integrating IaaS cloud systems. In Proceedings of the second international conference on cloud computing, GRIDs, and virtualization (Cloud Computing 2011), IARIA, pp 7–12, Rome, Italy

28. Kertesz A, Kecskemeti G, Oriol M, Kotcauer P, Acs S, Rodriguez M, Merce O, Marosi ACs, Marco J, Franch X (2013) Enhancing federated cloud management with an integrated service monitoring approach. J Grid Comput 11(4):699–720

29. Oriol M, Franch X, Marco J, Ameller D (2008) Monitoring adaptable soa-systems using salmon. In Workshop on service monitoring, adaptation and beyond (Mona+), pp 19–28

30. Varadi Sz, Kertesz A, Parkin M (2012) The necessity of legally compliant data management in European cloud architectures. Computer Law and Security Review 28(5):577–586 (Elsevier)

31. European Commission (Nov 1995) Directive 95/46/EC of the European Parliament and of the Council of 24 October 1995 on the protection of individuals with regard to the processing of personal data and on the free movement of such data, Off J L 281:31–50

32. Planzner T, Kertesz A (Aug 2013) Towards data interoperability of cloud infrastructures using cloud storage services, 1st workshop on dependability and interoperability in heterogeneous clouds in conjunction with EuroPar'13, Aachen, Germany
33. Kecskemeti G, Kertesz A, Marosi ACs, Nemeth Zs (2013) Strategies for increased energy awareness in cloud federations, in book: high-performance computing on complex environments, Wiley series on parallel and distributed computing, Accepted in 2013.

Chapter 13
Security Aspects of Database-as-a-Service (DBaaS) in Cloud Computing

**Faria Mehak, Rahat Masood, Yumna Ghazi, Muhammad Awais Shibli
and Sharifullah Khan**

Abstract Database-as-a-Service (DBaaS) provides a wide range of benefits such as data outsourcing, multi-tenancy and resource sharing. It has garnered a lot of hype, but while it is promising, it is also a mine-field of concerns and issues. Security is one of the most critical challenges in this domain, which has only begun to earn the academic attention that it needs. There is a serious lack of research in this area that collectively covers the security of DBaaS, from its various problems to the possible solutions. To this end, this chapter provides a holistic survey on the security aspects of the Cloud DBaaS, including key features, advantages and different compatible architectures for managing data in the Cloud DBaaS. Furthermore, we identify challenges and classify the security limitations in DBaaS paradigm. Security requirements that are being fulfilled by state-of-the-art mechanisms along with their in-depth description are also presented. Additionally, we provide insight to the future security perspective. Our work acts as a comprehensive guidance for the developers and researchers to help them understand the inherent security issues and the existent countermeasures in the DBaaS domain.

Keywords Cloud databases · Database-as-a-Service · NoSQL · Big data · Database security · Confidentiality · Integrity · Availability · Privacy

R. Masood (✉) · F. Mehak · Y. Ghazi · M. A. Shibli · S. Khan
School of Electrical Engineering and Computer Science, National University of Sciences and Technology, Sector H-12, Islamabad 44000, Pakistan
e-mail: rahat.masood@seecs.edu.pk

F. Mehak
e-mail: 12mscsfmehak@seecs.edu.pk

Y. Ghazi
e-mail: 09bicseyghazi@seecs.edu.pk

M. A. Shibli
e-mail: awais.shibli@seecs.edu.pk

S. Khan
e-mail: sharifullah.khan@seecs.edu.pk

© Springer International Publishing Switzerland 2014
Z. Mahmood (ed.), *Cloud Computing,* Computer Communications and Networks,
DOI 10.1007/978-3-319-10530-7_13

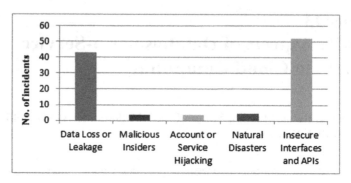

Fig. 13.1 Number of cloud security vulnerability incidents categorized by threats [33]

13.1 Introduction

One of the most attractive features of the cloud computing paradigm refers to its service-oriented architecture, wherein applications and resources are outsourced as services over the internet [68] as Software as a Service [27], Platform as a Service [22] and Infrastructure as a Service [97]. Likewise, *data outsourcing*, also called *Database-as-a-Service (DBaaS)*, is a new service model, which was proposed by Hacigumus et al. [51]. Based on Software-as-a-Service (SaaS), DBaaS moves database management system (DBMS) from a traditional client-server architecture, where the data owner is responsible for managing DBMS and responding to user's queries—to a third party architecture, where data management is not handled by the data owner. Data owners outsource their data to data service providers such as Google [84], Amazon [23], and Microsoft [76] etc., who have the facilities to manage large data sets [42]. DBaaS market is growing considerably and the trend of its adoption is not limited to large scale businesses such as IBM [57] and Microsoft [76], but also extends to small enterprises such as ZeusDB [108] and LongJump [65].

However, despite the various benefits offered by DBaaS over traditional data management systems, there are certain issues that hinder its wide adoption, of which security is one of the most critical concerns. According to International Data Corporation (IDC) Survey conducted in August 2008 [62], security of user data was identified as a major challenge in the IT industry. Moreover, the *Cloud Security Alliance (CSA)* [34] evaluated "Top Twelve" threats in the Cloud environment [33] which are shown in Fig. 13.1. It has been studied that from 2009 to 2011 the number of vulnerability incidents in Cloud has doubled most likely due to the phenomenal growth in the Cloud services [19]. Moreover, due to insecure interfaces/APIs, data loss and leakage have been reported to make up 29% and 25% of overall threats, respectively [33].

Data security, in particular, is rather crucial in the Cloud DBaaS paradigm because both the customer data and the code lie in the service provider's domain. One of the major factors behind data security issues is the lack of trust between service providers and consumers. Data outsourced to the third party is perceived as 'loss of control' by the data owner; therefore, consumers demand strong guarantees on the privacy and security of outsourced data [42]. Unauthorized access to data resources, misuse of data stored on third party platform, data confidentiality, integrity and availability are some of the major security challenges that ail this nascent Cloud service model.

Our research reveals that no extensive literature survey has been conducted so far which holistically covers security aspects of DBaaS. Moreover, there is a lack of research work which collectively enumerates the security requirements and the corresponding defense mechanisms devised till date for DBaaS. Therefore, we have conducted a holistic survey on DBaaS, in order to demystify the challenges and vulnerabilities—particularly those that are unique to the DBaaS environment—and categorized them, according to generic security requirements. We have studied different solutions addressing the security concerns and have clearly stated the security requirements satisfied by a particular technique. Furthermore, we have identified open issues and potential research directions in the area of DBaaS that need to be addressed by the Cloud community.

The rest of the chapter is organized as follows: Section 13.2 acts as a roadmap for the rest of the chapter and highlights the core features, main characteristics and advantages provided by DBaaS as well as the existing Cloud storage architectures suitable for the Cloud DBaaS environments. Section 13.3 discusses potential issues which are primary obstacles to the spacious adoption of DBaaS, with the major focus on the security challenges faced by DBaaS in Sect. 13.4. Section 13.5 reviews state-of-the-art in view of the identified security challenges. Section 13.6 throws light upon some future directions in order to make DBaaS more secure and help as a guideline to protect underlying data and finally Sect. 13.7 concludes the chapter.

13.2 Background of DBaaS

Since its genesis, the internet has undergone evolution at an unprecedented pace, and one of the significant byproducts of its advancement is the accumulation of exponential amounts of data referred to as *Big Data* [5, 89]. This growth in the volume of data shifted the trend from enterprise centric workloads to data centric workload [81], where organizations no longer have to manage their database locally and don't have to perform manual operations [81]. On-hand resources such as hardware and manual effort incur additional expense for organizations and thus, was the primary argument supporting the concept of third party data management applications. Thus, after 40 years of Relational DBMS rule in the industry, the concept of databases in the *Cloud* emerged [18, 40] in order to share and manage resources, software and information between devices over the internet [103].

Based on the data model, databases residing in the Cloud are divided into two major categories [24], i.e., *NoSQL* databases [78] such as Amazon [12], SimpleDB [13], Yahoo PNUT [37], CouchDB [16] and *SQL* databases such as Oracle [82] and MySQL [75]. SQL databases provide a way to store and communicate with relational databases. While in contrast, NoSQL (Not only SQL) databases have a flexible data model and are meant to provide elastic scaling for managing big data. Both types of Cloud databases, either SQL or NoSQL can be deployed in two ways. One method is to use a *Virtual Machine (VM)* instance, which users can purchase for a limited time period with a database installed in it [1, 56, 71]. Alternatively, the Cloud databases are outsourced to third parties, where data owners can manage data resources in a distributed environment [1]—more popularly known as *Database-as-a-Service (DBaaS)* [25, 85, 103].

DBaaS eliminates the need for installing, maintaining and storing data on the local database servers (hard drives or disks). Data is fully managed on the Cloud servers making the service independent of hardware [40]. Moreover, DBaaS supports structured, unstructured or semi-structured data, as opposed to conventional DBMS systems which deal only with structured data along with the metadata residing in the database [103]. It also takes advantage of the Cloud's elastic and scalable nature to cater to the problem of exponential data growth. It offers reduced cost and effort on the user's end via virtualization [90]. The subsequent section describes various major features and advantages of DBaaS.

13.2.1   Discerning Features and Advantages of DBaaS

DBaaS offers numerous features that make it a better alternative in the dynamic environment of Cloud. First of all, DBaaS provides DBMS as an *on-demand independent service* for managing data [40]. Consumers can access this *ubiquitous service* instantly via various devices such as desktop computers, laptops, mobiles, notebooks, tablets, etc. [103] with the sole requirement of internet connectivity. Consumers can perform desired operations on the *abstract resources* anytime, without any major configuration or deployment requirements [54, 100]. Thus, consumers do not need to be aware of the internal implementation and characteristics for framing up the environment [54]. *Resource pooling* is performed by the DBaaS providers to pool location-independent computing and data resources to a common repository [40, 103]. These shared resources and redundant infrastructures are managed across many data centers.

Another major feature of DBaaS is that service providers adapt to the workload changes, hence making the model *scalable*. They have the power to deal with load variations by allocating fewer resources to the tenants or by increasing them during peak hours without any service disruption [6]. The fact that DBaaS allows dynamic scaling up or down of resources as per consumer requirements makes the service *elastic*, as well [6, 58]. DBaaS follows the *"Pay Only for What You Use"* model of pricing [40], since data resources are tracked using meter [30], and consumers only pay for the exact amount of data resources/storage space they consume, acquire, and provision. The Cloud DBaaS applications are also *agile* in nature, they adapt seamlessly to any upgrades according to business or technology advancements. DBaaS allows rapid provisioning of database resources to provide new computing resources and storage facilities in minimum possible time [48, 55].

Table 13.1 Primary features of DBaaS

Sr. No	Features	Description
1	Self-Service	Instant and automatic service provisioning without major deployment or configuration Users can perform different tasks without cost and performance overhead
2	Broad Ubiquitous Network Access	Service accessible using different devices (Desktop Computers, Mobile, Tablet)
3	Abstract Resources	Device and location-independent abstract database resources Focus on user's needs instead of hardware utilization
4	Resource Pooling	Location-independent, remotely-hosted database resources pooled at distributed servers
5	Elasticity and Scalability	Automated and dynamic scaling Databases adapt to workload changes without service disruption
6	Pay As You Go Model	Tracking of data resources using meter Payment management according to data resources used
7	Agility	Adaptive to business changes Rapid provisioning of database resources

All the highlighted features in Table 13.1 make the DBaaS model, arguably, a far better alternative for managing databases than traditional DBMSs [104]. DBaaS also provides some additional advantages to its consumers and service providers, such as fast, transparent, and *automated failure recovery* to make applications resilient against failures [18]. DBaaS ensures *maximum availability* of data resources [79]. Many strategies are used to prevent data loss. For example, Elastic Book Store (EBS) [14] used by EC2 or Windows Azure Drives, Blob and Table Storage [36] used by Windows Azure [72], are real-life examples of storage in the Cloud, which follow redundant disk strategy. There is no *single point of failure* in this architecture because it is based on self-detective and self-aware mechanism to handle changes and to recognize extreme events before it is too late [44].

DBaaS also provides *GUI-based configuration* for managing backups, restoring databases, and automated scheduling in DBaaS [20, 55]. Operational burden of provisioning, performance tuning, configuration, privacy, backup, scaling, and access control to DBaaS services is alleviated, which means that organizations do not require a dedicated team of professionals to deal with the databases [93, 100]. Therefore, minimal service provider interaction is required, lowering the overall cost effectively [9, 106]. DBaaS is economically feasible for consumers as well because it liberates consumers from local hardware. A glimpse of numerous advantages of DBaaS is represented in Table 13.2 for quick overview and understanding.

13.2.2 Cloud Storage Architectures

DBaaS is based on the architectural and operational approach [80]. In this subsection, we discuss some of the well-known architectures for Cloud based storage environment that can be adopted by DBaaS vendors according to their requirements:

Table 13.2 Major advantages of DBaaS

Sr. No	Advantages	Description
1	Effective failure recovery	Fast, transparent, and automated recovery
		Data replication at multiple locations
		Regular backups
2	Non-stop availability	24/7/365
		No single point of failure
		Self-detective and self-aware mechanism
3	Simplified query interface and faster management approval	GUI-based configuration
		Management of data backups, data restores, and automated scheduling using user-friendly interfaces
		No shipping and framing up environment required
4	Economical choice	No hardware (storage devices) utilization by consumers
		Lesser number of professionals required to handle the databases
		No requirement of hardware or experts lowers the overall cost of maintaining databases

Fig. 13.2 Layered Architecture of the Cloud based DBMS [47]

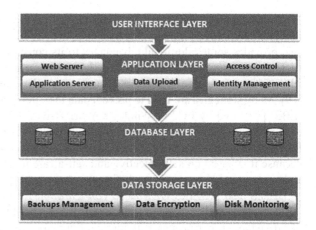

13.2.2.1   Layered Architecture for the Outsourced Cloud DBMS

The growing interest in outsourcing database management tasks to third parties provides the benefit of a significantly reduced operational cost, as discussed in Sect. 13.1. To manage such outsourced databases, there was a need for a newly designed DBMS, architected specifically for the Cloud computing platforms. Therefore, a layered architecture was proposed by Gelogo et al. [47] in 2012, specially designed for the Cloud based outsourced DBMS. There are three basic layers in the overall architecture as shown in Fig. 13.2, i.e., *Application Layer, Database Layer, and Storage Layer* [47] with an additional *User Interface Layer* to access the service via internet. The *Application layer* is used to access software services and storage space on the Cloud. The *Database layer* provides efficient and reliable service of managing database by reusing query statements residing in the storage, thus

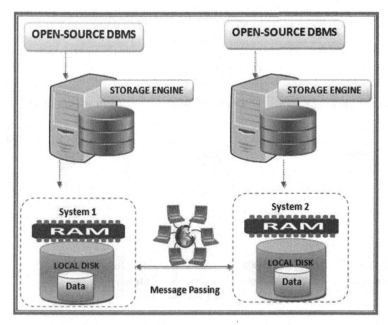

Fig. 13.3 Shared Nothing architecture [61]

saving time for querying and loading data. Data is encrypted when stored or backed up at *Data storage layer*, without any need for programming to encrypt and decrypt. Backup management and disk monitoring is also provided at this layer. The layered architecture helps to add more functionality at each layer; maintenance becomes easier and security threats are not compacted at one place, but are distributed at each layer. Therefore, addressing potential threats is easier using layered approach.

13.2.2.2   Shared-Disk vs Shared-Nothing Cloud Database Architecture

Shared-Nothing and *Shared-Disk* architectures [61] are also frequently employed for Cloud databases. *Shared-Nothing* architecture is based on the construct that every system contains its own private memory in one or more than one local disks. Database partitioning is performed wherein each database server processes and maintains its own data. The clustered processors running at each server communicate via messages over the network [18]. All the requests are automatically routed to the system and only one cluster at a time can own and consume resources. Thus, data consistency issue is avoided. As nothing is shared between the processors, interdependency of processors is prevented. There is fixed load balancing rather than dynamic load balancing, which means that each server has to handle peak load for its data. Scalability of processors is the core advantage provided by this architecture. Figure 13.3 shows the architecture of Shared-Nothing approach.

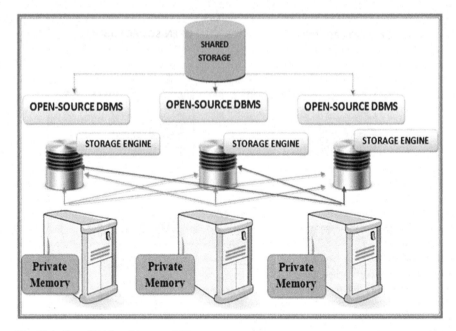

Fig. 13.4 Shared Disk architecture [61]

Shared-Disk architecture, as depicted by Fig. 13.4, not only uses its own private memory, but also allows connecting to other systems/disk memories [18]. Different database processes have access to all the system resources including data; therefore, any server (process) can become active at request and provide required database service. This provides fluidity to smoothly accommodate temporal and evolutionary changes. Overall performance is better with high availability and data does not need to be partitioned. But there may be interferences of one processor to another due to the shared disk [55].

13.3 Challenges Faced by DBaaS

Aside from the potential benefits DBaaS has to offer, there are tradeoffs attached with the paradigm, similar to every other Cloud service model. DBaaS model supports multi-tenancy [26, 92] which leads to interesting challenges at the administrator's end, such as *assigning logical resources to physical resources, configuring physical systems* (parameters, database design) and *load balancing* across physical resources [7, 20, 21, 68, 79, 98]. It demands that each tenant's network should be isolated from others and the tenants often need to have their own private address space. Therefore, multi-tenancy is difficult to manage in the dynamic environment of the Cloud where the number of tenants frequently varies.

The location of the data stored in Cloud is not known to organizations or data owners, which significantly *minimizes their control* over their data [87]. Consumers do not know the details pertaining to where actual physical machines, networking and storage devices are residing. In case of security breaches, it becomes difficult for them to identify the resource which has been compromised. In addition, consumers do not have fine-grained control over remote execution environment and the Cloud services; therefore, consumers cannot inspect the execution traces in order to detect occurrence of illegal operation [20, 21]. *Unavailability of database services* can also be faced from time to time affecting performance and any other linked service. Amazon has clearly mentioned in its licensing agreement that service unavailability may occur sometimes [11]. Furthermore, scalability promised by DBaaS is also difficult to manage by the service providers [35], particularly when scaling out causes *escalation in storage nodes* [92].

DBaaS consumers want to freely shift from one provider to another, in order to reuse their critical and redundant data across portable applications, such that components written for one DBaaS provider should run at the infrastructure of another DBaaS provider. In this respect, *vendor lock-in* is also a challenge in the DBaaS environment [18]. Another issue of concern is the *lack of interoperability* between DBaaS vendors [63]. DBaaS providers should be able to communicate with each other through API's and there must be a common front-end that would appear as a single homogenous entity with semantic calls [38]. Thus, there is a need to translate and transform standards with the objective to have native database driven interoperability standards [62].

The number of potential users simultaneously querying the database residing in Cloud is a variable in query workload; therefore, estimating the time required for *query workloads* is a challenge. This unpredictable behavior creates management problems and workload analysis at a particular time becomes difficult [7]. One of the barriers to the Cloud DBaaS performance is the *speed* with which data can be transferred between the database service providers and the consumers. However, internet transfer speed is not as high, compared with the speed required for transferring data, introducing performance overhead [7]. High speed internet connection and cables (modems) are used to achieve the desired speed, which in turn incur very high cost, diminishing the economic advantage of DBaaS.

Furthermore, the data in DBaaS can be confidential and any type of *Data loss* and *leakages* can cause financial and customer loss to the organization. Major causes for data loss in the Cloud are insufficient authorization, authentication, and accounting mechanisms, inconsistent use of encryption keys and techniques, alteration, or deletion of records without maintaining backup and operational failures [20]. There are many other technical and business risks, apart from the highlighted challenges which prevent customers from committing to the Cloud DBaaS. Table 13.3 shows the key challenges associated with DBaaS model that need to be addressed, along with their consequences and causes.

Table 13.3 Challenges faced by DBaaS

No.	Challenge	Consequences and causes
1	Resource allocation for multiple tenants: multi-tenancy	Problem faced in assigning logical resources to physical resources for multiple users accessing common data repository Configuration of physical systems becomes difficult Load balancing across physical resources becomes composite process
2	Loss of control	Lose control over location-independent data No fine-grained control for remote execution Difficult to determine source in case of failure
3	Service unavailability	Unavailability of services can affect performance Fault tolerant services are required
4	Escalation of data resources	Automatic scaling of data cause confidentiality issues
5	Vendor lock-in	Data shifting among vendors is not considered Data reusability across portable applications is not guaranteed
6	Lack of interoperability	Communication between multiple heterogeneous databases is required Need of mature standard notions of translation and transformations
7	Query and transactional workloads	Lack of management because number of users querying database is not known Time estimation is not possible in query workload
8	Internet speed	Data transfer requires high internet speed which will incur high cost Performance overhead
9	Data loss during migration	Alteration or deletion of records without a backup Insufficient authorization, authentication, and accounting control mechanisms Inconsistent use of encryption technique

13.4 Security Challenges Faced by DBaaS

The crux of the DBaaS security is to secure the data in transit, at rest, and in use. The security issues mainly include, risk from malicious outsiders and insiders, secure data management, confidentiality, integrity, and availability of personal and business critical information. Data owners delegate control of data over to the DBaaS providers, which may lead to compromised integrity, confidentiality, and availability of data [7, 43]. Moreover, if the DBaaS providers fail to deliver the relevant requirements/ evidence of their compliance such as Data Security Standard (DSS) or Payment Card Industry (PCI), then the resilience and continuity of business might be compromised. Thus, a road-map towards certification on key industry standards [86] is necessary to follow. Some data integrity and privacy issues arise due to the absence of authentication, authorization, and accounting controls, poor key management for encryption and decryption [20]. In this respect, the focus of this section is to look into different security concerns, categorized according to the *CIA principles*, i.e., *Confidentiality, Integrity, and Availability* [96], as well as some major privacy concerns.

13.4.1 Confidentiality

Confidentiality, in the context of data outsourcing, refers to secure execution of queries generated by trusted clients. It signifies that only authorized users should get access to the data. In DBaaS, data residing in an unencrypted form may be vulnerable to bugs, errors, and attacks from external entities, confronting data confidentiality issues. Frequent concerns related to confidentiality of data are described below:

Insider Threats Super users usually have the privilege to access all resources, due to maintenance purposes. However, if this privilege is misused, it poses a considerable threat to data in DBaaS [69]. Administrating the administrators is again an endless cycle. This key challenge might be addressed by enforcing strict supply chain management and by conducting a comprehensive supplier assessment. It will enable the Cloud DBaaS providers to hire people (contractors or vendors) who get through pre-defined characteristics, requirements testing or interviewing. In order to avoid espionage and intentional mal-behavior, resources can be tied to legal actions by specifying human resource requirements as part of the legal contracts [31].

Outside Malicious Attacks One of the problems in trusting DBaaS providers with confidential data is the potential of outside malicious attacks [20]. Malicious attacks such as fraud, phishing, scamming, and exploitation of the software vulnerabilities are also possible in the Cloud DBaaS. Malicious users can also execute spoofing, sniffing, man-in-the-middle attacks, side channeling [39] and illegal transactions to launch a *Denial of Service (DoS)* attack [20]. Data intrusion is another problem faced by DBaaS, where an intruder can get access to all of the instances and resources by illegally accessing login credentials. This way, any hacker can erase the information residing inside the data repositories and use it unethically for disabling/harm the services [9].

Access Control Issues In traditional data storage environment, organizations perform manual checks on locally-placed data, as well as on the super users by means of, e.g., security personnel or cameras [67]. However, organizations are not able to carry out the same level of monitoring and access control once the data is transferred to the Cloud DBaaS. This is because data is now outsourced to third parties and is not under possession of the owner. Big data, that is difficult to manage, is usually segregated into restrictive categories in order to ensure secure access to the data resources [35, 42, 54]. Moreover, access control policies are usually defined by the DBaaS providers and not by data owners; therefore, they cannot customize access policies if required.

Illegal Recovery of Data from Storage Devices DBaaS providers perform *data sanitization* to delete or remove data from their storage devices [88]. However, there are several techniques that can recover data that has not been properly discarded from the hard drives, which might introduce physical and logical security risks. Moreover, regular backups are maintained on multiple physical storage devices in order to physically colocate data from multiple customers and mitigate data losses [9]. Threats on this replicated data, stored on multiple locations are also possible.

Hence, data sanitization needs to be performed with a certain amount of caution. Physical security risks can be prevented by carefully destructing or overwriting critical data, such that information is not disclosed via unauthorized sources [88]. Requirements-specific regulations about performing sanitization should be formed in accordance with DBaaS.

Network Breaches In DBaaS model, all the data sent by users or enterprises is transferred through or by means of network. Communicating data over the network makes it prone to certain threats such as data modification and eavesdropping. Any weakness at the network level will give an opportunity to malicious users such that they can exploit data. Network packet sniffing is one of the exploitation techniques adopted by the malicious users for analyzing communications and gain information to crash or corrupt the network [15]. Eavesdropping, IP address spoofing, man in the middle attack, denial of service attack, SQL injection, cross side scripting, etc., are some other substantial network attacks. Therefore, it is necessary to secure the network in order to avoid the leakage of sensitive information in transit.

Data Provenance Data provenance refers to the tracing and recording process in order to find out the origin of data and its movement between databases [29]. DBaaS requires history of its digital data, such as details about its creator because this information is sometimes used to determine the data accuracy. Fast algorithms are needed to handle this metadata provenance which can be cumbersome [35]. Moreover, analysis of large graphs generated from provenance metadata is computationally expensive [32] and their security assessments are also time-sensitive in nature.

Supply Chain Failure DBaaS providers sometimes outsource certain specialized database tasks or all of their supply chain management functions to third parties. Therefore, their level of security in such situations may depend upon the security of these third party links. Lack of transparency in the contract can be the root cause of problems [99].

13.4.2 Integrity

Ensuring data integrity refers to protecting data from unauthorized modification, deletion, or fabrication. Therefore, accuracy and consistency of data should be guaranteed so that it remains intact and untouched from malicious activities at every location. Integrity of data can be breached when unauthorized parties, e.g., insiders such as disgruntled employees or outsiders such as hackers, intentionally modify data. Data tampering can happen at any level of storage in the Cloud DBaaS. If there is a security breach that affects the data of a consumer, the consequence could be damaging, not only for the consumer, but also for the service provider.

Moreover, the Cloud databases provide numerous configuration files assigned to consumers. These files represent specifications and access privileges. Modification of such files will result in improper functioning of the entire Cloud DBaaS. Fraud is the oldest form of attack on data integrity [46]. Phishing, trojan horses, denial of service attacks, or other unauthorized means can also impact data integrity through data modification. Attacks on the network also compromise data integrity by exposing the content to non-legitimate individuals [54, 64, 74, 110].

13.4.3 Availability

Availability is the extent to which a system's resources—mainly data resources in case of DBaaS—are accessible to its users [41]. It is considered to be a major security requirement which needs utmost attention from the Cloud DBaaS providers. Availability can be affected temporarily as well as permanently or it may be lost completely or partially, as a result of service failures [98, 107, 110]. Major threats to availability are DOS attacks, natural disasters, and equipment failures at the service provider's end [88]. Unavailability of a database for a long period would inevitably cause consumer applications to suffer. Long bouts of unavailability have been known to occur; for example, in February 2008, a major outage of 3 h was faced by Amazon S3 and that service breakdown in turn affected its consumers, mainly Twitter [105], and some other companies relying on their services [73]. Some of the relevant factors are listed below:

Resource Exhaustion It is simply a denial of service condition which usually prevents successful completion of DBaaS related activity because the required resources are completely consumed [83]. Due to resource exhaustion, imprecise interpretation of the customer service requests may lead to service unavailability, economic/reputation losses, and unauthorized access. As data resources are allocated according to statistical projections to each customer, a calculated risk is required in order to assign the resources to each of the consumer [99].

Consistency Management It is practically impossible for distributed computer systems to simultaneously provide *consistency, availability, and partition tolerance*, as per the *CAP Theorem*. DBaaS providers balance these properties by relaxing consistency and alleviating distributed replication issue. However, DBaaS consumers demand that they see a consistent view of the data, including visible changes made by every user who has access to this data [49]. A widely used strategy 'data replication' is used to achieve performance, availability and scalability goals. Synchronization of replicated data poses certain challenges because synchronizing big data results in a longer response time [85]. Moreover, DBaaS vendors need to maintain timely backups of all sensitive and confidential data in order to facilitate quick recovery in case of disasters [2]. Therefore, synchronizing the data backups is also equally problematic.

Internet Downtime Network issues affect the availability of DBaaS, since the service is dependent upon internet; therefore, data latency, and even application failure can be faced [54]. Network misconfiguration, lack of resource isolations, poor or untested business continuity, disaster recovery plan, system vulnerabilities, and network traffic modification are some other reasons for network failures engendering unavailability [102].

Data Lock-In APIs used by DBaaS are proprietary and are not subjected to active standardization; as a result, the issues of data lock-in arise. If customers want to shift the data from one DBaaS provider to another, they are responsible to extract the data they want to shift. Therefore, lack of data extraction is a restriction for organizations who are adopting any other Cloud database service provider. For example, "*Linkup*", an online storage service, shut down on August 8, 2008, causing loss of data access of 45 % of its customers [17]. "*Linkup*" had trusted "*Nirvanix*" [92] for storing customer data and was told to switch to another site for storage services. This switching raised an issue between two organizations as there was no standardization between the storage devices [17]. One possible way to solve this problem is a standardized API which DBaaS developers can use to deploy data services across multiple database vendors. Using this mechanism, failure of services provided by one vendor would not cause the failure of complete repository of customer data.

Natural Disasters Natural disasters such as lightning, earthquakes, storms are also regarded as risks. They affect the performance, security, and reputation of the DBaaS service. Such disasters can cause serious consequences if the database application is inadequately tested or if there is no disaster recovery plan. They also pose great threat to the availability of DBaaS and thus, demand precautions to avoid failures in extreme circumstances [99].

Lack of Auditing and Monitoring Mechanism Not all DBaaS providers offer their consumers the feature of auditing and monitoring, which is important to establish trust between the consumer and the provider [98]. Monitoring ensures high availability and helps avoid failures, backup maintenance, and configuring auto fail-over mechanisms. In the dynamic environment of the Cloud DBaaS, security risks related to auditing and monitoring of databases arise when conventional protecting and monitoring methods demand clear knowledge on network infrastructure and physical devices such as hardware-assisted SSL. Traditional approaches fail in such situations due to continuously changing configuration requirements.

Granular audit information is required when an attack takes place. It is also sometimes required to find the reason behind a missed attack with real-time security monitoring. For example, financial firms are obligated to provide granular auditing records [32, 91]. Auditing also ensures compliance, apart from providing forensic proof. Therefore, DBaaS providers must offer an auditing technique/tool that should be able to render full visibility into database activities, irrespective of the location.

13.4.4 Privacy Challenges

Privacy is the need of a person to control the disclosure of his personal information to another person or organization [103]. DBaaS has a number of privacy-related issues, which increase the risk of data breaches. Some of the crucial privacy challenges are discussed below:

Data Locality Raising Obligation Issues In DBaaS, consumers do not know where the data is actually stored [54, 87]. This can be the root cause of many problems. Compliance and data security/privacy laws are being followed in various countries giving data locality a high regulatory importance. For instance, there is a rule in many South American and European countries to prohibit certain types of sensitive data from being moved outside the country. Data locality issue also arises when no one takes responsibility of the misusage and disruption of data. It raises questions of whose jurisdiction the data falls under.

Varying Jurisdiction Some countries face high risks when they do not strictly follow legal frameworks and international agreements. Outsourced data in the Cloud DBaaS are stored at various location and thus, high risk and restrictions are faced when customer data is subjected to multiple jurisdictions. In such cases, customer data can be accessible by various parties irrespective of legal privacy policies and without customer's consent. Furthermore, certain countries have strict privacy policies/laws which demand customer's data to not be stored anywhere without their approval, where it can be tracked [99].

Table 13.4 highlights the security challenges along with their consequences and causes, which make DBaaS infrastructure vulnerable to threats.

13.5 Mechanisms to Overcome Security Challenges in DBaaS

So far, we have enlisted the major concerns and issues in DBaaS with emphasis on security challenges. It has been observed that despite quality research on secure data outsourcing and data services, security measures for protecting data have not evolved much. De-facto approaches on database encryption, authentication, digital signatures [70], contractual agreements, etc., have not gained much success in operations. Due to this, intelligence agencies, commercial entities and other private/public organizations are reluctant to adopt DBaaS. Thus, aside from the need for new security mechanisms, the existing counter measures also need to be modified and enhanced to cater to the requirements of DBaaS. This section focuses on comprehensive analysis of different approaches aiming to secure DBaaS. The literature we reviewed is discussed below according to the assorted categories of CIA principles.

13.5.1 Confidentiality and Privacy

Quite often, in research as well as industry, confidentiality and privacy are catered to in a single solution or system; therefore, we have dedicated this section to these significant security challenges. Recent solutions on the security of outsourced data mostly focus on confidentiality with respect to publishers only. Of those solutions, majority are based on traditional cryptographic techniques [95]. NetDB2 [50] was proposed to address the issue of data privacy by using encryption technique. User connects to NetDB2 service via Internet and performs queries through the API provided. The service is portable and users can benefit from any location with the help

Table 13.4 Security challenges faced by DBaaS

Category	Security challenge	Consequences and causes
Confidentiality	Insider threats	Employees can tap into sensitive and confidential data Strict supply chain management and assessment is required
	Outside malicious attackers	Malicious attacks by hackers Absence of authentication, authorization and accounting controls can result in such attacks
	Access control issues	Data owners cannot define or alter policies as per requirement Increased development and analysis cost is incurred when user management and granular access control is implemented
	Illegal recovery of data from storage devices	Perform degaussing, destruction and overwriting of data to avoid data leakages Recovery of data by malicious sources if not properly discarded
	Network breaches	Data flowing over the network (internet) is prone to hazardous circumstances and network performance issues. Possible network failure reasons are: misconfiguration, lack of resource isolations, poor or untested business continuity, disaster recovery plan, network traffic modification
	Data provenance	Complexity and time sensitiveness in provenance metadata Intensive computations involved in getting required history Fast algorithms, auto logs are needed
	Supply chain failure	Security is dependent on third parties when data is outsourced to them
Integrity	Integrity check	Modification of configuration, access and data files is a threat to data integrity Require accuracy and integrity of data
Availability	Resource exhaustion	Imprecise modeling of customer's requirements cause resource exhaustion
	Consistency management	Replications between multiple servers cause management as well as consistency issues
	Internet downtime	Network issues (internet) affect performance
	Data lock-in	Customers are unable to shift data from one site to another Failure of services provided by one vendor would result in complete loss of data Need of standard API to run under every provider's platform
	Natural disasters	Lack of disaster recovery plan Inadequately tested application can be a threat to availability of service.
	Lack of auditing and monitoring	Auditing is necessary for avoiding failures, backup maintenance, configuration of auto fail-over mechanisms for ensuring security of data Configuration requirements change continuously Require network and physical device, expertise and relevant resources

Table 13.4 (continued)

Category	Security challenge	Consequences and causes
Privacy	Data locality raising obligation issues	Compliance and data-security privacy laws prohibit movement of sensitive data among countries Issues faced when no one takes responsibility of data in location independent data storage
	Varying jurisdictions	Risks and restrictions faced when customer's data is subjected to multiple country's legal jurisdictions Data in this situation is accessible by multiple parties

of a web browser. Data privacy is ensured using Transport Layer Security (TSL) and Secure Socket Layer (SSL). Ge et al. [45] used homomorphic encryption in order to secure aggregate outsourcing of data. The proposed scheme operates on larger block size than single numeric data values. The basic underlying idea is to densely pack data values in an encryption block, and perform computation directly on the cipher-text using a secure homomorphic encryption scheme. Security is ensured as the database server performs the bulk of the computation without having access to the secret key or the sensitive data.

Similarly, Sion [94] proposed an approach which introduced the concept of query execution assurance in outsourced databases, such that database server guarantees that query requested by client is successfully executed on the database. Before the data is outsourced, an identity-hash is computed for each data segment. This identity-hash provides authentication for queries. For requested query, the data owner then picks a secret number and a one-time nonce to compute query token (to avoid replay attacks). The token is used by the service provider to prove actual query execution when the data owner submits a batch of queries. Verification of correct query is performed by the data owner when the service provider returns both the query execution proof and query results. Likewise, Hadavi et al. [53] proposed a scheme for preserving data confidentiality and correctness verifiability of query results for ensuring security in DBaaS. The distribution algorithm and redundant shares in the proposed *Secret Sharing Algorithm* are the basis for this approach. This algorithm works by splitting each attribute value between several different servers, located at distributed locations. The distribution of attribute values is based on customized threshold secret sharing mechanism. There are two main servers involved in the overall mechanism. *Data Server*: It has the same schema as the original relation in addition to a "TupleID" assigned to each data row with an incremental value to uniquely identify the row (tuple). Indexes of encrypted searchable attributes are maintained at *Index Server* which uses B+ trees for preserving the order of encrypted values of searchable attributes. Confidentiality is achieved by using secret sharing algorithm. Moreover, attribute values in the index tree and *TupleIDs* in the buckets are all in encrypted form.

Alzain et al. [8] proposed a new methodology called "*NetDB2-multi shares model*" which is appropriate for NetDB2 architecture. The model is based on secret sharing algorithm and multi-service providers. There are three main layers in the architecture, i.e., *Presentation Layer* for HTTP server and end user's browser,

Management Layer which consists of DBMS and database service provider and, lastly, the *Application Layer* where the actual application resides and runs. Private high speed network serves the purpose of secure communication between different components. Overall working involves the distribution of data divided into "n" shares, each stored on a different database server. Query is sent to all database servers to retrieve results without revealing any type of sensitive information (secret value) to the database service provider. *Cryptonite* is a solution proposed by Kumbhare et al. [60] for secure data storage. It also claims to address availability requirements. Cryptonite runs within Microsoft Azure and provides service APIs compatible with the existing Cloud storage services. Moreover, it provides pipelined and data parallel optimizations to reduce security overhead caused by encryption and key management. Basic tenets include file owner and repository where "File Owner" performs encryption and signs the data at the client side before storing in the Cloud. Client uploads plaintext data file on behalf of the owner, and the data file is encrypted. A random cryptographic public/private key pair is generated afterwards to sign the encrypted file. *Repository* offers scalability and user-friendly model for managing keys in an efficient and secure manner. This process ensures secure data file at client side and using the owner information stored in metadata; coarse grained access control is enforced. The technique claims to provide easy migration to the Cloud data storage clients by incorporating well-established cryptographic techniques and security standards.

It was later researched and investigated that performing data encryption itself is computationally expensive [3] and increases the response time of a query. Keeping this in mind, D. Agrawal et al. [4] proposed a scalable and privacy preserving algorithm for data outsourcing other than using encryption. In this simple but impractical solution, database service providers are primarily used to store data on servers. Data distribution is supported on multiple data provider sites where data divided into "n" shares is stored on different service providers. When a query is generated, relevant shares are retrieved from service providers and query result answer is reconstructed at a data source. *Data store* is considered as a client that wants to access the data. Service providers are not able to infer anything about the data content and *data store (client)* is still able to query the database by incurring reasonable computation and communication cost, quite similar to the overhead involved in the encryption approach. In the extended and improved information retrieval method based on this approach, only required tuples are retrieved from the service providers instead of whole superset.

Querying the encrypted data is also a challenge and various mechanisms have been proposed till now [79] in order to deal with this issue. It is believed that these mechanisms are able to secure DBaaS solutions. Therefore, in the successful adoption of homomorphic encryption, performing algebraic query processing is a challenge. In this regard, full homomorphic encryption proposed by Murali et al. [66] is a breakthrough, which supports operating on and querying encrypted data. Fully homomorphic encryption involves *Evaluate Algorithm* besides key generation, encryption and decryption techniques. This algorithm is capable of evaluating complete query along with the query literals sent by client, and as a result, produces correct and compact cipher texts which are returned to the client. There are two sub-parts involved in its working: a *Data Model*, which represents original tables, relational tables and intermediate results during query processing; and a *Computational Model*, which database service provider will use to perform query processing.

There are some other secure mechanisms which are based on *Third Party Auditors*. Auditors access the database on behalf of clients and perform auditing on the data. Ferretti et al [44] advised against using any intermediary component for accessing the database on behalf of the clients, since it becomes a single point of failure. Moreover, security of DBaaS is restricted by this trusted intermediary proxy server. In their proposed idea is to move the metadata to the Cloud database, while the encryption engine is executed by each client. Client machines execute a *client software component* that allows a user to connect and issue queries directly to the Cloud DBaaS. This component retrieves the necessary metadata from the untrusted database through SQL statements and makes them available to the encryption engine. Multiple clients can access the untrusted Cloud database independently, with the guarantee of the same level of availability, scalability and elasticity of the Cloud-based services. The solution depends on metadata as well; therefore, securing metadata is as critical as securing customer data.

13.5.2 Integrity

Protection of data integrity in a dynamic environment of the Cloud is a formidable task because users no longer have physical possession of the outsourced data. Data integrity demands consistency, accuracy, and validity of data. In this respect, Nithiavathy [77] proposed integrity auditing mechanism that utilizes distributed erasure-coded data (for employing redundancy) and homomorphic token. This technique allows third party auditors (TPA) and users to audit the logs and events at the Cloud storage using light weight communication protocol at low computation cost. The auditing result ensures storage correctness and it also helps to achieve fast data error localization. The scheme also supports efficient dynamic operations on secure outsourced data. TPAs do not know the secret key, so there is no way for them to breach the data. Wang et al. [101] proposed a similar approach which puts forth an idea of using TPAs and is suitable for preserving data integrity when data is outsourced to the DBaaS providers. This approach is different since it supports batch auditing by performing multiple auditing tasks simultaneously. Moreover, it utilizes the technique of public key-based homomorphic linear authenticator, which enables TPA to perform the auditing without demanding the local copy of data and thus, drastically reduces the communication and computation overhead as compared to the straightforward data auditing approaches. TPAs do not have any knowledge of data content and they perform audits for multiple users concurrently. Generally, a public auditing scheme consists of four algorithms. *KeyGen* is a key generation algorithm and is run by the user to setup the scheme. *SigGen* is used by the user to generate verification metadata and may consist of digital signatures. *GenProof* is run by the Cloud server to generate a proof of data storage correctness, while *VerifyProof* is run by the TPA to audit the proof.

Q Zheng et al. [109] also investigated the issue of query integrity and a solution was proposed which allows TPA/querier/data owner to verify executed queries in the Cloud database server. The proposed solution also provides additional support of flexible join and aggregate queries. The basic building block in this method is *Authenticated Outsourced Ordered*, which is based on different algorithms. *KeyGen* is the algorithm which takes the primary security parameter as input and outputs a pair of private and public keys. *SetUp* algorithm is executed by a data owner before outsourcing the database to the server. By taking as input the private key and the database, this algorithm outputs some cryptographic auxiliary information and state information. Both database and auxiliary information will be outsourced to the server and state information will be made public (so as to allow third parties to verify the query answers). *QueryVrfy* is the query protocol between a querier which issues a query, and the server which answers the query with the result and a proof. The querier verifies the result afterwards. Brzeźniak et al. [28] proposed a mechanism 'National Data Storage' which covers data key management, data encryption and data integrity and ensure high data security and access efficiency. They used on-the-fly client side encryption and cryptographic file systems for protecting the data in a transparent way. When a file is written into the directory, its symmetric key is encrypted using the directory's public key and stored in the system. Private Key of the file opened by the user is used to decode the private key of the directory. After that, the private key of the directory is used to decode the symmetric key of the file, which is in turn used to decode the file. AES-256 is used for encrypting the data files and SHA-512 algorithm is used for data integrity control. Symmetric and asymmetric cryptography is combined for managing complex key hierarchy.

Authors in [10] devised an approach for DBaaS in which they proposed searchable encryption scheme for ensuring authenticity (cipher text integrity) and privacy of data. Integrity is achieved without any additional communication and computational cost through the use of standard cryptographic primitives, such as block ciphers, symmetric encryption schemes, and message authentication codes. They also formulated an additional property of cipher text-integrity, and thus, the encryption algorithm should contain some redundancy at the end so that the ciphertext is verifiable. For catering the issue of consistency management, an approach was proposed in [52] based on the structure of tree. It basically helps to reduce interdependency between replica servers by ensuring maximum reliable path which is ensured from primary sever to all replica servers. Throughput and performance is increased as a result of reduced probability of transaction failure.

13.5.3   Availability

Availability in DBaaS is generally referred to as "Completeness" [42]. Completeness ensures that the user is provided with all the requested data if he has access privileges. Arjun Kumar et al. [59] proposed an approach which handles big data in the Cloud. The approach plays a vital role in dealing with availability of DBaaS because it supports three backup servers located at remote locations. In case of path failure, alternate paths are available for processing/querying data; therefore, data can be recovered in time. Data is stored in encrypted and compressed form in multi-server. This encryption is performed during backup operation by using secret key, before it is taken to multi-server and decrypted during recovery operation. Users send their data to the main servers after which backup of data is maintained at multiple servers. The main server is also contacted by users to retrieve the data. Lei Xu et al. [106] studied the overhead involved in encrypting, retrieving, decrypting and then performing operations on whole database. As a solution to overcome this overhead, authors proposed an approach called "Hub" which divides data into buckets in the form of tuples according to some attribute (column) values of the database. Original attribute values remain hidden by corresponding bucket indexes. For each attribute, a hard data copy will be stored, which is physically "bucketized" following the range of this attribute value. For query execution, each copy still carried bucket index of other attributes. Therefore, when query is executed, only required buckets are retrieved instead of whole database. This approach introduces privacy, backup efficiency and access performance as well. For replicas of data, a fine-grained private inter-backup between the heterogeneous copies is also designed using privacy preserving inter-backup protocol.

Table 13.5 summarizes possible defense mechanisms against some important security issues in DBaaS. Every technique primarily focuses on any one of the CIA aspect.

13.5.4 Future Directions

DBaaS is steadily gaining attraction in the market but despite the increasingly mature solutions, there are many critical challenges which require thorough research. It is necessary to devise strong security and privacy control mechanisms, in order to gain wide-scale acceptance of DBaaS in the Cloud paradigm. Various techniques have been proposed for securing relational data model so far. However, these techniques need improvement in order to make them more efficient and effective.

Majority of the existing techniques focus on security with respect to the service providers only. Therefore, approaches are required which focus on consumers too. Moreover, a majority of the available solutions are based on the traditional cryptographic techniques, where the general idea is that the owners can outsource the encrypted data. Publishers do not manage and encrypt the data and do not receive keys to decrypt it; therefore, it is recommended to devise such techniques which allow publishers to perform queries on the encrypted data. Furthermore, few techniques have also been proposed where data is encrypted by publishers using different keys and where user receives only the corresponding keys of data portions. Such techniques need improvement from the management perspective, as using large number of different keys creates difficulty in management. Important consideration is required for comparing different encryption algorithms in order to evaluate most appropriate one for the DBaaS environment. Until now, most of the simulations for the evaluation of the Cloud database security solutions are performed on test beds. This

Table 13.5 State-of-the-art mechanisms for securing DBaaS

Problem addressed	Defense mechanism	Description
Confidentiality and privacy	Net DB2 architecture [50]	Based on cryptography (Considered both RSA and Blowfish) TSL and SSL are used for privacy Information is not revealed to service providers
	Homomorphic encryption [45]	Operates on larger block size Computation applies directly on cipher-text Database server cannot see/access keys/data
	Query execution assurance [94]	Data owner ensures secure execution of query Based on hashing mechanism
	Secret sharing algorithm [53]	Secret sharing mechanism is used Data is divided into "n" shares and distributed into multiple servers hole database is retrieved for data reconstructions, processing overhead is involved B + Trees used for preserving order
	NetDB2 multi-shares model [8]	Supports NetDB2 architecture. Based on secret-sharing algorithm Secure network communication Data divided into 'n' shares as like previous approaches
	Cryptonite-secure data repository solution [60]	Addresses availability requirements File owner has permission to encrypt and audit the data StrongBox enables scalable key management and secures files
	Privacy preserving algorithm [4]	Encryption was not used Attribute values split to multiple distributed servers based on secret sharing mechanisms Service providers cannot infer data content Extension of this method retrieves only required tuples instead of whole database
	Full homo-morphic algorithm [66]	Querying encrypted data is possible *Evaluate Algorithm* is used besides key generation, encryption and decryption
	Proxy-less architecture [44]	Alleviate the need of using intermediate component Metadata is moved to database Encryption engine is executed by each client Scalability, security and consistency of data are provided
Integrity	Storage integrity auditing mechanism [77]	Distributed erasure-coded data is used for employing redundancy. Homomorphic token is used for dynamically storing data. TPA can audit logs and events but they do not know the encryption keys.
	Privacy-preserving public auditing for secure cloud storage [101]	Third party auditors are used for communication with users to check data integrity Batch auditing is used to perform delegated auditing tasks from different users Public key based homomorphic encryption linear authenticator is used

Table 13.5 (continued)

Problem addressed	Defense mechanism	Description
	Query integrity verifier [109]	TPA/Users/querier can verify executed queries Support for JOIN and AGGREGATE queries are a plus
	National data storage [28]	On the fly client side encryption is used SHA −512 algorithm for integrity control AES −256 is used for encryption Users no longer have to manage keys manually
	Searchable encryption scheme [10]	Standard cryptographic techniques such as block ciphers, symmetric encryption schemes, and message authentication codes are used Ensures authenticity (cipher text integrity) and privacy of data
	Consistency management [52]	Based on the data structure of trees Interdependency between replica servers is reduced There is maximum reliable path between primary sever to all replica servers
Availability	Backup approach	Three backup servers are maintained located at remote locations Traditional encryption and decryption method is used with two-step authentication Encryption is performed during backup operation
	Hub [106]	Data is divided into buckets such that only required tuples are retrieved from the hub Saves time to achieve performance Backups are easier to maintain Privacy preserving backup protocol between heterogeneous copies is designed

lack of testing in the actual environment should be mitigated by replacing test beds with real users/data and simulations with real database service providers in Cloud. Additionally, some solutions involve additional Third Party Auditors (TPA's) in which security of the whole architecture is dependent on the integrity of these TPAs and any security breach from TPAs will affect the whole storage mechanism. There is a need for more reliable and dependable auditor-less solutions. Additionally, performance issues are faced by most of the counter mechanisms when they have to process with big data, for which the techniques are not engineered. Secure APIs, auditing mechanisms and tools, data migration between DBaaS service providers and standards for permanent data deletion are some of the areas that are still unattended in DBaaS security. The practical and widely-adopted mechanisms which are meant to provide security for relational databases can also be adopted for the Cloud DBaaS model (database outsourcing) after transforming and customizing them accordingly.

Thus, after conducting a thorough study on DBaaS, it can be inferred that it is extremely important to holistically investigate the various DBaaS security related parameters such as threats, risks, challenges, vulnerabilities, and attacks. Moreover, majority of the extant mechanisms for mitigating security challenges have room for further improvement because none of them provide holistic solutions to cater every aspect of security concerns but address a particular preventive concern.

Secure mechanisms should be developed and evaluated according to a benchmark in order to make them more comprehensive, mature, practical and reliable. These security measures should be dynamic to adapt the changing requirements of the Cloud DBaaS.

13.6   Conclusion

Database-as-a-Service (DBaaS) is an increasingly popular Cloud service model, with attractive features like scalability, pay-as-you-go model and cost reduction; they make it suitable for most organizations with constantly changing requirements. There have been many data security breaches in the Cloud over the past few years, as mentioned in Sect. 13.1. Security is an active area of research but requires further investigation, especially in the domain of Cloud databases. No extensive research work has been done which meticulously covers security aspects of DBaaS. This chapter surveyed and presented in-depth survey of challenges faced by DBaaS including background knowledge of its evolution history, its major advantages, features, and characteristics, followed by different Cloud-compatible data storage architectures. Moreover, different inherent security issues faced by DBaaS are also enumerated. State-of-the-art techniques to secure DBaaS are also exemplified in this chapter. Some future directions are also given which will help researchers in exploring further research horizons and for devising solutions for the security of this model.

We have established that data storage security in the Cloud is a domain which is full of challenges and is of paramount importance as customers do not want to lose their data at any cost. It is also a major hurdle in the way of adopting the Cloud platform for storage services. Unfortunately, DBaaS is vulnerable to different attacks; thus, many research problems in this domain are yet to be investigated. There is a need for effective mechanisms and methodologies to mitigate security problems by having practices in the form of secure architectures so as to make DBaaS platform more secure, and ultimately, widely-adopted.

References

1. 万文典 (2011) Future trend of database: cloud database, http://toyhouse.cc/profiles/blogs/future-trend-of-database-Cloud-database. Accessed Aug 2013
2. Abadi DJ (2009) Data management in the cloud: limitations and opportunities. IEEE Data Eng 32(1):2009
3. Agrawal R, Evfimievski A, Srikant R (2003) Information sharing across private databases. In: Proceedings of the ACM SIGMOD conference, pp 86–97, 2003
4. Agrawal D, Abbadi AEl, Emekci F, Metwally A (2009) Database management as a service: challenges and opportunities, data engineering, ICDE'09. IEEE 25th international conference on IEEE, pp 1709–1716, 2009

5. Agrawal D, Das S, Abbadi AEl (2011) Big data and cloud computing: current state and future opportunities. Proceedings of the 14th international conference on extending database technology, ACM, pp 530–533, 2011
6. Agrawal D, Abbadi AEl, Das S, Elmore AJ (2011) Database scalability, elasticity, and autonomy in the cloud, database systems for advanced applications. Springer, Berlin, pp 1–14
7. Al Shehri W (2013) Cloud database Database-as-a-Service. Int J Database Manage Syst (IJDMS) 5(2):1–12
8. Alzain MA, Pardede E (2011) Using multi shares for ensuring privacy in Database-as-a-Service. Proceedings of 44th Hawaii international conference on system sciences, pp 1–9, 2011
9. AlZain MA, Pardede E, Soh B, Thom JA (2012) Cloud computing security: from single to multi-clouds. 45th Hawaii international conference on system sciences, pp 5490–5499, 2012
10. Amanatidis G, Boldyreva A, O'Neill A (2007) New security models and provably-secure schemes for basic query support in outsourced databases, 2007
11. Amazon (2006) Amazon web services. Web services licensing agreement, 2006
12. Amazon, Amazon Elastic Compute Cloud (Amazon EC2), http://aws.amazon.com/ec2/. Accessed Aug 2013
13. Amazon, Amazon SimpleDB, http://aws.amazon.com/simpledb/. Accessed Aug 2013
14. Amazon web services (2013) Amazon Elastic Block Store (EBS), 2013. http://aws.amazon.com/ebs/. Accessed Oct 2013
15. Ansari S, Rajeev SG, Chandrashekar HS (2002) Packet sniffing: a brief introduction. Potential IEEE 21(5):17–19
16. Apache, CouchDB. http://couchdb.apache.org/. Accessed Dec 2013
17. Armbrust M, Fox A, Griffith R, Joseph AD, Katz R, Konwinski A, Lee G, Patterson D, Rabkin A, Stoica I, Zaharia M (2010) A view of cloud computing. Commun ACM 53(4):50–58
18. Arora I, Gupta A (2012) Cloud databases: a paradigm shift in databases. Int J Comput Sci Issues 9(4):77–83
19. Babcock C (2012) Cloud implementation to double by 2012. http://www.informationweek.com/news/services/saas/214502033?queryText=cloud. Accessed Jan 2014
20. Behl A (2011) Emerging security challenges in cloud computing-an insight to cloud security challenges and their mitigation. Information and Communication Technologies (WICT), World Congress on IEEE, pp 217–222, 2011
21. Behl A, Behl K (2012) An analysis of cloud computing security issues. Information and Communication Technologies (WICT), World Congress on IEEE, pp 109–114, 2012
22. Beimborn D, Miletzki T, Wenzel S (2011) Platform as a service (PaaS). Bus Inf Syst Eng 3(6):381–384
23. Bezos J (1994) Amazon. http://www.amazon.com/. Accessed Nov 2013
24. Biswas A (2012) Cloud Database: Advantages and Disadvantages, 2012. http://www.itsabhik.com/Cloud-database-advangates-and-disadvantages/. Accessed Oct 2013
25. Bobrowski S (2008) Database-as-a-Service, 2008. http://dbaas.wordpress.com/2008/05/14/what-exactly-is-database-as-a-service/. Accessed Aug 2013
26. Bonnette R (2011) Top benefits of database cloud computing, 2011. http://blog.caspio.com/commentary/top-benefits-of-database-Cloud-computing/. Accessed Aug 2013
27. Brown WC, Nyarko K (2012) Software as a service (SaaS), cloud computing service and deployment models: layers and management, 2012
28. Brzeźniak M, Jankowski G, Jankowski M, Jankowski S, Jankowski T, Meyer N, Mikołajczak R, Zawada A, Zdanowski S (2013) National data storage 2: secure storage cloud with efficient and easy data access, 2013
29. Buneman P, Khanna S, Tan W-C (2000) Data provenance: some basic issues, FST TCS 2000: foundations of software technology and theoretical computer science. Springer, Berlin
30. Carrenza (2012) Database-as-a-Service, http://carrenza.com/services/use-cases/database-as-a-service/. Accessed Oct 2013
31. Cloudtweaks (2010) Top 10 cloud computing most promising adoption factors, 2010. http://www.Cloudtweaks.com/2010/08/top-10-Cloud-computing-most-promising-adoption-factors/. Accessed Sept 2013

32. Cloud Security Alliance (2012) Top ten big data security and privacy challenges, 2012. Accessed Oct 2013
33. Cloud Security Alliance, Cloud Vulnerabilities Working Group (2013) Cloud computing: vulnerability incidents: a statistical overview, 2013
34. Cloud Security Alliance, https://cloudsecurityalliance.org/, Accessed Feb 2013
35. Cloud Tweaks (2012) A hitchhikers guide to the cloud-database challenges to consider, 2012. http://www.cloudtweaks.com/2012/09/a-hitchhikers-guide-to-the-cloud-database-challenges -to-consider/. Accessed Oct 2013
36. Coleman C (2013) Why use a DBaaS instead of do-it-yourself MySQL in the cloud? https:// www.cleardb.com/blog/entry?id=pro-series/segment-101/why-use-a-database-as-a-service-instead-of-do-it-yourself-mysql-in-the-Cloud. Accessed Nov 2013
37. Cooper BF, Ramakrishnan R, Srivastava U, Silberstein A, Bohannon P, Jacobsen HA, Puz N, Weaver D, Yerneni R (2008) PNUTS: Yahoo!'s hosted data serving platform, 2008
38. David Linthicum-InfoWorld (2013) Interoperable database, 2013. http://dictionary.reference. com/browse/interoperable+database. Accessed Sept 2013
39. Dillon T, Wu C, Chang E (2012) Cloud computing: issues and challenges. 24th IEEE international conference on advanced information networking and applications, pp 27–33, 2012
40. Dimovski D (2013) Database management as a cloud based service for small and medium organizations, Dissertation/master thesis, Masaryk University Brno, 2013
41. Essner J (2011) Security in the Cloud. New Jersey Digital Government Summit, 2011
42. Ferrari E (2009) Database-as-a-Service: challenges and solutions for privacy and security, services computing conference, 2009. APSCC 2009. IEEE Asia-Pacific. IEEE, pp 46–51, 2009
43. Ferrari E (2010) Access control in data management systems. Morgan & Claypool, San Rafael
44. Ferretti L, Colajanni M, Marchetti M (2012) Supporting security and consistency for cloud database. Cyberspace Safe Secur Lect Notes Comput Sci 7672:179–193
45. Ge T, Zdonik SB (2007) Answering aggregation queries in a secure system model. In Proceedings of VLDB Conference, pp 519–530, 2007
46. Gelbstein E (2011) Data integrity-information security's poor relation. ISACA J 6:2011
47. Gelogo YE, Lee S (2012) Database management system as a cloud service. Int J Future Gener Commun Netw 5(2):71–76
48. Golden B (2010) Cloud computing: two kinds of agility, 2010. http://www.cio.com/article/599626/Cloud_Computing_Two_Kinds_of_Agility. Accessed Sept 2013
49. Gupta GKr, Sharma AK, Swaroop V (2010) Consistency and security in mobile real time distributed database (MRTDDB): a combinational giant challenge. AIP conference proceedings, vol 1324, 2010
50. Hacigumus H, Iyer B, Li C, Mehrotra S (2002) Executing SQL over encrypted data in the database service provider model. In: Proceedings of the ACM SIGMOD'200 conference, Madison, Wisconsin, pp 216–227, 2002
51. Hacigumus H, Iyer B, Mehrorta S (2002) Providing Database-as-a-Service, ICDE, pp 29–38, 2002
52. Hacigumus H, Iyer B, Mehrotra S (2002) Providing Database-as-a-Service. Proceedings of the 18th international conference on data engineering (ICDE.02), 2002
53. Hadavi MA, Noferesti M, Jalili R, Damiani E (2012) Database-as-a-Service: towards a unified solution for security requirements. IEEE 36th international conference on computer software and applications workshops, pp 415–420, 2012
54. Haughwout J (2011) Cloud computing: it's not just about access from anywhere, 2011. http:// technorati.com/technology/article/Cloud-computing-its-not-just-about/page-1/. Accessed Oct 2013
55. Hogan M (2008) Cloud computing & databases-how databases can meet the demands of Cloud computing, ScaleDB Inc, 2008
56. Holden EP, Kang JW, Bills DP, Ilyassov M (2009) Databases in the Cloud: a work in progress. Proceedings of the 10th ACM conference on SIG-information technology education, ACM, pp 138–143, 2009
57. IBM (1991) http://www.ibm.com/us/en/. Accessed Feb 2013

58. Kapa KK, Lopez R (2012) Database-as-a-Service (DBaaS) using enterprise manager 12c, Oracle Open World, 2012
59. Kumar A, Lee HJ, Singh RP (2012) Efficient and secure cloud storage for handling big data, information science and service science and data mining (ISSDM). 6th international conference on new trends in, pp 162–166, 2012
60. Kumbhare A, Simmhan Y, Prasanna V (2012) Cryptonite: a secure and performant data repository on public clouds, cloud computing (CLOUD), 2012 IEEE 5th international conference on IEEE, pp 510–517, 2012
61. Lee S (2011) Shared-nothing vs. shared-disk cloud database architecture. Int J Energy Inf Commun 2(4):211–216
62. Linthicum D (2010) The data interoperability challenge for Cloud computing, 2010. http://www.infoworld.com/d/Cloud-computing/data-interoperability-challenge-Cloud-computing-259. Accessed Oct 2013
63. Linthicum D (2010) The data interoperability challenge for cloud computing, http://www.infoworld.com/d/cloud-computing/data-interoperability-challenge-cloud-computing-259, 2010. Accessed Nov 2013
64. Liu W (2012) Research on cloud computing security problem and strategy, consumer electronics, communications and networks (CECNet), 2nd international conference on IEEE, pp 1216–1219, 2012
65. Longjump, http://www.softwareag.com/special/longjump/index.html. Accessed Feb 2013
66. Mani M, Shah K, Gunda M (2013) Enabling secure Database-as-a-Service using fully homomorphic encryption: challenges and opportunities, DanaC '13. Proceedings of the second workshop on data analytics in the cloud, pp 1–12, 2013
67. Markovich S (2011) Three clouds-computing data security risks that can't be overlooked, 2011. http://www.mcafee.com/us/products/databasesecurity/articles/20110321-01.aspx. Accessed Oct 2013
68. Mateljan V, Cisic D, Ogrizovid D (2010) Cloud Database-as-a-Service (DaaS)-ROI, MIPRO, Opatija, Croatia, pp 1185–1188, 2010
69. McAfee (2012) Data loss by the numbers. White paper, 2012.
70. Merkle RC (1989) A certified digital signature, advances in cryptology-CRYPTO '89. 9th annual international cryptology conference, Santa Barbara, California, USA, Proceedings vol 435, pp 218–238, 1989
71. Michel D (2010) Databases in the cloud, Doktorarbeit, HSR University of Applied Science Rapperswil, 2010
72. Microsoft, Windows Azure. http://www.windowsazure.com/en-us/. Accessed Nov 2013
73. Miller R (2008) Major outage for Amazon S3 and EC2, http://www.datacenterknowledge.com/archives/2008/02/15/major-outage-for-amazon-s3-and-ec2/,200. Accessed Oct 2013
74. Mitropoulos D (2013) Data security in the cloud environment vol 19, no 3, 2013
75. MySQL. http://www.mysql.com/products/enterprise/database/. Accessed Dec 2013
76. Nadella S (1975) Microsoft. http://www.microsoft.com/en-pk/default.aspx. Accessed Nov 2013
77. Nithiavathy R (2013) Data integrity and data dynamics with secure storage service in cloud. Proceedings of the 2013 international conference on pattern recognition, informatics and mobile engineering, IEEE, pp 125–130, 2013
78. NoSQL. http://nosql-database.org/. Accessed Nov 2013
79. Nuo DB (2013) 12 rules for a cloud data management system (CDMS), Cambridge Massachusetts (PRWEB), 2013
80. Oracle Corporation (2011) Database-as-a-Service: reference architecture-an overview, 2011
81. Oracle ® Database Security Guide 10 g Release 2 (10.2) (2013) 7 Security Policies, 2013. http://docs.oracle.com/cd/B19306_01/network.102/b14266/policies.htm. Accessed Aug 2013
82. Oracle, Oracle database, http://www.oracle.com/us/products/database/overview/index.html. Accessed Dec 2013
83. OWASP (2009) Resource exhaustion, https://www.owasp.org/index.php/Resource_exhaustion, 2009. Accessed Aug 2013

84.   Page L, Brin S (1998) Google. https://www.google.com.pk/. Accessed Oct 2013
85.   Pizette L, Cabot T (2012) Database-as-a-Service: a marketplace assessment, pp 1–4, 2012
86.   Posey M (2012) Database-as-a-Service: rightsizing database solutions, research vice president, hosting & managed network services, 2012
87.   Reddy Kandukuri B, Ramakrishna PV, Rakshit A (2009) Cloud security issues, IEEE, pp 517–520, 2009
88.   Sakhi I (2012) Databases security in cloud. Dissertation KTH, 2012
89.   Saravanan C, Sandya M (2011) Databases in the era of cloud computing and big data, features, open gurus, overview, technology, 2011. http://www.linuxforu.com/2011/05/databases-in-era-of-Cloud-computing-and-big-data. Accessed Aug 2013
90.   ScaleDB (2012) Database-as-a-Service (DBaaS), http://www.scaledb.com/DBaaS-Database-as-a-Service.php. Accessed Dec 2013
91.   Sengupta S, Kaulgud V, Sharma VS (2011) Cloud computing security-trends and research directions, services (SERVICES), IEEE World Congress on IEEE, pp 524–531, 2011
92.   Sharir R (2013) Nine cloudy challenges for databases, 2013. http://www.itbusinessedge.com/slideshows/show.aspx?c=96438. Accessed Nov 2013
93.   Sheldon R (2012) DBaaS pros and cons for solution providers, 2012. http://searchitchannel.techtarget.com/tip/DBaaS-pros-and-cons-for-solution-providers. Accessed Aug 2013
94.   Sion R (2005) Query execution assurance for outsourced database. In: Proceedings of VLDB conference, 2005
95.   Sion R (2007) Secure data outsourcing. In: Proceedings of the CLDB conference, pp 1431–1432, 2007
96.   Summers A, Tickner C (2004) What is security analysis? http://www.doc.ic.ac.uk/~ajs300/security/CIA.htm. Accessed Dec 2013
97.   Sushil B, Jain L, Jain S (2010) Cloud computing: a study of infrastructure as a service (IAAS). International journal of engineering and information technology 2.1, pp 60–63, 2010
98.   Tianfield H (2012) Security issues in cloud computing. IEEE international conference on systems, man, and cybernetics, pp 1082–1089, 2012
99.   Vacca JR (2012) Computer and information security handbook, second edition, Newnes, 2012
100. vFabric Team (2012) Why DBaaS? 5 trends pushing Database-as-a-Service, 2012. http://blogs.vmware.com/vfabric/2012/08/why-dbaas-6-trends-pushing-database-as-a-service.html. Accessed Sept 2013
101. Wang C, Chow SSM, Wang Q, Kui R, Wenjing L (2013) Privacy preserving public auditing for secure cloud storage. IEEE Trans Comput 62(2):362–375
102. Weis J, Alves-Foss J (2011) Securing Database-as-a-Service: issues and compromises, security & privacy, IEEE 9.6, pp 49–55, 2011
103. Wikia (2013) Cloud database, 2013. http://databasemanagement.wikia.com/wiki/Cloud_Database. Accessed Aug 2013
104. Wikipedia (2012) Cloud database, 2012. http://en.wikipedia.org/wiki/Cloud_database. Accessed Sept 2013
105. Williams E, Glass N, Dorsey J, Stone B (2006) Twitter. www.twitter.com. Accessed Nov 2013
106. Xu L, Wu X (2013) Hub: heterogeneous bucketization for database outsourcing, cloud computing'13, Hangzhou, China, pp 47–54, 2013
107. Yasin R (2013) 5 years down the road: the cloud of clouds, 2013. http://gcn.com/articles/2013/05/31/Cloud-of-Clouds-5-years-in-future.aspx. Accessed Oct 2013
108. ZeusDB. http://www.zeusdb.com. Accessed Feb, 2013
109. Zheng Q, Xu S, Ateniese G (2012) Efficient query integrity for outsourced dynamic databases, CCSW'12, Raleigh, North Carolina, USA, 2012
110. Zissis D, Lekkas D (2012) Addressing cloud computing security issues, future generation computer systems 3, pp 583–592, 2012

Chapter 14
Beyond the Clouds: How Should Next Generation Utility Computing Infrastructures Be Designed?

Marin Bertier, Frédéric Desprez, Gilles Fedak, Adrien Lebre, Anne-Cécile Orgerie, Jonathan Pastor, Flavien Quesnel, Jonathan Rouzaud-Cornabas and Cédric Tedeschi

Abstract To accommodate the ever-increasing demand for Utility Computing (UC) resources while taking into account both energy and economical issues, the current trend consists in building even larger data centers in a few strategic locations. Although, such an approach enables to cope with the actual demand while continuing to operate UC resources through centralized software system, it is far from delivering sustainable and efficient UC infrastructures. In this scenario, we claim that a disruptive change in UC infrastructures is required in the sense that UC resources should be managed differently, considering locality as a primary concern. To this aim, we propose to leverage any facilities available through the Internet in order to deliver widely

A. Lebre (✉) · M. Bertier · F. Desprez · G. Fedak · A.-C. Orgerie · J. Pastor · F. Quesnel · J. Rouzaud-Cornabas · C. Tedeschi
Inria, Campus universitaire de Beaulieu, 35042 Rennes, France
e-mail: Adrien.Lebre@inria.fr

M. Bertier
e-mail: Marin.Bertier@inria.fr

F. Desprez
e-mail: Frederic.Desprez@inria.fr

G. Fedak
e-mail: Gilles.Fedak@inria.fr

A.-C. Orgerie
e-mail: Anne-Cecile.Orgerie@inria.fr

J. Pastor
e-mail: Jonathan.Pastor@inria.fr

F. Quesnel
e-mail: Flavien.Quesnel@inria.fr

J. Rouzaud-Cornabas
e-mail: Jonathan.Rouzaud-Cornabas@inria.fr

C. Tedeschi
e-mail: Cedric.Tedeschi@inria.fr

© Springer International Publishing Switzerland 2014
Z. Mahmood, (ed.), *Cloud Computing,* Computer Communications and Networks,
DOI 10.1007/978-3-319-10530-7_14

distributed UC platforms that can better match the geographical dispersal of users as well as the unending resource demand. Critical to the emergence of such locality-based UC (LUC) platforms is the availability of appropriate operating mechanisms. We advocate the implementation of a unified system driving the use of resources at an unprecedented scale by turning a complex and diverse infrastructure into a collection of abstracted computing facilities that is both easy to operate and reliable. By deploying and using such a LUC Operating System on backbones, our ultimate vision is to make possible to host/operate a large part of the Internet by its internal structure itself: a scalable and nearly infinite set of resources delivered by any computing facilities forming the Internet, starting from the larger hubs operated by ISPs, governments, and academic institutions to any idle resources that may be provided by end users.

Keywords Utility Computing · UC · Locality-based UC · Distributed Cloud Computing · IaaS · Efficiency · Sustainability

14.1   Introduction

The success of Cloud Computing has driven the advent of Utility Computing (UC). However, Cloud Computing is a victim of its own success. In order to answer the escalating demand for computing resources, Cloud Computing providers must build data centers (DCs) of ever-increasing size. As a consequence, besides facing the well-known issues of large-scale platform management, large-scale DCs have now to deal with energy considerations that limit the number of physical resources that one location can host.

Instead of investigating alternative solutions that could tackle the aforementioned concerns, the current trend consists in deploying larger and larger DCs in few strategic locations presenting energy advantages. For example, Western North Carolina, USA, an attractive area due to its abundant capacity of coal and nuclear power, brought about the departure of the textile and furniture industry [21]. More recently, several proposals suggested building next generation DCs close to the polar circle in order to leverage free cooling techniques, considering that cooling accounts for a big part of the electricity consumption [24].

14.1.1   Inherent Limitations of Large-scale Data Centers

Although, building large-scale DCs enables to cope with the actual demand, it is far from delivering sustainable and efficient UC infrastructures. In addition to requiring the construction and the deployment of a complete network infrastructure to reach each DC, it exacerbates the inherent limitations of the Cloud Computing model:

- The externalization of private applications/data often faces legal issues that restrain companies from outsourcing them on external infrastructures, especially when located in other countries.

- The overhead implied by the unavoidable use of the Internet to reach distant platforms is wasteful and costly in several situations: Deploying a broadcasting service of local events or an online service to order pizzas at the edge of the polar circle, for instance, leads to important overheads since most of the users are *a priori* located in the neighborhood of the event/the pizzeria.
- The connectivity to the application/data cannot be ensured by centralized dedicated centers, especially if they are located in a similar geographical zone. The only way to ensure disaster recovery is to leverage distinct sites [23].

The two first points could be partially tackled by hybrid or federated Cloud solutions [4], that aim at extending the resources available on one Cloud with those of another one; however, the third one requires a disruptive change in the way UC resources are managed.

Another issue is that, according to some projections of a recent IEEE report [25], the network traffic has been doubling roughly every year. Consequently, bringing IT services closer to the end users is becoming crucial to limit the energy impact of these exchanges and to save the bandwidth of some links. Similarly, this notion of locality is critical for the adoption of the UC model by applications that need to deal with a large amount of data as getting them in and out using actual UC infrastructures may significantly impact the global performance [18].

The concept of micro/nano DCs at the edge of the backbone [24] may be seen as a complementary solution to hybrid platforms in order to reduce the overhead of network exchanges. However, operating multiple small DCs breaks somehow the idea of mutualization in terms of physical resources and administration simplicity, making this approach questionable.

14.1.2 Ubiquitous and Oversized Network Backbones

One way to partially solve the mutualization concern enlightened by the defenders of large-scale DCs is to directly deploy the concept of micro/nano DCs upon the Internet backbone. People are (and will be) more and more surrounded by computing resources, especially those in charge of interconnecting the IT equipment. Even though these small- and medium-sized facilities include resources that are barely used [3, 8], they can hardly be removed (e.g., routers). Considering this important aspect, we claim that a new generation of UC platforms can be delivered by leveraging existing network centers, starting from the core nodes of the backbone to the different network access points in charge of interconnecting public and private institutions. By such a mean, network and UC providers would be able to mutualize resources that are mandatory to operate network/data centers while delivering widely distributed UC platforms able to better match the geographical dispersal of users. Figure 14.1 allows to better capture the advantages of such a proposal. It shows a snapshot of the network weather map of RENATER, the backbone dedicated to universities and research institutes in France. It reveals several important points:

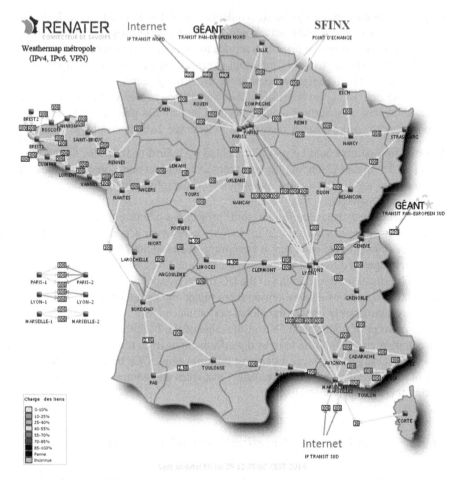

Fig. 14.1 The RENATER Weather Map on May 2013, the 27th, around 4 p.m. Each *red square* corresponds to a particular point of presence (PoP) of the network. The map is available in real-time at: http://www.renater.fr/raccourci

- As mentioned before, most of the resources are underutilized (only two links are used between 45 and 55 %, a few between 25 and 40 %, and the majority below the threshold of 25 %).
- The backbone was deployed and is renewed to match the demand: The density of points of presence (PoPs, i.e., small- or medium-sized network centers), as well as the bandwidth of each link, are more important on the edge of large cities such as Paris, Lyon, or Marseille.
- The backbone was designed to avoid disconnections, since 95 % of the PoPs can be reached by at least two distinct routes.

14.1.3 Locality-Based Utility Computing

This chapter aims at introducing locality-based UC (LUC) infrastructures, a new generation of UC platforms that solve inherent limitations of the Cloud Computing paradigm relying on large-scale DCs. Although, it involves radical changes in the way physical and virtual resources are managed, leveraging network centers is a promising way to deliver highly efficient and sustainable UC services.

From the physical point of view, network backbones provide appropriate infrastructures, i.e., reliable and efficient enough to operate UC resources spread across the different PoPs. Ideally, UC resources would be able to directly take advantage of computation cycles available on network active devices, i.e., those in charge of routing packets. However, leveraging network resources to make external computations may lead to important security concerns. Hence, we propose to extend each PoP with a number of servers dedicated to hosting virtual machines (VMs). As it is natural to assume that the network traffic and UC demands are proportional, larger network centers will be completed with more UC resources than the smaller ones. Moreover, by deploying UC services on relevant PoPs, a LUC infrastructure will be able to natively confine network exchanges to a minimal scope, minimizing altogether the energy footprint of the network, the impact on latency and the congestion phenomena that may occur on critical paths (for instance Paris and Marseille on RENATER).

From the software point of view, the main challenge is to design a comprehensive distributed system in charge of turning a complex and diverse network of resources into a collection of abstracted computing facilities that are both reliable and easy to operate.

The design of the LUC Operating System (OS), an advanced system being able to unify many UC resources distributed on distinct sites, would enable Internet service providers (ISPs) and other institutions in charge of operating a network backbone to build an extreme scale LUC infrastructure with a limited additional cost. Instead of redeploying a complete installation, they will be able to leverage IT resources and specific devices such as computer room air conditioning units, inverters, or redundant power supplies already present in each center of their backbone.

In addition to considering *locality* as a primary concern, the novelty of the LUC OS proposal is to consider the VM as the basic object it manipulates. Unlike existing research on distributed operating systems designed around the process concept, a LUC OS will manipulate VMs throughout a federation of widely distributed physical machines. Virtualization technologies abstract out hardware heterogeneity, and allow transparent deployment, preemption, and migration of virtual environments (VEs), i.e., a set of interconnected VMs. By dramatically increasing the flexibility of resource management, virtualization allows to leverage state-of-the-art results from other distributed systems areas such as autonomous and decentralized systems. Our goal is to build a system that allows end users to launch VEs over a distributed infrastructure as simply as they launch processes on a local machine, i.e., without the burden of dealing with resources availability or location.

14.1.4   Chapter Outline

Section 14.2 describes the key objectives of a LUC OS and the associated challenges. Section 14.3 explains why our vision differs from current and previous UC
solutions. In Section 14.4, we present how such a unified system may be designed
by delivering the premises of the DISCOVERY (DIStributed and COoperative
framework to manage Virtual EnviRonments autonomouslY) system, an agent-
based system enabling the distributed and cooperative management of virtual environments over a large-scale distributed infrastructure. Future work and opportunities
are addressed in Sect. 14.5. Finally, Sect. 14.6 concludes this chapter.

14.2   Overall Vision and Major Challenges

Similar to traditional operating systems (OSes), a LUC OS is composed of many
mechanisms. Trying to identify all of them and establishing how they interact is an
on-going work (see Sect. 14.4). However, we have pointed out the following key
objectives to be considered when designing a LUC OS:

- *Scalability*: A LUC OS must be able to manage hundreds of thousands of virtual
  machines (VMs) running on thousands of geographically distributed computing
  resources. These resources are small- or medium-sized computing facilities and
  may become highly volatile according to the network disconnections.
- *Reactivity*: To deal with the dynamicity of the infrastructure, a LUC OS should
  swiftly handle events that require to perform particular operations, either
  on virtual or on physical resources. This has to be done with the objective of
  maximizing the system utilization while meeting the Quality of Service (QoS)
  expectations of VEs. Some examples of operations that should be performed as
  fast as possible include: (i) the reconfiguration of VEs over distributed resources,
  sometimes spread across wide area networks (WANs), or (ii) the migration of
  VMs, while preserving their active connections.
- *Resiliency*: In addition to the inherent dynamicity of the infrastructure, failures,
  and faults should be considered as the norm rather than the exception at such a
  scale. The goal is therefore to transparently leverage the underlying infrastructure redundancy to: (i) allow the LUC OS to keep working despite node failures
  and network disconnections (LUC OS robustness), and to (ii) provide snapshotting as well as high availability mechanisms for VEs (VM robustness).
- *Sustainability*: Although the LUC approach would reduce the energy footprint of
  UC services by minimizing the cost of the network, it is important to go one step
  further by considering energy aspects at each level of a LUC OS and propose
  advanced mechanisms in charge of making an optimal usage of each source of
  energy. To achieve such an objective, the LUC OS should take account of data
  related to the energy consumption of the VEs and the computing resources, as
  well as the environmental conditions (computer room air conditioning unit, location of the site, etc.).

- *Security and Privacy*: Similar to resiliency, the security and privacy issues affect the LUC OS itself and the VEs running on it. Regarding the LUC OS, the goals are: (i) to create trust relationships between different locations, (ii) to secure the peer-to-peer layers, (iii) to include security and privacy decisions and enforcement points in the LUC OS, and (iv) to make them collaborate through the secured peer-to-peer layers to provide end-to-end security and privacy. Regarding the VEs, users should be able to express their requirements in terms of security and privacy; the LUC OS would then enforce these requirements.

In addition to the aforementioned objectives, working on a virtual infrastructure requires to deal with the management of VM images. Managing VM images in a distributed way across a wide area network (WAN) is a real challenge that will require adapting state-of-the-art techniques related to replication and deduplication. Also, the LUC OS must take into account VM images location, for instance: (i) to allocate the right resources to a VE, or (ii) to prefetch VM images, to improve deployment performance or VM relocations.

Finally, one last scientific and technical challenge is the lack of a global view of the infrastructure. Maintaining a global view would indeed limit the scalability of the LUC OS, which is inconsistent with our objective to manage large-scale geographically distributed systems. Therefore, we claim that the LUC OS should rely on decentralized and autonomous mechanisms, which can match and adapt to the volatile topology of the infrastructure. Several decentralized mechanisms are already used in production on large-scale systems; for instance, Amazon relies on the Dynamo service [15] to create distributed indexes and recover from data in-consistencies and Facebook uses Cassandra [29], a massive scale structured store that leverages peer-to-peer techniques. In a LUC OS, decentralized and self-organizing overlays will enable to maintain the information about the current state of both virtual and physical resources, their characteristics, and availabilities. Such information is mandatory to build higher level mechanisms ensuring the correct execution of VEs throughout the whole infrastructure.

14.3 Background

Several generations of UC infrastructures have been proposed and still coexist [19]. However, neither Desktop, Grid, nor Cloud Computing platforms provide a satisfying UC model. Contrary to the current trend that promotes large offshore-centralized DCs as the UC platform of choice, we claim that the only way to achieve sustainable and highly efficient UC services is to target a new infrastructure that better matches the Internet structure. As it aims at gathering an unprecedented amount of widely distributed computing resources into a single platform providing UC services close to the end users, a LUC infrastructure is fundamentally different from existing ones. Keeping in mind the aforementioned objectives, recycling UC resource management solutions developed in the past is doomed to failure.

As previously mentioned, our vision significantly differs from hybrid Cloud Computing solutions. Although these research activities address important concerns related to the use of federated Cloud platforms, such as interface standardization for supporting cooperation and resource sharing, their propositions are incremental improvements of existing UC models. Recent investigations on hybrid Clouds and Cloud federation are comparable in some ways to previous works done on Grids, since the purpose of a Grid middleware is to interact with each resource management system composing the Grid [11, 49, 55].

By taking into account the network issues, in addition to traditional computing and storage concerns in Cloud Computing systems, the European SAIL project [50] is probably the one which targets the biggest advances with regard to previous works on Grid systems. More concretely, this project investigates new network technologies to provide end users of hybrid/federated Clouds with the possibility to configure and virtually operate the network backbone interconnecting the different sites they use [37].

More recently, the *Fog Computing* concept has been proposed as a promising solution to applications and services that cannot be put into the Cloud due to locality issues (mainly the latency and mobility concerns) [10]. Although it might look similar to our vision as they propose to extend the Cloud Computing paradigm to the edge of the network, *Fog Computing* does not target a unified system but rather proposes to add a third party layer (i.e., the *Fog*) between Cloud vendors and end users.

In our vision, UC resources (i.e., Cloud Computing ones) should be repacked in the different points of presence of backbones and operated through a unified system, the LUC OS. As far as we know, the only system that investigated whether a widely distributed infrastructure can be operated by a single system was the XtreemOS Project [36]. Although this project shared some of the goals of the LUC OS, it did not investigate how the geographical distribution of resources can be leveraged to deliver more efficient and sustainable UC infrastructures.

To sum up, we argue for the design and the implementation of a kind of distributed OS, manipulating VEs instead of processes, and considering locality as a primary concern. Referred to as a LUC OS, such a system will include most of the mechanisms that are common to current UC management systems [17, 32, 35, 39–41]. However, each of them will have to be rethought in order to leverage peer-to-peer algorithms. While largely unexplored for building operating systems, peer-to-peer/decentralized mechanisms have the potential to achieve the scalability required to manage LUC infrastructures. Using this technology for establishing the base mechanisms of a massive-scale LUC OS will be a major breakthrough from current static, centralized, or hierarchical management solutions.

14.4   Premise of a LUC OS: The DISCOVERY Proposal

In this section, we propose to go one step further by discussing preliminary investigations around the design and implementation of a first LUC OS proposal: the DISCOVERY system. We draw the premises of the DISCOVERY system by emphasizing some of the challenges as well as some research directions to solve them. Finally, we give some details regarding the prototype that is under development and how we are going to evaluate it.

14.4.1 Overview

The DISCOVERY system relies on a multi-agent peer-to-peer system deployed on each physical resource composing the LUC infrastructure. Agents are autonomous entities that collaborate with one another to efficiently use the LUC resources. In our context, efficiency means that a good trade-off is found between users' expectations, reliability, reactivity, and availability, while limiting the energy consumption of the system and providing scalability.

In DISCOVERY, each agent has two purposes: (i) maintaining a knowledge base on the composition of the LUC platform, and (ii) ensuring the correct execution of VEs. This includes the configuration, deployment, and monitoring of VEs as well as the dynamic allocation or relocation of VMs to adapt to changes in VEs requirements and physical resources availability. To this end, agents will rely on dedicated mechanisms related to:

- The localization and monitoring of physical resources
- The management of VEs
- The management of VM images
- Reliability
- Security and privacy

14.4.2 Resource Localization and Monitoring Mechanisms

Keeping in mind that DISCOVERY should be designed in a fully decentralized fashion, its mechanisms should be built on top of an overlay network able to abstract out changes that occur at the physical level. The specific requirements of this platform will lead to the development of a novel kind of overlay networks based on locality and a minimalistic design. More concretely, the first step is to design, at the lowest level, an overlay layer intended to hide the details of the physical routes and computing utilities, while satisfying some basic requirements such as locality and availability. This overlay needs to enable the communications between any two nodes in the platform. While overlay computing has been extensively studied over the last decade, we emphasize here on minimalism, especially on one key feature to implement a LUC OS: retrieving nodes that are geographically close to a given departure node.

14.4.2.1 Giving Nodes a Position

The initial configuration of the physical network can take an arbitrary shape. We choose to rely on the Vivaldi protocol [14]. *Vivaldi* is a distributed algorithm

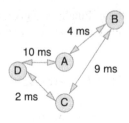

Fig. 14.2 Vivaldi plot before updating positions. Each node pings other nodes. Each node maintains a map of distance

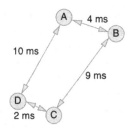

Fig. 14.3 Vivaldi plot after updating positions. The computed positions of other nodes have been updated

as-signing coordinates in the plane to nodes of a distributed system. Each node is equipped with a *view* of the network, i.e., a set of nodes it knows. This view is initially assumed as random. Coordinates obtained by a node reflect its *position* in the network, i.e., close nodes in the network are given close coordinates in the plane. To achieve this, each node periodically checks the round trip time between itself and another node (randomly chosen among nodes in its view) and adapts its distance (by changing its coordinates) with this node in the plane accordingly. Refer to Figs. 14.2 and 14.3 for an illustration of four nodes (A, B, C, and D) moving according to the Vivaldi protocol. A globally accurate positioning of nodes can be obtained if nodes have a few long-distance nodes in their view [14]. These long-distance links can be easily maintained by means of a simple gossip protocol.

14.4.2.2 Searching for Close Nodes

Once the map is achieved (each node knows its coordinates), we are able to decide whether two nodes are *close* by calculating their distance. However, the view of each node does not a priori contain its closest nodes. Therefore, we need additional mechanisms to locate a set of nodes that are close to a given initial node—Vivaldi gives a *location* to each node, but not to the neighborhood. To achieve this, we use a modified distributed version of the classic Dijkstra's algorithm used to find the shortest path between two nodes in a graph. The goal is to build a *spiral* interconnecting the nodes in the plane that are the closest ones to a given initial node. Note that the term *spiral* is here a misuse of language, since the graph actually drawn in the plane might contain crossing edges. The only guarantee is that when following the path constructed, the nodes are always further from the initial node.

Let us consider that our initial point is a node called *I*. The first step is to find a node to build a two-node spiral with *I*. Such a node is sought in the view of *I* by selecting the node, say S, having the smallest distance with I. I then sends its view to S, I stores S as its successor in the spiral, and S adds I as its predecessor in the spiral. Then I forwards its view to S. S creates a new view by keeping the n nodes which are the closest to I in the views of I and S. This last view is then referred to as the *spiral view* and is intended to contain a set of nodes among which to find the next step of the spiral. Then S restarts the same process: Among the spiral view, it chooses the node with the smallest distance to I, say S', and adds it in the spiral—S becomes the predecessor of S' and S' becomes the successor of S. Then, the spiral view is sent to S' which updates it with the nodes it has in its own view. The process is repeated until we consider that enough nodes have been gathered (a parameter sent by the application).

Note that one risk is to be blocked by having a spiral view containing only nodes that are already in the spiral, leading to the impossibility to build the spiral further. However, this problem can be easily addressed by forcing the presence of a few long-distance nodes whenever it is updated.

14.4.2.3   Learning

Applying the protocol described above, the quality of the spiral is questionable in the sense that the nodes that are actually close to the starting node s may not be included. The only property ensured is that one step forward on the built path always takes us further from the initial node.

To improve the *quality* of the spiral, i.e., reduce the average distance between the nodes it comprises and the initial node, we add a learning mechanism coming with no extra communication cost: when a node is contacted to become the next node in one spiral, and receives the associated spiral view, it can also keep the nodes that are the closest to itself, thus potentially increasing the quality of a future spiral construction.

14.4.2.4   Routing

In the context of a LUC infrastructure, one crucial feature is to be able to locate an existing VM. Having the same strategy consisting in improving the performance of the overlay based on the activity of the application, we envision a routing mechanism which will be improved by past routing requests. By means of the spiral mechanism, a node is able to contact its neighboring nodes to start routing a message.

This initial routing mechanism can be very expensive as the number of hops can be linear in the size of the network. However, from previous communications, a node is able to memorize long links to different locations of the network. Consequently, from each routing request, the source of the request and each node on the path to the destination are able to learn long links, which will significantly reduce the number of hops of future requests. We are currently studying the amount of requests needed to get close to a logarithmic routing complexity. More generally, we are working on the estimation if the activity of the application is required to: (i) guarantee the constant efficiency of the overlay, and (ii) converge, starting from a random configuration, to a fully efficient overlay network.

14.4.3   VEs Management Mechanisms

In the DISCOVERY system, we define a VE as a set of VMs that may have specific requirements in terms of hardware, software, and also in terms of placement: For instance, some VMs must be on the same node/site to cope with performance objectives while others should not be collocated to ensure high-availability criteria [26]. As operations on a VE may occur in any place from any location, each agent should provide the capability to configure and start a VE, to suspend/resume/stop it, to relocate some of its VMs if the need arises, or simply to retrieve the location of a particular VE. Most of these mechanisms are provided by current UC platforms. However, as mentioned before, they should be revisited to leverage peer-to-peer mechanisms to correctly run on the infrastructure we target (i.e., in terms of scalability, resiliency, and reliability).

As a first example, placing the VMs of a VE requires the ability to find the available nodes that fulfill the VM's needs (in terms of resource requirements as well as placement constraints). Such a placement can start locally, close to the client application requesting it, i.e., in its local group. If no such node is found, a simple navigation ensures that the request will encounter a bridge, leading to the exploration of further nodes. This navigation goes on until an adequate node is found. A similar process is performed by the mechanism in charge of dynamically controlling and adapting the placement of VEs during their lifetime. For instance, to ensure the particular needs of a VM, it can be necessary to relocate other VMs. According to the predefined constraints of VEs, some VMs might be relocated on far nodes while others would prefer to be suspended. Such a mechanism has been deeply studied in the DVMS framework [16, 46]. DVMS (Distributed Virtual Machine Scheduler) is able to dynamically schedule a significant number of VMs throughout a large-scale distributed infrastructure while guaranteeing VM resource expectations.

A second example regards the networking configuration of VEs. Although it might look simple, assigning the right IP to each VM as well as maintaining the intraconnectivity of a VE becomes a bit more complex than in the case of a single network domain, i.e., a single site deployment. Keeping in mind that a LUC infrastructure is, by definition, spread WANwide, a VE can be hosted between distinct network domains during its lifetime. No solution has been chosen yet. Our first investigations led us to leverage techniques such as the IP over P2P project [20]. However, software-defined networking becomes more and more important; investigating proposals such as the Open vSwitch project [44] looks promising to solve such an issue.

14.4.4   VM Images Management

In a LUC infrastructure, VM images could be deployed in any place from any other location. However, being in a decentralized, large-scale, heterogeneous, and widely spread environment makes the management of VM images more difficult than with conventional centralized repositories. At coarse grain: (i) the management of the VM images should be consistent with regard to the location of each VM in the DISCOVERY infrastructure, and (ii) each VM image should remain reachable or at least recoverable in case of failures. The envisioned mechanisms to manage VM images have been classified into two categories. First, some mechanisms are required to efficiently upload VM images and replicate them across many nodes, to ensure efficiency as well as reliability. Second, other mechanisms are needed to schedule VM image transfers. Advanced policies are important to improve the efficiency of each transfer that may occur either during the first deployment of a VM or during its relocations.

Regarding the storage and replication mechanisms, an analysis of an IBM Cloud concludes that a fully distributed approach using peer-to-peer technology is not the best choice to manage VM images, since the number of instances of the same VM image is rather small [42]. However, central or hierarchical solutions are not suited for the infrastructure we target. Consequently, an improved peer-to-peer solution working with replicas and deduplication has to be investigated to provide more reliability, speed, and scalability to the system. For example, analyzing different VM images shows that at least 30% of the image is shared between different VMs [28]. This 30% can become a 30% reduction in space, or a 30% increase in reliability, or in transfer speed. Depending on the situation, we should decide to go from one scenario to another.

Regarding the scheduling mechanisms, a study showed that VM boot time could be increased from 10 to 240 s when multiple VMs running I/O intensive tasks use the same storage system [53]. Some actions can provide a performance boost and limit the overhead that is still observed in commercial Clouds [33], like providing the image chunks needed to boot first [54], defining a new image format, and pausing the rest of the I/O operations.

More generally, the amount of data linked with VM images is significant. Actions involving data should be aware of consequences on metrics like (but not limited to): energy efficiency, reliability, proximity, bandwidth, and hardware usage. The scheduler could also anticipate actions, for instance, moving images when the load is low or the energy is cheap.

14.4.5   Reliability Mechanisms

Although, we can expect that the frequency of failures on LUC resources should be similar to that in current UC platforms, it is noteworthy to mention that the expected mean time to repair failed equipment might be much higher since resources will be highly distributed. For these reasons, specific mechanisms should be designed to manage failures transparently with a minimum downtime.

Ensuring the high availability of the DISCOVERY system requires the ability to autonomously relocate and restart any service on a healthy node in case of failure. Moreover, a Cassandra-like framework [29] is required to avoid losing or corrupting information belonging to stateful services, since it provides a reliable and highly available back-end.

Regarding the VEs reliability, leveraging periodical VM snapshotting capabilities can provide a first level of fault tolerance. In case of failure, a VE can be restarted from its latest snapshot. Performing VM snapshotting in a large-scale, heterogeneous, and widely spread environment, is a challenging task. However, we believe that adapting ideas that were recently proposed in this field [38] would allow us to provide such a feature.

Snapshotting is not enough for services that should be made highly available, but a promising solution is to use VM replication [43]. To implement VM replication in a WAN, solutions to optimize synchronizations between replicas [22, 47] should be investigated. Also, we think that a LUC infrastructure has a major advantage over other UC platforms, since it is tightly coupled with the network infrastructure. As such, we can expect *low* latencies between nodes which would enable us to provide a strong consistency between replicas while achieving acceptable response time for the replicated services.

Reliability techniques will of course make use of the overlays for resource localization and monitoring. Replicated VMs should be hosted on nodes that have a low probability to fail simultaneously. Following the previously defined overlay structure, this can be done through a navigation scheme where at least one bridge is encountered. A replica can then be monitored by a *watcher*, which is in the same local group as the replica.

14.4.6 Security and Privacy Mechanisms

To be successful, DISCOVERY needs to provide mechanisms and methods to construct trust relationships between resource providers. Trust relationships are known to be complex to build [34]. Providing strong authentication, assurance, and certification mechanisms to providers and users is required, but is definitely not enough. Trust covers socioeconomic aspects that must be addressed but are out of the scope of this chapter. The challenge is to provide a trusted DISCOVERY base.

As overlays are fundamentals to all DISCOVERY mechanisms, another challenge is to ensure that they are not compromised. Recent advances [12] might enable to tackle such concerns.

The third challenge will consist in: (i) providing end users with a way to define their own security and privacy policies, and (ii) ensuring that these policies are enforced. The expression of these policies itself is a complex task, as it requires to improve the current trade-off between security (and privacy) and usability. To ease the expression of these policies, we are currently designing a domain-specific language to define high-level security and privacy requirements [9, 30]. These policies will be enforced in a decentralized manner, by distributed security and privacy decision and enforcement points (SPDEPs) during the lifetime of the VEs. Implementing such SPDEP mechanisms in a distributed fashion will require conducting specific research, as currently there are only prospective proposals for classic UC infrastructures [5, 51]. Therefore, we need to investigate whether such proposals can be adapted to the LUC infrastructure by leveraging appropriate overlays.

Fig. 14.4 The *Peer Actor*
Model. The *Supervisor Actor*
monitors all the actors it
encapsulates while the *Peer
Actor* acts as an interface
between the services and the
overlay

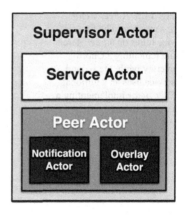

14.4.7 Towards a First Proof of Concept

The first prototype is under heavy development. It aims at delivering a simple
mock-up for integration/collaboration purposes. Following the coarse-grained architecture described in the previous sections, we have started to identify all the
components participating in the system, their relationships, as well as the resulting
interfaces. Conducting such a work now is mandatory to move towards a more
complete as well as more complex system.

To ensure a scalable and reliable design, we chose to rely on the use of high-level
programming abstractions. More precisely, we are using distributed complex event
programming [27] in association with the actor model [1]. This enables us to easily
switch between a push- and a pull-oriented approach depending on our needs.

Our preliminary studies showed that a common building block is mandatory
to handle resiliency concerns in all components. Concretely, it corresponds to a
mechanism in charge of throwing notifications that are triggered by the low level
network overlay each time a node joins or leaves it. Such a mechanism makes the
design and the development of higher building blocks easier as they do not have to
provide specific portions of code to monitor infrastructure changes.

This building block has been designed around the *Peer Actor* concept (see
Figs. 14.4 and 14.5). The *Peer Actor* serves as an interface between higher services
and the communication layer. It provides methods that enable to define the behaviors of a service when a resource joins or leaves a particular peer-to-peer overlay
as well as when neighbors change. Considering that several overlays may coexist
in the DISCOVERY system, the association between a *Peer Actor* and its *Overlay
Actor* is done at runtime and can be changed on the fly if need be. However, it is
noteworthy that each *Peer Actor* takes part to one and only one overlay at the same
time. In addition to the *Overlay Actor*, a *Peer Actor* is composed of a *Notification
Actor* that processes events and notifies registered actors. As illustrated in Fig. 14.5,
a service can use more than one *Peer Actor* (and reciprocally). Mutualizing a *Peer
Actor* enables for instance to reduce the network overhead implied by the maintenance of the overlays. In the example, the first service relies on a *Peer Actor*

Fig. 14.5 A *Peer Actor*
instantiation. The first service relies on a *Peer Actor*
implementing a Chord
overlay while the second
service uses an additional
Peer Actor implementing a
CAN structure

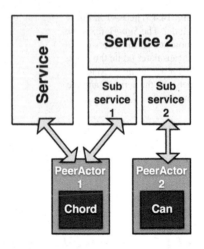

implementing a Chord overlay [52], while the second service uses an additional
Peer Actor implementing a CAN structure [48].

By such a mean, higher-level services can take the advantage of the advanced
communication layers without dealing with the burden of managing the different
overlays. As an example, when a node disappears, all services that have been registered as dependent on such an event are notified. Service actors can thus react
accordingly to the behavior that has been specified.

Regarding the design and the implementation of the DISCOVERY system, each
service is executed inside its own actor and communicates by exchanging messages
with the other ones. This ensures that each service is isolated from the others: When
a service crashes and needs to be restarted, the execution of other services is not affected. As previously mentioned, we consider that at the LUC infrastructure scale,
failures are the norm rather than the exception; hence, we decided that a *Supervisor
Actor* would monitor each actor (see Fig. 14.4). DISCOVERY services are under
the supervision of the DISCOVERY agent: This design allows to precisely define
a strategy that will be executed in case of service failures. This will be the way to
introduce self-healing and self-organizing properties to the DISCOVERY system.

This building block has been fully implemented by leveraging the Akka/Scala
framework [2], and is available online at https://github.com/BeyondTheClouds.

As a proof of concept (POC), we are implementing a first high-level service in
charge of dynamically scheduling VMs across a LUC infrastructure by leveraging
the DVMS [46] proposal (see Sect. 14.4.3). The low-level overlay that is being currently implemented is a robust ring based on the Chord algorithm combined with
the Vivaldi positioning system: It enables services to select nodes that have low
latency, so that collaboration will be more efficient.

To validate the behavior, the performance as well as the reliability of our proof of
concept, we are performing several experiments on the Grid'5000 test bed [6] that
comprises hundreds of nodes distributed on 10 computing sites that are geographically spread across France. To make experiments with DISCOVERY easier, we
developed a set of scripts that can deploy thousands of VMs throughout the whole

infrastructure in a *one-click* fashion [7]. By deploying our POC on each node and by leveraging the VM deployment scripts, we can evaluate real scenario by injecting specific workloads in the different VMs. The validation of this first POC is almost completed. The resulting system will be the first to provide reactive, reliable, and scalable reconfiguration mechanisms of virtual machines in a fully distributed and autonomous way. This new result will pave the way for a complete proposal of the DISCOVERY system.

14.5 Future Work/Opportunities

14.5.1 Geo-diversification as a Key Element

The Cloud Computing paradigm is changing the way applications are designed. In order to benefit from elasticity capabilities of Cloud systems, applications integrate or leverage mechanisms to provision resources, i.e., starting or stopping VMs, according to their fluctuating needs. The ConPaaS system [45] is one of the promising systems for elastic Cloud applications. At the same time, a few projects have started investigating distributed/collaborative ways of hosting famous applications such as Wikipedia or Facebook-like systems by leveraging volunteer computing techniques. However, considering that resources provided by end users were not reliable enough, only few contributions have been done yet. By providing a system that will enable to operate widely spread but more reliable resources closer to the end users, the LUC OS proposal may strongly benefit to this research area. Investigating the benefit of locality provisioning (i.e., combining elasticity and distributed/collaborative hosting) is a promising direction for all Web services that are embarrassingly distributed [13]. Image sharing systems, such as Google Picasa or Flickr, are examples of applications where leveraging locality will enable to limit network exchanges: Users could upload their images on a peer that is close to them, and images would be transferred to other locations only when required (pulling versus pushing model).

LUC infrastructures will allow envisioning a wider range of services that may answer specific SMEs requests such as data archiving or backup solutions, while significantly reducing the network overhead as well as legal concerns. Moreover, it will make the deployment of UC services easier by relieving developers of the burden of dealing with multi-Cloud vendors. Of course, this will require software engineering and middleware advances to easily take advantage of locality. But proposing LUC OS solutions, such as the DISCOVERY project, is the mandatory step before investigating new APIs enabling applications to directly interact with the LUC OS internals.

14.5.2 Energy, a Primary Concern for Modern Societies

The energy footprint of current UC infrastructures, and more generally of the Internet, is a major concern for the society. Although we need to conduct deeper investigations, we clearly expect that by its design and the way to operate it, a LUC infrastructure will have a smaller impact with a better integration in the whole Internet ecosystem.

Moreover, the LUC proposal is an interesting way to deploy the data furnaces proposal [31]. Concretely, following the Smart City recommendations (i.e., delivering efficient and sustainable ICT services), the construction of new districts in metropolises may take advantage of each LUC/Network PoP in order to heat buildings while operating UC resources remotely by means of a LUC OS. Finally, taking into account recent results about passive data centers, such as solar-powered micro-data centers, might extend this idea. The idea behind passive computing facilities is to limit as much as possible the energy footprint of major hubs and DSLAMS by taking advantage of renewable energies to power them, and by using the heat they produce as a source of energy. Combining such ideas with the LUC approach would allow reaching an unprecedented level of energy efficiency for UC platforms.

14.6 Conclusion

Cloud Computing has entered into our daily life with a great speed. From classic high performance computing simulations to the management of huge amounts of data coming from mobile devices and sensors, its impact can no longer be disregarded. While a lot of progress has already been made in Cloud technologies, there are several concerns that limit the complete adoption of the Cloud Computing paradigm.

In this chapter, we have outlined that, in addition to these concerns, intrinsic issues limit the current model of UC. Instead of following the current trend by trying to cope with existing platforms and network interfaces, we proposed to take a different direction by promoting the design of a system that will be efficient and sustainable at the same time, putting knowledge and intelligence directly into the network backbone itself.

The innovative approach, we introduced, will definitely tackle and go beyond Cloud Computing limitations. Our objective is to pave the way for a new generation of Utility Computing infrastructures that better match the Internet structure by means of advanced operating mechanisms. By offering the possibility to tightly couple UC servers and network backbones throughout distinct sites and operate them remotely, the LUC OS technology may lead to major changes in the design of UC infrastructures as well as in their environmental impact. The internal mechanisms of the LUC OS should be topology-dependent and resources-efficient. The natural distribution of the nodes through the different points of presence should be an advantage, which allows to process a request according to its scale: Local requests should be computed locally, while large computations should benefit from a large number of nodes.

Finally, we believe that LUC investigations may contribute to fill the gap between the distributed computing community and the networked ones. This connection between these two communities has already started with the different activities around Software-Defined Networking and Network as a Service. In the long term, this may result in a new community dealing with UC challenges where network and computational concerns are fully integrated. Such a new community may leverage the background of both areas to propose new systems that are more suitable to accommodate the needs of our modern societies.

We are well aware that the design of a complete LUC OS and its adoption by companies and network providers require several big changes in the way UC infrastructures are managed and WANs are operated. However, we are convinced that such an approach will pave the way towards highly efficient and sustainable UC infrastructures, coping with heterogeneity, scale, and faults.

References

1. Agha G (1986) Actors: a model of concurrent computation in distributed systems. MIT Press, Cambridge
2. Akka (2013) Build powerful concurrent & distributed applications more easily. http://www.akka.io. Accessed: March 2013
3. Andrew O (2003) Data networks are lightly utilized, and will stay that way. review of network economics. Rev Netw Econ 2(3):210–237
4. Armbrust M, Fox A, Griffith R, Joseph AD, Katz R, Konwinski A, Lee G, Patterson D, Rabkin A, Stoica I, Zaharia M (2010) A view of cloud computing. Commun ACM 53(4):50–58
5. Bacon J, Evans D, Eyers DM, Migliavacca M, Pietzuch P, Shand B (2010) Enforcing end-to-end application security in the cloud (big ideas paper). In: Proceedings of the ACM/IFIP/USENIX 11th International Conference on Middleware, Springer-Verlag, Berlin, Middleware'10, pp 293–312
6. Balouek D, Carpen Amarie A, Charrier G, Desprez F, Jeannot E, Jeanvoine E, Lèbre A, Margery D, Niclausse N, Nussbaum L et al (2013) Adding virtualization capabilities to the Grid'5000 testbed. In: Ivanov I, Sinderen M, Leymann F, Shan T (eds) Cloud computing and services science, Springer, Berlin
7. Balouek D, Lebre A, Quesnel F (2013) Flauncher and DVMS: deploying and scheduling thousands of virtual machines on hundreds of nodes distributed geographically. In: The sixth IEEE international scalable computing challenge (collocated with CCGRID), Delft, The Netherlands
8. Benson T, Akella A, Maltz DA (2010) Network traffic characteristics of data centers in the wild. In: Proceedings of the 10th ACM SIGCOMM Conference on Internet Measurement, ACM, New York, IMC'10, pp 267–280
9. Blanc M, Briffaut J, Clevy L, Gros D, Rouzaud-Cornabas J, Toinard C, Venelle B (2013) Mandatory protection within clouds. In: Nepal S, Pathan M (eds) Security, privacy and trust in cloud systems, Springer, Berlin
10. Bonomi F, Milito R, Zhu J, Addepalli S (2012) Fog computing and its role in the internet of things. In: Proceedings of the first edition of the MCC workshop on mobile cloud computing, ACM, New York, USA, MCC'12, pp 13–16
11. Buyya R, Ranjan R, Calheiros RN (2010) InterCloud: utility-oriented federation of cloud computing environments for scaling of application services. In: Proceedings of the 10th international conference on algorithms and architectures for parallel processing, Springer-Verlag, Berlin, ICA3PP'10, pp 13–31
12. Castro M, Druschel P, Ganesh A, Rowstron A, Wallach DS (2002) Secure routing for structured peer-to-peer overlay networks. SIGOPS Oper Syst Rev 36(SI):299–314

13. Church K, Greenberg A, Hamilton J (2008) On delivering embarrassingly distributed cloud services. In: HotNets
14. Dabek F, Cox R, Kaashoek MF, Morris R (2004) Vivaldi: a decentralized network coordinate system. In: Proceedings of the 2004 conference on applications, technologies, architectures, and protocols for computer communications, SIGCOMM'04, pp 15–26
15. DeCandia G, Hastorun D, Jampani M, Kakulapati G, Lakshman A, Pilchin A, Sivasubramanian S, Vosshall P, Vogels W (2007) Dynamo: Amazon's highly available key-value store. In: Proceedings of twenty-first ACM SIGOPS symposium on operating systems principles, ACM, SOSP'07, pp 205–220
16. Discovery (2013) Distributed VM scheduler. http://beyondtheclouds.github.io/DVMS/. Accessed: March 2013
17. CloudStack (2013) CloudStack, open source cloud computing. http://cloudstack.apache.org. Accessed: March 2013
18. Foster I (2011) Globus online: accelerating and democratizing science through cloud-based services. IEEE Internet Comput 15(3):70–73
19. Foster I, Kesselman C (2011) The history of the grid. In: Foster I, Gentzsch W, Grandinetti L, Joubert GR (eds) Advances in parallel computing—volume 20: HPC: from grids and clouds to exascale. IOS Press, Amsterdam
20. Ganguly A, Agrawal A, Boykin PO, Figueiredo R (2006) IP over P2P: enabling self-configuring virtual IP networks for grid computing. In: Proceedings of the 20th international conference on Parallel and distributed processing, IEEE Computer Society, Washington, DC, USA, IPDPS'06
21. Gary Cook JVH (2013) How dirty is your data? Greenpeace International report
22. Gerofi B, Ishikawa Y (2012) Enhancing TCP throughput of highly available virtual machines via speculative communication. In: Proceedings of the 8th ACM SIGPLAN/SIGOPS conference on Virtual Execution Environments, NY, USA, VEE'12
23. Gigaom Consortium (2012) Amazon outages—lessons learned. http://gigaom.com/cloud/amazon-outages-lessons-learned/. Accessed: 23 Feb. 2014
24. Greenberg A, Hamilton J, Maltz DA, Patel P (2008) The cost of a cloud: research problems in data center networks. SIGCOMM Comput Commun Rev 39(1):68–73
25. Group IEW (2012) IEEE 802.3TM industry connections ethernet bandwidth assessment
26. Hermenier F, Lawall J, Muller G (2013) BtrPlace: a flexible consolidation manager for highly available applications. IEEE Transactions on Dependable and Secure Computing
27. Janiesch C, Matzner M, Muller O (2011) A blueprint for event-driven business activity management. In: Proceedings of the 9th international conference on business process management, Springer-Verlag, BPM'11, pp 17–28
28. Jin K, Miller EL (2009) The effectiveness of deduplication on virtual machine disk images. In: Proceedings of SYSTOR 2009: the Israeli Experimental Systems Conference, ACM, New York, USA, SYSTOR'09, pp 7:1–7:12
29. Lakshman A, Malik P (2010) Cassandra: a decentralized structured storage system. SIGOPS Oper Syst Rev 44(2):35–40
30. Lefray A, Caron E, Rouzaud-Cornabas J, Zhang HY, Bousquet A, Briffaut J, Toinard C (2013) Security-aware models for clouds. In: Poster Session of IEEE Symposium on High Performance Distributed Computing (HPDC)
31. Liu J, Goraczko M, James S, Belady C, Lu J, Whitehouse K (2011) The data furnace: heating up with cloud computing. In: Proceedings of the 3rd USENIX conference on hot topics in cloud computing, HotCloud'11
32. Lowe S (2011) Mastering VMware vSphere. Wiley: Indianapolis
33. Mao M, Humphrey M (2012) A performance study on the VM startup time in the cloud. In: Proceedings of the 2012 IEEE Fifth International Conference on Cloud Computing, IEEE Computer Society, CLOUD'12, pp 423–430
34. Miller KW, Voas J, Laplante P (2010) In trust we trust. Computer 43:85–87
35. Moreno-Vozmediano R, Montero R, Llorente I (2012) IaaS cloud architecture: from virtualized datacenters to federated cloud infrastructures. Computer 45(12):65–72

36. Morin C (2007) XtreemOS: a grid operating system making your computer ready for partici-
    pating in virtual organizations. In: Proceedings of the 10th IEEE International Symposium
    on Object and Component-Oriented Real-Time Distributed Computing, IEEE Computer So-
    ciety, ISORC'07, pp 393–402
37. Murray P, Sefidcon A, Steinert R, Fusenig V, Carapinha J (2012) Cloud networking: an infra-
    structure service architecture for the wide area. HP Labs Tech Report-HPL-2012-111R1
38. Nicolae B, Bresnahan J, Keahey K, Antoniu G (2011) Going back and forth: efficient mul-
    tideployment and multisnapshotting on clouds. In: Proceedings of the 20th international
    symposium on High performance distributed computing, ACM, New York, USA, HPDC'11,
    pp 147–158
39. Nimbus (2013) Nimbus is cloud computing for science. http://www.nimbusproject.org.
    Accessed: March 2013
40. OpenNebula (2013) Open source data center virtualization. http://www.opennebula.org.
    Accessed: March 2013
41. OpenStack (2013) The open source, open standards cloud. http://www.openstack.org. Accessed:
    March 2013
42. Peng C, Kim M, Zhang Z, Lei H (2012) VDN: virtual machine image distribution network
    for cloud data centers. In: INFOCOM, 2012, pp 181–189
43. Petrovic D, Schiper A (2012) Implementing virtual machine replication: a case study using
    Xen and Kvm. In: Proceedings of the 2012 IEEE 26th International Conference on Advanced
    Information Networking and Applications, pp 73–80
44. Pfaff B, Pettit J, Koponen T, Amidon K, Casado M, Shenker S (2009) Extending networking
    into the virtualization layer. In: ACM HotNets
45. Pierre G, Stratan C (2012) ConPaaS: a platform for hosting elastic cloud applications. IEEE
    Internet Comput 16(5):88–92
46. Quesnel F, Lebre A, Sudholt M (2012) Cooperative and reactive scheduling in large-scale
    virtualized platforms with DVMS. Concurr Comput Pract Exp 25(12):1643–1655
47. Rajagopalan S, Cully B, O'Connor R, Warfield A (2012) SecondSite: disaster tolerance as a
    service. In: Proceedings of the 8th ACM SIGPLAN/SIGOPS conference on Virtual Execu-
    tion Environments, ACM, VEE'12, pp 97–108
48. Ratnasamy S, Francis P, Handley M, Karp R, Shenker S (2001) A scalable content-address-
    able network. In: SIGCOMM'01: Proceedings of the conference on applications, technolo-
    gies, architectures, and protocols for computer communications, ACM, New York, USA,
    SIGCOMM'01, pp 161–172
49. Rochwerger B, Breitgand D, Levy E, Galis A, Nagin K, Llorente IM, Montero R, Wolfsthal
    Y, Elmroth E, Caceres J, Ben-Yehuda M, Emmerich W, Galan F (2009) The reservoir model
    and architecture for open federated cloud computing. IBM J Res Dev 53(4):4:1–4:11
50. Sail Consortium (2012) Scalable and adaptive internet solutions—European Project FP7 pro-
    gram. http://www.sail-project.eu. Accessed: March 2014
51. Sandhu R, Boppana R, Krishnan R, Reich J, Wolff T, Zachry J (2010) Towards a discipline
    of mission-aware cloud computing. In: Proceedings of the 2010 ACM workshop on cloud
    computing security workshop, pp 13–18
52. Stoica I, Morris R, Karger D, Kaashoek MF, Balakrishnan H (2001) Chord: a scalable peer-
    to-peer lookup service for internet applications. In: Proceedings of the 2001 conference
    on Applications, technologies, architectures, and protocols for computer communications,
    ACM, New York, USA, SIGCOMM'01, pp 149–160
53. Tan T, Simmonds R, Arlt B, Arlitt M, Walker B (2008) Image management in a virtualized
    data center. SIGMETRICS Perform Eval Rev 36(2):4–9
54. Tang C (2011) FVD: a high-performance virtual machine image format for cloud. In:
    Proceedings of the 2011 USENIX conference on USENIX annual technical conference,
    USENIX Association, USENIXATC'11
55. Zhao H, Yu Z, Tiwari S, Mao X, Lee K, Wolinsky D, Li X, Figueiredo R (2012) CloudBay:
    enabling an online resource market place for open clouds. In: Proceedings of the 2012 IEEE/
    ACM Fifth International Conference on Utility and Cloud Computing, UCC'12

Index

1-Copy Equivalence, 28
2-Phase Commit (2PC), 26, 29
2-Phase Locking (2PL), 30
3-Phase Commit, 30

A
A-C systems, 42
Access control, 106, 108
  grade-based, 110, 114, 122
  issues, 307, 312
  role-based, 111
ACID, 26, 28, 40
  semantics, 42, 43
Active,
  networking, 213
  replication, 33
A-L systems, 42, 44
Amazon EC2, 14, 16
  hypervisor scheduler, 13
  IaaS model, 5
  mitigation technique in, 10
  virtual machine, 12
Amazon Elastic Compute, 214
Analysis, 261, 262
AndJoin, 262
AndSplit, 262
Apache Cassandra, 225
Apache Zookeeper, 225
API network, 216
Application, 258
  driven networking, 227, 232
ARM,
  architecture, 247, 248
  CPUs, 251
Aruba networks, 230
Asymmetric update processing, 38
Asynchronous, 220
Atomicity, 28

Atomicity, Consistency, Isolation and
  Durability *See* ACID, 26
Attack, 10, 17
  Cloud malware injection, 13
  Cloud-specific, 12, 16
  DDoS, 8, 9, 11, 18
  FRC, 16
  hypervisor, 13
  in Cloud, 4, 7
  keystroke timing, 12
  offline, 15
  resource-freeing attacks (RFAs), 15
  side-channel, 10, 12
  VM DoS, 12, 18
  VM image, 14
Automatic provisioning, 222
Availability, 6, 17, 266, 299, 304
  address, 314, 318
  data, 306
  in the Cloud, 6
  issues, 7
  of DBaaS, 310
  role in VM DoS attack, 18
  security, third-party security and, 7
  threats to, 309
  use of 'data replication' strategy in, 309
  violation, 18
Average relative error, 161

B
Bandwidth-hungry applications, 144, 169
BASE, 40–42, 44, 48
Basically Available, Soft state, Eventually
  consistent *See* BASE, 40
BestPractice, 266
Black-Box replication, 36
BLADE network technologies, 147
Border gateway protocol, 224

Bring Your Own Device *See* BYOD, 246
Broker, 260
Broker cloud communication
      paradigm, 118, 121
Business, 262
BYOD, 246, 247, 249

C
CAP, 27
  principle, 27
  reasoning, 40
  theorem, 27, 42, 45, 48
Casual consistency, 41
C-C systems, 43–45
CDF, 148
Cipher text policy attribute based
      encryption, 107
Ciphertext, 107, 108, 110
C-L systems, 43–45
Cloud,
  broker, 280, 281
  computing, 52, 54, 59, 61, 63, 69, 75, 258,
      326, 329, 331, 332, 341, 342
  databases, 299, 308
  DBaaS security challenges, 306, 311
  federations, 278, 288–294
  provider, 287, 289
Cloud SLA *See* CSLA, 65
CloudReports simulation tool, 131
Clouds@Home, 252
CloudSim framework, 129
CloudSim toolkit, 129
Compliance, 266
Composition, 261
Compute time, 161
Confidentiality, 6, 10, 18, 299, 306, 307
  and privacy, 311
  in VMs, 18
  security fundamental, 17
  using Trusted Cloud Computing Platform
     (TCCP) for, 13
Congestion, 144, 150, 153, 160, 169
Conservative update, 145, 147, 154
Consistency, 28
Consistency, Availability and Partition *See*
     CAP, 27
Content Delivery Network *See* CDN, 24
Co-residency, 9, 10, 12, 15
Count-Min, 145, 147, 153
CP-ABE *See* Cipher text policy attribute based
     encryption, 107
CPU, 242, 247, 251
Cryptographic technique, 109
CSLA, 65, 69

CSV format, 148, 150
Cube, 262
Cumulative distribution function *See* CDF, 148
Cursor Stability (CS), 31
Customer, 260

D
Data,
  identifier, 112, 113
  network, 216
  protection, 278, 290, 291, 294
Data Center (DC), 326, 327, 329, 331
Data Center Network *See* DCN, 144
Database, 215, 220, 222, 224–226, 230, 258
Datacenter, 281, 292, 293
DBaaS, 300, 301, 317
  advantages of, 300, 304
  applications, 300
  authenticity in, 316
  availability in, 316
  concept of, 301, 320
  consumers, 305
  data provenance, 308
  future prospects of, 317
  model, 304, 305, 308
  providers, 300, 306–310, 315
  security aspects of, 299, 306, 311,
     313–315
  services, 310
  studies on, 319
DCN, 144, 146, 148, 150, 153, 158
  architecture, 144
  bandwidth-hungry applications in, 169
  hosting, 147, 148
  management of, 159
  performance, 145
  traffic data set, 145, 146
  workload, 148, 150
DDoS, 8, 9, 11, 16–19
Decryption key, 106, 108, 109
Deployment models, 5, 8, 278, 280
Dirty Read, 32
DISCOVERY, 338
  infrastructure, 337
  mechanism of, 338
  monitoring mechanisms, 333
  project, 341
  proposal, 332
  purpose of, 333
  resource localization, 333
  system, 330, 332, 333, 336, 337, 339, 340
Distributed,
  algorithms, 144
  Logical Router, 224

Documentation, 266
DoS, 244, 247
Durability, 28
Dynamic, 258, 259

E
EC2, 214
Ecosystem, 282, 286, 294
EDoS, 16, 17, 19
Encryption, 106, 107, 112, 117, 119, 122,
        306, 314, 315, 319
    database, 311
    keys and techniques, 305, 306
    of data, 316, 317
    timings, 117
Energy, 341
    consumption, 278, 292, 293
    efficiency, 278, 292, 294
Enterprise,
    architectures, 108
    software, 222
Environment, 260
Equal Cost MultiPath, 225
Error performance, 145, 155, 156, 158, 162,
        167, 170
Eventual Consistency, 41

F
Floodlight, 213, 221, 222
Floodlight SDN controller, 220
Forensics, 245–247
Full replication, 38
Functional, 260

G
GPU, 251, 252
Graph, 262, 264
Graphical user interface, 136
Gray-Box replication, 36
GreenCloud simulator, 129
GridSim toolkit, 129

H
HAProxy load balancer, 217
Hash functions, 147, 153, 154
Hedera, 146
Helios, 146
High,
    availability, 24
    scalability, 24
Honeypot, 246, 247
Horizontal partitioning, 38
Hot-spotted partition, 46

HTTP, 147, 148, 150, 151, 156, 167, 215
Hybrid, 248
    partial replication, 39
Hypervisor, 5, 6, 10–13, 15, 18, 238, 245

I
IaaS, 4, 5, 12, 107, 210, 214, 238, 252, 258,
        278, 285–287, 291–293
    advantages of, 105
    attacks in, 6
    examples of, 10, 13
    models of, 19
    providers, 287, 293
    security in, 6
    service model, 8
    services, 11, 13
    systems, 289
iCanCloud platform, 129
Identity management, 106, 108, 111–113,
        122, 214
IFPIX, 144
Information, 260
Infrastructure, 260
    provider, 180, 281, 282, 284, 291, 294
Inputs, 260
Integrity, 6, 13, 17, 18, 299, 306, 312, 315,
        316, 318, 319
InterCloud, 108
Interoperability, 288
Introspection, 243, 245, 249
IP-based voice networking, 231, 232
IPv4, 216
IPv6, 216
Isolation, 28

K
Key Policy attribute based encryption, 107
Keystroke timing, 10, 12, 18
Knowledge, 265

L
Latency, 266
Layer, 261
Lazy replication, 33, 34
Leakage, 241
Level, 260
Link discovery, 221
Link layer discovery protocol, 221
Locality-based UC (LUC), 329–333,
        335–338, 340–343
Loop, 262
Lossy counting, 145, 147
Lost update, 32

M
MapReduce, 144
Massively Multi-player Online Role Playing
        Games *See* MMOG, 46
Media access control, 216
Midokura's MidoNet, 224
MMOG, 46
Mobile, 246, 247
Model, 258, 259
Monotonic,
    read consistency, 41
    write consistency, 41
mSSE, 112, 113
Multi-cloud, 282, 283, 287, 294
Multidimensional, 266
Multi-tenancy, 5, 6, 8, 10–12, 18, 239
Multi-version Concurrency Control, 32

N
NetFlow, 144
Network,
    backbone, 327
    functions virtualization, 224
    performance, 144, 153
    Point of Presence (PoP), 328, 329, 342
    virtualization, 222
Neutron (OpenStack), 216
Neutron Floodlight plugin, 222
NIST, 4, 7
Non-repeatable read, 32
Northbound API (SDN controller), 220
NoSQL, 299
NOX, 213

O
OF/SDN architecture, 212
OL/SDN, 211
OLAP, 265
Open Networking Foundation (ONF), 213
OpenFlow, 210, 213, 217–221, 224
    protocol, 213, 219
OpenFlow switch, 217
OpenStack, 210, 214–217, 222, 224
Operations, 260
Optimal, 259
Optimistic concurrency control, 30
Orchestration, 214
Outputs, 260

P
PaaS, 238, 252, 258
PACELC, 42
Parser, 262

Partial replication, 38
Paxos, 30, 35
Pay-as-you-go, 12
PDF, 148
Performance, 259
Pessimistic concurrency control, 30
Platform, 260
Policy-driven networking, 227
Primary copy update, 33
Privacy, 106, 311, 318, 331, 338
Private, 248
    cloud, 280, 282
Probability distribution function *See* PDF, 148
Process, 259, 262
Profile, 260
Properties, 260
Provider lock-in, 278, 283, 288, 294
Public, 248
Public cloud, 280
Pure partial replication, 39
Python, 222

Q
QoS, 228–231, 258, 259
QoSDW, 262, 263, 265
Quality, 262
Quality of Service, 52, 228, 231, 330

R
Race Condition, 31
Rackspace, 214
Randomness, 251, 252
Reactivity, 330
Read skew, 33
Read-your-writes consistency, 41
Real-time,
    moving average, 158, 167
    Wi-Fi, 230
Recall, 161
Registry, 259
Reliability, 266
Report, 262
Resiliency, 330
ResponseTime, 266
REST, 222
Risk,
    evaluation, 94
    modelling, 94
Role-based,
    access, 111
    encryption, 108
ROWA/ROWAA, 35

S
S3, 214
SaaS, 45, 238, 252, 258
Scalability, 330
Schema, 262
SCSRA, 150, 151
SDN, 210, 213, 214, 217, 222, 223, 225, 227,
    228, 230, 232
  controller, 212, 213, 220
  implementation challenges, 210, 226
  UC applications in, 231, 232
Searchable encryption, 107, 108, 116, 122
SecDSIM, 113, 116–118, 122
  framework, 117, 119
Security, 76, 78, 83, 84, 88, 90, 102, 260, 298,
    307–311, 313, 314, 318, 331, 338
  and data protection, 86
  control mechanisms, 317
  data, 316
  for relational databases, 319
  issues in DBaaS, 320
  risk assessment, 84, 86
  solutions, 317
  testing, 98
Selection, 259, 262
Semantic, 262, 265
Sequence, 262
Server virtualization, 214
Service, 258, 259
  lifecycle, 77, 83, 89, 99
  model, 5, 8
  monitoring, 278, 289, 294
  providers, 281, 282, 305, 314, 317–319
Service Level Objective *See* SLO, 44
ServiceFlow, 262
Service-level agreement, 281
Session consistency, 41
sFlow, 144, 147, 159
  datagram, 159
Shards, 24, 37
Shared-lock, 30
Side-channel, 12, 15
  attack, 10
SimGrid framework, 128
Simple storage service, 214
Sketch-based algorithms, 145–147, 161
Sketching algorithms, 146, 153, 158, 160
SLA, 52, 54, 55, 258
  and cloud, 55
  based cloud architecture, 56
  challenges, 62
  concept of, 52
  deviation, 60
  levels, 58

  management, 56
  manager, 68
  mechanisms, 53
  metrics in, 59
  of cloud provider, 57
  potential barriers/issues of, 65
SLO, 44, 46
Snapshot,
  reads, 32
  writes, 32
Software-defined,
  data centre, 210, 222
  networking, 210
Space,
  cost, 161
  saving, 147
State, 262
Storage virtualization, 214
Streaming algorithms, 144–146, 158, 162
Sub-service, 261
Successability, 266
Supercomputing, 238
Sustainability, 330
Symmetric, 220
  encryption, 106, 107, 109, 122
  update processing, 38

T
Throughput, 266
Time complexity, 145, 147, 155–157, 162,
    167, 170
Top-K, 153, 162
ToR, 144
Traffic engineering, 225
Tree, 262

U
Ubiquitous network, 5, 11
UC,
  application, 228, 231
  Interoperability Forum (UCIF), 227
  SDN interaction model, 231
Unified Communications, 210, 227, 232
Update anywhere, 33
  approach, 34
Update throughput, 161
User,
  identity, 112
Utility,
  computing, 180, 326, 327, 329–332,
    336–338, 341–343
  challenges, 343
  infrastructures, 326, 331, 338,
    341–343

    locality-based, 329
    management systems, 332
    models, 327, 332, 342
    operation of, 329
    platforms, 327, 336–338
    resources, 327, 329, 332, 342
    services, 330, 341
    solutions, 330
Utility pricing, 6, 12, 16, 18, 19

V
Values, 265
Vertical,
    partitioning, 37
    replication pattern, 39
Virtual Environment (VE), 329–333, 336, 338
Virtual eXtensible Local Area Network, 216
Virtual Local Area Network, 216
Virtual Machine (VM), 214, 290, 329–331,
            333, 335–338, 340, 341
Virtualization, 4, 6–8, 12, 238–240, 245,
            246, 284
Vivaldi, 333, 334, 340

VLAN, 216, 219, 222
VM images, 214
VMM, 5
VXLAN, 216, 223, 224

W
Web, 259
Write skew, 33

X
Xen, 10, 11, 13, 15, 16
XorJoin, 262
XorSplit, 262

Z
Zipfian,
        distribution, 150, 167
        parameter, 147, 170

Printed in the United States
By Bookmasters